AN INTRODUCTION TO
THE BIBLE

AN INTRODUCTION TO
THE BIBLE

Sacred Texts and Imperial Contexts

DAVID M. CARR AND COLLEEN M. CONWAY

A John Wiley & Sons, Ltd., Publication

This edition first published 2010
© 2010 David M. Carr & Colleen M. Conway

Blackwell Publishing was acquired by John Wiley & Sons in February 2007. Blackwell's publishing program has been merged with Wiley's global Scientific, Technical, and Medical business to form Wiley-Blackwell.

Registered Office
John Wiley & Sons Ltd, The Atrium, Southern Gate, Chichester, West Sussex, PO19 8SQ, United Kingdom

Editorial Offices
350 Main Street, Malden, MA 02148-5020, USA
9600 Garsington Road, Oxford, OX4 2DQ, UK
The Atrium, Southern Gate, Chichester, West Sussex, PO19 8SQ, UK

For details of our global editorial offices, for customer services, and for information about how to apply for permission to reuse the copyright material in this book please see our website at www.wiley.com/wiley-blackwell.

Library of Congress Cataloging-in-Publication Data

Carr, David McLain, 1961–
    An introduction to the Bible : sacred texts and imperial contexts / David M. Carr and Colleen M. Conway.
        p. cm.
    Includes bibliographical references and index.
    ISBN 978-1-4051-6738-3 (hardcover : alk. paper) – ISBN 978-1-4051-6737-6 (pbk. : alk. paper)   1. Bible – History.   2. Bible – History of contemporary events. 3. Bible – Introductions.   I. Conway, Colleen M.   II. Title.
    BS445.C35 2010
    221.09–dc22

                                                                    2009041255

A catalogue record for this book is available from the British Library.

Set in 10/13 pt Minion by Graphicraft Limited, Hong Kong
Printed in the USA

2   2014

CONTENTS

FIGURES

MAPS

BOXES

---

basics **What is a Basics Box?**

These boxes give a brief overview of basic information about a biblical book or other major text under discussion. This includes an outline of the book or text, information about the time(s) in which it was written, and (usually) a discussion of a major issue in interpretation of the book or text.

WHAT IS A MORE ON METHOD BOX?

These boxes give a brief introduction to methods used to interpret the Hebrew Bible. They detail the sorts of questions that each method attempts to answer, give an example of how the method has been applied, and include a reference to an article or book with more information about the method under discussion.

What is in Miscellaneous Boxes?

These boxes offer extra information relevant to the broader discussion. Some pull together relevant dates for a period, while others show parallels between texts, or summarize information on a theme or question that relates to the topic at hand. This information is not optional or superfluous. Instead, these boxes highlight topics that are worth focused attention.

PREFACE

This book introduces students to the books of the Bible as shaped in the crucible of the history of Israel and the early church. A prominent theme throughout is the way the books of the Bible reflect quite different sorts of interaction with empires that dominated the ancient Near East and Mediterranean. At first some students and professors may find this approach unusual, since we do not begin with Genesis and do not proceed through biblical books in order. The group of texts introduced early on in this textbook is quite different from the Bible they now know. So why have we chosen this approach? There are many advantages. On the basis of our experience with using this approach we have seen that the picture of the Bible's development comes into focus as the narrative of its formation unfolds. By the end, students should find meaning in aspects of the Bible that they once overlooked, even as they also understand that much of the power of the Bible has been its capability to transcend the original contexts in which it was written. Moreover, through discussion of the history of Jewish and Christian interpretation of focus texts toward the end of many chapters, students will gain a taste of how faith communities have used the Bible in creative, inspired, and sometimes death-dealing ways to guide and make sense of their lives. Given the already large scope of this *Introduction*, we have focused on texts included in the Old and New Testaments, with a particular emphasis – in the case of the Old Testament – on books included in the scriptures of Judaism and various forms of Christianity. This meant that we could not give sustained attention to apocryphal/deutero-canonical books of the Old Testament, or to the range of non-canonical early Christian works that did not end up being included in the Christian Bible.

The date framework given in this textbook follows that of Anson Rainey and Steven Notley's *The Sacred Bridge: Carta's Atlas of the Biblical World* (Jerusalem: Carta, 2005). In many cases specific dates are uncertain, but Rainey and Notley provide a recent, solid framework to start from on an introductory level. Unless otherwise indicated, the translations from Hebrew and Greek are our own.

As with any such textbook, particularly a first edition, there is always room for improvement. We know that there are multiple ways in which virtually everything that is written here could be footnoted, qualified, and balanced with other perspectives. What this introduction provides is one general outline of a historical approach to the Bible which students can then supplement, correct, and balance in their future studies. We certainly invite all possible suggestions for correction and improvement of future editions of this textbook.

We have been helped by many people in writing this textbook. In particular, several colleagues – Benjamin Sommer, Kent Reynolds, Mark Smith, and Marvin Sweeney –

generously reviewed portions of chapters on the Hebrew Bible. In addition, students over the last two years at Union Theological Seminary and Seton Hall University have read earlier drafts and suggested corrections. Some students and teaching assistants who have offered a particularly large volume of helpful corrections are Mary Ellen Kris, Candice Olson, Lizzie Berne-DeGear, Laurel Koepf, Meagan Manas, and Todd Kennedy. Maia Kotrosits provided timely assistance with the glossary and web materials. Our thanks to all for their generous help in this project.

Finally, with love we dedicate this volume to our parents, James and Patricia Conway, John and Adrienne Carr, whose love of teaching and care for their students helped inspire this book.

Colleen Conway and David Carr

ACKNOWLEDGMENTS

The author and publisher gratefully acknowledge the permission granted to reproduce the copyrighted material in this book:

Figure 0.1	© John C. Trever, Ph.D., digital image by James E. Trever.
Figure 0.2	Biblia Hebraica Stuttgartensia, edited by Karl Elliger and Wilhelm Rudolph, Fifth Revised Edition, edited by Adrian Schenker, © 1977 and 1997 Deutsche Bibelgesellschaft, Stuttgart. Used by permission.
Figure 2.1	Z. Radovan/www.BibleLandPictures.com
Figure 2.3	bpk / Vorderasiatisches Museum, SMB / Gudrun Stenzel
Figure 2.4	Jürgen Liepe
Figure 3.1	© Lloyd K Townsend
Figure 3.2	William Schniedewind
Figure 3.3	akg-images / Erich Lessing
Figure 3.4	Courtesy of R. E. Tappy and The Zeitah Excavations. Photograph by B. Zuckerman and M. Lundberg, overlay by P. K. McCarter, Jr
Figure 3.5	Z. Radovan/www.BibleLandPictures.com
Figure 3.6	© The Trustees of the British Museum
Figure 3.7	The Granger Collection / Topfoto
Figure 3.8	Image by © Francis G. Mayer/CORBIS
Figure 4.1	Z. Radovan/www.BibleLandPictures.com
Figure 4.2	akg-images / Erich Lessing
Figure 4.3	Z. Radovan/www.BibleLandPictures.com
Figure 4.4	Image by © The Gallery Collection/CORBIS
Figure 4.5	Stiftung BIBEL+ORIENT
Figure 4.6	Photo © The Israel Museum, Jerusalem
Figure 4.7	Stiftung BIBEL+ORIENT
Figure 5.1	Stiftung BIBEL+ORIENT
Figure 6.1	Z. Radovan/www.BibleLandPictures.com
Figure 6.2	akg-images / Erich Lessing
Figure 6.3	Stiftung BIBEL+ORIENT
Figure 7.1	Image by © Gianni Dagli Orti/CORBIS
Figure 7.2	akg-images / Erich Lessing
Figure 8.1	Photo © The Israel Museum, Jerusalem
Figure 8.2	Courtesy of Carta, Jerusalem
Figure 9.1	Todd Bolen / BiblePlaces.com
Figure 9.2	© Bojan Brecelj/CORBIS

Figure 9.3	© David Rubinger/CORBIS
Figure 9.4	Mary Evans Picture Library
Figure 10.1	Todd Bolen / BiblePlaces.com
Figure 10.2	© Tim Thompson/CORBIS
Figure 10.3	akg-images / Electa
Figure 10.5	Mary Evans Picture Library / Alinari
Figure 11.1	Courtesy of the American Numismatic Society
Figure 11.2	Mary Evans Picture Library / Alinari
Figure 11.3	Courtesy of the Hecht Museum, University of Haifa, Israel
Figure 12.2	Sammlung von Fotos und Abgüssen antiker Münzen der Goethe-Universität Frankfurt am Main
Figure 13.1	Deutsches Archäologisches Institut Rome, D-DAI-ROM 1975.1289 / photo Rossa
Figure 13.2	© The Trustees of the British Museum
Figure 13.3	Photo Scala, Florence
Figure 14.1	Reproduced by courtesy of the University Librarian and Director, The John Rylands University Library, The University of Manchester
Figure 14.2	bpk / Gemäldegalerie, SMB / Jörg P. Anders
Figure 15.1	Photo: akg-images / Pirozzi
Figure 15.2	© The Trustees of the British Museum
Figure 16.1	Andre Nantel / Shutterstock
Figure 16.2	The Granger Collection/Topfoto

Chapter opener photo © Joseph Chalev/Shutterstock

The Pharaoh Merneptah hymn in Chapter 3, page 64, and the Cyrus cylinder text in Chapter 7, page 187: Pritchard, James; *Ancient Near Eastern Texts Relating to the Old Testament – Third Edition with Supplement.* © 1950, 1955, 1969, renewed 1978 by Princeton University Press. Reprinted by permission of Princeton University Press.

At a few points throughout the book extracts have been used from the Revised Standard Version of the Bible: Revised Standard Version of the Bible, copyright 1952 [2nd edition, 1971] by the Division of Christian Education of the National Council of the Churches of Christ in the United States of America. Used by permission. All rights reserved.

The publisher apologizes for any errors or omissions in the above list and would be grateful if notified of any corrections that should be incorporated in future reprints or editions of this book.

ABBREVIATIONS

ANET   James Pritchard (ed.), *Ancient Near Eastern Texts Relating to the Old Testament with Supplement*. Princeton: Princeton University Press, 1969.

George   Andrew George, *The Babylonian Gilgamesh Epic: Introduction, Critical Edition and Cuneiform Texts*. New York: Oxford University Press, 2003.

Livingstone Alasdair Livingstone (ed.), *Court Poetry and Literary Miscellanea* State Archives of Assyria, 3. Helsinki: Helsinki University Press, 1989.

NJPS   *The New Jewish Publication Society Tanach Translation*. Philadelphia: Jewish Publication Society, 1985.

NRSV   *The New Revised Standard Version of the Bible*. New York: National Council of Churches, 1989.

NT   New Testament

OT   Old Testament

OT Parallels Victor Matthews and Don Benjamin, *Old Testament Parallels: Laws and Stories from the Ancient Near East* (3rd revised and expanded edition). Mahwah, NJ: Paulist Press, 2007.

For Bible abbreviations, see Chapter 1, Box 1.2.

Asterisks after Bible citations, e.g. "Genesis 12–50*," indicate that only parts of the cited texts are included.

// indicate that the texts before and after the slashes are parallel to each other.

OVERVIEW OF THE HISTORICAL PERIOD

This shows major periods and corresponding texts covered in this book.

Dates	1250–1000 BCE (13th–11th centuries)	1000–930 (10th century)	930–800 (10th–9th centuries)	800–700 (8th century)	700–597 (7th and early 6th centuries)	586–538 (6th century)	538–332 (6th–4th centuries)	332–63 (4th–1st centuries)	63 BCE–100 CE (1st century BCE to 1st century CE)
Chapter	2	3	4	4	5	6	7	8	9–15
Major events (in chronological order)	Spread of villages in hill country. Tribal "Israel" emerges. Saul's chieftainship	Formation of Davidic monarchy. Jerusalem taken as capital of Judah/Israel. David and Solomon	Formation of northern kingdom of "Israel". Rise and Fall of Omride dynasty	Domination and destruction of northern "Israel" by Assyria. Domination of Judah by Assyria	Eventual decline of Assyrian power. Enactment of Josiah's "reform". Decline of Judah into domination by Babylon. First wave of exile	Destruction of Jerusalem and its Temple. Second and third waves of exile of elites to Babylon	Persian victory, waves of return, rebuilding of Temple. Nehemiah's rebuilding of the wall. Divorce of foreign wives under Ezra and elevation of Torah	Hellenistic rule. Hellenizing crisis. Hasmonean kingdom	Roman rule
Major writings (and oral traditions)	(No writings, but oral traditions about exodus, trickster ancestors)	Royal and Zion psalms. Proverbs. J primeval history. ?Covenant Code. ?Song of Songs. ?Ecclesiastes	Jacob narrative. Joseph narrative. Exodus–wilderness story. Song of Deborah	Prophecy to the north by Amos and Hosea. Prophecy to the south by Micah and Isaiah	Early edition of Deuteronomistic history (Deut–2 Kings) that led from Deuteronomy to Josiah's reform (and no further). Nahum. Zephaniah. Early prophecies from Jeremiah	Exilic Deuteronomistic history. Lamentations. Ezekiel and Second Isaiah. L story of creation to Israel. P counter-story of creation to Israel	Haggai. Zechariah. Nehemiah memoir. Temple rebuilding/Ezra narrative. Third Isaiah. Combined L/P Pentateuch. Psalter	Early parts of Enoch. Ben Sira. Ezra–Nehemiah. Esther. 1–2 Chronicles. Daniel	Most of the New Testament
Major new ideas and themes	Election theology	Royal/Zion theology			Exclusive devotion to Yahweh enforced (briefly) by Josiah	Monotheism	Dual Temple–Torah focus	Judaism. Resurrection	Emergent belief in Jesus as messiah and Son of God

TIMELINE

Important texts are noted in blue.

BCE	SOUTH (Judah)	NORTH ("Israel" in narrower sense)
1300	(Waning Egyptian domination of Canaan)	
		Spread of villages in Israelite hill county
1200		Merneptah Stela
		(Assorted battles, e.g. Deborah, of hill-country Israelites with neighbors)
		Oral exodus traditions
		Oral ancestral traditions
1100		**Oral victory traditions**
	Saul's "chieftainship"	
	David (Hebron; 1010–1002)	
1000	David (Jerusalem; 1002–970)	
	Royal psalms, Zion psalms	
	Solomon (Jerusalem; 970–930)	
	Proverb collections, J primeval history	
	?Covenant Code, ?Song of Songs, ?Ecclesiastes	
	Rehoboam (Jerusalem)	Jeroboam founds northern monarchy
900		**Jacob narrative**
		Joseph narrative
		Exodus narrative
		(written) Song of Deborah
		Omride dynasty (880–841)
		Jehu's coup (841)
800		
		Jeroboam II (782–753)
	Isaiah start	**Amos**
	Syro-Ephraimite war (735–734)	Assyrian domination of Israel begins (745–)
		Hosea
	Assyrian domination of Judah begins (734–)	
	Isaiah (cont.), Micah	
	Hezekiah (715–686)	Assyrian destruction of Israel (722)
	Hezekiah's rebellion and reform (705)	
700	Sennacherib's attack and mysterious withdrawal (701)	
	Manasseh (697–642)	
	Amon (642–640)	(Waning of Assyrian power)
	Josiah (640–609)	
	Zephaniah	
	Josiah's reform (623)	
	Josianic edition of Deuteronomistic history	
		(Fall of Nineveh, Assyria's capital)
	Nahum	
	Jeremiah	
	Domination of Judah by Babylonia	
600	First wave of exiles (586)	
	Ezekiel's early prophecy	
	Lay/Non-Priestly Pentateuchal Source	
	Destruction of Jerusalem and second wave of exiles (586)	
	Lamentations and Psalm 137	
	Ezekiel's later prophecy	
	Third wave of exiles (582)	
	Exilic edition of Deuteronomistic history	

Lay Pentateuchal Source (incorporating modified
    forms of older J primeval history, Jacob–Joseph story,
    Moses story, and Deuteronomy)

Priestly Pentateuchal Source

Second Isaiah
Persian conquering of Babylonian empire (539)
    First wave of returnees (538)
    Another wave, beginning of Temple restoration (532)
    Another wave with Zerubbabel, completion of Temple rebuilding (520–515)
      Haggai and Zechariah (1–9)

500

    Nehemiah's return and governorships (445–425)
      (rebuilding wall, purification of priesthood)
      Nehemiah memoir

400   Return with Ezra, divorce of foreign wives, elevation of Torah (397–)
      Combined (L/P) Pentateuch
      Temple-rebuilding/Ezra narrative
      Third Isaiah
      Psalter
Greek conquering of Persian empire (332)

300   (Shifting domination of Palestine by Greek Ptolemies
(Egypt) and Seleucids (Mesopotamia); 332–142)

      Early parts of Enoch

      1–2 Chronicles

      Wisdom of Ben Sira

200   Jason purchase of high priesthood, attempt to Hellenize Jerusalem (174)

    Menelaus purchase of high priesthood (171) and Judean rebellion against him

      Daniel

    Antiochus Epiphanes IV campaign to eradicate observant Judaism and beginning of Hasmonean-led
      rebellion against Hellenistic rule (167–)
    Purification and rededication of Temple (164)

    Hasmonean independence and rule (142–63)

      Ezra–Nehemiah

      Esther

100   Roman takeover of Palestine (63)

    Rule of Herod in Palestine (40–4)

    Beginning of Roman empire with reign of Caesar Augustus (Octavian) (27)

    Birth of Jesus (4?)

CE   Paul's letters (50s)

    Jewish War (first Jewish revolt) (66–70)

    Destruction of the Temple (70)

      Gospel of Mark

      Gospels of Matthew and Luke

      Acts of the Apostles

      Revelation of John

      Gospel of John

      Pastoral Epistles
    Second Jewish revolt (132–5)

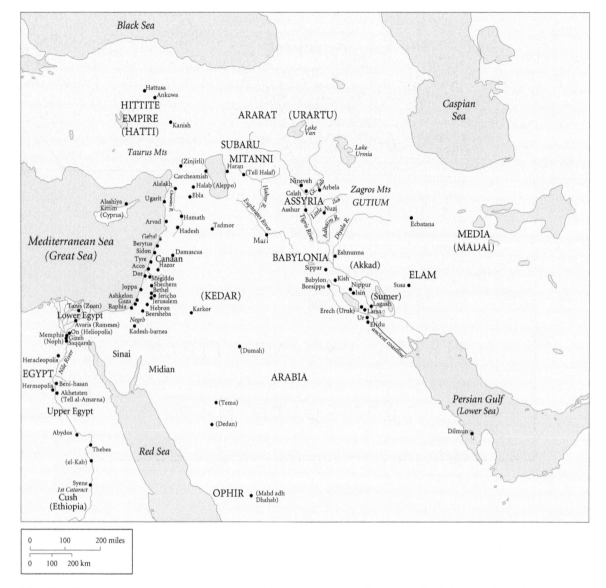

Map 0.1 The ancient Near East. Redrawn from Adrian Curtis (ed.), *Oxford Bible Atlas* (4th edition). Oxford, New York: Oxford University Press, 2007, page 67.

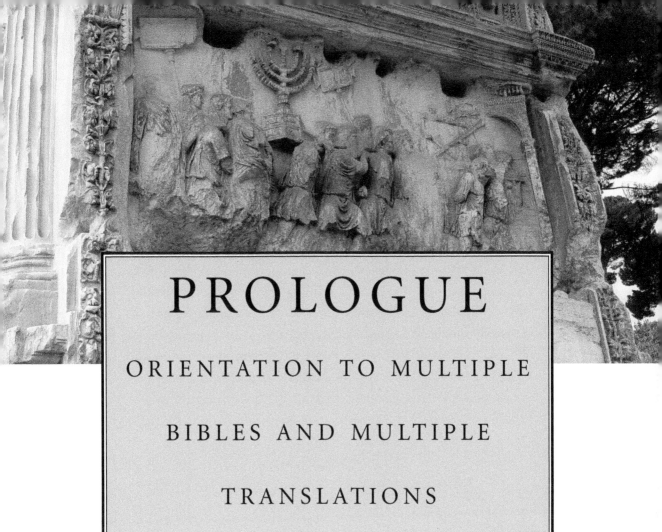

PROLOGUE

ORIENTATION TO MULTIPLE BIBLES AND MULTIPLE TRANSLATIONS

Chapter Outline

CHAPTER OVERVIEW

This chapter answers the questions: "What are the biggest differences between the scriptures revered in Judaism, Christianity and Islam?" and "What should I know about in choosing an English translation of the Bible?" By the end of this chapter you should know the differences between the bibles of Judaism and Christianity, as well as the relationship of the Muslim Koran to both sets of scriptures. You will also learn about how study of different readings of ancient manuscripts of the Bible, "textual criticism," and advances in knowledge of ancient languages have led to major progress in translation of the Bible since the King James Version was completed in 1611. Finally, you will learn some basic things to look for in choosing an up-to-date English translation of the Bible.

EXERCISE

Using the parallels provided at the end of the chapter in Appendix 1, compare the translations (and paraphrase) of Isa 52:13–15. What differences do you notice?

Take a look at two pages of a biblical book in your Bible. Make a list of *all* types of elements on those pages aside from the actual text of the Bible. Using the discussions in this chapter, identify where those elements came from.

The Different Scriptures of Judaism and Christianity

To begin, it is important to get acquainted with the different forms of the Old Testament/ Hebrew Bible recognized by different faith communities. These are referred to as different "canons" of the Bible, with "**canon**" meaning a collection of books that are recognized as divinely inspired scripture by a given religious community. Such books are recognized as "**canonical**."

The Jewish people calls its Scriptures the "**TaNaK**" (or "**Tanach**," with the ch pronounced like the ch in Bach). This is a word formed out of the first letters of the three main parts of the Jewish Bible: *Torah* (Genesis, Exodus, Leviticus, Numbers, and Deuteronomy), *Neviim* ("Prophets"), and *Ketuvim* ("Writings"). See the Miscellaneous Box on "Contents of the Hebrew Bible/Tanach/Old Testament" for an overview of the contents of each of these three parts. The Torah, otherwise known as the **Pentateuch**, is the centerpiece of the Jewish Tanach, while the prophets and writings are understood as commentary on it. In accordance with the emphasis in Judaism on temple and purity, the Tanach concludes on a hopeful note, as 2 Chronicles anticipates a new rebuilding of the Temple (2 Chr 36:22–3).

The Christian version of these scriptures, the "**Old Testament**" (OT), is organized quite differently from the Jewish Tanach. This is especially clear in the case of Protestant Bibles, which contain the very same books as the Jewish Tanach, but in a different order. Like the Jewish Bible, the Protestant "Old Testament" starts with the books of Genesis Exodus, Leviticus, Numbers, and Deuteronomy and then moves to Joshua through 2 Kings and then the parallel history found in 1–2 Chronicles and Ezra–Nehemiah. The rest of the books in the Old Testament are put in the order of their traditional authors, starting with the book of Job (an early Edomite sage), and moving through Psalms (David as traditional author), Proverbs, Ecclesiastes, and Song of Songs (Solomon as traditional author), and on to the major (Isaiah, Jeremiah, Ezekiel) and minor (Hosea, etc.) prophets. As in the case of the Jewish Tanach, the ending of the Christian

Contents of the Hebrew Bible/Tanach/Old Testament

Jewish Tanach	Protestant OT	Roman Catholic OT (*italics* = not in Tanach)	Eastern Orthodox OT (*italics* = not in Tanach)
Torah Genesis, Exodus, Leviticus, Numbers, Deuteronomy	**(Pentateuch)** Genesis, Exodus, Leviticus, Numbers, Deuteronomy	**(Pentateuch)** Genesis, Exodus, Leviticus, Numbers, Deuteronomy	**(Pentateuch)** Genesis, Exodus, Leviticus, Numbers, Deuteronomy
Prophets (Neviim)	**(Historical Books)**	**(Historical Books)**	**(Historical Books)**
Former prophets Joshua, Judges	Joshua, Judges, Ruth	Joshua, Judges, Ruth	Joshua, Judges, Ruth
1–2 Samuel 1–2 Kings	1–2 Samuel 1–2 Kings 1–2 Chronicles Ezra–Nehemiah	1–2 Samuel 1–2 Kings 1–2 Chronicles Ezra–Nehemiah	1–2 Samuel 1–2 Kings 1–2 Chronicles Ezra–Nehemiah *1 Esdras (2 Esdras in Russian Orthodox)*
Latter prophets			
Major prophets		*Tobit* *Judith*	*Tobit* *Judith*
Isaiah Jeremiah Ezekiel	Esther	Esther *(with additions)* *1–2 Maccabees*	Esther *(with additions)* *1–3 Maccabees*
Minor prophets/ book of the twelve	**(Poetical Books)**	**(Poetical Books)**	**(Poetical Books)**
Hosea, Joel, Amos, Obadiah, Jonah, Micah, Nahum, Habakkuk, Zephaniah, Haggai, Zechariah, Malachi	Job Psalms Proverbs Ecclesiastes Song of Solomon	Job Psalms Proverbs Ecclesiastes Song of Solomon *Wisdom of Solomon* *Sirach*	Job Psalms (with Psalm 151) Proverbs Ecclesiastes Song of Solomon *Wisdom of Solomon* *Sirach*

Writings (Ketuvim)
Psalms
Proverbs
Job
	(Prophets)
	Isaiah
	Jeremiah
	Lamentations
		(Prophets)
		Isaiah
		Jeremiah
		Lamentations
		Baruch
		   Letter of Jeremiah
			(Prophets)
			Isaiah
			Jeremiah
			Lamentations
			Baruch
			   Letter of Jeremiah

Five festal scrolls Song of Songs Ruth Lamentations Ecclesiastes Esther	Ezekiel Daniel Hosea, Joel, Amos, Obadiah, Jonah, Micah, Nahum, Habakkuk, Zephaniah, Haggai, Zechariah, Malachi	Ezekiel Daniel *(with additions)* Hosea, Joel, Amos, Obadiah, Jonah, Micah, Nahum, Habakkuk, Zephaniah, Haggai, Zechariah, Malachi	Ezekiel Daniel *(with additions)* Hosea, Joel, Amos, Obadiah, Jonah, Micah, Nahum, Habakkuk, Zephaniah, Haggai, Zechariah, Malachi
Daniel Ezra–Nehemiah 1–2 Chronicles			*4 Maccabees* (appendix)

Old Testament is revealing. It concludes with the last chapter of Malachi, a prediction of the second coming of Elijah (Mal 4:5). This ending leads nicely into the first book of the New Testament (NT), the Gospel of Matthew, which describes the coming of John the Baptist, who is clothed like Elijah and prophesies the coming of Jesus (Matt 3:1–6).

Other Christian churches organize their "Old Testament" similarly, but recognize additional books as part of it, books not included in the Jewish or the Protestant Scriptures. For example, the Roman Catholic church also includes books such as 1 and 2 Maccabees, Sirach, and the Wisdom of Solomon. The Ethiopic church recognizes the book of Enoch as part of its Old Testament, and various forms of Orthodox Christianity likewise recognize slightly different groups of additional books. For the Roman Catholics, such additional books are "**deutero-canonical**," which means that they belong to a "second canon." For Protestants, such books not in the Jewish Tanach are not considered true scripture, but "**apocrypha**," which means "books hidden away." We will not hide such books away in this textbook, but neither will we be able to discuss them at length. Instead, we will discuss briefly a sampling of them: Sirach, Enoch, and the books of Maccabees.

"**Hebrew Bible**" is yet another term that is often used to designate the scriptures shared by Jews and Christians. Many people prefer the expression "Hebrew Bible" because it avoids the pejorative connotations that the term "Old Testament" has assumed in some Christian circles. Christianity has long struggled with a tendency toward what is called "**supersessionism**" – the idea that Christianity and the Christian church have superseded and thus replaced Judaism and the people of Israel. For Christians who subscribe to this idea, the Old Testament is often treated as the *Old* and superseded Testament. It is seen as the outdated book of the "law," as opposed to the New Testament, which is understood to be the truly scriptural word about Jesus, love, and grace. Such views reflect a lack of close reading of either the Old or the New Testament, but they are widespread and influential. Therefore, some avoid the term "Old Testament," with its possible implications of supersessionism, and prefer terms such as "Hebrew Bible" or "First Testament" instead. Other Christians find these terms odd and/or inaccurate (for example, several chapters in the Tanach/Old Testament are not in Hebrew, but Aramaic). They prefer sticking with the Christian term "Old Testament," but emphasize the more ancient understanding of "Old" as implying something good, rather than the more contemporary idea of "Old" being something that is outdated.

The important thing for academic study of the Bible is to understand the meanings of these different terms for the Tanach/Old Testament/Hebrew scriptures and the slight differences in contents and order of these otherwise similar collections. These differences reflect the fact that these scriptures have come to belong to multiple faith communities. In addition, the religion of Islam sees the scriptures of Judaism and Christianity as possessing a secondary authority to that of its central text, the **Koran**. From the Muslim perspective, the Koran represents in pure form revelations about the one true god, Allah (Arabic for "the God"), revelations present in diluted form in the Jewish Tanach and Christian Old and New Testaments. This Koran is quite different in contents from the Tanach/Old Testament, containing a set of Arabic poems attributed to the prophet

Muhammad. It is not a parallel "Old Testament" or "Tanach." Nevertheless, parts of the Koran reflect post-biblical Jewish traditions about history up to Moses, and other Muslim traditions have elaborated on stories about Adam, Abraham, Ishmael, Joseph, and other biblical figures up to and including Moses. Thus Islam represents another strand of history of interpretation of scripture, alongside Judaism and Christianity.

Thus we see that there is no one "Bible" or "Old Testament" shared by Judaism and Christianity, let alone Islam. Despite major overlaps in the contents of the Jewish Tanach and Christian Old Testament, there are significant differences in order and (occasionally) content as well. This is an initial indicator of the quite different readings that Christians and Jews give to the texts they hold in common. We will see others along the way. Moreover, this diversity of Jewish and Christian Bibles is preceded by a diversity of perspectives and voices found within the Hebrew scriptures themselves. In the following chapters, we will see this diversity in texts written at different times and even in texts offering different perspectives on the same time.

Basics on Bible Translations

Since most students do not know Hebrew or Greek, they can only read a Bible in translation. There are several things that every user of such Bible translations should know about them in order to be an informed user.

Figure 0.1 One of our earliest manuscripts of the book of Isaiah, dated to the early first century BCE. Note how the letters are hung from lines on the parchment and a scribe has added a verse into the middle.

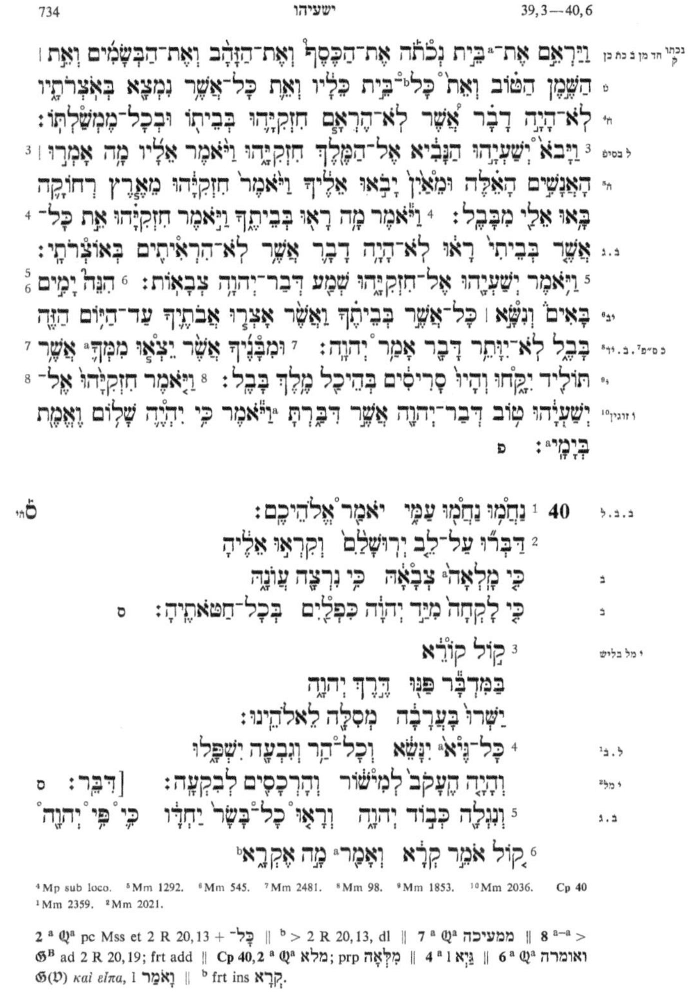

734   ישעיהו   39,3—40,6

וַיַּרְאֵם אֶת־בֵּית נְכֹתֹה אֶת־הַכֶּסֶף וְאֶת־הַזָּהָב וְאֶת־הַבְּשָׂמִים וְאֵת |

הַשֶּׁמֶן הַטּוֹב וְאֵת כָּל־בֵּית כֵּלָיו וְאֵת כָּל־אֲשֶׁר נִמְצָא בְּאֹצְרֹתָיו

לֹא־הָיָה דָבָר אֲשֶׁר לֹא־הֶרְאָם חִזְקִיָּהוּ בְּבֵיתוֹ וּבְכָל־מֶמְשַׁלְתּוֹ:

3 וַיָּבֹא יְשַׁעְיָהוּ הַנָּבִיא אֶל־הַמֶּלֶךְ חִזְקִיָּהוּ וַיֹּאמֶר אֵלָיו מָה אָמְרוּ |

הָאֲנָשִׁים הָאֵלֶּה וּמֵאַיִן יָבֹאוּ אֵלֶיךָ וַיֹּאמֶר חִזְקִיָּהוּ מֵאֶרֶץ רְחוֹקָה

בָּאוּ אֵלַי מִבָּבֶל: 4 וַיֹּאמֶר מָה רָאוּ בְּבֵיתֶךָ וַיֹּאמֶר חִזְקִיָּהוּ אֵת כָּל־

אֲשֶׁר בְּבֵיתִי רָאוּ לֹא־הָיָה דָבָר אֲשֶׁר לֹא־הִרְאִיתִים בְּאוֹצְרֹתָי:

5 וַיֹּאמֶר יְשַׁעְיָהוּ אֶל־חִזְקִיָּהוּ שְׁמַע דְּבַר־יְהוָה צְבָאוֹת: 6 הִנֵּה יָמִים

בָּאִים וְנִשָּׂא | כָּל־אֲשֶׁר בְּבֵיתֶךָ וַאֲשֶׁר אָצְרוּ אֲבֹתֶיךָ עַד־הַיּוֹם הַזֶּה

בָּבֶל לֹא־יִוָּתֵר דָּבָר אָמַר יְהוָה: 7 וּמִבָּנֶיךָ אֲשֶׁר יֵצְאוּ מִמְּךָ אֲשֶׁר

תּוֹלִיד יִקָּחוּ וְהָיוּ סָרִיסִים בְּהֵיכַל מֶלֶךְ בָּבֶל: 8 וַיֹּאמֶר חִזְקִיָּהוּ אֶל־

יְשַׁעְיָהוּ טוֹב דְּבַר־יְהוָה אֲשֶׁר דִּבַּרְתָּ וַיֹּאמֶר כִּי יִהְיֶה שָׁלוֹם וֶאֱמֶת

בְּיָמָי:
פ

40 1 נַחֲמוּ נַחֲמוּ עַמִּי   יֹאמַר אֱלֹהֵיכֶם:

2 דַּבְּרוּ עַל־לֵב יְרוּשָׁלִַם   וְקִרְאוּ אֵלֶיהָ

כִּי מָלְאָה צְבָאָהּ   כִּי נִרְצָה עֲוֹנָהּ

כִּי לָקְחָה מִיַּד יְהוָה כִּפְלַיִם   בְּכָל־חַטֹּאתֶיהָ:

3 קוֹל קוֹרֵא

בַּמִּדְבָּר פַּנּוּ   דֶּרֶךְ יְהוָה

יַשְּׁרוּ בָּעֲרָבָה   מְסִלָּה לֵאלֹהֵינוּ:

4 כָּל־גֶּיא יִנָּשֵׂא   וְכָל־הַר וְגִבְעָה יִשְׁפָּלוּ

וְהָיָה הֶעָקֹב לְמִישׁוֹר   וְהָרְכָסִים לְבִקְעָה: [דִּבֵּר: ס

5 וְנִגְלָה כְּבוֹד יְהוָה   וְרָאוּ כָל־בָּשָׂר יַחְדָּו   כִּי פִּי יְהוָה

6 קוֹל אֹמֵר קְרָא   וְאָמַר מָה אֶקְרָא

4 Mp sub loco. 5 Mm 1292. 7 Mm 2481. 8 Mm 98. 9 Mm 1853. 10 Mm 2036.   Cp 40
1 Mm 2359. 2 Mm 2021.

2 a Qa pc Mss et 2 R 20,13 + כֹּל b > 2 R 20,13, dl ‖ 7 a Qa ממעיכה ‖ 8 a–a >
GB ad 2 R 20,19; frt add ‖ Cp 40,2 a Qa מלא; prp מִלְאָה 4 a 1 גֵּיא Qa ‖ 6 a Qa ואומרה
G(V) καὶ εἶπα, 1 וָאֹמַר b frt ins קְרָא.

Figure 0.2 Scholarly edition of the same text as in Figure 0.1. In contrast to the early manuscript it has chapter and verse numbers along with scholarly notes at the bottom about alternative Hebrew readings to the ones given in the body of the text.

First, every translation involves many decisions by the translator about the Hebrew, Greek, or (in a few cases) Aramaic text. Scholars are still not sure about the meanings of some words, and the biblical languages do not translate precisely into English (or other modern languages). In addition, we have no original manuscript of any biblical book, and the existing biblical manuscripts disagree with each other at many points. This means that scholars must use **textual criticism** to decide the best Hebrew or Greek text in each case where the manuscripts disagree with each other. Luckily, over the last several centuries much progress has been made in uncovering ancient manuscripts and learning to identify copying errors and other changes in such manuscripts. In addition, there has been a huge growth in knowledge about the biblical languages.

MORE ON METHOD: TEXTUAL CRITICISM

As indicated in the text, "textual criticism" is not general study of a text. Instead, textual criticism focuses exclusively on getting the best textual reading for a given biblical text in its original language. Over the centuries scribes have introduced tens of thousands of minor changes into biblical texts as they copied them. Some were introduced by accident, as when a scribe might accidentally copy a given line twice or confuse letters. Other changes seem more intentional, where a scribe seems to have added a clarification of a place name or a theological correction or expansion.

In search of the best reading

Textual critics use two main methods to uncover the best reading for a Hebrew, Greek, or Aramaic biblical text. The first method is to compare ancient manuscripts of a given passage with each other, seeing if one or more **manuscript witnesses** to the passage seem to preserve a better reading. For example, one major witness for the Hebrew Bible is the **Masoretic text** (**MT**), the authoritative version of the Hebrew text that was produced by Jewish scribes in the medieval period. Other important witnesses for the Hebrew Bible are the biblical manuscripts found at the Dead Sea (Qumran), the Pentateuch preserved by the Samaritan community (around Samaria in the north), and even ancient translations of early Hebrew manuscripts, especially the **Septuagint** (**LXX**), an ancient set of translations of various biblical books into Greek.

On occasion, a biblical scholar may judge that all of the textual witnesses preserve an error. In such cases, that scholar may propose a reading that is not preserved in any manuscript. This second method of correction is called **conjectural emendation**.

These advances in knowledge about the text and language of the Bible mean that academic study of the Bible requires use of up-to-date translations of the biblical text. The **King James Version** (also known as the "Authorized Version"), though beautiful and cherished by many, is not an up-to-date translation. It was done four hundred years ago. Scholars knew far less about Hebrew and Greek then than they do now. Moreover, the translation is based on manuscripts with more errors and expansions than the manuscripts used for translations today. Therefore, the King James Version should not be used for readings in a twenty-first-century academic course on the Bible.

Translations also vary in religious perspective. The New Jewish Publication Society translation (NJPS) obviously comes out of a tradition of Jewish interpretation of the Tanach. The New Jerusalem Bible (NJB) and New American Bible (NAB) were produced by Catholic scholars. The New Revised Standard Version (NRSV; preceded by the Revised Standard Version – RSV) aims to be an ecumenical translation, but it is part of a line of Protestant revisions of the King James Version. The New International Version

(NIV; now available in updated form as Today's New International Version) is also Protestant and was conceived as an evangelical alternative to the RSV/NRSV.

Translations also vary in style: whether they aim to stay as close to the biblical languages as possible or whether they aim for maximum readability. **Formal correspondence** translations aim to stay as close as possible to word-for-word translation of the Hebrew, Aramaic, or Greek text. This can make them good tools for study, but it also makes them more difficult to understand. Translations that tend toward formal correspondence include the NRSV, NIV, and the New American Standard Bible (NASB). Other translations tend toward **dynamic equivalence**, which aims for equivalent meaning, but not a word-for-word translation. This results in translations that are more readable, but also contain more interpretation on the part of translators. Examples of translations that tend toward dynamic equivalence include the NJB, NAB, and several other translations produced by Protestant groups, such as the Good News Translation (GNT; also known as the "Good News Bible" and TEV – Today's English Version) and the Contemporary English Version (CEV). These translations should be distinguished from resources such as the Living Bible or Amplified Bible. The latter are not direct translations of the Hebrew and Greek texts, but paraphrases or expansions of other translations. For example, the Living Bible is a paraphrase of the nineteenth-century American Standard Version. Such paraphrase subtly adds yet another level of interpretation between the reader and the original text and is not helpful for academic work on the Bible.

One more way that contemporary Bible translations vary is in the extent to which they aim to use gender-neutral language, such as "humanity" instead of "mankind." Though older writing conventions endorsed the use of "man" for "human" or "he" for "he or she," many now argue that general use of such male-focused language reinforces male domination of women. This has led to two levels of revision of older translations that used such male-specific language. In some cases, past English translators had used male-specific words to translate Hebrew or Greek expressions that were gender neutral. The recent revision of the NIV translation, Today's New International Version, aims to correct such mistranslations to what is termed "gender-accurate" English expressions. Some other translations revise yet other references to people toward gender-neutral English terms, even in cases where the original biblical languages use masculine nouns. Examples of such translations include the NRSV, NJB, and the Contemporary Torah, a "gender-sensitive" revision of the NJPS. We generally follow that policy in this textbook, using "God" rather than "he" or "him" and preferring gender-neutral references to human beings. Nevertheless, the Bible was formed in a culture that privileged masculinity and conceived its God in largely masculine terms, and this is reflected at points in the translations included in this textbook.

Finally, readers should recognize that all these translations are published in different editions, each with its own perspective and added resources. For example, the *New Oxford Annotated Bible* and the *HarperCollins Study Bible* are not different translations, but different editions of the NRSV. Each one has a different introductory essay, introductions to the biblical books, and brief commentary on the biblical text written by biblical scholars commissioned by the publisher. Indeed, whenever you use a given translation, it usually includes many other elements that were added by the publisher of the particular edition that you are using: headings for different sections of the biblical text, marginal references to other biblical passages, maps, and other additions. These can be helpful resources. Nevertheless, users of such editions should be aware of how these additional elements – none of which is actually part of the Bible per se – can subtly influence how one reads a given biblical passage. They should be used critically.

As time allows, it is often a good idea to compare multiple good translations with each other to see where there are significant differences. Some like to use online resources for this, such as Crosswire's "Bible Tool" (www.crosswire.org/study) or the Bible Gateway (www.biblegateway.com), though these resources are generally limited to older, out-of-date translations. Better alternatives are *The Complete Parallel Bible*, which contains four recent translations of the whole Bible (NRSV, NJB, New English Bible [NEB], and NAB), or a Bible software tool (such as Accordance, Bible Works, or Logos) that is equipped with multiple, recent translations. Such comparison can reveal major differences between translations, and the more one finds such differences, the more one wonders how to decide between the alternatives. This is ideally solved by learning biblical languages! Many students, however, lack time and/or interest in going that far with biblical studies. For those lacking knowledge of biblical languages it is important to know where a given translation is but one possible rendering in English of a phrase in Hebrew, Aramaic, or Greek that could also be rendered, perhaps better, in another way. Comparison of Bible translations shows this.

PROLOGUE REVIEW

1. Know the meaning and significance of the following terms discussed in this chapter:

- apocrypha
- canon and canonical
- conjectural emendation
- deutero-canonical books
- dynamic equivalence translation
- formal correspondence translation
- Hebrew Bible
- King James Version
- Koran
- LXX
- manuscript witness
- Masoretic text
- MT
- Old Testament
- Pentateuch
- Septuagint
- supersessionism
- Tanach or TaNaK
- textual criticism
- Torah

RESOURCES FOR FURTHER STUDY

Editions of translations

The first edition listed provides an overview of several translations; some good editions follow.

The Complete Parallel Bible. New York: Oxford University Press, 1993.

The New Jerusalem Bible. New York: Doubleday, 1985. This is the NJB.

The New Oxford Annotated Bible (3rd edition), eds. Michael Coogan et al. New York: Oxford University Press, 2001. This contains the NRSV.

The Jewish Study Bible, eds. A. Berlin et al. New York: Oxford University Press, 2004. This contains the NJPS.

The HarperCollins Study Bible (fully revised and updated), eds. Harold W. Attridge et al. San Francisco: Harper SanFrancisco, 2006. This contains the NRSV.

One-volume commentaries

Mays, James L., ed. *HarperCollin's Bible Commentary* (revised edition). San Francisco: Harper & Row, 2000.

Newsom, Carol A., and Ringe, Sharon H., *The Women's Bible Commentary* (2nd edition). Louisville, KY: Westminster John Knox Press, 1998.

The formation of the Jewish and Christian scriptures

Barton, John. *How the Bible Came to Be*. Louisville, KY: Westminster John Knox Press, 1997.

Bible software packages for searches and initial work with biblical languages

For Mac (and Windows with a free Mac Emulator):
The "Introductory Level" of the "Scholars Collection" of Accordance software from Oaktree Software (www. accordancebible.com). Be sure to specify that you want the NRSV, NJB, or other up-to-date translation. Otherwise you are given the King James Version by default.

Only for Windows:
Bible Works (www.bibleworks.com)
Bibloi (www.silvermnt.com; this was formerly "Bible Windows")
Logos (www.logos.com)
You can also obtain free software for searching and reading the Bible at www.crosswire.org.

Useful websites for translation comparison

Note that these mainly feature old translations.
Crosswire – www.crosswire.org/study
The Bible Gateway – www.biblegateway.com
Studylight (more up-to-date translations) – www. studylight.org

APPENDIX 1: TRANSLATION AND PARAPHRASE COMPARISON OF ISA 52:13–15

ISA Chapter and Verse	Revised Standard Version	New American Standard Version	New International Version	Today's English Version (Good News Bible)
52:13	Behold my servant shall prosper, he shall be exalted and lifted up, and shall be very high.	Behold my servant will prosper, He will be high and lifted up, and greatly exalted.	See, my servant will act wisely; he will be raised and lifted up and highly exalted.	The Lord says, My servant will succeed in his task; he will be highly honored.
52:14	As many were astonished at him – his appearance was so marred, beyond human semblance, and his form beyond that of the sons of men –	Just as many were astonished at you, *My People*, so His appearance was marred more than any man, And his form more than the sons of men.	Just as there were many who were appalled at him – his appearance was so disfigured beyond that of any man and his form marred beyond human likeness –	Many people were shocked when they saw him; he was so disfigured that he hardly looked human.
52:15	so shall he startle many nations; kings shall shut their mouths because of him; for that which has not been told them they shall see, and that which they have not heard they shall understand.	Thus he will sprinkle many nations, Kings will shut their mouths on account of Him; For what had not been told them they will see, And what they had not heard they will understand.	so will he sprinkle many nations, and kings will shut their mouths because of him. For what they were not told, they will see, and what they have not heard, they will understand.	But now many nations will marvel at him, and kings will be speechless with amazement. They will see and understand something they had never known.

ISA Chapter and Verse	New English Bible	Living Bible	Tanakh	New Jerusalem Bible
52:13	Behold, my servant shall prosper, he shall be lifted up, exalted to the heights.	See, my Servant shall prosper; he shall be highly exalted.	Indeed, My servant shall prosper, be exalted and raised to great heights.	Look, my servant will prosper, will grow great, will rise to great heights.
52:14	Time was when many were aghast at you, my people;	Yet many shall be amazed when they see him – yes, even far-off foreign nations and their kings; [See the end of 52:15 for the rest]	Just as the many were appalled at him – So marred was his appearance, unlike that of man, His form, beyond human semblance –	As many people were aghast at him – he was so inhumanly disfigured that he no longer looked like a man –
52:15	. . . so now many nations recoil at the sight of him, and kings curl their lips in disgust. For they see what they had never been told and things unheard before fill their thoughts.	. . . they shall stand dumbfounded, speechless in his presence. For they shall see and understand what they had not been told before. They shall see my Servant beaten and bloodied, so disfigured one would scarcely know it was a person standing there. So shall he cleanse many nations.	Just so he shall startle many nations. Kings shall be silenced because of him, For they shall see what has not been told them, Shall behold what they never have heard.	so many nations will be astonished and kings will stay tight-lipped before him, seeing what had never been told them, learning what they had not heard before.

APPENDIX 2: CHARACTERISTICS OF SELECT ENGLISH TRANSLATIONS OF THE BIBLE

Translation	Background	Style	Use of MT (with translation of Isa 7:14 as indicator of theological leanings)	Gender language
NJPS (1985)	Jewish Publication Society	Formal correspondence, colloquial	No deviation from MT and uses Jewish chapter/verse numbering	Aims at "gender accuracy" (Note: 2006 JPS *Contemporary Torah* with more changes)
NRSV (1989)	Protestant, National Council of Churches	Formal correspondence, literary	Some deviation from MT in light of Dead Sea scrolls and LXX	Modest move toward inclusive language
NIV (1978)	Protestant Evangelical, International Bible Society	Formal correspondence, literary	Very modest deviation from MT, mostly in notes. Modifies Hebrew of Isa 7:14 to match Matthew	
Today's NIV (TNIV) (2005)	Protestant Evangelical, International Bible Society	Formal correspondence, literary	Very modest deviation from MT, mostly in notes. Modifies Hebrew of Isa 7:14 to match Matthew	Modest move toward "gender-accurate" language
NASB (1971)	Protestant Evangelical, Lockman Foundation	Formal correspondence, quite literal and often awkward	Little revision of MT. Modifies Hebrew of Isa 7:14 to match Matthew	
GNT (formerly TEV) (1992)	Protestant, American Bible Society (particularly for missionaries)	Dynamic equivalence, colloquial and simple vocabulary	Little deviation from MT	Includes revisions toward gender-inclusive language
CEV (1999)	Protestant, American Bible Society	Dynamic equivalence, colloquial, yet more simple vocabulary and syntax	Little deviation from MT. Modifies Hebrew of Isa 7:14 to match Matthew	Moves toward gender-inclusive language for humans
REB (1989), revision of NEB (1970)	British Protestant and Roman Catholic churches	Dynamic equivalence, literary	Substantial deviations from MT	Moves in 1989 revision toward gender-inclusive language
NJB (1985)	European Roman Catholic	Dynamic equivalence, but literary	Some substantial deviations from the MT	Very modest moves toward gender-inclusive language
NAB (1991)	United States Roman Catholic	Mix of dynamic equivalence and formal correspondence (the latter especially in NT)	Some substantial deviations from the MT. Modifies Hebrew of Isa 7:14 to match Matthew	Modest moves toward gender-inclusive language in NT and Psalms

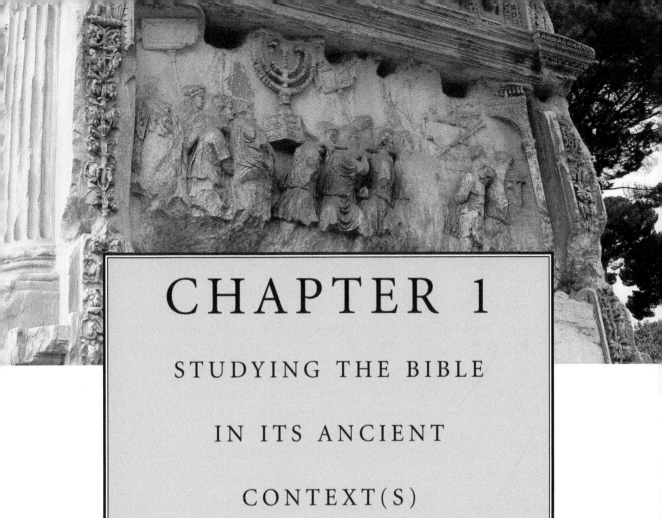

CHAPTER 1

STUDYING THE BIBLE

IN ITS ANCIENT

CONTEXT(S)

Chapter Outline

CHAPTER OVERVIEW

This chapter introduces the basic orientation of the textbook and sets the stage for what follows with three overviews: geographical, historical, and methodological. The beginning of the chapter answers the questions "What makes academic study of the Bible different from typical 'bible study?'" and "Why is such academic study important?" Next you gain a bird's-eye view of the major regions of the land of Israel, the major periods of Israel's history, and the major methods used by scholars to analyze the Bible. Your future study will be helped in particular by learning the location of the two major regions of ancient Israel – the heartland of tribal Israel to the north and the area of David's clan, Judah, to the south (with the famous city of Jerusalem between these two areas) – and by memorizing the dates of the major periods in the history of Israel (see also the appendix to this chapter).

READING

Exodus 14–15.
Scholars see two
accounts of
deliverance in
Exodus 14: can you?

EXERCISE

Write a half-page to one-page statement or mini-autobiography of your
past encounters with the Bible. Which parts of it have been most central
in such encounters? Have you studied the Bible in an academic context
before? Have you had unusually positive or negative experiences with the
Bible or people citing it?

Why History Is Important in Studying the Bible

At first glance, the Bible is one of the most familiar of books. Most families own a copy.
Every weekend, Jews and Christians read from it at worship. There are echoes of the
Bible in all kinds of music, from Handel's *Messiah* to reggae and hip hop. Popular
expressions, such as "Thou shalt not" or "Love thy neighbor as thyself," come from the
Bible. Movies are often filled with biblical allusions. And you still can find a copy of
the Bible, or at least the New Testament and Psalms, in many hotels.

AD, BC, BCE, and CE

The older expressions for dates, BC and AD, are explicitly Christian in orientation.
BC comes from "Before Christ," and AD comes from the Latin *anno Domini*, which
means "in the year of the Lord."

Over the last decades scholarly works have tended to use the more neutral
terms BCE and CE, which refer to "Before the Common Era" and "Common Era"
respectively. The year references are the same, but the labels are not specifically
Christian.

This *Introduction* uses the standard scholarly BCE and CE abbreviations.

At second glance, the Bible is one of the most foreign of books. Its language, even
in English translation, is often difficult to understand, especially if you are using the
King James Translation (1611), with its beautiful, but often obscure, seventeenth-century
cadences and words. The biblical texts that are translated in the King James and other
versions are still older. The New Testament was written in Greek, and its texts date from
about two thousand years ago (50–200 CE). The Old Testament was written in Hebrew,

and some of its parts date as far back as three thousand years (1000–164 BCE). Both testaments reflect their ancient origins in many ways. They use ancient literary forms and images that are not common now. They come out of religious contexts much different from contemporary Judaism or Christianity. And they are addressed to historical struggles and circumstances that most readers of the Bible do not know.

Bible Abbreviations, Verses, and Chapters

When books and articles cite biblical passages by chapter and verse, they usually follow this order: abbreviation for the biblical book, followed by the chapter number, followed by the verse. An example is Isa 44:28 (chapter 44, verse 28). If more than one verse is cited, dashes and commas can be used: Isa 44:20, 28 or Isa 44:10–13, 28. When scholars want to refer to the bulk of a passage without detailing specific verses left out, they will add an asterisk to indicate that some verses are not meant to be included in the reference, e.g. Genesis 28*.

Here are standard abbreviations for biblical books shared by Jewish and Christian Bibles (given in the Old Testament order):

Gen = Genesis	Esther = Esther	Hos = Hosea
Exod = Exodus	Job = Job	Joel = Joel
Lev = Leviticus	Ps or Pss = Psalms	Amos = Amos
Num = Numbers	Prov = Proverbs	Ob = Obadiah
Deut = Deuteronomy	Eccl = Ecclesiastes	Jon = Jonah
Josh = Joshua	Song = Song of Songs	Micah = Micah
Judg = Judges	(also known as Canticles,	Nah = Nahum
Ruth = Ruth	and Song of Solomon)	Hab = Habakkuk
Sam = Samuel	Isa = Isaiah	Zeph = Zephaniah
Kgs = Kings	Jer = Jeremiah	Hag = Haggai
Chr = Chronicles	Lam = Lamentations	Zech = Zechariah
Ezra = Ezra	Ezek = Ezekiel	
Neh = Nehemiah	Dan = Daniel	

Here are the abbreviations for books in the New Testament:

Matt = Matthew	Eph = Ephesians	Heb = Hebrews
Mark = Mark	Phil = Philippians	Jas = James
Luke = Luke	Col = Colossians	1–2 Pet = 1–2 Peter
John = John	1–2 Thess = 1–2	1–2–3 John = 1–2–3 John
Acts = Acts	Thessalonians	Jude = Jude
Rom = Romans	1–2 Tim = 1–2 Timothy	Rev = Revelation
1–2 Cor = 1–2 Corinthians	Titus = Titus	
Gal = Galatians	Phlm = Philemon	

The ancient aspects of the Bible are part of what give it its holy aura, but they also make biblical texts difficult to understand. If someone sees a reference to "Cyrus" in Isa 44:28 and 45:1, that person likely will have few associations with who "Cyrus" was and what he meant to the writer of this text. Most readers have even fewer associations with places and empires mentioned in the Bible, such as "Ephraim" or "Assyria." Usually, their only acquaintance with "Egypt" or "Babylonia" is a brief discussion in some kind of world history class. Furthermore, other aspects of biblical texts are often hard for readers to get much out of now – such as the genealogies of Genesis or the harsh words about enemies in the psalms. This means that large portions of the Bible mean little or nothing to many readers. Few people who try to read the Bible from beginning to end actually get very far, and those who do often fail to make much sense out of what they have read.

This book will give you keys to understand the often obscure parts of the Bible. Names (e.g. Cyrus), events (e.g. the liberation from Babylonian captivity), and general perspectives in the Bible that previously you might have skipped past or not noticed should come into focus and make sense. For many, the experience of reading the Bible in historical context is much like finally getting to see a movie in color that beforehand had only been available in black and white. It is not at all that the meaning of the Bible can or should be limited to the settings in which it was originally composed. On the contrary: along the way we will see how the Bible is an important document now thanks to the fact that it has been radically *re*interpreted over centuries, first by successive communities of ancient Israelites and later by Jewish and Christian communities who cherished the Bible. Still, learning to see scriptures in relation to ancient history and culture can make previously bland or puzzling biblical texts come alive.

The Origins of Verses and Chapters

The earliest Hebrew and Greek manuscripts of the Bible lack any chapter or verse markings or numberings. The Hebrew Bible/Old Testament was divided into sections for reading in the synagogue, and the Greek New Testament was divided into sections as well, but there were no numbers in these early manuscripts.

Verses were first added into the Hebrew Bible (without numbers) by the Masoretes, a group of Jewish scholars who worked in the seventh to tenth centuries CE and produced the standard edition of the Hebrew Bible now used in Judaism. The chapter divisions we now have were developed in 1205 by Stephen Langton, a professor in Paris and eventually an archbishop of the Church of England.

The first Old Testament and New Testament Bible with verses was produced in 1555 by a Parisian book seller, Robert Estienne (also known as Stephanus). He is reported to have divided a copy of his New Testament into the present 7,959 verses while riding horseback from Paris to Lyon. He also numbered the chapters and verses of both the Old and New Testament.

To pursue this historical approach, we will *not* read the Bible from beginning to end. Instead, we will look at biblical texts in relationship to the different historical contexts that they addressed. This means that rather than starting with the creation stories of Genesis 1–3, this book starts with remnants of Israel's earliest oral traditions. These are songs and sagas from the time when Israel had no cities and was still a purely tribal people. Our next stop will be texts from the rise of Israel's first monarchies, particularly certain "royal" psalms that celebrate God's choice of Jerusalem and anointing of kings there. When we move to the New Testament, it will mean beginning with Paul's letters, all of which were written before the gospels. As we move on through Israelite and early Christian history, we will see how biblical texts reflect the very different influences of major world empires: the Mesopotamian empires of Assyria and Babylonia, and then the Persian, Hellenistic (Greek), and Roman empires. The common thread will be historical, and this will mean starting most chapters with some discussion of the historical and cultural context of the biblical texts to be discussed there.

Overview: Order of Main Discussions of Biblical Books

Period of the Judges: Chapter 2. Oral traditions in Genesis 12–35, Exodus, and Judges 5.

Early monarchy/David and Solomon: Chapter 3. 1–2 Samuel, texts attributed to David and Solomon (Psalms [especially royal and Zion psalms], Proverbs, Ecclesiastes, Song of Songs), and Genesis 2–4 and parts of 6–11 (an early primeval history).

Later northern and southern monarchies: Chapter 4. Amos, Hosea, Micah, and early parts of Isaiah (along with possible northern traditions in Exodus, Genesis 25–35, etc.).

Twilight of the Monarchy in Jerusalem: Chapter 5. Deuteronomy through 2 Kings, Jeremiah, Nahum, and Zephaniah.

Exile of Judeans to Babylon: Chapter 6. Lamentations, Ezekiel, Isaiah 40–55, and major parts of Genesis through Numbers (especially the Abraham story in Genesis 12–25 and the book of Leviticus).

Return of exiles and rebuilding: Chapter 7. Haggai, Zechariah, Isaiah 56–66, Jonah, Ruth, Job, and the book of Psalms (along with parts of Ezra–Nehemiah and Genesis through Numbers).

The Hellenistic empires and crisis: Chapter 8. Sirach, Enoch, Daniel, Ezra–Nehemiah, 1–2 Chronicles, Esther, and the final formation of the Hebrew Bible (along with some on Ecclesiastes and Song of Songs).

The Roman empire: Chapters 9–15. The books of the New Testament, starting with Paul and then moving to the gospels and select other writings.

At first this approach may be disorienting, since it involves placing familiar biblical texts in a different order and in new contexts. Take the example of the story of creation in Gen 1:1–2:3. It seems straightforward enough as it is. Why wait to talk much about this opening story of the Bible until Chapter 6 of this *Introduction*? As we will see, one reason is that reading Gen 1:1–2:3 in relation to the Judeans' experience of forced exile in Babylonia (the focus of Chapter 6) explains the major emphasis in this text on the Sabbath. This is an aspect of the text that many people, especially non-Jews, completely miss, since it has little meaning for them. But the whole seven-day structure of the story is meant to lead up to one thing: God's rest on the seventh day and blessing of it (Gen 2:1–3). Reading this text in relation to the Babylonian exile highlights this important feature and makes sense of other aspects of the creation story as well.

This is just one way in which academic study of the Bible is quite a different thing from study of the Bible in Sunday school or even high school religion classes in parochial schools. Many people come to a university or seminary class on the Bible expecting a summary of the contents of the Bible or indoctrination into biblical theologies or values. Others expect a devotional approach that they have learned in church Bible studies where the Bible often is read as a lesson book for life. All these approaches have their value and place, but they differ from the academic approach of a college or seminary course. Moreover, they are misleading indicators of what to expect out of such a course. Where a student might expect to work hard in a history or organic chemistry class, study of the "Bible" – especially if it's imagined on the basis of earlier experience with religious education – promises to be easy. Yet an *academic* course on the Bible offers its own set of challenges, somewhat similar to those of a good course in history or English literature. Indeed, some students find academic study of the Bible especially difficult because it offers alternatives to their past interpretations of biblical texts that they cherish. These students not only must learn the course material about the Bible, but must integrate this knowledge with their beliefs and values.

The benefits of such study are substantial. Familiar texts offer new meanings. Difficult biblical texts start to make better sense when placed in their original historical contexts. Where once the Bible might have seemed a monolithic, ancient set of rules, it becomes a rich variety of different perspectives that have stood the test of time. We encourage you to be open to this approach and learn for yourself what it has to offer.

The Geography and Major Characters of the Biblical Drama

We start by setting the scene for the drama of biblical history, looking at the geography of the biblical world, major nations, and major historical periods. This information is important, because it will orient you to the quite different world in which the Bible was created.

Asked to picture the land of Israel, many would conjure up images from TV specials or popular movies where biblical events occur amidst sand dunes, palm trees, and small villages. The reality is that the area of Israel encompasses sharp contrasts in topography, rainfall, and vegetation. Imagine Map 1.1 as divided into four narrow strips running up and down. The strip to the left is the *coastal plain* along the Mediterranean sea. It is low, flat, and fertile and receives relatively regular rainfall. Non-Israelites lived here through most of Israelite history, and it was ruled from Jerusalem only for short

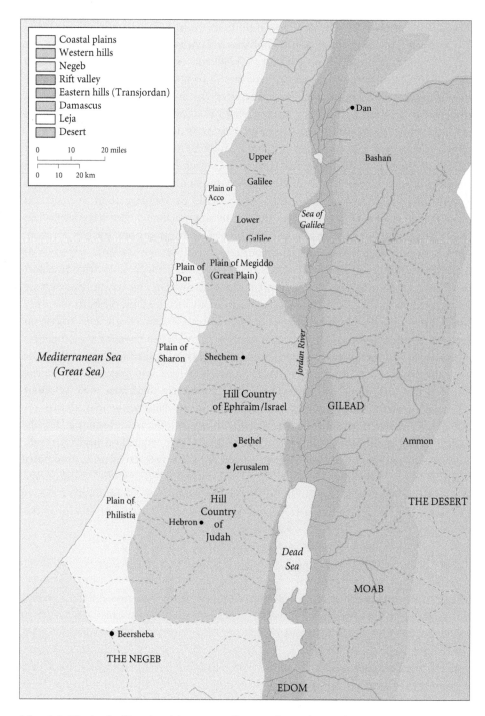

Map 1.1 The land of Israel and its surroundings. Redrawn from Adrian Curtis (ed.), *Oxford Bible Atlas* (4th edition). Oxford, New York: Oxford University Press, 2007.

periods. The next strip is the *central hill country* and runs down the middle of the map, encompassing the hill country of Judah, hill country of Ephraim (Israel), and Galilee. This is an area of rocky hills, rising up to 3,000 feet, where most of Israelite history took place. It is drier and less accessible than the coastal plain to the west. The third strip is the *Jordan Valley*, encompassing the Dead Sea, Jordan River, and Sea of Galilee (from north to south). This is one of the lowest places on earth, about 1,000 feet below sea level, and – aside from some oases – it is very dry and barren. The fourth strip is the *Transjordanian Plateau*, including Edom, Moab, Ammon, and the Gilead region (where Israelites settled). This plateau, now in the contemporary nation of Jordan, has similar characteristics to the central highlands of Israel. To the east of it (and off the map) lies the desert.

Before looking more broadly at the world of the ancient Near East, it is important to get a preliminary understanding of the different parts of the land of Israel and the peoples who lived there. Though people often apply the term "Israel" to this entire area, this term often refers more narrowly to the peoples who settled in the *northern* highlands described above ("Hill country of Ephraim/Israel" on Map 1.1, with Shechem at its center) along with parts of the Gilead of the Transjordan. For much of biblical history, this area and this people are to be distinguished from "Judah," which is located in the *southern* highlands of the map ("Hill country of Judah;" Hebron is a Judean city). Note that Jerusalem lay between Israel and Judah and was not "Israelite"/"Judean" until David conquered it by stealth at the outset of his monarchy. This distinction between "Judah" in the south and "Israel" in the north is important for much of Israel's early history. Later on, the term "Israel" came to encompass Judah as well, and the narratives of the Hebrew Bible – many of them written later – project that picture onto the earliest history of the people. Therefore, the word "**Israel**" has at least two major meanings in the Bible: a narrow sense referring to the ancient tribal groups settled in the northern highlands and a broader sense referring to Judah along with those other tribal groups. When people refer to the "land of Israel" or the "people of Israel," they usually are using the word "Israel" in the broader sense, but there will be numerous times in this *Introduction* when it will be important to remember the narrower sense of "Israel" (in the north) as opposed to "Judah" (in the south).

The "land of Israel" where most biblical events take place is actually relatively small. As you can see on Map 1.1, the Sea of Galilee is only 30 miles from the Mediterranean Sea, and the Dead Sea is only 60 miles away. The distance from the area around Shechem in the north to Beersheba in the south is about 90 miles. This means that the main setting of biblical history, the area of the central highlands (thus excluding the non-Israelite coastal plains), is about 40 miles by 90 miles – not much bigger than many large metropolitan areas. This tiny area is the site where texts and religious ideas were formed that would change world history. Notably, this highland area also encompasses many areas most in dispute in the contemporary Middle East, areas that are variously designated as "the West Bank," "occupied territories," and "Judea and Samaria." Before 1967 these regions were not part of the modern nation of Israel, but they were seized by Israel from Jordan during the 1967 war, and their status is a major issue in the ongoing Middle East conflict.

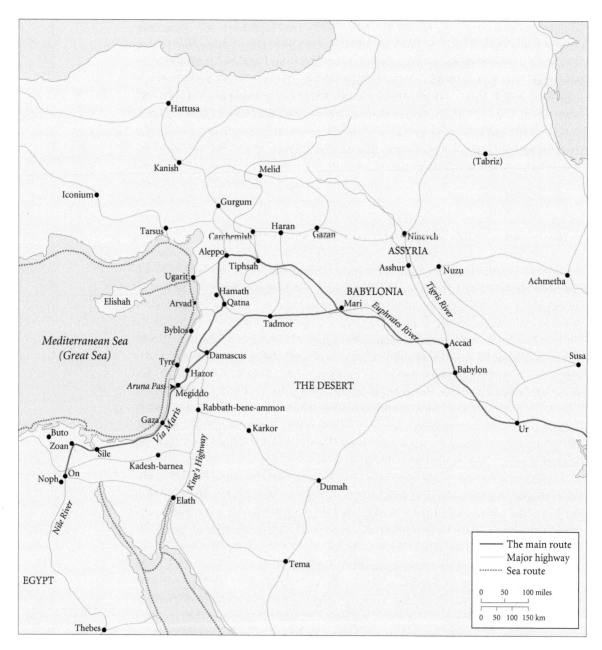

Map 1.2 The major routes of the ancient Near East. Note how the major routes move from Egypt on the left through Judah/Israel near the Mediterranean to Syria and Mesopotamia to the northeast and east. Redrawn from Yohanan Aharoni and Michael Avi-Yonah (eds.), *The Macmillan Bible Atlas* (revised edition). New York, Macmillan, 1977, map 9.

This recent dispute is only the latest chapter in thousands of years of struggles for control of this narrow strip of land. In ancient times, the land of Israel occupied a strategic location along the "Fertile Crescent" extending from Egypt in the southwest to the Mesopotamian empires of Assyria and Babylonia in the northeast. Because much of the area east of Israel was impassable desert, the major roads between Egypt and Mesopotamia had to cross the narrow strip of land between the Mediterranean Sea and the desert (see Map 1.2). Israel lay right along those roads and often got run over by the armies of its more powerful neighbors. The various empires of the ancient Near East were almost always laying claim to Israel and the surrounding areas, and the peoples of Israel got caught in the middle.

Major Periods in the Biblical Drama

The major turns in biblical history can be seen in this context. The Egyptian empire dominated the area of ancient Israel from around 1450 to 1200 BCE, the years when most scholars think the biblical exodus may have happened. Then, a series of catastrophes ended Egyptian rule over the area and inaugurated a power vacuum in the land of Israel. This is when we first see identifiable archaeological evidence of a "people of Israel." We first see this people settled in small villages in the hill country of Judah and Israel during the **pre-state tribal period** (1250–1000 BCE, including the time of the chieftain, Saul), then kings David and Solomon ruled this whole area for about a century from their capital in Jerusalem (**united monarchy**, 1000–930 BCE), and finally the northern tribes split from this monarchy (930 BCE). Thus began the period of the **divided monarchy**, where there were two kingdoms in broader Israel: a kingdom of Israel in the north, and a kingdom of Judah in the south (930–722 BCE).

This window of freedom from imperial domination, however, was not to last. Especially in the late eighth century (745 BCE and onward), the Assyrian empire, based in what is now northern Iraq, gained control of both Israel and (later) Judah (see Map 1.3). This empire completely destroyed the kingdom of Israel in 722 BCE and dominated the kingdom of Judah for decades. Indeed, from 745 to 586 BCE, Israel and Judah were dominated by a series of brutal empires – Assyria, Egypt (for a couple of years), and Babylonia (based in middle Iraq). Though Judah enjoyed brief independence between domination by the Assyrians and Egyptians, the nation was dominated and eventually destroyed by the Babylonian empire, which reduced Jerusalem, along with its Temple, to rubble in 586 BCE (**destruction of Jerusalem**, ending a period of "Judah alone," 722–586 BCE). Thus began one of the most important periods of biblical history, the **Babylonian exile** (586–538). At the outset of this period, most of the elite who had lived in Judah were forcibly deported to Babylon, and in many cases neither they nor their children ever returned.

The story of Israel and empires, however, was not over. Just decades later, the Persian ruler, Cyrus, conquered the Babylonian empire, ushering in a period of Persian rule of Judah that lasted from 538 to 332 BCE (the **Persian period**, the beginning of the **post-exilic period** starting 538 BCE). The Bible records a number of ways in which Cyrus

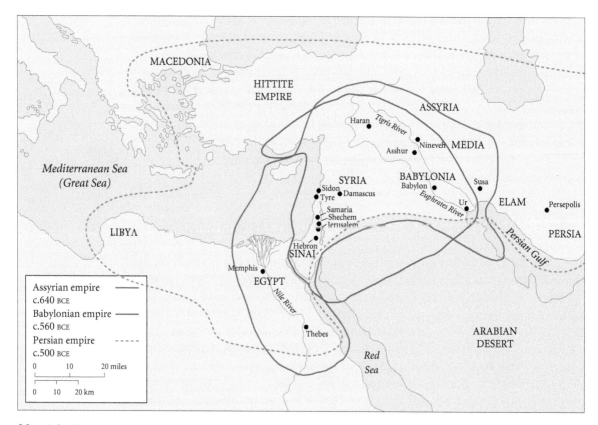

Map 1.3 The reach of three of the major empires that dominated Israel and/or Judah: the Assyrian, Babylonian, and Persian empires. Redrawn from www.bible.ca, Abingdon Press, 1994.

and his successors helped former exiles in Babylon rebuild the Temple and rebuild their community. Later, Alexander the Great conquered the area in 333 BCE, beginning a period of Hellenistic rule, and it appears that Alexander and his successors generally continued the Persian policies of support of Jerusalem and its leadership during their rule of Judah and Jerusalem (**Hellenistic period**, 332–167 BCE). Nevertheless, in the late second century (starting in 167 BCE), there was a major crisis in Judah, precipitated by the efforts of some elite Judeans to turn the city of Jerusalem into a Greek city. This crisis eventually led to the formation, for a brief period, of another monarchy in Judah, this one led by a priestly family called the **Hasmoneans** (also known as the **Maccabees**). This **Hasmonean monarchy** continued from 142 to 63 BCE, when the Romans took control of the area, which they named "Palestine" and put under control of a series of governors. The year 63 BCE represents the beginning of the **Roman period** in Palestine.

With this, "Palestine" joined much of the surrounding world as part of the Roman empire. This is the time when Jesus lived, the early church formed in the wake of his crucifixion by the Romans, and the Christian movement spread across the Mediterranean Sea to cities around the Roman empire. This was also the time of multiple Judean revolts against Roman control that eventually led to the destruction in 70 CE of the Jerusalem Temple rebuilt under the Persians (**destruction of the Second Temple**) and the complete destruction of Jewish Jerusalem in 135 CE. Thus the Jewish temple state was completely destroyed. In the wake of this destruction, the Jewish people were once again faced with the issue of survival. The main form of Jewish life to survive this catastrophe was rabbinic Judaism, which grew out of the Torah-centered scholarship and leadership of the earlier, popular movement of the Pharisees. As we will see, the early followers of Jesus offered a different way forward in the wake of this disaster – belief in the resurrected Jesus as the expected messiah and divine Son of God.

Later chapters of this *Introduction* will give details about all of these historical periods, correlating each of them with biblical texts. The aim here is to give a sense of how much Israelite history was shaped by relationships with various empires. Though "Israel" (and "Judah") emerged as recognizable peoples and states during an imperial power vacuum (1200–745 BCE), the books of the Bible were largely written during the periods of imperial domination by Assyrian, Babylonian, Persian, Hellenistic, and Roman empires. We gain a much deeper understanding of the Bible the more we see how diverse biblical pictures of the "empire of God" were formed in response to domination by these powerful empires in the ancient world.

Multiple Contexts, Multiple Methods

Reading biblical texts in relation to their original contexts can make many aspects of them come alive, but the reason such texts are read now is that they have remained meaningful to diverse communities in much later contexts. These texts are in the Bible because they have consistently transcended their origins. This *Introduction* will discuss both aspects of the Bible: its origins in the ancient Near East and its later interpretation by Jewish, Christian, and even Muslim communities today. Knowing more about the Bible's early contexts gives some perspective on contemporary differences in interpretation. The more you know about the antiquity of the Bible, the more you may appreciate both the care and the creativity with which it has been read and reread over time by different communities.

This can be illustrated through a brief look at how different methods of biblical criticism might look at Israel's "exodus," the story of **Yahweh**'s (see the Miscellaneous Box on "The Name of Israel's God: Yahweh/the LORD") liberation of the people from Egypt that is now found in the first chapters of the book of Exodus (Exodus 1–15). To start, some scholars try to reconstruct whether and when this exodus actually happened. Such academic study of the history of Israel uses biblical texts as one among multiple sources for the reconstruction of "what probably happened." So far, the results of such study have been inconclusive. On the one hand, many scholars believe some sort of exodus out of Egypt happened, probably during the centuries just before the emergence of the people of "Israel" as a distinct group in the highlands of Canaan. On the other hand, most academic scholars of the Bible also believe that the written texts of the Bible are so far removed from the events that they describe that they are not useful for precise retelling of what actually happened back then: who said what, how many and who were involved, etc. The biblical texts are not reliable for such details because they have been filtered by centuries of oral retelling and written expansions by later Israelites. Imagine a game of "telephone" with hundreds of people over a period of five hundred years passing along a story that is important to them to the next generation. Unlike the game of telephone, this process of retelling would involve deliberate changes to the story so that it spoke to the particular concerns of each generation. Now imagine trying to use the end result of this process for historical analysis. Because biblical texts are so shaped by time, scholars studying the history of Israel attempt to reconstruct what happened through analyzing them and comparing them – where possible – with archaeological records and non-biblical historical sources.

The Name of Israel's God: Yahweh/the LORD

The name of Israel's God in Hebrew is Yahweh, but you will not see this name written out in most English translations of the Bible. Instead, most translations have "the LORD" where the Hebrew manuscripts have a strange combination of the consonants for Yahweh (YHWH) and the vowels for the Hebrew word "lord." Why this combination?

The consonants are earlier, since the earliest Hebrew Bible manuscripts were written in all consonants. When Jewish scholars started producing manuscripts with vowels, the divine name Yahweh had become so holy that they did not pronounce it out loud (This is still true for many Jews.) Therefore, they added the vowels for "lord" in every place where the consonants for Yahweh occurred so that readers would say "lord" rather than the holy name. English translations reflect this combination when they put "lord" in all capital letters (LORD), indicating that this particular "lord" is Yahweh. (Note "Jehovah" is the word that is produced when you simply pronounce the consonants of YHWH with the vowels for the Hebrew word for "lord.")

We will be focusing here on the state of the Bible before such prohibitions on pronouncing the divine name existed. So there will be occasions where it will be helpful to refer to Israel's God by the name Yahweh.

Historical criticism is a family of historical methods that analyzes how and where the biblical texts (and oral traditions in them) were composed. "Criticism" in this case does not mean that historical-critics find fault with the biblical texts that they study, but that they use academically critical analysis to arrive at their conclusions rather than starting on the basis of faith assumptions. Through **tradition criticism** and **form criticism** biblical scholars attempt to identify early oral traditions standing behind the biblical text. For example, past tradition and form critics have supposed that the following song of Miriam may be one of the earliest traditions in the Bible to speak of the defeat of the Egyptian army at the Red sea:

> Sing to Yahweh, for he has been victorious
> Horse and rider, he has thrown into the sea. (Exod 15:21)

Form critics study different types of texts in the Bible and their likely social contexts. They would argue that the text above was the kind of "victory song" that was sung by women upon return of men from battle. Tradition critics investigate the telling and retelling process of early biblical traditions, often analyzing written texts to uncover the centuries-long evolution of oral traditions (and sometimes written traditions) about an event such as the exodus. **Source criticism** and **redaction criticism** attempt to reconstruct the literary development of such biblical texts. For example, more than two hundred years ago source critics discovered that the story of Israel's deliverance from Egypt in Exodus 14 is actually an interweaving of two, originally separate written accounts of the same event, one source which tells of the sea waters being driven back by a strong wind, and another source which tells of the Israelites being led through the sea between two walls of water. Redaction critics study the final formation of the biblical text through the combination of such sources and literary expansions of them. Where source critics study the written building blocks of the biblical text, redaction critics examine how those building blocks were put together and added onto. The broad term for this kind of study of the formation of the Bible out of both oral and written traditions is "**transmission history**."

Many scholars, however, focus not on how the Bible was formed, but on what it means and has meant to generations of readers of the Bible. For example, **literary criticism** has drawn on methods in study of modern literature to study the plot, characterization, pacing, and shape of biblical texts. Such critics have examined Exodus 1–15 as if it were a novel, looking at *how* the story is artfully told: how is Moses introduced and characterized? How does this contrast with the characterization of the Egyptians and their leaders? What does the reader expect and learn as the narrative unfolds? Such study of the poetic and narrative dynamics of biblical texts is distinct from study of how such texts have been interpreted by later readers, which is the **history of interpretation**. Historians of interpretation study how the story of the Exodus is featured in Islam, as well as its becoming central to both Judaism and Christianity. The exodus story is the centerpiece of the Jewish celebration of Passover and is a founding story for the Christian practices of baptism and eucharist. Meanwhile, **cultural criticism** has studied ways the exodus story is not just read in faith communities, but has entered popular culture, through media such as reggae music or movies like *The Ten Commandments* and *The Prince of Egypt*. Both history of interpretation and cultural criticism are embraced in the overall study in **reception history** of how biblical texts have been used and consciously interpreted.

Finally, various forms of **ideological criticism** analyze ways that the exodus story can be, has been, and should be read in the midst of systematic structures of power.

For example, early **feminist criticism** lifted up the importance of the story of the mid-wives in the lead-up to the exodus (Exod 1:15–21), and later feminist critics have raised questions about the male focus of the exodus story and most other parts of the Bible. **Gender criticism** analyzes biblical depictions of both male and female gender in the Bible, including the implicit characterization of God in the exodus as a masculine, militaristic God, "a man of war" (Exod 15:3). Finally, **postcolonial criticism** has examined how texts like the exodus story were formed in response to imperial dynamics and later played a role in colonial imperialism. Thus, a postcolonial critic could look at how the biblical exodus story was written hundreds of years after the events it describes as a response to Assyrian, Babylonian, or other domination. But postcolonial critics have also looked at ways Christian missionaries and European colonial powers justified their domination of other peoples through depicting themselves as the true heirs of the "Israel" depicted as favored by God in the Exodus story. Thus "postcolonial" criticism adds a particular perspective to both study of the formation of the biblical text and study of its history of interpretation.

Looking Forward to the Big Picture

This chapter has given an overview which will be filled in by the following textbook. It may be disorienting to encounter so many terms and dates at once. Nevertheless, it is important to get this larger picture in order to understand the details of what follows. The first eight chapters of this *Introduction* will unfold the story of the creation of the Hebrew Bible/Old Testament. This story moves from discussion of oral traditions in pre-literate Israel all the way through to the final formation of the Hebrew Bible in the kingdom of the Hasmoneans. Though the first chapters will uncover a strange and different ancient Israel unfamiliar to many readers, this historical approach will illuminate many aspects of the Bible that otherwise make little sense. In addition, it will provide a starting point for engaging other scholarly methods of looking at biblical texts in new ways. Similarly, Chapters 9–15 will trace the development of the New Testament writings, beginning with a discussion of the earliest oral traditions about Jesus.

Of course, the analysis of the formation of the Bible and its texts is always in flux. Within the space of this brief *Introduction* we can touch on only a few of the major debates. Nevertheless, scholars have been doing this kind of historical analysis of the Bible for about three hundred years, and these efforts have produced some interesting and important results. This textbook draws on the breadth of that scholarship in giving a historical orientation to the Bible that can be a starting point for further study, questioning, and correction.

CHAPTER ONE REVIEW

1. Know the meaning and significance of the following terms discussed in this chapter:
- cultural criticism
- feminist criticism
- form criticism
- gender criticism
- historical criticism
- history of interpretation
- ideological criticism
- Israel [two meanings]
- literary criticism
- postcolonial criticism
- reception history
- redaction criticism
- source criticism
- tradition criticism
- transmission history
- Yahweh

2. Be able to identify the following areas on a map and describe their general characteristics:
- coastal plain
- central hill country
- Jordan valley
- Judah
- Transjordan

3. Know the dates and basic significance of the following overall periods of history:
- pre-state tribal period
- united monarchy
- divided monarchy
- destruction of Jerusalem
- Babylonian exile
- Persian period
- post-exilic period
- Hellenistic period
- Hasmonean (Maccabean) monarchy
- beginning of the Roman period
- destruction of the Second Temple

4. Know the order in which the following empires dominated Israel and Judah:
- Assyrian
- Babylonian
- Persian
- Hellenistic (or Greek)
- Roman

RESOURCES FOR FURTHER STUDY

Overviews of the history of Israel

Miller, J. Maxwell. *The History of Israel: An Essential Guide.* Nashville: Abingdon, 1997.

Shanks, Hershel. *Ancient Israel: From Abraham to the Roman Destruction of the Temple* (2nd edition). Washington, DC: Biblical Archaeology Society, 1999.

Geography of lands and places featured in the Bible

Atlas of the Bible Lands (revised edition). Maplewood, NJ: Hammond, 1990.

Rainey, Anson F., and Notley, R. Steven. *The Sacred Bridge: Carta's Atlas of the Biblical World.* Jerusalem: Carta, 2006. Detailed. Much focus on reconstructing history.

Rogerson, John. *The New Atlas of the Bible.* London: McDonald, 1985. Organized not by historical periods, but by regions. Excellent photographs and art.

Discussions of methods in biblical interpretation

Barry, Peter. *Beginning Theory: An Introduction to Literary and Cultural Theory* (2nd edition). Manchester: Manchester University Press, 2002. Excellent, accessible overview of more recent literary theory and methods of interpretation.

McKenzie, Steven L., and Haynes, Stephen R. *To Each Its Own Meaning: An Introduction to Biblical Criticisms and Their Application* (2nd edition). Louisville, KY: Westminster John Knox Press, 1999.

Book of Exodus, problems of history, and history of interpretation

Johnstone, William. *Exodus.* Old Testament Guides. Sheffield: Sheffield Academic Press, 1990. Especially pp. 31–8.

Langston, Scott M. *Exodus.* Blackwell Commentary Series. Oxford: Blackwell, 2006. History of interpretation.

APPENDIX: ISRAEL'S HISTORY AND EMPIRES

(Prehistory of Israel: domination of Canaan by Egypt, 1450–1200 BCE)

Emergence of "Israel" in imperial power vacuum
    Appearance of Israelite villages in unsettled hill country (1250–1000 BCE)
    David and Solomon's united monarchy in Jerusalem (1000–930 BCE)
    Divided monarchy: southern Judah and northern Israel (930–722 BCE)

Oppression by successive empires: Assyria, Egypt, and Babylonia (745–586 BCE)
    Fall of northern kingdom (722 BCE)
    Destruction of Jerusalem and exile of its leadership (586 BCE; also other waves of exile)

Imperial sponsorship of (formerly exiled) Judeans: post-exilic period (starting 538 BCE)
    Persian-sponsored rebuilding and rule of Judah (538–332 BCE)
    Hellenistic continuation of Persian policies until Hellenistic crisis (332–167 BCE)
    Hellenistic crisis and emergence of Hasmonean/Maccabean monarchy (167–63 BCE)

Roman rule (starting 63 BCE with different dates of end)
    Destruction of the Second Temple (70 CE)
    Total destruction of Jerusalem (135 CE)

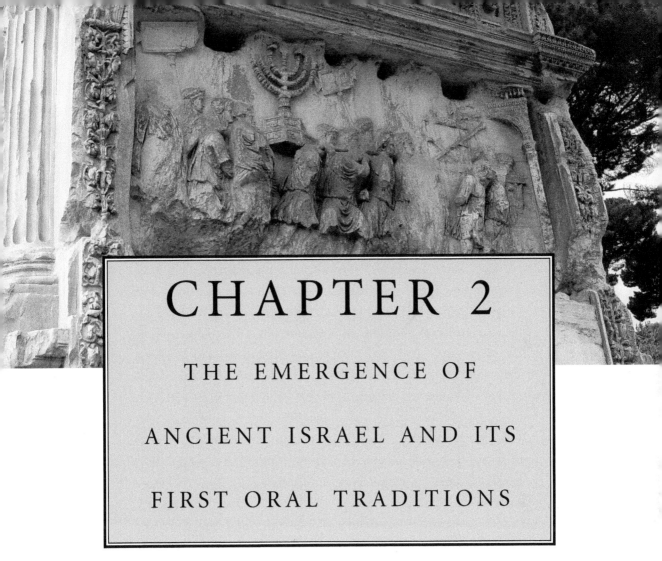

CHAPTER 2

THE EMERGENCE OF

ANCIENT ISRAEL AND ITS

FIRST ORAL TRADITIONS

Chapter Outline

CHAPTER OVERVIEW

This chapter addresses the questions "How did the earliest Israelites live?" and "What were some of Israel's most ancient traditions?" You will learn about ancient Israelite tribal life and how that form of social organization is distinguished from two other forms of social life important in later chapters of Israel's history: the monarchal city-state and the empire. The chapter discusses some unique characteristics of the kind of oral tradition typical of such tribal groups, and it finds evidence of such oral traditions embedded in biblical texts about Jacob, exodus from Egypt, and Deborah's victory over the armies of Hazor. In their early oral form (no longer available to us), these stories and poems, often celebrating devious "tricksters" who triumph over all odds, formed part of a "cultural memory" that helped distinguish the tribal-culture Israelites from the Canaanites surrounding them. At the same time, despite these differences in social organization and tribal tradition, you will also discover in this chapter ways that early Israel was more "Canaanite" in its religion and culture than you previously thought. Read both for ways ancient Israel was different from its neighbors and ways it was similar.

Imagining Early Israel

We begin with a look at the stories and songs treasured by Israel at the outset of its history. More than anywhere else in this book this requires a lot of imagination, since we have no Israelite writings from this period. Therefore, we must piece together a picture of Israel based on a combination of archaeology, some material from neighboring cultures, and distant echoes of early Israel in the much later writings now found in our Bible.

So we start with imagination – a creative reconstruction of the kind of village where Israel's first oral traditions might have developed. It is a journey back to the time described in the Bible in the books of Joshua and Judges. Nevertheless, there are major contrasts between what these books say about this "period of the Judges" and what historians reconstruct of it. Later, in Chapter 5 of this *Introduction*, we will discuss the later writing of Joshua and Judges, along with the Pentateuch that comes before them (Genesis–Deuteronomy). For now, however, the focus is not on the written books of the Bible, but on the oral culture that produced Israel's first traditions. Here is a picture based on archaeology and careful analysis of the Bible and non-biblical texts.

If we were to take a time machine back to Israel's beginnings, the journey probably would take us to one of the hilltop villages in the hill country that existed in the late second millennium (1250–1000 BCE) between the coastal plains and Jordan valley (see Figure 2.1). The early Israelites in the **village** lived on a subsistence level, surviving

Figure 2.1 Part of the hill country of central Israel. Notice the ancient terraces cut into the limestone hills to help in farming them.

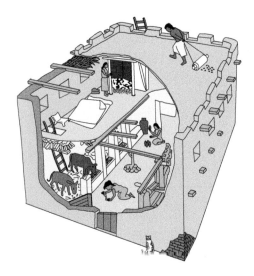

Figure 2.2 Typical pillared house of the Israelites. The bottom floor had stables for animals, cistern for water, and areas for cooking and food preparation. The top floor was where the family slept, dined, and entertained. Redrawn from Philip J. King and Lawrence E. Stager, *Life in Biblical Israel*. Louisville, KY: Westminster John Knox Press, 2001, page 29.

largely on the crops that they grew. Generally there were two main seasons, a dry summer–fall season and a rainy winter–spring season culminating in the harvest of barley, then wheat and other crops. The rain on which they depended was fickle. They would store water from the rainy season in sealed underground holes, "cisterns." They used large pottery jars to store food produced from the harvest. Nevertheless, about every three or four years there would be too little rain for crops. Life would be especially hard then, with families struggling to keep from starving until another year, a better rainy season, and the first harvests from that next year's crop. In such times they might sacrifice and eat one of their precious animals in order to survive. Otherwise, animals were primarily sources of milk and clothing (wool or skins).

Our village would have only a few homes, housing a handful of clans, settled in separate households where extended families lived together: grandparents, their sons and sons' wives, unmarried daughters, and dependents. Only about 50–300 people would have lived in each such village, and their lives were short and hard (as everywhere else in the ancient world). Though a few lucky individuals lived much longer, most males who survived early childhood typically lived into their mid-thirties, while most women died already in their late twenties, half of them in childbirth. They were vulnerable to starvation, diseases, warfare, and (for women) the hazards of childbirth.

Because a village lacked a wall or many men of fighting age, it was vulnerable to raids from other areas or attacks by the organized armies of the city-states in the

What Was Earliest "Israel" and Who Were "Judges"?

Though the Bible portrays "Israel" as a coherent group of 12 tribes descended from Jacob, most scholars now agree that this is not an accurate historical portrayal. Instead, as we will see later (in our look at Judges 5), earliest "Israel" was a loosely organized group of tribes who shared a way of life (in villages) and helped in each other's military defense. Anthropologists use the term "**segmentary society**" to describe the kind of decentralized social grouping that was early Israel.

One distinctive element of such segmentary societies is the lack of a permanent power structure, such as a kingship. Instead, the villages and larger groupings were guided in their day-to-day life by elders. In times of great need, charismatic leaders, such as Deborah, would arise to join the different groups of "Israel" into a common army. They are referred to in English biblical translations as "judges," but a better – though awkward – translation probably would be "temporary leaders."

coastal areas and lowlands. Their only hope of defense was divine help, along with assistance from banding together with other villages in their tribe (e.g. Ephraim, Manasseh, Asher). In times of particular crisis, the villages of multiple tribes might join together in a temporary military alliance led by a charismatic individual. As we will see in the Song of Deborah, it was not always easy to pull together these scattered tribes and villages into a coordinated defense. Such texts show that – contrary to some other biblical portrayals – earliest "Israel" was a very loosely organized whole. Villages and tribes bonded together to counter the unpredictabilities of military or agricultural catastrophe. Still, the primary social reality for most people in early Israel would have been their village and its clans. They would have spent the vast bulk of their lives living and working within the confines of the village itself and the surrounding hills.

This way of life contrasted with that of non-Israelite **monarchal city-states** near Israel. Ancient Near Eastern city-states were territories controlled by a city, generally cities ruled by kings. Such cities could amass resources and achieve levels of organization that were impossible in more decentralized systems such as tribal Israel. The walls around cities gave them immense defensive advantages over forces attacking with superior numbers. City-states usually had a professional army, whose training and equipment gave them an advantage over more disorganized voluntary forces like those of Israel. Their greater military power and social organization allowed them to dominate surrounding areas, requiring peasants under their domination to help build fortifications in the city and provide regular deliveries of a certain amount of their produce. Even though the stories of the book of Judges come from a later time, we can read between the lines to see signs of struggle by Israelites against the attempts of surrounding city-states (e.g. Hazor) to dominate them. These threats, along with raids from groups such as the Midianites and Amalekites, created the need for charismatic leaders in crisis, "judges" such as Deborah or Samson, to rally disparate villages and tribes together, pooling their resources to repel a common enemy.

One enemy these Israelites did not have to face – in stark contrast to later periods in the history of Israel – was the might of a major ancient Near Eastern **empire** such as Egypt or Babylonia. The most this village culture would have known of such superpowers would have been distant echoes of Egyptian influence in some of the cities against which the villages had to fight for survival. Before the Israelite settlements emerged, Egypt had dominated the area for about two hundred years, subduing and demanding allegiance from the rulers of its major cities. Eventually, Egypt lost control

Figure 2.3 Tablet containing a letter from Abdi-heba, the ruler of Jerusalem while it was still a Jebusite city, before David captured it. In it the ruler reports on the area to his overlords in Egypt.

of the area. Nevertheless, Egyptian influence continued for centuries in major coastal cities such as Byblos, and elsewhere in Palestine.

Unfortunately, we lack written texts from the Israelites of this period. Like other peoples of small villages across the Near East, the early Israelites almost certainly did not have time or need to learn to read and write extensive literary texts. We know from both comparative and archaeological evidence that writing – when it occurs – is primarily connected to centralized and hierarchical urban forms of social organization (e.g. Jerusalem). Nevertheless, like other small groups throughout time, our early Israelite villagers would have had a rich and varied cultural life. Rather than writing texts, they passed on traditions orally from one generation to another. These traditions would have included genealogical trees organizing clans and villages into tribal groups and sub-groups, stories of cultural heroes such as Jacob, and songs of deliverance about the exodus or the victory under Deborah.

History and the Books of Joshua and Judges

At this point we are discussing Israel's earliest history in the land. This is the time when Israel lived in villages and did not yet have a king, a period described in the biblical books of Joshua and Judges. These books, however, date from around 600 BCE at the earliest, at least five hundred years after the events they describe. They are different from each other, and each builds on diverse oral and written traditions to tell its stories. For example, the books tell up to three different stories of the conquest of several cities: e.g. Hebron in Josh 10:36–7, 15:13–14, and Judg 1:10 or Debir in Josh 10:38–9, 15:15–17, and Judg 1:11. Therefore, historians of ancient Israel are ever more careful about how they use information from Joshua and Judges. Also, the discipline of archaeology has provided an important control for helping such historians evaluate the historical usefulness of biblical traditions. Later in this *Introduction* we will return to look at the books of Joshua and Judges as theological texts addressed to the people of the seventh century.

These **oral traditions** were in flux, as they were sung and told from year to year amidst constantly cycling generations. At one time scholars used to think that non-literate cultures, such as the early Israelites, had unusual powers of memory that allowed them to memorize and precisely recite oral traditions over hundreds of years. Careful study of such cultures, however, has revealed that people who memorize traditions through purely oral means change them constantly and substantially. To be sure, some elements may be preserved because they are anchored in a name, topographical feature, or ongoing cultural practice. Nevertheless, the singers of oral cultures constantly adapt the traditions they receive, and they only partially can correct for this process of adaptation through consultation with networks of other oral singers and storytellers.

This means that the early traditions of ancient Israel, whatever they were, evolved in their journey across the centuries of the late second millennium, passing from one set of lips to another. A name such as "Moses" might stick, even the name of a long-abandoned Egyptian city – "Rameses" – but the story of the Israelites' exodus out of Egypt would evolve as they faced new enemies and challenges in later centuries. In the process of oral telling and retelling, the "Moses" of the story might start to resemble leaders or liberators at the time of retelling, and the "Egypt" of the retold story might resemble later enemies. Similarly, the story of Jacob wrestling God at the Jabbok (now in Gen 32:22–32) explains the place name "Penuel," and because the place name implies a divine encounter (Penuel is interpreted as Hebrew for "face of God"), that part of the story may have stayed stable over time while other details changed in the retelling process.

MORE ON METHOD: TRADITION HISTORY AND TRANSMISSION HISTORY

Though traditions can be written as well as oral, many scholars use the term "**tradition history**" to refer to the history of oral traditions that existed before and alongside the written texts now in the Bible. Different versions of an oral tradition can be recognized by the combination of thematic or plot parallels on the one hand and variation in characters, setting, and especially wording on the other. Take the example of the parallel stories of Abraham and Sarah at Philistine Gerar with King Abimelech (Gen 20:1–18, 21:22–34) and Isaac and Rebekah at the same place and with the same king (Gen 26:6–33). Look at the similarities and differences! Though the two sets of stories are remarkably parallel, they diverge enough from each other that many believe them to be oral variants of the same tales.

Scholars can use the term "transmission history" to refer more broadly to the history of the transmission of oral *and written* biblical traditions. Later in this *Introduction* we will discuss numerous examples of the growth of written texts through combination or expansion of earlier sources.

One characteristic appears to have been remarkably frequent, particularly in Israel's early traditions: the **trickster** – that is, a character whose ability to survive through trickery and even lawbreaking is celebrated in religion, literature, or another part of culture. Anthropologists have long noted that many cultures, particularly cultures of more vulnerable groups, celebrate such tricksters who survive against difficult odds through cunning and sometimes deceptive behavior. Figures such as the Plains Indian Coyote demonstrate to their people how one can survive in a hostile environment where the rules are stacked against you. Throughout time people in vulnerable circumstances have celebrated such tricksters, who are often heroes within their own group. In home rituals, agricultural celebrations, weddings and other rites of passage, and other events, they would tell and sing stories of how their ancestors had triumphed against all odds, often tricking and defeating their more powerful opponents.

Problems in Reconstructing Early Israel

READING

The Merneptah Stela (www. wiley.com/go/ carr).

EXERCISE

Read Joshua 11. What impression do you get from this chapter of the Israelites' military accomplishments? How does this compare with the picture of these as summarized in Judges 1? As indicated in the discussion below, both these narratives about Israel's origins were written centuries after the events they describe and are historically problematic.

Figure 2.4 Stela listing Egyptian conquests, dating to around 1200 BCE. It contains the earliest mention of "Israel" outside the Bible.

The village described above is forever lost for us, if it ever existed in anything like that form. At the most we have fragments of its existence. Archaeological surveys have uncovered the remains of hundreds of settlements in the northern hill country of Israel that suddenly sprang up in unusual numbers around 1250 BCE. Strikingly, this also happens to be around the time when we see the first mention of the name "Israel" in a datable ancient document. A stone monument set up by Pharaoh Merneptah (see Figure 2.4) celebrates his army's victory over cities and other groups in Syria-Palestine, saying:

> I have plundered Canaan from one end to the other, taken slaves from the city of Ashkelon [a coastal Philistine settlement] and conquered the city of Gezer. I have razed Yanoam to the ground. I have decimated the people of Israel and put their children to death . . . All Canaan has been pacified. (Translation, *OT Parallels*)

The stela commemorates an Egyptian campaign carried out sometime around 1220 BCE. Interestingly, the Egyptian writing system clearly indicates that this "Israel" is a tribal people, not a territory. The next securely datable mention of anything specifically Israelite comes four hundred years later. So this mention of a people, "Israel," in the Merneptah stela of 1207 is a precious clue. It helps us interpret the village settlements across the hill country in 1250–1000 BCE as the earliest remains of "Israel," the people who would later create the Hebrew Bible/Old Testament.

The earlier history of this people cannot be recovered. This is as far back as we can go using academic methods of historical reconstruction. Through a combination of archaeological evidence for early hilltop villages and the Merneptah stela, we have good reason to think that some kind of village culture "Israel" already lived in the hill country of Palestine from around 1300 onward (see Map 2.1). Nevertheless, we do not have the kind of secure written or other sources that historians would typically rely on to tell us where these people came from or how they got there.

To be sure, the Bible tells a story of how this people was formed from ancestors of Jacob's sons, who went down into Egypt, emerged in the exodus, and wandered in the wilderness, before entering Canaan through a triumphant military conquest of all of the area and destruction of all its inhabitants. Scholars once thought that archaeological remains confirmed this picture of external origins and total conquest, since there are destruction layers in many Canaanite towns in the late second millennium. Some thought these destruction layers were evidence of an Israelite onslaught. Nevertheless, others have rightly argued that the cities where destruction layers were found are not generally cities mentioned in the Bible. Moreover, their destructions apparently occurred over a period of over one hundred years rather than in a single conquest as related in the book of Joshua. This calls into question the idea that they are the result of a coordinated Israelite conquest of the sort described in Joshua. Instead, many of these cities probably disappeared as part of a more widespread destruction of major urban centers that occurred toward the end of the second millennium, a destruction caused by a combination of environmental catastrophe and invasions of "sea peoples" from the western Mediterranean. Furthermore, of the nineteen cities mentioned in the Bible as destroyed by the Israelites, only three were clearly destroyed, while the rest either were not destroyed or were abandoned at the times when most scholars think the conquest could have occurred. In sum, the archaeological evidence, if anything, contradicts rather than confirms the picture of total destruction of the Canaanite people given in Joshua. Indeed, it better matches the picture of the coexistence of Israelites and Canaanites in the land given in Judges 1, a biblical text which contrasts with the account of total conquest in Joshua.

So, one might ask, where did the biblical stories in Joshua come from? There are different explanations for individual stories on the one hand and of the broader account of total conquest on the other. For example, many scholars now understand individual stories such as the conquest of Jericho as tales of triumph that were built up to explain ancient ruins. Much later in Israel's history an Israelite storyteller, unaware that the ruins at Jericho long predated the presence of Israel in the land, told a story that explained those ruins as the remains of a great victory by God when Israel entered the land. This story developed over time until it was included in a broader story of Israel's conquest of the whole land under Joshua. This story of total conquest of the land (Joshua 1–12) in response to God's command (Deuteronomy 7) is even further from being a photographic reproduction of ancient events. The language and theology of Joshua 1–12 make clear that it was a story composed to empower a much later Israelite

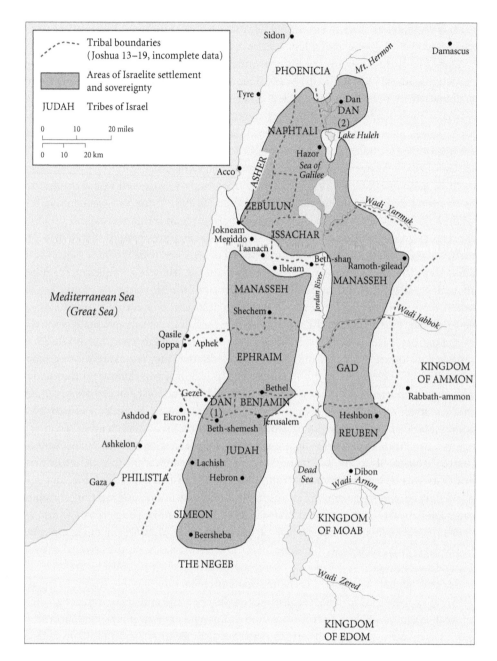

Map 2.1 Areas of the hill country occupied by the Israelites and Judeans, and where the tribes are said to have been located in the pre-state period. Redrawn from Norman Gottwald, *The Hebrew Bible: A Socio-Literary Introduction*. Minneapolis: Fortress, 1985, page 133.

people who had been repeatedly humiliated and oppressed by the superpowers of their day. Chapter 5 of this textbook will feature more discussion of the biblical picture of conquest, since it focuses on the time in which the book of Joshua was written.

All this leads us back to the origins of Israel – *in* Canaan. Our evidence shows every sign that the vast bulk of the earliest Israelites came from Canaan and shared its language, its material culture, and – to some extent – its religion. To be sure, there may have been a "Moses group," themselves of Canaanite extraction, who experienced slavery and liberation from Egypt, but most scholars believe that such a group – if it existed – was only a small minority in early Israel, even though their story came to be claimed by all. The rest of early Israelites did not come from outside the land through conquest or gradual settlement. The architecture and pottery of early Israelite settlements show close connections to pre-Israelite, "Canaanite" architecture and pottery. Prior attempts to identify a distinctively different "Israelite" pottery, house type, or other feature have failed. The Hebrew language, including its more ancient forms, is so closely related to neighboring languages that a student who learns Hebrew is well on his or her way to reading Phoenician, Moabite, Ammonite, etc.

Finally, both archaeological remains and the much later evidence from the Hebrew Bible indicate that the oldest forms of Israelite religion were not as distinct from non-Israelite, "Canaanite" religion as scholars once thought. The Canaanites worshipped various gods, such as the creator and father god, **El**, his wife **Asherah**, the storm god **Baal**, and the goddess of love and war Anat. Anat is not particularly prominent in biblical traditions, but the other three all appear to have played significant roles in early Israel, alongside Israelite worship of a non-Canaanite God, "Yahweh." For example, ancient Israelites often expressed their theology by giving their children pious sentence-names. The Bible records that Saul, one of Israel's earliest leaders, had descendents named "Ishbaal" (Hebrew for "man of Baal") and "Mephibaal" ("from the mouth of Baal"). In this case, these names of Saul's descendents probably indicate reverence for Baal in his family. The name "El" is yet more prominent in biblical tradition, forming part of the name "Isra*el*," and of several important place names (e.g. Bethel – "house of El"). One biblical text even uses a frequent epithet of El, "the Most High," to describe how El assigned Yahweh to Israel:

> When the Most High assigned the nations,
>   when he divided humankind,
> He determined the boundaries of the peoples
>   according to the number of the gods.
> Yahweh's own portion was his people,
>   Jacob was his assigned share. (Deut 32:8–9)

Israel's worship probably was not confined to male deities such as Baal, El, or Yahweh. Archaeologists have found remains in early Israelite settlements both of female figurines and of early Israelite depictions of trees, a frequent symbol in ancient Canaan of female reproductive power (see Figure 2.5). Many scholars think these early images of trees/women were representations of the goddess Asherah, the wife of the

Figure 2.5 Animals feeding on trees, an early Israelite reflection of a yet earlier artistic pattern seen in pre-Israelite remains where the same animals were fed by a goddess figure, possibly Asherah. Redrawn from Othmar Keel and Christoph Uehlinger, *Göttinnen, Götter und Gottessymbole: neue Erkenntnisse zur Religionsgeschichte Kanaans und Israels aufgrund bislang unerschlossener ikonographischer Quellen* (Quaestiones disputatae). Freiburg im Breisgau: Herder, 1992, page 134.

The Name "Israel"

The name "Israel," like most ancient Hebrew names, is a sentence. It is formed from the divine name "El," and may mean "El rules" or "May El prove his rulership." It reflects the potential focus in earliest Israel on El's role in helping early tribal groups resist the "rulership" of surrounding cities and their armies.

creator god El. Worship of Asherah appears to have been widespread in earliest Israel. Each ancient village probably had its own hilltop sanctuary, a raised platform for sacrifice, featuring both a pillar to symbolize male deity and a tree to symbolize divine female power. Asherah, whose symbol is the tree, was the probable focus of the tree symbolism.

Traces of the Most Ancient Israelite Oral Traditions in the Bible

Such archaeological evidence helps us reconstruct aspects of Israel's origins not reflected in the Bible, which – after all – is a corpus of texts written down after the conclusion of the tribal period. It gives us a glimpse of tribal Israel that resembles the pre-Israelite culture from which it emerged. One might say that ancient Israelites were a sub-group of "Canaanites" living in hill-country villages. These ancient villagers, however, had their own traditions, passed down by word of mouth from generation to generation. These traditions, constantly evolving to fit the hopes and fears of the performers and their audiences, expressed the deepest values of their community. The following sections of this chapter discuss three sets of Biblical texts that are good candidates for providing a view, however blurry and indistinct, of distinctive elements of early Israel's theology and traditions.

The Exodus from Egypt

As already suggested in Chapter 1, the narratives in Exodus 1–15 all come from centuries after this pre-state period in ancient Israel. Yet many indicators suggest that these traditions were present in ancient Israel from a very early period, probably when an "exodus group" of prisoners who had escaped from Egypt joined others living in hill-country villages and told their story of liberation from Pharaoh under the leadership of Moses. The indicators of historicity in the exodus story suggest that it was not made up by later authors, and those indicators point back to the late Bronze Age.

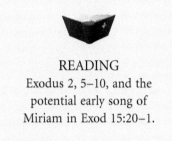

READING
Exodus 2, 5–10, and the potential early song of Miriam in Exod 15:20–1.

Yet, even assuming that some sort of exodus from Egypt occurred historically, the story about it would not have survived if it had not also spoken an important new word to the people living in the hill-country villages. And there are good reasons to think it did. For these village-culture Israelites had "pharaohs" of their own day, the rulers of the city-states surrounding them, whom they needed to resist. The Song of Deborah in Judges 5 (and the later accompanying story in Judges 4) vividly describes the kind of threat posed by such cities, with their professional armies and chariots. Furthermore, it is likely that some such formerly Egyptian-dominated cities, such as Jerusalem or Shechem, preserved remnants of the Egyptian culture. At the least, these former outposts of Egyptian domination of Canaan would have been perceived by villagers as the closest oppressive counterpart to the Egypt that had once dominated the area.

The story of Yahweh's deliverance of slaves from Egypt would have served as a powerful rallying cry for villagers now fighting for survival against such city-states. The story became the property of all "Israel," not just former slaves and their descendants. We see this sort of community claiming of an older story today, for example, in the way later African-Americans have claimed the stories of the Old Testament for themselves. In his August, 2008 speech on race, "A More Perfect Union," Barack Obama drew on his autobiography to describe how he found hope in the merging of biblical stories and contemporary lives in the black church:

People began to shout, to rise from their seats and clap and cry out, a forceful wind carrying the reverend's voice up into the rafters . . . And in that single note – hope! – I heard something else; at the foot of that cross, inside the thousands of churches across the city, I imagined the stories of ordinary black people merging with the stories of David and Goliath, Moses and Pharaoh, the Christians in the lion's den, Ezekiel's field of dry bones. Those stories – of survival, and freedom, and hope – became our story, my story; the blood that had spilled was our blood, the tears our tears; until this black church, on this bright day, seemed once more a vessel carrying the story of a people into future generations and into a larger world. Our trials and triumphs became at once unique and universal, black and more than black; in chronicling our journey, the stories and songs gave us a means to reclaim memories that we didn't need to feel shame about . . . memories that all people might study and cherish – and with which we could start to rebuild.

This claiming of older stories by new groups is hardly limited to the black church. Much as many Americans now claim for themselves the story of the *Mayflower* and Puritan holiday of thanksgiving, despite the fact that many descend from immigrants of the last century, so also Israelite villagers of varied origins claimed the exodus story as their own. That story celebrated the god, Yahweh, who had liberated "them" from Egypt, and it expressed their confidence that this exodus God would also fight on their behalf against their contemporary "pharaohs," the local city-states.

Yet we should be clear, as was stressed in the first chapter of this textbook, that the exodus story (or stories) that ancient Israelites claimed almost certainly was not identical with the story found in the Bible in Exodus 1–15. No one would have been writing such texts in the villages of early Israel. Moreover, there are numerous signs – to be discussed elsewhere in this book – that these stories in the book of Exodus were shaped into their present form by much later Israelites rereading the story of exodus in relation to ever new "pharaohs": the "pharaoh" of Solomon and his kingdom, the "pharaoh" of Assyrian and Babylonian superpowers, etc. This process of merging of stories described by Barack Obama has been going on a very long time.

That said, there are some trickster elements in the biblical exodus story that may point to early oral elements lying in some form behind the text in Exodus 1–15. Take, for example, the tale of the tricky midwives, Shiphrah and Puah (Exod 1:15–22), who disobey Pharaoh's command to kill all male Israelite babies, claiming "Hebrew women are not like Egyptian women; they are so strong that they give birth before the midwife has a chance to get to them." Later on, fully intending to depart for good, Moses nevertheless tries to get the Israelites free by asking Pharaoh for a three-day vacation in the wilderness so they can fulfill God's command to worship there (Exod 5:1–5). Later, when Pharaoh agrees to let the Israelites have a three-day festival in Egypt rather than going away, Moses claims that they cannot do so because the Israelite sacrifices would be too distasteful to the Egyptians (8:21–23). When the plagues finally persuade Pharaoh to let the male Israelites go on their supposed worship pilgrimage, Moses slyly insists that the men cannot adequately observe this particular festival without all of their families and livestock along (10:7–10). All these elements are now found in much later, written biblical texts. Nevertheless, they reflect a tone of trickery particularly characteristic of early oral traditions. They indicate the persistence of trickster components later in Israel's history, but they may also be trickster tastes of early elements embedded in Israel's later exodus traditions.

Traditions surrounding Jacob

Such trickster elements are even more prominent in the traditions surrounding Jacob and his family in Genesis 25–35. Jacob cleverly gets a hungry Esau to sell his birthright for a pot of lentil stew in Genesis 25. Then, in Genesis 27, Rebekah, Jacob's mother, develops a tricky ruse to get Jacob's father, Isaac, to give Jacob the superior blessing that he meant to give to Esau. At Rebekah's urging, Jacob flees to escape Esau's plan to murder him, and he gets a taste of his own medicine in Haran, where his father in law, Laban, gets him to work seven years to marry Rachel, but then slips Leah into Jacob's marriage bed instead (Genesis 29). Soon Jacob turns the tables on Laban, using magical means to outwit Laban's plan to deprive Jacob of his wages in livestock (Genesis 30) and later escaping with Laban's daughters without Laban's knowledge (Genesis 31). In the process, Rachel shows her own capacity for trickery, stealing her father's household gods and then preventing him from finding them by sitting on them and then telling her father that she cannot get up because she has her period ("the way of woman is on me"; Gen 31:35). In these ways and others, the story depicts Jacob and his closest family as crafty tricksters, able to survive and flourish in the face of difficult odds. Not only is he himself a trickster, but his mother helped get him started, and he worked 14 years to marry a woman, Rachel, who continues the tradition.

Such traditions of trickery are not the sort of thing typically focused on in sermons and Sunday school lessons. Many within dominant cultures are not used to celebrations of culture heroes like this who trick and even lie to get their way. Nevertheless, such stories can be empowering to people who feel that they will inevitably perish if they play by "the rules" of their social context. Whether Native American or ancient Israelite, vulnerable people often gain empowerment through celebrating ancestors who made their way in the world through using cleverness to overcome impossible odds. For people on top, such trickster stories can appear to be embarrassing elements in an otherwise tidy Bible. For people on the bottom, such stories can be a major way of gaining hope and resisting domination.

In either case, the stories found in Genesis 25–35 are substantially different from Jacob, Rebekah, and Rachel stories told in villages of early Israel. On the one hand, we know that early Israel almost certainly told stories about Jacob, who happens to be a namesake of early "Israel." Moreover, the stories in Genesis are related in some way to those early tales. On the other hand, those stories changed radically over the centuries of oral and then oral-written tradition, and there are numerous elements in them that point specifically to later periods in Israel's history. For example, several place names that are now prominent in the Genesis Jacob story, e.g. Bethel and Penuel, may reveal a shaping of the story in the context of the later northern monarchy in Israel, where Bethel was one of the main royal sanctuaries and Penuel was a capital for a few years. In addition, in Chapter 6 we will see how people in exile probably added to the Jacob story the promise theme now found throughout Gen 26:1–33 along with several other isolated places in the Jacob story (e.g. 28:13–16; 32:10–13; 35:9–15).

In these and probably many other ways, the story of Jacob and his family has been so shaped by its journey through the centuries that we no longer can identify the parts that come from Israel's earliest history. The most we can say is that the people of Israel probably told trickster stories about Rebekah, Jacob, Rachel, and others from the beginning of their history, a time when they did not yet have a king and were living in vulnerable, unwalled villages of the hill country of Canaan.

FOCUS
TEXT

READING
Judges 5 (note that this potentially early poem is different from the later account in Judges 4).

The Song of Deborah

The Song of Deborah in Judges 5 is the one of the best candidates for being a biblical text that might more closely reflect an ancient village-culture tradition than the (prose) narratives discussed so far. Unlike the above texts, the Song of Deborah is a poem, and its poetic – and perhaps sung – form could aid more precise memorization and recitation over the years. In addition, the song contains archaic elements of Hebrew language, and the list of tribes and other groups in Judges 5 only partially overlaps with later lists of tribes that made up early Israel (an example can be found in Numbers 1). Judges 5 does not even mention some of the southern tribes, and it mentions other names not typically found in 12-tribe lists such as that in Numbers 1 (e.g. Machir = Manasseh; and Meroz). These are among some of our first clues that this text may reflect a very early poem. Open up your Bible to Judges 5 and we will use this text as an evocative window to a time long before texts of our Bible began to be written down.

5:2–5: The song opens with a hymn of praise describing Yahweh's triumphant appearance from the southern desert regions of Seir and Edom (5:4–5). It is one of several potentially early texts that locate Sinai and Yahweh's origins in the desert regions south of Palestine (Deut 33:2; Hab 3:3; Ps 68:7–9). Our ancient text envisions Yahweh as a powerful storm god, whose arrival is marked by earthquakes and torrential floods. Yet there is also a focus here and throughout the poem on the people. The first verse of the poem celebrates the way leaders took the lead and the people responded willingly (5:2), and the second verse (5:3) calls on the powerful "kings and princes" of the world to hear this "song" about the triumph of a kingless group of tribal villagers.

5:6–12: The next section of the poem celebrates the emergence of leadership in this otherwise disorganized group: the rise of Deborah. Beforehand, trails had become unsafe, settlements were defenseless, and the people had no weapons (5:6–7a). But then Deborah arose "as a mother in Israel." The poem then again calls on those who volunteered in the effort to offer praise (5:9), along with other groups (5:10–11), and Deborah and Barak themselves (5:12).

5:13–18 and 5:23: The poem then details which tribal groups answered the call to battle willingly, and which did not. Six tribes came when called: Ephraim, Benjamin, Machir (related to Manasseh; Num 26:29), Zebulon, Issachar and Naphtali. Four did not: Reuben, Gilead (perhaps in place of Gad in the standard lists of tribes), Dan, and Asher. Two southern tribes are not even mentioned: Judah and Simeon. Apparently at the time the Song was written they were not even envisioned as potential partners in this kind of military effort. Even the northern groups that appear here are clearly not unified. Only six out of ten answered the call to battle. Indeed, from the initial call to praise those who volunteered (5:2) to the contrast of those who volunteered and those who did not (5:13–18), much of Deborah's song seems aimed at encouraging the separate tribes to affirm their common destiny. It calls on villagers to sing praises to God for a victory where six tribes joined together to defeat – with God's help – the mighty forces of Sisera. And it soon calls on them to curse "Meroz," an unknown group who failed to answer the call (5:23).

5:19–22: The actual description of the battle occurs only in these four verses. They move beyond the conflict between Israel and Sisera to juxtapose the "kings of Canaan" with their horses, on the one hand, with the cosmic powers of Yahweh, on the other. The kings may have the superior military technology, but they have no chance against the power of stars fighting from heaven and the force of the Kishon River (5:19–21). Soon the once powerful stallions were fleeing (5:22).

5:24–31: In two scenes, 5:24–7 and 28–30, the poet concludes with vignettes about the aftermath of the battle. The first blesses Jael, of the Kenites, for aiding in the effort by cleverly tricking Sisera into enjoying her hospitality and then killing him with a mallet (5:24–7). Again, there is an element of the trickster here, since hospitality is otherwise celebrated as a profound value, not just in surrounding cultures, but in Israelite traditions as well. Nevertheless, Jael welcomes Sisera into her tent and feeds him, before killing him with a mallet. Like a slow-motion movie, the poetry uses repetition to focus in on the moment.

> Between her feet he sank, he sank, he fell
> He lay between her feet, he sank, he fell
> Where he sank, there he fell, killed.

Meanwhile, in 5:28–30 the poet offers another vision featuring a woman, this time, the mother of Sisera, waiting for him to return triumphant from battle, not knowing of his recent death. As she wonders at his delay, her "wise women" speculate that he is probably delayed by dividing spoil: a few Israelite maidens for each warrior and some nice cloth to bring back to the women at home.

In this way, "Deborah's song" uses two scenes involving women to illustrate the contrast between the destinies of Yahweh's friends and enemies. Yahweh's enemies will perish and their women (like Sisera's mother) will mourn, but those who join in the effort to fight, like Jael, will be "like the sun when it rises with all its might." (5:31)

This belief in the triumph of the people that God chooses is an early form of what is often termed "**election theology**" – that is, the idea that God has chosen a particular people to care for and defend. This idea is present in the affirmation of the exodus tradition that Yahweh delivered Israel from Egypt. And it is implicit in the stories of God's protection and provision for Israel's trickster ancestor, Jacob, and his family.

In all these traditions, God chooses not a place, nor a territorial nation, but a people, and protects them against seemingly impossible odds. This belief in God's choosing of a particular people, rooted in tribal traditions like the Song of Deborah and the exodus story, is a fundamental bedrock of later Israelite theology, especially in the northern part of Israel. Moreover, this idea of the distinctiveness and chosenness of a *people*, election theology, may have distinguished early Israel from some of the monarchal nation states that surrounded it. Those states were more focused on how their gods chose a particular city and/or royal-priestly dynasty.

The Creation of "Israel" Through Cultural Memory of Resistance to Domination

All this is a prelude to the gradual creation of the Hebrew Bible/Old Testament. At this point in the history of Israel no books, not even chapters, had been written. "Israel" was only a very loose association of village-tribal groups. These villages shared, however, a common way of life. They aided each other in times of famine, and charismatic leaders such as Deborah rose up in times of crisis to fight common enemies. Whatever their diverse origins, these village-dwellers came to claim a common story of liberation from Egypt. They claimed a common ancestor, Jacob, along with the rest of his trickster family. And through poems like the Song of Deborah, they celebrated those occasions where they joined together to experience Yahweh's deliverance against the more powerful city-states around them.

Some scholars, such as Maurice Halbwachs (*On Collective Memory* [Chicago: University of Chicago Press, 1992]) and Jan Assmann (*Religion and Cultural Memory* [Stanford: University of Stanford Press, 2005]), have argued persuasively that such common memories are what form groups of people. Such **cultural memory** is reinforced through parental teaching, schools, festivals, and other practices in which people in groups recite or act out their common heritage. For example, national holidays, such as July 4 in the US, are occasions when national identity is reinforced through various festivities, in this case marking the day when the nation was born. New citizens are required to learn the common story before they can become "Americans." Similarly, the worship year in Jewish synagogues and Christian churches continually reminds those communities of their stories, having them relive the events of the Torah (for synagogues) or the life of Jesus (for churches) and reinforce their sense of a particular religious identity. You become a "Jew" or "Christian" partly through learning the story of that group and claiming it as your own.

We do not know exactly how the oral versions of the texts about exodus, Jacob's family, and Deborah's victory were used, but they appear to have served a similar purpose in helping to create and reinforce a sense of common "Israelite" identity out of varied groups. Whether taught to children, recited at clan worship, sung at festivals, or used in some other way, the ancient oral traditions discussed in this chapter helped turn the people living in the hill country of Syro-Palestine into the "Israelites" who would create the later Bible.

The shared oral memories discussed in this chapter made for a particular kind of community: one that celebrated powerful work by God on the one hand and the clever action of tricksters on the other. In the midst of the pluralistic Canaanite religious environment, these traditions praise the liberative work of Yahweh, a god known from the southern deserts. Yet they also celebrate Israelite resourcefulness and wit. In particular, they empower people living on the margins by celebrating clever underdogs such as Jacob or Jael. Women are quite prominent in these traditions, as mothers, tricksters, and even military leaders (Deborah). Meanwhile, "kings" and their representatives are the opponents in these village-culture traditions, whether Pharaoh or Hazor's general Sisera.

Even when Israel developed writing, the stories of these oral traditions – in highly varied forms – continued to be told and sung among Israelites, many of whom never learned to write. We must keep in mind that our written Bible is but the tip of the iceberg of a largely lost oral tradition in ancient Israel. The process started not with writing, but with telling tales of Israelite liberation, survival, and victory.

CHAPTER TWO REVIEW

1. Know the meaning and significance of the following terms discussed in this chapter:

- Asherah
- Baal
- cultural memory
- El
- election theology
- empire
- monarchal city-state
- oral traditions
- segmentary society
- trickster
- village

2. Know the main differences between the following three ancient forms of social organization:

- empire
- monarchal city-state
- village

3. What is "tradition history," and what is an example of the sort of phenomenon in the Bible that it would study? What is the difference between "tradition history" and "transmission history"? Do the terms overlap?

4. What do anthropologists now know about the character of oral traditions? How does this affect their usability for reconstructing early traditions? How specifically are such oral traditions reflected in Genesis 12–25 or Exodus 1–15?

5. What are the main issues surrounding the reconstruction of a historical "conquest" of all of Canaan by all of Israel?

RESOURCES FOR FURTHER STUDY

Commentaries and other books on Joshua

Hawk, Daniel L. *Every Promise Fulfilled: Contesting Plots in the Book of Joshua*. Literary Currents in Biblical Interpretation. Louisville, KY: Westminster John Knox Press, 1991.

Nelson, Richard D. *Joshua: A Commentary*. Old Testament Library. Louisville, KY: Westminster John Knox Press, 1997.

Niditch, Susan. "Joshua" in the *Oxford Bible Commentary* (revised edition), eds. John Barton and John Muddiman. New York: Oxford University Press, 2007.

Commentaries and other books on Judges

Hamlin, John E. *At Risk in the Promised Land: A Commentary on the Book of Judges*. Grand Rapids: Eerdmans, 1990.

McCann, J. Clinton. *Judges*. Interpretation. Louisville, KY: Westminster John Knox Press, 2002.

Soggin, J. Alberto. *Judges*. Old Testament Library. Philadelphia: Westminster Press, 1981.

Trible, Phyllis. *Texts of Terror: Literary-Feminist Readings of Biblical Narratives*. Philadelphia: Fortress, 1984. Chapters on the Levite's wife and Jephthah's daughter.

Everyday life in ancient Israel

King, Philip J., and Stager, Lawrence E. *Life in Biblical Israel*. Library of Ancient Israel. Louisville, KY: Westminster John Knox Press, 2001.

The history of Israelite religion

Keel, Othmar, and Uehlinger, Christoph. *Gods, Goddesses, and Images of God in Ancient Israel*, trans. Allan W. Mahnke. Minneapolis: Fortress, 1997. Difficult, but good.

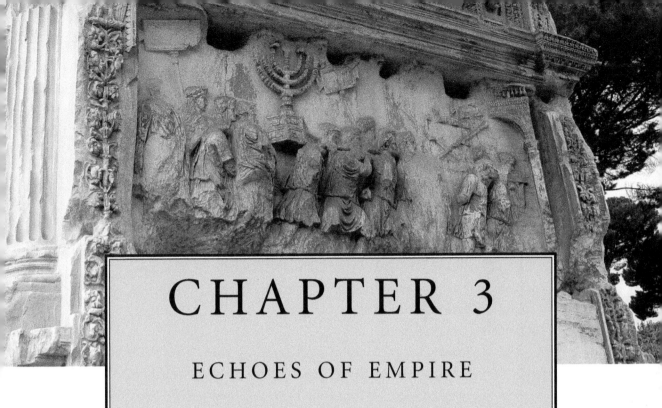

CHAPTER 3

ECHOES OF EMPIRE

IN MONARCHAL ISRAEL

Chapter Outline

CHAPTER OVERVIEW

This chapter outlines the huge changes in Israelite culture that led to the writing of the first books of the Hebrew Bible. Up to this point, Israelite village culture had many and varied oral traditions. Texts were something that empires and some smaller city-states had. But by the tenth century – the 900s BCE – the Israelites are being ruled by a Davidic monarchy based in Jerusalem. Moreover, this new Israelite state appears to have modeled itself on the older empires that preceded it, dominating nearby regions.

This is the time when scribes in early Israel began to develop the very first corpus of written Hebrew texts, often modeling their new compositions on yet older writings from Egypt and Mesopotamia. The scribes created something like a "bible before our Bible." But as we will see, this "bible" was still a long way from the Old Testament as we have it now. We can find traces of this shorter, older "bible before our Bible" in several texts now in the Old Testament that "echo" written traditions of more ancient cultures.

Imagining Early Monarchal Israel

Once again, we start with an imaginary reconstruction of the context in which these biblical traditions were written. Our sources are few, varied, and disputed. Although the Bible describes Israel as a world power at the time of David and Solomon, archaeologists have not succeeded in finding extensive remains of their kingdoms. Some even suspect that the Bible's entire picture of their glory is a fictional creation of an Israelite golden age. This book, however, takes another perspective. Certainly, the stories surrounding David and Solomon grew over time, and their reputation was enhanced. Nevertheless, a combination of archaeology and a critical reading of biblical texts suggests that Israel under David and Solomon did develop the beginnings of a city-state monarchy, a monarchy that apparently included short-lived domination of some neighboring nations as well. The following imaginary reconstruction is based on this combination of archaeological and biblical evidence.

Our journey takes us back to another hilltop in ancient Canaan, this time Mount **Zion**, a hilltop to the south of the heartland of tribal Israel. Generally speaking, "Zion" and the city associated with it, "Jerusalem," are synonymous in the Bible. What is less well known is that Jerusalem had a long history as a city before David conquered it and made it the capital of his kingdom. This pre-Davidic city had its own cultural and political traditions, some of which may have been adapted by David and his successors in the process of setting up their fledgling kingdom. For example, the Bible contains a tantalizing suggestion that the pre-Israelite (Jebusite) inhabitants of the city already had a belief in Jerusalem's invulnerability. When David laid siege to Jerusalem, the Jebusites are said to have told David that "you will not come in, even the blind and lame will ward you off" (2 Sam 5:6). Such a claim that Jerusalem was unconquerable anticipates later biblical **Zion theology** – that is, theology about Jerusalem's specialness and invulnerability – that we will see in some of Israel's psalms and other literature.

Let us return now to imagining the Jerusalem of later, Solomonic, times. As it turned out, the Jebusites were wrong. David conquered Jerusalem by stealth and made it the capital of his kingdom uniting Judah in the south and Israel in the north. In our imagining exercise, we visit Jerusalem at the time of Solomon, David's son and successor. By this time, Jerusalem has become the center of a fledgling mini-empire. Not only does the city have its ancient wall and traditions, but Solomon has built a new palace for the king and a temple to Yahweh (see Figure 3.1). The temple contains the "ark of the covenant," a symbol of older Israel's tribal-Exodus god.

Solomon, the king, serves as both high priest and commander of the army. Below him is a small but expanding class of priestly, royal, and military officials. This is a new form of leadership, showing an evolution under David from tribal structures to foreign models of monarchy, particularly as seen in Egypt. Solomon's court bears a strong resemblance to the Egyptian royal court, and many of its positions are filled by the sons of officials who served in David's court. Indeed, one of Solomon's scribes may even have had an Egyptian father, David's scribe "Shisha," whose name is quite similar to

Figure 3.1 Artist's reconstruction of Solomon's Jerusalem. The Temple is on the upper right, next down is the palace, and then the citadel of David with a stepped-stone structure supporting it.

the Egyptian word for "scribe." These officials and those under them administrated the complex kingdom. They were the glue that held this broad kingdom of varied tribes and territories together.

This nation, indeed this mini-empire, had many provisions for continuity across space and time. Where tribal culture had charismatic leaders such as Deborah who galvanized the people in a time of crisis, this kind of monarchy achieved political stability through an ongoing royal dynasty. Where tribal culture depended on tribes volunteering to join others in resisting enemies, this monarchy had a standing army. And where groups in tribal culture shared ever-fluid *oral* traditions, this monarchy resembled other such monarchies in using *written* texts to reinforce and standardize oral memory. These written texts were not accessible to everyone in a largely non-literate society, but they provided an essential way to educate the new ruling class for this more expansive realm. By memorizing a specific collection of written texts, youths preparing to be leaders learned a common worldview that persisted across space and time. David's and Solomon's scribes are the probable authors of the first such collection of Hebrew, written literary-theological texts.

The Rise of the Monarchy and Resistance to It

READING

1 Samuel 8–12,
16–20, 31; 2 Samuel
2–10 and 1 Kings
1–10.

EXERCISE

The readings above are narratives about the rise of kingship told centuries after the events they describe. The authors of these narratives reveal much about their values in the different reasons they give for why a monarchy rose in Israel. As you read 1 Samuel 8–12 make a list of the different reasons given for the rise of the monarchy (including chapter and verse) and note any other clues you can find to whether the authors of these texts approved or disapproved of the monarchy. Extrapolating from these narratives, do you think the authors of these texts thought the monarchy was a good idea?

Before looking at the earliest Hebrew texts, we need to appreciate the city-state context in which they were created. In Chapter 2 we saw how Israel emerged as a loose association of villages organized into tribes, settled largely in the northern hill country of Palestine. They were a "people," not a city-state or nation. Their limited resources and social organization made it difficult for them to resist raids by neighboring tribes or attempts to dominate them by nearby city-states. Aside from the rise of temporary leaders in times of crisis, "judges" in the Bible, there were no elite classes. The people shared common access to the orally transmitted "cultural memory" that helped identify them as Israelites.

The book of 1 Samuel, written hundreds of years after the period it narrates, gives many explanations for why this tribal existence under judges came to an end: the people requested a king because Samuel's sons were corrupt, or because they wanted to imitate other nations, or because they wanted a human king instead of Yahweh as king (see the exercise at the outset of this section). Nevertheless, the explanation for kingship that most scholars find compelling is the following: the Israelites accepted kingship because it was the only form of social organization that was centralized enough to repel the Philistine invasions into the hill country of central Palestine. The Bible records clashes between Israelites and Philistines in stories about Samson (Judges 14–16), the time of Samuel (1 Sam 4:1–7:1), Saul (1 Samuel 13–31), and David (2 Samuel 5 and 8). Saul, a member of the tribe of Benjamin, was anointed as "king" to repel the Philistines; he really was little more than a warlord. He did not develop a city capital or a professional army, and he achieved only limited success before being killed in battle with the Philistines, along with his heir Jonathan (1 Samuel 31//2 Chronicles 10). Saul's leadership was not the sort of "kingship" needed to repel the Philistines. It was really more of a "chieftainship."

Kingship would come under David and especially his heir, Solomon. Within the much later biblical texts, David is remembered as a paradoxical mix. On the one hand, several texts depict him as a king "faithful" to Yahweh (e.g. 1 Kgs 3:6). On the other hand, he is flawed enough to seduce an officer's wife, Bathsheba, and send her husband to certain death in order to be able to marry her (2 Samuel 11–12). In the broader scheme of things, however, David appears to have been an extraordinarily gifted military commander who took the first steps of establishing a monarchy that would last over four hundred years.

Timeline: Rise of the Monarchy

Saul's chieftainship	1025–1010* BCE
David's reign	1010–970
In Hebron	1010–1002
In Jerusalem	1002–970

(*Note this date range is particularly uncertain because of incomplete preservation of 1 Sam 13:1.)

David started as an officer in Saul's Israelite army, and he was so militarily successful against the Philistines that he had to flee Saul's jealous wrath (see 1 Samuel 16–29). Later, when Saul died, David ruled his tribe, Judah, for a few years from the Judean town of Hebron, while Saul's son Eshbaal ruled Israel (2 Samuel 2–3). Then, when Eshbaal was assassinated, the Israelite leaders anointed David as king over them, so that David became king of both Judah and Israel (2 Sam 4:1–5:5). One of the first things he did as ruler of both peoples was to start a series of campaigns against the Philistines that permanently ended their threat to Judah and Israel (2 Sam 5:17–25; 8:1; see also 2 Sam 21:15–22).

Yet David did much more than defeat the Philistines. In contrast to (warlord) Saul, David introduced societal changes associated with true kingship: establishment of a state based in a walled city, organization of a professional army, and enforcement of taxes on the people to support the fortified city (or cities) and army. First, David captured the Jebusite city of Jerusalem, by stealth, and made it the capital of his new kingdom (2 Samuel 5:6–16). This was a politically smart move for a Judean king claiming authority over Israel. Jerusalem was not identified with the southern tribe of Judah the way that Hebron was. Second, David solidified Jerusalem's claim as the new capital of "Israel" by bringing into it the ark of the covenant, an object sacred to all the Israelite tribes (2 Samuel 6). Third, he achieved additional military success, subduing neighboring kingdoms such as Moab, Edom, Ammon, and even Damascus (which was allied with Ammon; 2 Samuel 8, 10–12). This allowed him to pay members of his army with land grants and support his fledgling state with tribute from neighboring groups. Fourth and finally, he started to build longer-term city-state structures: he started plans for a temple (2 Sam 24:18), solidified ties with neighboring groups through marriage alliances (2 Sam 3:2–5), developed a professional army, and prepared for formal taxation through instituting a census of the people (2 Sam 24:1–9). He even appears to have followed Egyptian models in developing a royal court, eventually one that included a position for "forced labor" of his citizens to help with fortifying the country (2 Sam 20:23–6; compare with 2 Sam 8:16–18). Map 3.1 surveys his kingdom.

David's successor, Solomon, went yet further in developing a city-state based in Jerusalem. After being put in power by a virtual coup d'etat implemented by his mother, Bathsheba (working in concert with several of David's close associates; see 1 Kings 1–2), Solomon began building a full-fledged ancient Near Eastern city-state. He continued and expanded the royal cabinet, appointing sons of David's officials to several crucial positions, and adding some new positions, again along the Egyptian model. He expanded the army and added chariots. He made marriage alliances with foreign kings. He started lucrative trade exchanges with Tyre, Arabia, and others. He engaged in major construction projects in Jerusalem and several fortress cities, Hazor, Gezer, and possibly Megiddo (see Map 2.1, p. 42). Most importantly, drawing heavily on the material and technical resources of the Tyrian king Hiram, Solomon built the Jerusalem Temple for Yahweh and a palace for himself.

To do this, Solomon required significant resources. He divided the kingdom into 12 districts, each with a governor and each responsible for providing for the royal apparatus for one month. Many scholars see this 12-district system, organized in correspondence with the lunar month cycle, as the beginning of the idea that Israel originated as *12* tribes. Only later was this 12-tribe idea projected back into Israel's earlier history – the time of the judges and before. The most important shift for village-culture Israelites was that they now had a new burden to add to the struggle for everyday existence. Not only did they need to find a way to provide for their kin each year, but they also had to provide substantial resources to the king and his city-state.

Not all Israelites were happy with the changes that came with David's and Solomon's kingship. Though surely they were glad to see the Philistine threat contained, many perceived David and especially Solomon as Judean versions of the oppressive kings they had just defeated. This led to several rebellions, mainly centered in the north, where people in the heartland of ancient tribal "Israel" were the least happy with being ruled by Judah. One was led by Absalom, David's own son; another was led by Sheba, a leader from the Israelite north; and the final and successful one was led by Jeroboam, who will be discussed more in Chapter 4. What is important for our purposes now is an appreciation that the leaders in this early monarchy had to contend with opponents, particularly those associated with the Israelite north, who doubted the benefits of this new monarchy. The monarchy was a major new form of communal life, with many foreign elements, that involved many costs as well as benefits.

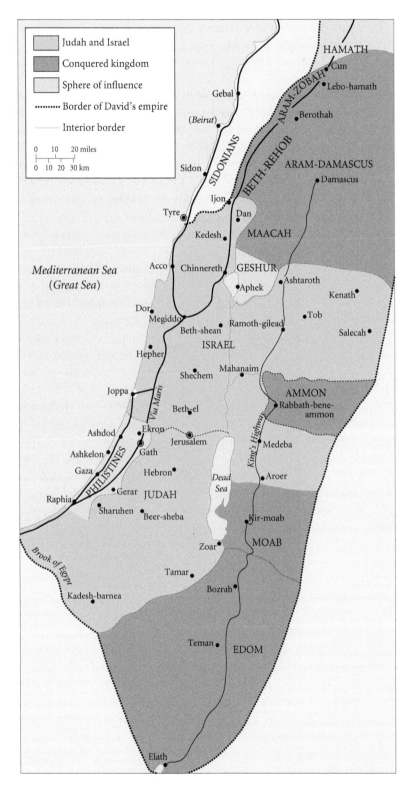

Map 3.1 Areas ruled and dominated by David and Solomon. Redrawn from
Yohanan Aharoni and Michael Avi-Yonah (eds.), *The Macmillan Bible Atlas* (revised edition).
New York: Macmillan, 1977, map 104.

Influence of Ancient Empires on Early Israel's Monarchy and Writings

David and Solomon did not start from scratch when they started to develop the Israelite monarchy and associated Jerusalemite city-state. They were adopting a more ancient social form that was known elsewhere. After all, city-states had been around in Mesopotamia, Syria, Egypt, and even Palestine from the third millennium onward. Indeed, as mentioned before, Jerusalem itself was the site of a small, pre-Israelite, Jebusite city-state which had once been dominated by Egypt. There are numerous signs that David and Solomon drew deeply on older Egyptian and other models in building the monarchy in Jerusalem: the make-up of their royal court, the models used for construction of temple and palace, etc. These are non-textual "echoes of empire" seen in the emergent Davidic monarchy in Jerusalem.

Yet there is another sort of "echo of empire" to be discussed here, and that is the way some biblical texts appear to echo pre-Israelite texts that were used in the much older empires of Mesopotamia and Egypt. One thing that distinguished many ancient monarchies from the tribal groups surrounding them was their use of written texts, including the sorts of texts found in the Bible: wisdom sayings, psalms, myths, and stories (see Figure 3.2). These written texts were a form of cultural memory like the oral traditions that continued to exist. Nevertheless, there were important differences. Most importantly, the relative firmness of written traditions made them good tools for shaping elites across time and across space. Written texts do not change as readily as oral traditions do. This was important in city-states and empires, which spanned large distances and joined disparate groups together. An empire or even a centralized city-state could bind together its different parts by making sure that its leaders all learned writing and memorized the same educational texts.

Our best examples of such literary education come from Egypt and Mesopotamia, much larger civilizations whose texts are better preserved (in Egypt because of climate, in Mesopotamia because they used clay tablets). The evidence from Egypt and Mesopotamia shows how students learned in family-based schools, often learning to read texts from either their own fathers or teachers whom they called "father." Ancient education in Egypt and Mesopotamia followed a similar pattern, a pattern probably common across the ancient world. Students started by learning to write and read basic symbols. The next step was memorizing and reciting basic "wisdom" instructions on how to live, and the final and most advanced stage was internalizing and performing other types of texts, such as royal hymns or stories of creation and flood. Careful analysis of student exercises from Mesopotamia, such as that seen in Figure 3.3, has allowed scholars to see how students in these cultures were taught to memorize their culture's texts line by line. Only a few in any ancient society had time to acquire such knowledge, but it was an important means by which Egypt, Mesopotamia, and other cultures trained future leaders.

This background from the cultures of Egypt and Mesopotamia is important because their educational-literary systems were used as models for the monarchies of Syro-

Figure 3.2 Scribe standing before the king of a small neighboring kingdom
with a scroll in his hand, dating from about a century after David and Solomon.
The image shows the prestige attached to scribal writing even in the small
kingdoms of the area.

Palestine in the centuries just before Israel emerged. The kingdom of David and Solomon
was too small to develop its own brand-new counterpart to the massive literatures
of those ancient empires. Thus when scribes began writing the first Hebrew texts in
the time of David and Solomon (see Figures 3.4 and 3.5 for scribal exercises from that
period), it seems that they did *not* focus on creating textual versions of earlier Israelite
oral traditions about ancestors, exodus, or the like. Instead, the earliest authors of
Hebrew literature were dependent on *foreign* models for literary education and imitated
foreign texts from Egypt and Mesopotamia. Why? Perhaps because in creating Israel's
first written literature these early Judean scribes were most interested in adapting
earlier examples of such writings (all of which were foreign), rather than transforming
properly oral traditions from the Israelite north. So they wrote Hebrew versions of the

sorts of texts used elsewhere to educate leaders for their emergent monarchy: creation and flood myths, hymns about the king, instructions on proper living, etc.

In this chapter we will look at two types of texts that show particularly close links to the monarchy and some reliance on foreign models as well: royal and Zion psalms. Though some of these texts are attributed to David or Solomon (see the Miscellaneous Box below on "Labels (e.g. 'Psalm of David'): What They (Don't) Tell Us"), we cannot be sure that all come from that time. To some extent, because the first monarchal scribes were particularly dependent on foreign models (and later scribes often had a more complicated perspective on foreign influence), one possible indicator that a biblical text is early is a set of specific echoes of foreign texts and traditions. Nevertheless, whenever one dates the texts to be discussed here, a study of them in relationship to their non-biblical counterparts can teach us much about how these biblical texts were used and what made them special.

Figure 3.3 Student exercise tablet where the teacher wrote a couple of lines of an educational text on the top half and the student copied below.

Figure 3.4 Letters inscribed into the surface of a stone, with overlay indicating their shape. The stone was found embedded in a wall from the tenth century BCE.

Figure 3.5 The "Gezer Calendar." This may be a school exercise from the time of Solomon. It lists what was done in the months of the agricultural year of ancient Canaan.

Echoes of Near Eastern Royal Theology in the Royal and Zion Psalms

EXERCISE

Read the following (royal) psalms and make a list of ideas that come up two or more times in them: 2 Sam 23:1–7; Psalms 2, 21, 72, and 110. Include citations in your notes of where each idea occurred. Then read the following (Zion) psalms and list ideas that occur two or more times in them: Pss 9, 15, 46, and 48. Finally, how do all these texts contrast with the values implicit in the narratives about the rise of kingship in 1 Samuel 8–12? Make a list of similarities and (especially) differences.

One of the main emphases in the literature of ancient empires was the monarchy. For example, Egyptian enthronement texts describe the new king (Pharaoh) receiving a document on which was written his throne names, climaxing with the throne name that marked his status as the only begotten son of the sun god, Re. Temple reliefs show the process by which Re conceived the king, not through intercourse, but through spreading his aroma over the king's mother. By the end of the process Re equipped the king with all he needed to rule the world in Re's place, proclaiming:

> Son of my body, beloved, lord of the righteousness [Maat] of Re, whose body I have made with me in the palace, I give you all life and wellbeing, to appear as the king of upper and lower Egypt on the throne of Horus.

Meanwhile, we also have hymns used in Egyptian education that taught students to celebrate the Egyptian king's power to vanquish wrongdoing and establish prosperity. The following one focuses on the Pharaoh Merneptah:

> Be glad of heart, the entire land! The good times have come. A lord – life, prosperity, health – is given in all lands, and normality has returned to its place. The king of Upper and Lower Egypt, the lord of millions of years, great of kingship like Horus … he who bestows happiness on Egypt, the son of Re, most competent of any king, Merneptah – life, prosperity, health.

All you who are righteous, come that you may see! Right has banished wrong. Evildoers have fallen on their faces. The oppressors are ignored. (ANET 378, adapted)

Similar themes appear in the royal literature of ancient Mesopotamia. For example, we find the following proclamation to the king in an ancient Babylonian coronation ritual:

May Assur and Ninlil, the lords of your crown, set your crown on your head for a hundred years! May your foot in Ekur and your hands stretched toward the breast of Assur, your God, be pleasing! May your priesthood and the priesthood of your sons be pleasing to Assur, your god! With your straight scepter widen your land! May Assur give you authority, obedience, concord, justice and peace! (Translation: Livingstone, 472)

Royal texts from both ancient Mesopotamia and Egypt emphasized the choosing of the king by the high god of the pantheon, the king's appointment as the highest authority and priest of the land, his overcoming of all enemies in the name of the god, and his bestowing of justice and peace on the land through his rule. Together, these and other themes comprise what is meant here by **royal theology**.

Labels (e.g. "Psalm of David"): What They (Don't) Tell Us

The attentive reader will notice that many of the texts to be discussed in this chapter are attributed to David and Solomon. For example, the book of Proverbs starts with the following label: "The proverbs of Solomon, son of David, king of Israel." From this label we might conclude that everything in the book of Proverbs was written by Solomon. Nevertheless, we must be careful about how much weight we put on such ancient attributions of authorship. Ancient texts could be attributed to authors for a variety of reasons – to continue a stream of tradition associated with a given ancient figure, to gain authority through being associated with an ancient figure, etc.

Therefore, when we see a text such as Psalm 110 assigned to David, this may mean that it was written at the time of David by one of David's scribes, or it may just mean that this psalm was seen as part of a longer tradition of Davidic psalms.

Similarly, labels that assign the Song of Songs, Ecclesiastes, and most parts of Proverbs to Solomon probably do not mean that Solomon wrote all these texts. Instead, some may have been written at the time of Solomon, while others may just be part of a broader stream of "Solomonic" tradition extending even to apocryphal texts, such as the Wisdom of Solomon.

That said, the Bible's attribution of texts to figures such as David or Solomon can still be significant. For one thing, they are the first Judean or Israelite figures in the Bible to have whole biblical texts attributed to them (Moses only becomes the author of the Pentateuch in *post*-biblical tradition). The attributions of texts to David and Solomon may be recollections, preserved in the Bible, that David and Solomon's time was the first phase of the development of Israelite literature.

Many elements of Egyptian and Mesopotamian royal theology are common in the **royal psalms** of the Hebrew Bible (Psalms 2, 18, 20, 21, 45, 72, 89, 110, and 144; along with 2 Sam 23:1–7). These poetic texts feature a distinctive focus on the king and his relationship with God. For example, Psalm 110 opens with a call for the king to sit at the right hand of God (Ps 110:1), a common motif in ancient Egyptian royal art. Its picture of the king subduing his enemies (Ps 110:1–3a) is typical of ancient royal literature, whether Egyptian or Mesopotamian. The latter part of verse 3, however, contains an obscure text whose meaning may be clarified when we look back to Egyptian royal ideology. God proclaims to the king: "from the womb of dawn, I fathered you like dew." Recall that the sun God, Re, in Egypt conceived the king through spreading his aroma over the king's mother. The Egyptian word for "aroma" rhymes with the word for "dew." In speaking of Yahweh "fathering" the king "like dew" (see "aroma" in the Egyptian materials) "before the womb of the dawn," Psalm 110 seems to apply these ideas to the Judean king. The psalm then hearkens back to the pre-Israelite royal traditions of Jerusalem in reporting God's oath to give the king eternal priesthood "according to the order of Melkizedeq" (110:4), a figure remembered elsewhere in the Bible as one of Jerusalem's kings in the time before David (Gen 14:18). Next come pictures of the king destroying his enemies (Ps 110:5–6) that are quite typical of ancient royal literature, before the psalm concludes with a reference to the king's drinking from Jerusalem's spring (Ps 110:7). Apparently the Judean king was anointed by the Gihon spring in Jerusalem (1 Kgs 1:33–4, 38–9). Thus Psalm 110 is a good example of a psalm whose obscure references can be understood when we see how it adapts ancient ideas about kingship recalled from pre-Davidic Jerusalem and the yet older royal theologies of Egypt and Mesopotamia. It does not depend on any specific pre-Israelite text, but in a broader way it contains "echoes of ancient empires."

The same can be said of many other biblical royal psalms. Just as the Egyptian king received a written decree from the gods proclaiming his status as the "son of Re," so Psalm 2 has the king report receiving a similar decree from Yahweh:

> I will proclaim the decree of Yahweh.
> He said to me, "You are my son,
>   I have fathered you today.
> Ask me, and I will give nations as your birthright,
>   The entire world as your possession." (Ps 2:7–8)

This theme of God offering the king whatever he wants, especially military victory (Ps 2:8), is found in other royal psalms as well (Ps 21:2; see also 1 Kgs 3:5), and is a major feature of ancient Egyptian and Mesopotamian royal theology. Over and over again the texts of these ancient empires emphasize that it is the king who is authorized to call on God for military help. The king, and the king alone, is authorized by God to ask for and achieve military success for his people, and one of the main jobs of the king in ancient Egyptian and Mesopotamian royal texts is to destroy the people's enemies.

This emphasis in royal psalms on the king's violent power can seem harsh to contemporary readers, particularly those in Europe or North America who have not experienced the direct threat of military attack. To ancient Israelites, however, such words sounded differently. Though many may have been inclined to follow calls such as Absalom or Sheba's to reject the monarchy, these royal psalms insist that the king was appointed by God and would protect and defend them against any threat like the Philistines. In the process, the psalms draw on older Near Eastern royal imagery – e.g. divine "fathering" of the king, setting the king at God's right hand, the grant of the king's wishes – to justify the Jerusalem monarchy to skeptical Israelites.

basics	Book of Psalms: Part 1

(For "Book of Psalms: Part 2," see Basics Box on p. 201.)

Multiple levels in the book of Psalms

The book of Psalms was created over a very long period of time. It contains some of Israel's earliest texts. Yet it was still being expanded late into Israel's history. This mix of ancient and later texts in Psalms reflects the fact that these texts were integrally linked to and reflected shifts in the lives of Israelites as they faced ever different individual and national challenges.

Tracking down the earliest psalms

It is impossible to be sure whether a given Psalm comes from the pre-exilic period, let alone from the time of David and Solomon. Nevertheless, most scholars agree that some psalms are good candidates for being among Israel's earliest literature. Some hymns, such as the praise of the storm god in Psalm 29 or the praise of God's power for fertility in Psalm 104, may have originated as pre-Israelite hymns to other gods before being adapted for Israelite use. Some other potentially early psalms mention the king, ark, or Zion, such as the celebration in Psalm 132 of Yahweh's choice of Zion and David's moving of the ark there. It is relatively unlikely that an author wrote such references after the destruction of the monarchy and the Zion Temple with its ark.

Other potentially early psalms?

The psalms discussed above point to the probable existence of early psalms across the book of Psalms. They stand as potential indicators that *some* of the other psalms that lack such historical references, such as some psalms of lament or trust, may also date from Israel's early periods. Such texts about individual suffering or rescue are inherently difficult to date. Luckily, such dating is relatively unimportant for their interpretation.

One other important theme in these royal psalms is the emphasis on the importance to the kingship of "social responsibility" – Hebrew **tsedeqah**. This Hebrew word is usually translated into English as "righteousness," but it refers more specifically to the virtue of fulfilling one's social obligations to others, particularly defending those most vulnerable in ancient society: the orphan, widow, and foreign immigrant (the "stranger" or "alien"). For example, 2 Sam 23:3 notes that the king must rule with such "social solidarity" to dawn on his people like the morning light, and virtually all of Psalm 72, a "Psalm of Solomon," is a prayer that God may give the king the power to rule his people with such *tsedeqah*:

> Give the king your justice, O God,
>   and your social solidarity to the royal son!
> May he judge your people with social solidarity [*tsedeqah*],
>   and your poor with justice! (Ps 72:1–2)

MORE ON METHOD: POETIC ANALYSIS

Poetry in the Bible does not have the kind of sound rhymes found in much English-language poetry. Instead, it is characterized by a phenomenon called "**seconding**," where the second line of a poetic **couplet** – or pair of lines – builds on the idea or imagery of the first line, but somehow takes it further. Some poems may have a **triplet** (or more). In triplets the stress is on the final, third line, which builds on and advances the idea(s) or imagery of the first two. Take the example of the following triplet from Psalm 110, a royal psalm:

> 2) The LORD sends out from Zion
>   your mighty scepter
>   *Rule in the midst of your foes.* (NRSV)

Note how a translation like the NRSV marks a triplet like this through slightly indenting the second and third lines. These indentations of about 2 spaces indicate where the translators locate the Hebrew line breaks.

The example above uses italics for the third and climactic, seconding, line of the triplet. If you are analyzing a couplet or triplet, it is a good idea to write it out this way and underline or highlight the final line. Look at the parallels and differences between this final line and the two lines that precede it. How do the first two lines prepare for the final line and what is the impact of concluding the triplet this way? Can you identify an emotional impact of this poetic couplet in addition to summarizing it?

Take a Bible with the NRSV and try to find and analyze the poetic units in verse 3 of Psalm 110. (Hint: according to the NRSV, there is a triplet and a couplet here.)

For more see Robert Alter, *The Art of Biblical Poetry* (New York: Basic Books, 1985).

These texts show that Israelite kingship aimed to be an institution that protected the formerly vulnerable peoples of Israel's hill country and provided true justice. As we will see in Chapter 4, the monarchy – like all human institutions – did not always live up to its highest aims, and Israelites rebelled against the monarchy several times. Nevertheless, these psalms show how Israel's kingship was meant to be an institution through which God provided both protection and care for the most vulnerable of God's people.

These same values of justice and social solidarity are also prominent in another group of psalms, often termed "**Zion psalms**" because of their common emphasis on the special significance of Zion/Jerusalem, the capital of the new monarchy. For example, Psalm 9 describes how God who dwells in Zion "judges the peoples with social solidarity" (9:8) and is "a stronghold for the oppressed" (9:9). Psalms 15 and 24 are ancient liturgies for those making a pilgrimage to Zion. These psalms bar from Zion those who cannot affirm that they have "clean hands and a pure heart" (24:4) and do not exploit others through lending practices (15:5). Zion, at the heart of ancient Jerusalem, was the mountain where God dwelt. Those who would come there had to hold themselves to a higher standard of behavior. They were expected to be just as the God of Zion is just. Furthermore, these and other psalms repeatedly assert what will be one of the most important claims of Zion theology: that Jerusalem, the dwelling place of God, is invulnerable to foreign attack. See, for example, the description of Jerusalem/Zion in Psalm 46:

> There is a river whose streams bring joy to the city of God,
>   The holy dwelling of the most high.
> God is in the midst of her [the city], she shall not fall.
>   God will rescue her at the break of day. (46:4–5)

Though parts of these royal and Zion psalms may have been written at later points in the history of the Jerusalem monarchy, they stand as excellent examples of how early Israelites – who had lived for hundreds of years in hilltop villages – made theological sense of this new social form: a new monarchy set in a new capital city, Jerusalem. Later Jewish and Christian interpreters, of course, have reinterpreted many of these psalms, so that – for example – the king praised in texts such as Psalm 2 or 110 is understood to be the Messiah. Such reinterpretations can be legitimate, since these texts would not have survived and become part of the Hebrew Bible if later readers had understood them only to be relevant to a monarchy that would eventually perish. Yet these texts should also be understood in their historical context. As such, they are a witness to some of Israel's earliest ideas about power and community, ideas which would prove very important to the later writers of prophecies and histories.

Echoes of Ancient Empires in Writings Attributed to Solomon

Some of the most striking echoes of ancient empires in the entire Old Testament are found in books associated with Solomon, David's

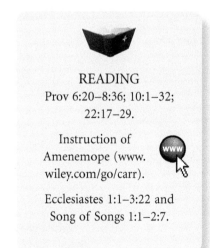

READING
Prov 6:20–8:36; 10:1–32; 22:17–29.

Instruction of Amenemope (www. wiley.com/go/carr).

Ecclesiastes 1:1–3:22 and Song of Songs 1:1–2:7.

successor: Proverbs, Song of Songs, and Ecclesiastes. This is a bit of a surprise, since virtually all historical-critics do not think Solomon actually wrote all three books, and most would date these books to widely different periods. Nevertheless, despite their differences, these "Solomonic" books each echo traditions that were prominent in the ancient Near East.

basics   Song of Songs

It has proven difficult to find a systematic pattern in the loosely connected love poems that make up the Song of Songs. The following is a rough overview based particularly on the striking set of parallel refrains across the Song (2:7; 3:5; 8:4).

Outline

I	Introduction of themes	1:1–2:7
	Seeking day/night scenes	2:8–3:5
	Riches and praise	3:6–5:1
	Seeking night scene	5:2–6:3
	Riches and praise	6:4–8:3
II	Concluding statements on themes	8:4–14

Date

Most scholars would date the Song of Songs to the third or fourth centuries BCE, centuries after Solomon, particularly because of late features in its language. A minority see indicators of earlier origins of these materials, such as the way they resemble Egyptian and other early love songs.

Theme: sex, God, and the poetics of the Song

Many readers insist that one must decide that the Song is *either* about human desire *or* about divine–human love. The poetry of the Song, however, is more elusive. The dense metaphors and disconnected dialogues invite readers to build their own images of what is happening. The lack of explicit divine references and other features of the Song suggest that the book was meant to evoke the drama of human love. Still, the poetry allows multiple readings, especially now that the Song stands in a Bible that elsewhere depicts God's love for God's people (e.g. the book of Hosea, to be discussed later in this textbook).

Take, for example, the Song of Songs (otherwise known as Song of Solomon or Canticles), an often overlooked book of passionate love poetry at the heart of the Old Testament. Though early Jewish and Christian communities often read this book as a love dialogue between God and God's beloved community (whether church or synagogue), the book's closest parallels are secular love songs found in Egypt just before the emergence of Israel. Those ancient Egyptian love poems and their parallels in the biblical Song of Songs do not describe the love affairs of gods. The Song of Songs does not ever clearly refer to Yahweh! Instead, like the Egyptian love poetry it most resembles, the Song of Songs is focused on the drama of human physical love: desiring, seeking, losing, and seeking again human passion with one's true love. Moreover, like the love literature that it echoes, the Song of Songs presents a positive, not fearful, picture of female desire. The woman of the Song of Songs is a powerful figure, not afraid to ask her lover for what she wants and speaking more than half of the words of the book. Nowhere in the book is she judged for her desire, nor is her lover, even though their love remains frustratingly secret and forbidden (Song 8:1–2). Scholars are not sure when to date the book, but its unique poetic picture of human love is deeply indebted to poetry about human love found elsewhere in the Near East.

Ecclesiastes (also known by its Hebrew name "Qohelet") is similarly difficult to date, and it likewise echoes literature from the ancient Near East. Though the book is attributed to "the teacher, the son of David in Jerusalem" (traditionally Solomon), its date and authorship are debated. What we can say is that Ecclesiastes/Qohelet is a complex combination of skepticism about wisdom and affirmation of life's small joys. Its main idea is the way all values are called into question by the fact that everyone dies and "you can't take it with you." During ancient Israel's history, there was no belief in a heaven or hell where people would be rewarded or punished for their behavior during life. In light of this, the "teacher" of Ecclesiastes ends up deciding that "emptiness, emptiness, all is emptiness" (Eccl 1:2, 14; 2:1; etc.). Since everyone dies sooner or later, both frantic pleasure seeking (Eccl 2:1–11) and excessive wisdom and righteousness (2:12–23) are pointless, "chasing after wind." Rather than getting too attached to any great project, the teacher of this text urges all to enjoy each day's moderate pleasures:

> Go, eat your food with pleasure, and drink your wine with a happy heart; for God has long approved what you do. Let your clothing always be white, do not let oil be lacking on your head. Enjoy life with the woman you love, all the days of your empty life that you are given under the sun. For that is your portion in life and your work which you work under the sun. (Eccl. 9:7–9; see also 2:24–5; 5:18–20; 8:15)

This kind of day-to-day living, eating, drinking, and enjoying romantic love, this "imperative of joy" (as one scholar has called it), is the "teacher's" prescription for life lived in a world where "emptiness, emptiness, all is emptiness." Moreover, we find a close parallel to both the concern about death and Ecclesiastes/Qohelet's "imperative of joy" in a very ancient Mesopotamian text, the epic of Gilgamesh. There Gilgamesh expresses his terror in the face of mortality and is told, "let your belly be full, . . . every day make merry . . . let your clothes be clean, let your head be washed, . . . let a wife enjoy your repeated embrace."

Whenever one dates Ecclesiastes/Qohelet, that book seems to be responding with skepticism to older wisdom of the kind seen in Proverbs, the "Solomonic" book with the best claim to being datable (at least in part) to the time of David and Solomon. This one biblical book actually contains multiple collections, many of which are identified by separate headings: "the Proverbs of Solomon, son of David, king of Israel" *basics* Ecclesiastes/Qohelet

Outline:	I	Introductory royal testament	1:1–2:26
counter-wisdom	II	Instruction in skeptical wisdom	3:1–12:8
instruction	III	Epilogue with later affirmations	12:9–14

Date Most scholars consider Ecclesiastes/Qohelet to be among the latest books in the Hebrew Bible. The Hebrew in which it is written is unusual for an early text, and many would see its perspective to be Greek. As in the case of the Song of Songs, however, there are some reasons to think a form of Ecclesiastes may have been earlier, such as its resemblance to the older form of the Gilgamesh epic (see below).

Major themes: The lead themes through most of Ecclesiastes are the absurdity of all human striv-
Qohelet's ing (Eccl 1:2, 14; 2:1; etc.) and the benefits of daily pleasures in life (2:24–5; 5:18–20;
contradictions etc.). Yet the last verses of the book (12:13–14) as well as isolated sections in its midst (e.g. 2:26; 3:17) affirm the more traditional idea that good eventually is rewarded and evil punished. Many would take these more traditional affirmations to be late additions to the book.

(Prov 1:1–9:18), "the Proverbs of Solomon" (Prov 10:1–22:16), "the Proverbs of Solomon that were collected by Hezekiah's men" (Prov 25:1ff.), and so on. What we have in Proverbs, then, is a collection of collections of ancient Israel's educational materials.

This collection of collections in Proverbs contains some of the clearest echoes of foreign educational texts found in the Bible. For example, we find a collection of "words of the wise" in Proverbs 22:17–24:22 whose "thirty sayings" (Prov 22:20) loosely adapt and echo some of the 30 chapters of the Egyptian Instruction of Amenemope (see Figure 3.6). Both collections begin with a call to memorize the following instruction (Amenemope chapter 1; Prov 22:17–21), and continue with similar instructions not to oppress the poor (Amenemope 2; Prov 22:22–3), not to move boundary stones (Amenemope 6; Prov 22:28), not get tied up in pursuing wealth (Amenemope 7; Prov 23:4–5), to avoid fools (Amenemope 9; Prov 22:24–5), and to take care in eating in front of nobles (Amenemope 23; Prov 23:1–3). To be sure, the author of Proverbs did not translate the ancient Egyptian instruction. The existing parallels between the texts are parallels in general content, and there are many parts of Prov 22:17–24:22 that have no counterpart in the Instruction of Amenenope. Nevertheless, the shared concept of 30 sayings and multiple parallels between these texts are good reason to conclude that the author of Prov 22:17–24:22 knew of and loosely appropriated parts of the Egyptian

Figure 3.6 Copy of the Egyptian Instruction of Amenemope, dated approximately 1200 BCE. The topics of its 30 sayings (cf. Prov 22:20) loosely parallel those found in Prov 22:17–24:22.

basics	Book of Proverbs		
Outline: treasury of ancient Israelite wisdom	I Introductory instruction: seek wisdom!		1:1–9:18
	II Additional wisdom collections		10:1–31:9
	III A good woman as embodiment of wisdom		31:10–31

Date Most scholars see a great diversity of date in the material of Proverbs. Sections such as Proverbs 1–9 are dated many centuries after Solomon, while parts of other sections, such as Prov 22:17–24:22, are thought to be among the earliest parts of the Bible. A minority of scholars, however, find indicators of early date in sections such as Proverbs 1–9 as well.

Major themes Since Proverbs is a collection of collections, it is particularly difficult to summarize with a single theme or set of themes. Nevertheless, major features of the book include its prominent focus on female figures toward the beginning (Proverbs 1–9) and end (Prov 31:10–31), and its repeated emphasis on the importance of "fear of Yahweh" (Prov 1:7, 29; 2:5; etc.) throughout.

instruction of Amenemope, along with other wisdom traditions, in composing his own version of "30" sayings. In this sense Prov 22:17–24:22 is an important "echo of ancient [Egyptian] empire" in the Bible.

The book of Proverbs also shows the importance of female wisdom in ancient Israel. Proverbs starts and continues with calls for students to attend to both the father's *and* the mother's wisdom (Prov 1:8; 6:20; 23:22). The early chapters of Proverbs feature a powerful depiction of wisdom as a female, semi-divine figure (e.g. Prov 1:20–33; 8:1–36). And Proverbs concludes with an instruction attributed to King Lemuel's *mother* (Prov 31:1–9) and an A–Z praise of the "woman of power" which Jewish men often sing to their wives over the table of the Friday evening Sabbath meal (Prov 31:10–31).

Alongside all this, there also is a religious element. Both the instructions and proverbs in the book of Proverbs have a distinctive emphasis on the "fear of Yahweh" as crucial to the successful life (Prov 1:7, 29; 14:26–7; 23:17; etc.). Nevertheless, the collections of educational texts in Proverbs are broader instruction in how to succeed with both god and human beings. Combined with assertions of the importance of fearing Yahweh (e.g. Prov 14:26) are pragmatic sayings such as the affirmation in Prov 17:8 that bribes often work well. All these materials in Proverbs (in contrast to Qohelet) affirm the basic idea of **moral act-consequence**: the idea that fear of God and/or good actions produce good results, while bad behavior leads to disaster. The task of the student is to walk the path toward success, not toward death.

Uncovering Echoes of Past Empires Elsewhere in the Bible

READING
Genesis 1–11, Gilgamesh (tablet 11), and Atrahasis (www.wiley.com/go/carr).

EXERCISE
Before reading this section, read Gen 6:5–9:17 and note every place where the same or quite similar event is narrated twice. An example would be God's announcement of the flood both in Gen 6:13 and in 7:4. Another is Noah's multiple entries into the ark in 7:7 and 7:13. Once you have developed a list of such doubly narrated events, see whether "God" or "LORD" is used to refer to God in any of these doublets. Come up with your own theory about how the biblical flood story ended up this way.

So far we have found echoes of ancient empires in entire texts (e.g. royal psalms) or books (e.g. Song of Songs) that are associated in different ways with the time of David and Solomon. Nevertheless, other texts from the Bible also contain strong echoes of ancient Near Eastern literature, many of which similarly may be datable to the beginnings of the monarchy. For example, recent scholarship by David Wright (*Inventing God's Law: How the Covenant Code of the Bible Used and Revised the Laws of Hammurabi* [New York: Oxford University Press, 2009]) has identified multiple and specific parallels between the ancient Mesopotamian code of Hammurabi (www.wiley.com/go/carr) and a collection of biblical laws in Exodus 20:22–23:33 called the "**Covenant Code**" (see Exod 24:7). For over a century scholars have judged that this "Covenant Code" was one of the earliest collections of laws in the Bible, because its laws about topics such as building altars (Exod 20:24–6) and celebrating festivals (Exod 23:14–17) reflect early practices of offering sacrifices all over the land and not just in Jerusalem. Only recently, however, have scholars seen ways that the Covenant Code may be loosely modeled on parts of the Code of Hammurabi (see Figure 3.7), much as Prov 22:17–24:22 was modeled partially on the Instruction of Amenemope. Indeed, it is likely that many of the purity and ritual regulations of Leviticus and Numbers also had ancient precursors, since we have extensive examples of similar sorts of documents about priestly matters found among the remains of the peoples preceding and surrounding ancient Israel. Law, whether royal decree or priestly instruction, was one of the most important forms of ancient writing.

Perhaps the most famous echoes of texts from ancient empires are found at the very beginning of the Bible, in the **primeval history** (Genesis 1–11), which tells the stories about the whole earth and its peoples. Before looking at these echoes, however, it is important to realize that these chapters of Genesis contain *two* parallel sets of stories about the early history of the world. Lots of things are described twice in these chapters. "God" creates plants, animals, and humans (male and female) in Genesis 1, and then "LORD God" creates the first man, animals, and then woman in Genesis 2. Genesis 3–4 tell stories about these first humans and their descendants up to the time of Noah, and then Genesis 5 gives a genealogy from Adam to

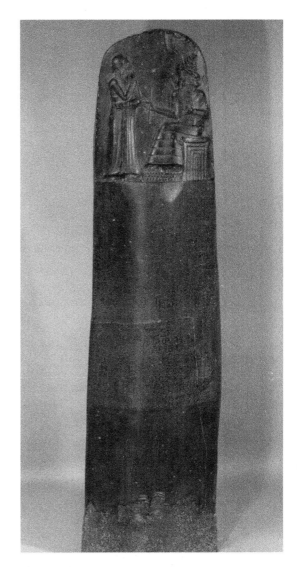

Figure 3.7 The stela of Hammurabi (c.1700 BCE). The top image depicts the king showing respect before the enthroned Mesopotamian god of justice, Shamash. The text below describes his appointment by the gods to give justice and then quotes his proclamation of laws that roughly parallel (in topic) parts of the Covenant Code in Exod 20:22–23:33.

Noah. Then, the flood story of Genesis 6–9 is full of doubly narrated events: two descriptions of the problem leading to the flood (6:1–4 and 6:11), two descriptions of God's perception of the problem (6:5 and 6:12), two assertions that Noah was exceptional in his righteousness (6:8 and 9), and so on. Looking at these duplicate narratives in the flood and across Genesis 1–11 more generally, it appears as if an Israelite author had two complete, written stories of creation and flood, and that author wove those older written stories, these ancient "sources" of Genesis, together to create the present biblical text.

Over the last two hundred years, biblical scholars have reached a high level of agreement on how to untangle these interwoven creation and flood writings (sources) embedded in Genesis 1–11. They call one of these sources "**P**" or the **Priestly Source**, because its sequence of stories (Gen 1:1–2:3; 5:1–32; 6:9–22; 7:6, 11, and other parts of the flood up through 9:1–17) links with other parts of the **Tetrateuch** (Genesis, Exodus, Leviticus, and Numbers) that focus on priests. The other source starts with the garden of Eden story in Genesis 2:4–3:24, continues with the Cain and Abel story and genealogies of Genesis 4, includes its own flood narrative (Gen 6:1–8; 7:1–5, 10, 12, and other parts up through 8:20–2), and contains an epilogue about Noah and his sons (Gen 9:18–27). This source is often called "**J**" or the "**Yahwistic Source,**" since this source uses the holy Hebrew name Yahweh to refer to God. (The German scholars who first discovered the "J" source two hundred years ago used the letter "j" for their "y" sound and spelled the name Yahwist "Jahwist.") As will be discussed later, in the Miscellaneous Box in Chapter 6 on "The L Source: Terms for It and Pictures of Its Formation," many scholars see this J source, like P, continuing across the Tetrateuch, but there are good reasons to be skeptical of their claims. Instead, this textbook considers any early "J" source to be limited to a "J primeval history" found exclusively in Genesis 1–11.

Both of these sources, J and P, echo texts from ancient empires that preceded Israel. For example, the P creation story in Genesis 1:1–2:3 echoes aspects of the ancient Mesopotamian Enuma Elish epic (www.wiley.com/go/carr). Both texts describe the beginning of creation as a watery chaos before the god(s) spoke the world into being:

Enuma Elish	Genesis 1:1–3
When on high no heaven had been named, when no earth had been called, When there were no divine elders . . . When there was nothing, nothing but . . . Godfather Apsu and Mummu-Tiamat, Godmother of All Living, two bodies of water becoming one . . . When there were no divine warriors, When no names had been called, When no tasks had been assigned . . . (Translation: *OT Parallels* 12)	When God first created the heaven and the earth, and the earth was completely without form and darkness was on the face of the deep, and a divine wind howled over the face of the water . . . God said, ["let there be light . . ."]

The Enuma Elish goes on to describe the creation of the inhabited world out of a conflict between the gods, including the triumph of the god Marduk over the goddess

MORE ON METHOD: SOURCE CRITICISM

The term "source criticism" refers to the scholarly attempt to identify separate sources standing behind the existing biblical text. As discussed in the main text, we have no manuscripts of these earlier sources. Instead, scholars must examine the biblical text we now have and look for clues to earlier sources, such as doublets, contradictions, and major shifts in language. Sometimes scholars can achieve substantial consensus in reconstructing hypothetical earlier documents, such as the Priestly/P and Yahwistic/J primeval history sources discussed in this chapter. As we will see in later chapters, the picture is less clear as we move beyond Genesis 1–11.

of the primeval salt water, Tiamat. Such a focus on divine conflict is absent from the biblical story, but Tiamat is distantly echoed in the Hebrew word for "deep" that appears in the initial description of chaotic waters in Gen 1:2. Moreover, the biblical chapter shares with its Mesopotamian counterpart a picture of creation that moves from watery chaos to the creation of light, then a heavenly domed ceiling to separate the two primeval oceans (the "firmament" of Gen 1:6 and following), dry ground, and humans. In these and other ways the story of creation of the cosmos in Genesis 1 echoes multiple elements of the Enuma Elish epic, even as the biblical story also has its own distinctive emphases, some of which will be discussed when we return to the P document in Chapter 6.

Meanwhile, the echoes of ancient empires are just as widespread in the J primeval history. Many scholars have noted that this strand of Genesis 1–11 links at multiple points with the ancient Mesopotamian Atrahasis epic, written almost one thousand years before the time of David and Solomon. That epic starts with a creation story that resembles parts of the garden of Eden story (Gen 2:4–25), continues with multiple accounts of human multiplication that anticipate the biblical report of human multiplication (Gen 6:1), and concludes with an ancient Mesopotamian story of the flood with multiple links to the story of Noah and the flood. In Atrahasis the gods ordain a flood, the flood is announced to a flood hero, the hero builds an ark and survives the flood, the flood eventually abates and the ark lands on a mountain, the flood hero offers a sacrifice, and the god(s) resolve never to send another flood once they smell the sacrifice. Sometimes, the links can be very specific. For example, a version of the Atrahasis flood narrative that was included in the Gilgamesh epic tells of how the flood hero, Utnapishtim in that story, sent forth a dove, a swallow, and a raven to find out if the flood was over, closely paralleling the story (in J) of Noah sending birds to find out the same thing (Gen 8:6–12). These and other parallels have convinced many scholars that the author of the J primeval history knew some form of these ancient Mesopotamian traditions. He may even have been crafting his own distinctively Israelite version of the Atrahasis primeval history.

We do not know for sure when the authors of the J and P narratives did their work. Most would date the overall P source to a relatively late period in Israelite history, but there are signs that some parts of the P source, including some form of the Genesis 1 creation story, may have existed much earlier. Meanwhile, many would date the J primeval history early in Israelite history, possibly as early as the time of Solomon. Its widespread and specific dependence on older non-biblical Mesopotamian texts makes good sense in the early period of the monarchy, and it does not clearly anticipate or refer to themes of Torah and law that are important in later periods of Israelite history. In sum, if there is material from around the time of David or Solomon in the book of Genesis, the J primeval history is one of the most likely places to find it.

FOCUS
TEXT

The Garden of Eden Story (Gen 2:4–3:24)

We turn next to look more closely at the text that opens the J/Yahwistic source discussed above: the garden of Eden story in Gen 2:4–3:24. Most people approach this text with presuppositions shaped by its history of interpretation. For example, if asked to name the fruit that Adam and Eve ate in the garden, most would instantly reply "an apple." The Genesis text, however, does not say this. Similarly, though many assume that the snake in the garden was "Satan," that is never specified in the Bible. These and other elements were added to the biblical story by later interpreters (see Figure 3.8).

This history of interpretation of the garden of Eden text has also influenced what people think the whole story is about. For example, many have understood Paul in Rom 5:18–21 to imply that Genesis 2–3 is a tale of how sin entered the world, putting all humans under the curse of death. In the post-Pauline letter of 1 Timothy, this tragedy is blamed on women, who must now pay the price by bearing children:

> For Adam was formed first, then Eve; and Adam was not deceived, but the woman was deceived and became a transgressor. Yet she will be saved through childbearing, provided they continue in faith and love and holiness, with modesty. (1 Tim 2:13–15; translation: NRSV)

Later Christian interpreters expanded on this type of interpretation, with the early theologian Gregory Nazianzen talking of how Eve "beguiled the man by means of pleasure" and Tertullian saying to a group of women, "Are not each of you an Eve? . . . You are the Devil's gateway." With these and many other interpretations setting the stage for contemporary readings, it is little wonder that many people today assume that this text is an anti-female text blaming Eve for seducing Adam and introducing sin and death into the world.

Yet particularly thanks to groundbreaking work by Phyllis Trible (*God and the Rhetoric of Sexuality* [Philadelphia: Fortress, 1978]) and others in the mid-1970s, scholars have gradually recognized that there is no more basis for that reading in the text itself than there is for the idea that the fruit which the first humans ate was an "apple" (that word

Figure 3.8 Titian's painting of Adam and Eve taking the apple from a snake-tailed cherubic Satan. It well illustrates how later interpretation of Genesis 2–3 influenced people's visions of the scene.

never occurs in Genesis 3). Both of these ideas are later interpretations that have been laid on a text that has very different concerns. Trible and others have pointed out that the text actually celebrates the woman as the culmination of creation. "Sin" is never mentioned in it, and the woman and man share responsibility for the garden crime. Moreover, the consequences for this act that come on them are depicted in the text as tragic, not divinely willed elements of creation. Let us now take a new look at this often-interpreted text.

The story is organized into three main parts: a description of God's creation of a deeply connected partnership of men and women working the earth (Gen 2:4–25), a crime scene describing their disobedience of God's one prohibition (3:1–6), and an account of the tragic loss of original connectedness to each other and the earth as a result of the crime (3:7–25). The story opens with God creating the first "human" (Hebrew *Adam*) out of the earth (Hebrew *adamah*), and giving him life through breathing the divine breath into him. God sets him in the garden to work and protect it, and the word play on *Adam/Adamah* (much like "human" and "humus") emphasizes the original connectedness of the human to the earth he was destined to work.

Yet God immediately recognizes that there is a problem with this picture: "It is not good for the human to be alone" (Gen 2:18). God then decides to create a partner "corresponding to him." God creates the animals, and brings each to the human for him to name them, but none truly "corresponds" to him (Gen 2:19–20). So God tries a new approach, anesthetizing the first human by putting him to sleep, removing a rib, and "building" the woman out of it. When the human awakens and sees the woman, he sings the first song of creation, one that emphasizes the connectedness they share:

> This is it! Bone of my bones, flesh of my flesh;
> This one will be called woman [Hebrew *ishah*]
> for out of man [Hebrew *ish*] she was taken. (Gen 2:23)

The text concludes by saying that this is the origin of love and marriage, it is the reason a man leaves his parents and "clings to his wife and they become one flesh." In stark contrast to many other world-creation stories, sex is not connected at all here to having children. Instead, sex is a sign of the original connectedness of the man and the woman created out of a part of him so that they would truly correspond to each other. This is a story of God's will that humans be in close relationship with each other and the earth. In the wake of this creation, both man and woman "were naked and not ashamed" (Gen 2:25). They may work the garden together and eat of its fruit, with one exception: they may not eat of the "tree of knowledge of good and evil" on penalty of death (Gen 2:17).

The scene shifts in Gen 3:1–6 to a new cast of characters, the man, woman, and now a "clever" snake in place of God (Gen 3:1). Again, the history of interpretation has often pictured Satan as the snake, but there is no basis for that in the Hebrew text. Instead, the snake stands as an ancient symbol of wisdom and immortality, and the adjective used to describe him – *arum* ("clever") – is a virtue frequently praised in the wisdom writings of Proverbs. Furthermore, though interpreters have often supposed that the sin of the first humans somehow consisted of sex or desire, there is no hint of that here. As we saw, Genesis 2 already explains the first sexual partnership of humans as the result of God's creation of a woman out of part of a man. Instead, the issue is human acquisition of godlike "wisdom." Not only is the "clever" snake associated with wisdom, but the "tree of knowledge of good and evil" is a symbol of wisdom's fruits. This then is underlined when the snake convinces the woman to consider eating of the tree, and she sees that the "tree was good for food, a delight to the eyes, and good for becoming wise" (Gen 3:6). She eats of the fruit of wisdom, gives fruit to her husband and he does the same, and the text says that "the eyes of both were opened" (Gen 3:7). This is a frequent expression for gaining education. Thus Gen 3:1–7 describes the first act of human disobedience as the defiance of God and the gaining of a form of "wisdom" that shows many signs of being associated with the ancient Israelite textual wisdom we have seen in books such as Proverbs.

This then sets in motion a tragic unraveling of much of the connectedness that God had created at the outset. The text already illustrates this when God arrives in the garden, the humans hide, and when questioned about why they are hiding, begin to blame each other. The man blames both the woman and God who made the woman (3:12), and the woman blames the snake (3:13). In response, God proclaims consequences for all three. The snake will now crawl on the ground and be an eternal enemy of humans. The woman will not longer enjoy idyllic life in the garden, but God will "multiply her toil and pregnancies" (not "increase pangs in childbearing" as often translated). And the idyllic life of the man likewise will come to an end. His toil is to work the ground from which he was made until he dies and returns to it. Where once there was mutual desire, now the woman's desire will be for her husband, and where once there was mutuality between corresponding partners, now the husband will "rule" over his wife (3:16). The story goes on to describe Adam's naming of his wife "Eve" (a name made from the Hebrew word for "life") to reflect her new job of producing children (3:20). God gives the human pair clothes (3:21) – a sign of human civilization that is also seen in ancient non-biblical texts such as the Gilgamesh epic. Finally, God expels them from the garden for fear that they might gain godlike immortality much as they had already gained godlike wisdom (Gen 3:22–4).

In this way the text accurately depicts the non-ideal world that actual Israelites lived in, but with a twist. Most Israelites still lived lives closely tied to the land, working it by the sweat of their brow until they returned to it. The work was hard, famine was frequent, and death came much sooner than it does for people in the developed world today. Women lived in patriarchal marriages, sustaining the household with their work, while undergoing an endless series of pregnancies, many of which were very dangerous. Analysis of female remains has suggested that as many as half of women eventually died in childbirth. In this sense, the realities described in the latter part of Genesis 3 all held true for the ancient Israelite men and women. Yet what is remarkable about this text is its suggestion that this often harsh and patriarchal reality is not what God originally intended for humans. God originally made humans for fruitful farming, long life, and mutual, truly corresponding life and desire between men and women. It was only with the human step toward godlike wisdom that they emerged into the harsh reality that they experience today. "Wisdom" – not women – is the source of the tragic endless labor, patriarchy, and death that characterize the present.

This kind of narrative about human origins is as timeless as many texts discussed above, but it may also stand as a reflection on what "wisdom" was coming to mean in monarchal Israel. Though most still lived in villages, Judah and Israel were increasingly dominated by urban elites who were educated in new literary traditions modeled on non-biblical sources. The leaders of Israel who were touched by this process were undergoing a momentous shift in their collective memory. Before this monarchy, tribal villages all had their oral traditions, such as tales of trickster ancestors, the exodus, or military triumph. But now – with the monarchy – we have seen the emergence of an early Israelite literary tradition recited and memorized from *written* texts: royal psalms, stories of royalty, royal wisdom and (possibly) early love literature, stories of creation and flood. Moreover, many of these written texts were based on educational literature from outside Israel, such as Egyptian wisdom and love songs or Mesopotamian traditions about creation and flood. This growing Israelite literary corpus, so difficult to identify precisely now, was the means by which a small and growing number of literate Israelites gained "knowledge of good and evil" and had their "eyes" "opened."

Read in this context, the garden of Eden story – itself a text – suggests that wisdom is both an essential part of human growing up and a source of many human ills. On the one hand, it suggests that there is no return to an idyllic life in the garden, munching on fruit and obeying God's one clear command – not to eat of the tree of knowledge of good and evil. On the other hand, this enlightenment, this human journey to mature civilization, has brought many of the ills of adult life with it: endless pregnancies and agricultural work. The marks of original creation persist, such as the way humans still are drawn to "cleave to each other" and "become one flesh." Yet the story recognizes that adult life also has its toil and tragic imperfections. The journey out of the garden has brought a life where humans have work in place of leisure, "wisdom" in place of the single garden command, and – all too often – male rule over women in place of the connectedness that God originally wished.

Conclusion

Ultimately, we cannot know for sure whether any of the texts discussed in this chapter date from the time of David or Solomon's monarchy. Some texts are associated with David or Solomon, but this is not a sufficient basis for dating them to that time. The form of the Hebrew language can be another clue, but it is not reliable for dating texts transmitted – often by memory – over centuries. Even the tracing of "echoes" of ancient non-biblical texts in the Bible is not a sure sign of early dating. In sum, there are no sure guideposts for dating biblical texts, particularly to a period so long before our earliest manuscripts. The most we could do in this chapter is focus on a few biblical texts, some associated with David and Solomon and some not, that show a distinctive "echoing" of foreign, pre-Israelite traditions. Such non-polemical echoing, we are suggesting, would be most typical of writings formed at the outset of Israelite writing and less typical of later times when hostility toward foreign culture was greater.

These echoes of ancient texts can teach us about how ancient Israelites used the sorts of written texts now in the Bible. For example, the Instruction of Amenemope, the epic of Atrahasis, and the laws in the Code of Hammurabi were all used in ancient Egyptian or Mesopotamian education. Mesopotamian and Egyptian leaders were qualified for their jobs by learning to read and memorize these texts. When we turn to similar biblical texts, such as the "words of the wise" in Prov 22:17–24:34 that echo Amenemope, it is logical to hypothesize that such biblical texts likewise were used to educate leaders in the early monarchy. Whatever the original function of earlier oral traditions now embedded in such biblical texts, as *writings* they probably helped educate the leadership elite in an emergent monarchy.

Meanwhile, the differences between biblical texts and their non-biblical counterparts are as important as the similarities. We can learn much about the particular values and perspectives of biblical authors through comparing the Covenant Code with Hammurabi, the "words of the wise" in Prov 22:17–24:34 with the Instruction of Amenemope, the J source in Genesis 1–11 with Atrahasis, and so on. Biblical authors did not just copy major texts of Mesopotamia and Egypt. They reframed non-biblical traditions in light of their particular values. There is a major difference, for example, between the biblical story of the flood in Genesis 6–9, where just one god brings the flood and rescues a human from it, and the polytheistic tale in Atrahasis, where most of the gods bring the flood while one god rescues a human from it. In this and other biblical texts discussed here, we see ancient Israelite authors building freely on and yet radically adapting more ancient literary traditions from elsewhere. These unknown authors, the earliest of whom worked in the time of David and Solomon, are responsible for writing the first building blocks for what would much later become the Hebrew Bible.

CHAPTER THREE REVIEW

1. Know the meaning and significance of the following terms discussed in this chapter:

- couplet
- Covenant Code
- J
- moral act-consequence
- P
- Priestly Source
- primeval history
- royal psalms
- royal theology
- seconding
- Tetrateuch
- triplet
- *tsedeqah*
- Yahwistic Source
- Zion
- Zion psalms
- Zion theology

2. What are two different ways in which comparison of a biblical text with an ancient non-biblical text can be useful? Give two examples of such comparison from this chapter.

3. What are the multiple clues to the presence of two sources in Genesis 1–11?

4. What is source criticism and how does it compare to tradition history and transmission history? What is an example of a conclusion from source criticism?

5. Know the basic character of the following ancient Near Eastern texts and how they are related by scholars to biblical texts that were discussed in this chapter:

- Atrahasis Epic
- Code of Hammurabi
- Egyptian love songs
- Gilgamesh epic
- Instruction of Amenemope

RESOURCES FOR FURTHER STUDY

General introductions to wisdom literature

Crenshaw, James. *Old Testament Wisdom: An Introduction.* Louisville, KY: Westminster John Knox Press, 1998.

Murphy, Roland. *The Tree of Life: An Exploration of Biblical Wisdom Literature.* New York: Doubleday, 1990.

Proverbs

Fox, Michael V. *Proverbs.* 2 volumes. Anchor Bible. New York: Doubleday, 2000–9.

Leeuwen, Raymond C. Van. "Proverbs." Pp. 17–264 in vol. 5 of the *New Interpreters Bible.* Nashville: Abingdon, 1997.

Newsom, Carol A. "Woman and the Discourse of Patriarchal Wisdom: A Study of Proverbs 1–9." Pp. 142–60 in Peggy L. Day (ed.), *Gender and Difference in Ancient Israel.* Philadelphia: Fortress, 1989.

Ecclesiastes

Brown, William. *Ecclesiastes.* Interpretation. Louisville, KY: Westminster John Knox Press, 2000.

Crenshaw, James L. *Ecclesiastes.* Old Testament Library. Philadelphia: Westminster Press, 1987.

Gordis, R. *Kohelet: The Man and His World: A Study of Ecclesiastes* (revised edition). New York: Schocken Books, 1988.

Lohfink, Norbert. *Qohelet: A Continental Commentary,* trans. Sean McEvenue. Minneapolis, MN: Fortress, 2003. Translation of a 1980 original.

Song of Songs

Exum, Cheryl. *Song of Songs.* Old Testament Library. Louisville, KY: Westminster John Knox Press, 2005.

Keel, Othmar. *Song of Songs: A Continental Commentary,* trans. Frederick J. Gaiser. Minneapolis: MN: Fortress, 1997. Translation of a 1986 original.

Weems, Renita. "Song of Songs." Pp. 361–434 in vol. 5 of the *New Interpreters Bible.* Nashville: Abingdon, 1997.

Genesis 1–11

Carr, David. *Reading the Fractures of Genesis.* Louisville, KY: Westminster John Knox Press, 1996. For more detail on indicators of sources in Genesis 1–11.

Gowan, Donald E. *From Eden to Babel: A Commentary on the Book of Genesis 1–11.* International Theological Commentary. Grand Rapids: Eerdmans, 1988.

Discussion of Song of Songs, Genesis, and other texts relating to sexuality

Carr, David M. *The Erotic Word: Sexuality and Spirituality in the Hebrew Bible.* New York: Oxford University Press, 2003.

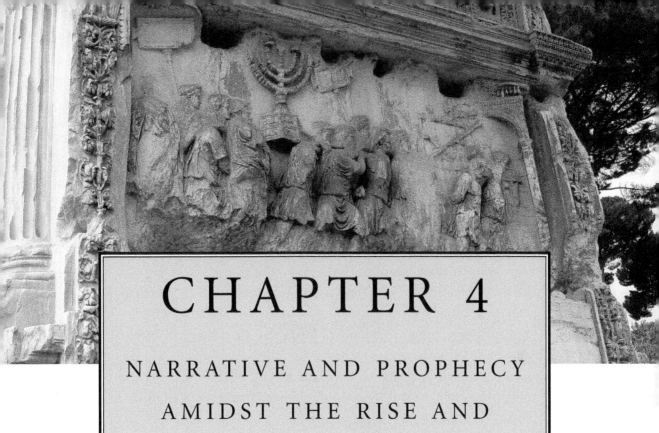

CHAPTER 4

NARRATIVE AND PROPHECY AMIDST THE RISE AND FALL OF THE NORTHERN KINGDOM

Chapter Outline

CHAPTER OVERVIEW

Chapter 3 traced echoes of past empires in the Hebrew Bible, while this one focuses on the reverberations of an imperial onslaught. The time to be reviewed here is the ninth and eighth centuries BCE (800s and 700s). The attacking empire was **Assyria**, a Mesopotamian state based in what is now northern Iraq. By this point there was no longer a "kingdom of Israel and Judah" based in Jerusalem. Instead, there were two kingdoms. A new kingdom of Israel had risen up in the north, while a southern kingdom of Judah was still ruled by descendants of David in Jerusalem. Initially, this northern kingdom (Israel) became stronger than its southern counterpart, while developing its own corpus of texts that were largely distinct from those used in the south. Yet ultimately the northern kingdom was destroyed by Assyria, and the southern kingdom barely survived the decades it spent under Assyrian domination.

The Hebrew Bible reflects this initial imperial encounter in at least two main ways. First, although the Hebrew Bible is a collection of Judean texts, it preserves some remnants of texts from the destroyed northern kingdom, texts that have been appropriated and adapted by Judean scribes. Second, the Bible's first prophetic books came from this time of imperial encounter. The books of Amos, Hosea, Micah, and Isaiah all contain early prophecies that reflect the crises faced by Judah and Israel leading up to and during the Assyrian onslaught. Knowing more about the origins of these texts – whether northern texts now embedded in the Hebrew Bible (e.g. an early Jacob story) or prophetic writings formed in the crucible of imperial crisis – can help us understand them in new ways.

Setting the Stage: The Rise of the Northern Kingdom of Israel and Its Texts

READING
1 Kings 12; 2 Kgs 14:23–9; 15:17–31; 17:1–6 (from Jeroboam of Israel to the fall of the north). Review Genesis 25–35 and Exodus 2–14.

EXERCISE
Compare 1 Kgs 11:26–8, 40, and 12 with Exodus 2 and 4–5. What parallels do you see between how 1 Kings 11–12 describe Jeroboam's story and how Exodus 2 and 4–5 describe the story of Moses?

Our journey toward greater understanding of these texts starts with the story of the emergence of a monarchy in the Israelite north. This monarchy was the ultimate outgrowth of a long process of tribal rebellion. Groups in Israel had tried in the past to gain liberty from the Davidic monarchy, but they did not succeed in breaking free until Solomon's death, around 927 BCE.

According to the description of this event in 1 Kings 12 (//2 Chronicles 10), Solomon's son, Rehoboam, went to the ancient tribal center of Shechem to be anointed by the elders of northern Israel. Instead, they ended up having a confrontation. The elders asked if Rehoboam's "yoke," that is his domination of them, would be as heavy as that of his father. Against the advice of his older advisors, Rehoboam is reported to have said: "I will add to your yoke; my father disciplined you with whips, but I will discipline you with scorpions" (1 Kgs 12:11//2 Chr 10:14). As one might expect, this did not get a good response. The elders called for withdrawal of support of the Davidic monarchy in Jerusalem, saying "To your tents, oh Israel. Look to your own house, David" (1 Kgs 12:16; cf. 2 Sam 20:1). When Rehoboam sent his chief of forced labor to bring the northerners back in line, they stoned him to death (1 Kgs 12:18).

The elders of Israel, however, appear to have started a new monarchy rather than trying to return to the tribal life they had before kingship. In place of Rehoboam, they anointed one of their own countrymen as king, Jeroboam, who was a man from the tribe of Ephraim. Earlier he had worked for Solomon as chief of forced labor, but rebelled and fled to Egypt when Solomon tried to kill him (1 Kgs 11:26–7). As a new king of Israel, Jeroboam first established Shechem as his capital, then moved to Penuel, and he established royal sanctuaries at the towns of Bethel (toward the south of Israel) and Dan (in the north; see Map 4.1). He installed statues of calves at each sanctuary and proclaimed "Here are your gods, Oh Israel, who led you out of Egypt" (1 Kgs 12:28).

This narrative in 1 Kings 12 represents a perspective by later southern scribes on how awful it was that Israel in the north broke away from Judah. Nevertheless, even this unsympathetic narrative preserves a memory that this Israelite northern monarchy was different from the Davidic monarchy in the south. Having gained liberty, Jeroboam

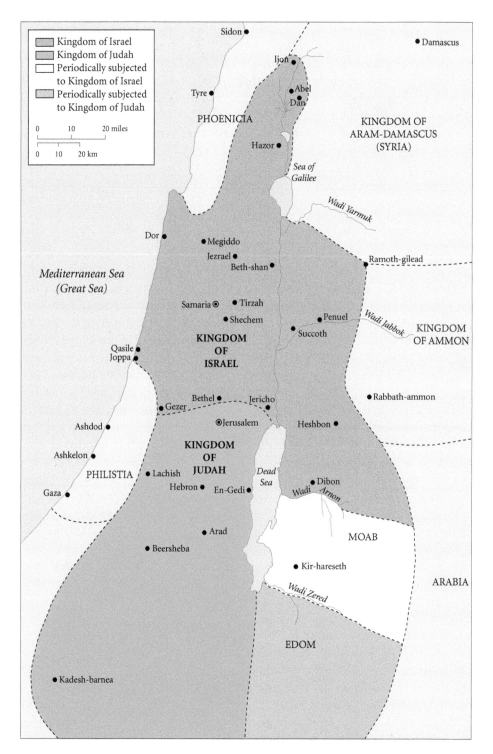

Map 4.1 The divided kingdoms of Israel and Judah. Redrawn from Norman Gottwald, *The Hebrew Bible: A Socio-Literary Introduction*. Minneapolis: Fortress, 1985, page 291.

invoked exodus traditions in setting up royal sanctuaries in Bethel and Dan ("Here are your gods . . . who led you out of Egypt"). He picked ancient northern cities as capitals for his new kingdom, cities such as Shechem and then Penuel. And though Jeroboam's "calves" are viewed negatively in these chapters of the Bible, archaeological finds of ancient statues of bulls in Israelite sites suggest that they were one of the most ancient symbols of divinity known in early Israel.

There is one other way in which Jeroboam and other northerners forged a new path in founding the northern monarchy: *they appear to have developed their own corpus of written texts.* This corpus could be a "counter-curriculum" to replace many of the Davidic and Zion texts that had been taught in the north during David and Solomon's rule. Those texts remained important in Judah, and many are preserved in the Bible. The split-off kingdom of "Israel," however, created its own distinctive texts, featuring north-ern themes, places, and heroes.

Indeed, some chapters in the Bible probably were written in the north as part of this distinctive counter-curriculum. A good example is the story of Jacob found in Genesis (Genesis 25–35), a story built on the trickster traditions about Jacob discussed in Chap-ter 2. It features Jeroboam's royal sanctuary city of Bethel and early northern capitals such as Penuel (where Jacob wrestles God – Gen 32:22–32). Indeed, the story of Jacob in Genesis counters the claims of the older monarchy in Jerusalem. Where Jerusalem Zion traditions claimed that Yahweh dwelled at Mount Zion (Pss 9:11; 135:21), the Jacob

basics	**Jacob Story**

Design: the Jacob story chiasm	A Encounter Jacob/Esau (25:21–34; 27:1–45)
	   B Divine encounter, departure (28*)
	      C Wives acquisition (29:1–30)
	         D Fertility: children (29:31–30:24)
	         D′ Fertility: flocks (30:25–43)
	      C′ Wives extrication (31:1–32:1)
	   B′ Divine encounter, return (32:22–32)
	A′ Encounter Jacob/Esau (33:1–17)

Defining "chiasm"	A **chiasm** is a circular literary form that moves through a set of themes to the cen-ter (e.g. A, B, C, D) and then goes through similar themes in reverse order after the center (e.g. D′, C′, B′, A′). Major emphasis is often put on the texts that occur at the center of a chiasm.
Major themes of the Jacob story	The center of this early Jacob story is the fertility of Jacob's family and flocks (Gen 29:31–30:43). This is a major theme of the story, alongside emphasis on his (and his women's) resourcefulness amidst conflict and danger.

story embedded in Genesis has God (quoted by Jacob) say, "I am the God who dwells in Bethel" (Gen 31:13). These clues suggest that the bulk of the Jacob story now in Genesis was written in the north as a counterpoint to the writings of the Davidic monarchy in the south. To be sure, as we saw in Chapter 2, the Genesis Jacob story builds on more ancient trickster and other oral traditions about Jacob and his family. Nevertheless, most of the *written* story of Jacob probably originates from the time of the early northern monarchy as part of Jeroboam's counter-curriculum. It even seems as if the northern prophet, Hosea, studied this story and could refer specifically to it (Hosea 12:3–4, 12).

MORE ON METHOD: THE JOSEPH STORY AND LITERARY APPROACHES

The Joseph story as a potential early northern text

The Joseph story (minus probable later additions such as chapters 38, 46, and 48–9) is another good candidate for being an early northern text. These chapters tell a tale that starts with a pair of dreams that Joseph has. In one, the sheaves of grain belonging to Joseph's brothers bow down in obedience to Joseph's sheaf. In the other dream, 11 stars and the sun and moon bow down to Joseph. His (11) brothers interpret these dreams as claims by Joseph that he will dominate them, and their murderous resentment about these claims results in Joseph being taken into slavery in Egypt (Genesis 37). There he rises to prominence, is able to provide food for his family when they flee a famine in Israel, and is reconciled to his brothers (Genesis 45 and 50).

Especially since Joseph was an ancestor of Jeroboam, tribal groups of the north could have seen this narrative as an allegory of power. It may have been designed to help them recognize Jeroboam's ultimate destiny to rule and provide for them the way Joseph, Jeroboam's ancestor, was destined to rule and provide for his brothers. As such, an early form of the Joseph narrative now in Genesis may have been part of the early northern literary corpus.

Literary approaches and Joseph

Meanwhile, the Joseph story has been a major focus of literary study of the Bible. No matter when one dates the Joseph story (and there is debate), there is much room for analysis of its characterization of Joseph and his brothers, the contrast between what the storyteller says happened at points and what different brothers report about what happened, and the move of the plot from brotherly resentment to reconciliation. Literary study of biblical narrative draws on the study of modern literature to reach insights about texts like the Joseph story that are not related to particular theories about dating or social context.

Such literary approaches to biblical narrative have grown ever more varied as study of literature in the humanities itself has evolved. For more on diverse literary approaches to narrative, see David Gunn, "Narrative Criticism," pp. 201–29 in S. McKenzie and S. Haynes (eds.), *To Each Its Own Meaning* (Louisville, KY: Westminster John Knox Press, 1999).

It is difficult to know exactly what other biblical texts were composed in the north, but there are many other chapters of the Old Testament that show strong northern connections. Chapter 2 of this textbook discussed one of those chapters, Deborah's victory song in Judges 5, which focuses exclusively on northern tribes. This early song probably was written down in the northern kingdom started by Jeroboam. Some form of the book of Deuteronomy may have started in the north as well. It includes a scene of covenant making on northern mountains (Deut 27:1–13) that almost certainly would not have been composed by later Judean scribes.

We may even have hints of fragments of an early northern exodus story in the book of Exodus. As you may have seen in the exercise comparing 1 Kings 11–12 and Exodus 2, 4–5, the story in Exodus is written in a way that makes Moses's liberation of Israel from Egypt sound a lot like Jeroboam's liberation of Israel from Rehoboam. Both grow up in privileged households, identify with the people being oppressed, flee from the oppressive ruler, return when that ruler dies, appeal to the new ruler to lighten the oppression, and eventually lead their people out from under oppression when the new ruler refuses. It is possible that Jeroboam's liberation of the north just happened to parallel Moses's liberation of Israel. It is more likely, however, that these parallels in stories came about because scribes working for Jeroboam in the early northern kingdom shaped the ancient exodus traditions of the north in light of the recent "exodus" they had experienced under Jeroboam from oppression by Solomon and his son, Rehoboam.

Does this mean that the ancient northern scribes just "made up" stories about Jacob or exodus in the process of writing their counter-curriculum? Not really. There is a contemporary analogy to this process of shaping ancient stories in light of recent experience. In the 1950s and 1960s, many fighting for civil rights would cite the biblical story of the exodus as a warrant for their struggle for freedom. In doing so, they selectively drew on the parts of the story that most matched their current experience. An example was Martin Luther King Jr.'s famous final speech in Memphis, just before he died, about standing, like Moses, on the mountain, looking over into a promised land that he would not get to see himself. The parallels between the biblical stories of Moses and Jeroboam probably were caused by a similar process of linking past to present: northern scribes who were writing down ancient oral traditions about the exodus retold the story so that it celebrated a "Moses" who now looked much like Jeroboam, their new king. The written results of their work, an early northern "exodus story," are preserved – very fragmentarily – in parts of Exodus 2, 4–5.

It should be no surprise that there are many traces of northern texts in the Bible, in Genesis, Exodus, and many other books of the Old Testament. There is much archaeological evidence that the kingdom of Israel, during its two centuries of existence, was more powerful and prominent than the kingdom of Judah to the south. In particular, the northern kingdom reached a zenith of power during the time of king Omri and his son, Ahab (see Figure 4.1). Omri established a massive new capital in Samaria, made a major marriage alliance with Phoenicia (Ahab's wife Jezebel was from Sidon), and dominated the smaller, southern kingdom of Judah, which was still ruled by descendants of David. Though the Omride dynasty was eventually brought down through a coup d'etat led by a general Jehu (841 BCE), years afterward, Mesopotamian kings would still refer to the whole area as "the house of Omri." The northern kingdom of Israel could

Figure 4.1 One of the ivory carvings found in Samaria, the site of Ahab's famous "ivory palace" (1 Kgs 22:39). Originally covered in gold, these objects illustrate the kind of wealth and power possessed by the northern kingdom, particularly under Omri and Ahab.

achieve such prominence during this time partly because it had more land and population than the kingdom of Judah and controlled more central trade routes. Judging from this, many scholars believe that the northern kingdom of Israel had a more active literary tradition during this time than Judah did. The kingdom of Israel became the central place for writing and developing written traditions common to north and south, while Judah played a more peripheral role until the late eighth century.

Imperial clouds, however, were on the horizon. In the second half of the eighth century, the Assyrian empire under King Tiglath-Pileser III began extending its reach westward to secure access to resources and trade routes in the area of Israel. The Assyrians had long been a major trading power in the Near East, but by this time they also had assembled an extremely efficient army that was the terror of their neighbors. Figure 4.2 shows an Assyrian depiction of an attack on a Judean city in 701. Other parts of the same set of reliefs show Judean resisters being impaled and inhabitants of the town being led away in chains. Through such attacks, and reports and depictions of them, the Assyrians terrorized the area and enforced their domination. One Assyrian king brags, "Many of the captives . . . I took alive; from some of these I cut off their hands to the wrist, from others I cut off their noses, ears, and fingers; I put out the eyes of many of the soldiers." Another reports, "I fixed up a pile of corpses in front of the gate. I flayed the nobles, as many as had rebelled and spread their skins out on the piles of corpses." It was in the face of threats like these that central parts of the biblical tradition were formed.

Facing the prospect of possible Assyrian invasion, many countries voluntarily submitted to Assyria and promised to send regular tribute to the Assyrian king. This

Figure 4.2 Detail from a wall-sized panorama, in the palace of the Assyrian king Sennacherib, of the defeat of the town of Lachish in Judah. The Assyrians are pushing a siege engine up a ramp to break a hole in the wall of Lachish while the Judean defenders attempt to set the engine on fire by throwing torches down from the wall.

Figure 4.3 Panel from the Black Obelisk of the Assyrian king Shalmaneser III, depicting the Israelite king Jehu offering tribute to and kissing the ground before the Assyrian king. It documents the brief subservience of the northern kingdom to Assyria about a hundred years before Assyria dominated and eventually destroyed the kingdom of Israel in the late eighth century.

happened first in the north, perhaps already in the ninth century with Jehu (as in Figure 4.3), but first in an ongoing way when king Menahem of Israel started paying substantial tribute to Assyria around 738 BCE. But Menahem died, and the kingship was soon taken over around 735 BCE by Pekah, who aimed to join Syria and other nations in rebelling from Assyria and stopping payment of the onerous tribute. In what is called the **Syro-Ephraimite war** (735–734 BCE) this new anti-Assyrian coalition even laid siege to Jerusalem in the south in an attempt to force similar anti-Assyrian policies on Ahaz, who was king of Judah at the time. Ahaz escaped the Israelite and Syrian forces by appealing for Assyrian help, thus defeating those besieging him, but also falling under Assyrian domination himself. Thus began a process where the northern kingdom was gradually reduced in size and eventually totally destroyed in 722, while Judah barely survived its period of Assyrian rule.

A few years later Hezekiah, king of Judah, also rebelled. In retaliation, the Assyrians destroyed virtually all the towns of Judah and were poised to destroy Jerusalem as well. Nevertheless, they pulled back – for unknown reasons. The account of his attack and withdrawal is found in both an Assyrian version and multiple biblical versions (see the Miscellaneous Box on "A View from the Assyrian Imperial Court: The Annals of Sennacherib"). The kingdom of Judah barely survived, and Hezekiah and, later, his son Manasseh ruled for decades as vassals of Assyria over a much reduced kingdom of Judah. Zion theology was apparently affirmed, but Judah was forever wounded.

A View from the Assyrian Imperial Court: The Annals of Sennacherib

Figure 4.4 The Sennacherib prism.

ramps and battering rams. These siege engines were supported by infantry who tunneled under the walls. I took 200,150 prisoners of war, young and old, male and female, from these places. I also plundered more horses, mules, donkeys, camels, large and small cattle than we could count. I imprisoned Hezekiah in Jerusalem like a bird in a cage. I erected siege works to prevent anyone escaping through the city gates.

The cities in Judah which I captured I gave to Mitinti, King of Ashdod, and to Padi, King of Ekron, and to Sillibel, King of Gaza. Thus I reduced the land of Hezekiah in this campaign, and I also increased Hezekiah's annual tribute payments.

Hezekiah, who was overwhelmed by my terror-inspiring splendor, was deserted by his elite troops, which he had brought into Jerusalem. He was forced to send me 420 pounds [Akkadian 30 talents] of gold . . . and all kinds of valuable treasures, his daughters, wives, and male and female musicians. He sent his personal messenger to deliver this tribute and bow down to me. (Translation: *OT Parallels 191–2*)

Exercise

Because Hezekiah of Judah did not submit to my yoke, I laid siege to forty-six of his fortified cities, and walled forts, and to the countless villages in their vicinity. I conquered them using earthen

How does this description compare with Isaiah 36–7 (parallel to 2 Kgs 18:13, 17–19:37)? How does it compare to 2 Kgs 18:14–16 (material not found in Isaiah)?

This whole process decisively affected the formation of the Hebrew Bible. Whatever texts we now have from the northern kingdom were preserved – in tatters and fragments – in the texts of the kingdom of Judah. Moreover, this drama of Assyrian invasions, anti-Assyrian coalitions, and switching between pro-Assyrian and anti-Assyrian kings forms the backdrop for much of Israel's earliest written prophecy. The prophecies of

Hosea, Micah, and Isaiah, in particular, are difficult to understand without a sense of the political turmoil their countries were facing. Even the harsh prophecy of Amos, which was delivered prior to the Assyrian onslaught, probably became as important as it did as an explanation of the Assyrian destruction of the north.

In sum, much of the Hebrew Bible was formed in the shadow of Assyria's imperial domination of Israel and Judah. The rich literature of the north was destroyed as such, only to be preserved in fragments strewn across Judah's later Bible. In addition, this Assyrian crisis was the starting point for the development of written prophecy in ancient Israel and Judah. Prophets such as Hosea and Amos, Micah and Isaiah, may not have gotten much of a hearing in their own day. Nevertheless, the writings attributed to them became very important to later generations of Judeans who had to endure yet more catastrophes like the eighth-century Assyrian onslaught. We turn now to look at the phenomenon of such written prophecy.

Ancient Near Eastern Prophecy

Prophecy was a widespread phenomenon in the Near East. Egypt, Phoenicia, Syria, and the kingdoms of Mesopotamia all knew people, some amateurs and some professionals, who pronounced oracles from the gods. This was part of a broader system by which kings and others tried to divine the future. Much as some people learn to read scrolls, these scholars aimed to learn to "read" clues in the cosmos to the gods' intentions, clues encoded in dreams, omens, parts of special animals sacrificed to divine the future, and other means. Life was unpredictable, and the people of the Near East marshaled every resource they could to understand more about what the gods were doing and what they wished. Verbal prophecies from human mediums were a major way of gaining such information.

Most such prophecies were oral, but sometimes they were written down. The archives at Mari, a Syrian city that became very powerful in the second millennium BCE, contain hundreds of records of prophecies given there, just in case such prophecies might be useful in future. Later Mesopotamian archives likewise contain careful records of prophetic oracles and even a few small collections of oracles. Perhaps one of the most interesting written prophecies, however, is an early eighth-century wall inscription dating from just a few decades before the time of the biblical prophets and found in the Transjordan, just across from Israel, in a crossroads village now known as Deir Alla. This inscription, dated a few decades before those of the biblical prophets to be discussed here, gives the contents of a scroll describing how "Balaam, son of Beor" (a figure known as a seer in Numbers 22–4) received a vision of judgment much like the Hebrew prophets to be discussed below. Together, the DeirAlla text and early prophetic collections in the Hebrew Bible show peoples in the neighborhood of Israel collecting and studying prophetic words of judgment, not just hearing those words preached. Let us turn now for a closer look at the earliest of the prophetic teachings preserved in the Hebrew Bible.

Overview of the Four Eighth-Century Prophets

	Prophecy addressed to Israel (the northern kingdom)	Prophecy addressed to Judah (the southern kingdom)
Prediction of doom	Amos	Micah
Prediction of hope on other side of painful judgment	Hosea	Isaiah

Amos, a Southern Prophet Preaching Justice and Doom to the North

The prophet Amos may be best known right now – insofar as he is known at all – as a prophet of social justice. No other prophet packs so much social critique in so little space. The book starts and finishes with similar divine critiques of elites of northern Israel taking advantage of their power to exploit the poor:

READING
Amos 1–2 and 7–9.

> For the three crimes of Israel and for four,
>   I will not turn back the punishment.
> Because they sell those who act rightly for silver
>   And the poor for a pair of sandals.
> They trample the head of the poor into the dust of the earth
>   And push the oppressed out of their way. (Amos 2:6–7; also 8:4–6)

Later, Amos proclaims disaster on the women of the capital city of Samaria, who "oppress the poor and crush the needy" (4:1). He announces disaster against those "who turn justice into wormwood and bring down social solidarity" (5:7). In a passage later echoed by Martin Luther King and others, he calls for "justice [to] roll down like waters and righteousness like an everflowing stream" (5:24).

This prophecy by Amos does not seem to have been received positively in his own time. To start with, he was an outsider in northern Israel. The Bible records that he came from Judah, having been a shepherd near the small town of Tekoa (Amos 1:1; 7:14). Moreover, most of his prophecies to the north were uncompromisingly harsh, often undermining the ancient traditions most dear to his audience. The Israelites might have thought they were safe because the God of the exodus was on their side, but Amos suggested that this exodus was nothing special:

> Are you not like the Ethiopians to me, Oh Israel?
> Did I not bring Israel out of Egypt
> And the Philistines from Caphtor
> And the Arameans from Kir? (Amos 9:7)

The Israelites might have thought that God's choosing of them would protect them ("election theology"), but the book of Amos quotes God giving an interesting twist on such northern election theology:

> You only have I known among all the nations of the earth,
> Therefore, I will hold you accountable for all your crimes. (Amos 3:2)

A later story about Amos in Amos 7:10–17 gives a vivid picture of one response to his message. It starts by telling how Amos went to the royal sanctuary at Bethel, and announced that the king of Israel at the time, Jeroboam II, would die by the sword, while his people would go into exile. The high priest at Bethel, Amaziah, sent a message about this to the king and then said to Amos:

> Go away, seer, flee to Judah, eat bread there and prophesy, but don't ever again prophesy at Bethel because it is the king's sanctuary and the temple of the kingdom. (7:12–13)

Amos in this story responds that he is – or was – not a professional prophet just trying to prophesy anywhere. Instead, God called him from his farmwork in Tekoa to go prophesy to "God's people, Israel" (Amos 7:14–15). But now that Amaziah has told him to stop prophesying in Israel, Amos adds to his former prophesy that the priest's wife will become a city prostitute, his sons will die in battle, and he, a priest, will die "in an unclean land" (7:17).

There is no hint in this and many other prophecies that Amos aimed to change the ways of his Israelite audience. To be sure, there are some isolated calls for the people to change in chapter 5 (Amos 5:4, 6, and 14) and some predictions of hope for Judah added to the end of the book (Amos 9:8b, 11–15). These fragments, however, hardly outweigh the book's general tone of doom. It starts with a set of prophecies where God proclaims that "for three crimes and for four" God will not turn back the punishment (Amos 1–2). It ends with a series of four visions: in the first two Amos turns back God's punishment through his pleas on Israel's behalf (Amos 7:1–6), but in the "third" and "fourth" visions God will not turn back the punishment (7:7–9; 8:1–8). Instead, God has a "plumbline of justice" by which God has measured Israel (7:7–9), and it will be struck by a horrible earthquake (8:8; see also 2:13).

As it turns out, Israel actually was hit by an earthquake around the time of Amos. This has been confirmed by a combination of archaeological and geological data. This fulfillment of Amos's prophecy was never forgotten (Amos 1:1). Yet his prophecies of disaster proved to be correct in a broader way as well. As Amos had predicted (Amos 2:13–16; 3:11–15; 6:1–7), the northern kingdom was completely destroyed, though not

basics   Book of Amos

How Amos was adapted for the south

Most specialists in Amos agree that the book of Amos contains numerous additions that adapted his prophecy to the north so that it could speak to the south as well. For example, the oracle of judgment against Judah in Amos 2:4–5 stands out from the other oracles in 1:3–16 and is probably an addition designed to include Judah among the nations judged by Amos. Likewise, the concluding promise that the "booth of David" will be rebuilt (Amos 9:11–15, also introduced by 8b) was probably added to provide a word of hope for Judah (and "Israel" in the wider sense) in contrast to the word of judgment throughout the rest of the book on the northern kingdom of Israel.

More information: Amos and praise?

The middle of the book is punctuated by three similar praises of Yahweh: 4:13; 5:8–9; 9:5–6. Read them and see the similarities. These late elements of Amos challenge the reader to praise the awesome God who brings such judgment on Israel and set that judgment in the context of God's creation.

in a way he envisioned. Amos prophesied in a time before the Assyrians' dominance and does not mention them, but in 722 they invaded, destroyed Israel's sanctuaries and palaces, and carried into exile its surviving leaders.

By this time Amos had returned to Judah, and his written prophecy was a form of prophetic "teaching" that Judeans could reinterpret – now in relation to the threat (and later reality) of Assyrian domination. Like teachings seen in Proverbs, these sayings by Amos followed a format of "3 and 4" (Prov 30:15–31; cf. Amos 1–2; 7:1–9 and 8:1–8), rhetorical questions (Amos 3:4–6), and riddles (Amos 3:12; 6:12). Yet this written prophetic teaching of Amos consists of quotations of God, not a sage like Solomon. And the focus of the teaching is on social acts and their national consequences, not the smaller scale "moral act-consequence" of an individual student emphasized in Proverbs (see Chapter 3 on moral act-consequence). In the end, this written form of Amos's prophecy had a more lasting effect than any oral words that he delivered. Though told to go home by the northern high priest Amaziah, Amos's words are still being read more than two and a half thousand years after they were written.

Hosea, the Northern Prophet, Calling for Israel's Devotion to Yahweh Alone

READING
Hosea 1–2 and 11–12.

The book of Hosea was also addressed to the kingdom of Israel around this time, but it is quite different from the prophecy of Amos. Where Amos emphasized judgment for Israel's injustice, Hosea pleaded for his own people to change, to "sow social solidarity" (10:12) and "protect justice" (12:6). Where Amos announced irreversible disaster, Hosea predicted restoration on the other side of God's punishment. And where Amos inverted and critiqued his audience's deep belief in their chosenness (ancient "election theology"), Hosea found new ways of describing that chosenness, ways that emphasized God's love for Israel and God's wish for Israel's devotion to God. For Hosea, Israel's main failing was a lack of devotion to God and a love of false gods instead.

This is most vividly illustrated at the outset of the book with Hosea's image of God's broken marriage to Israel. The book starts with the story of a rather remarkable and personal act of symbolic prophecy – yet one that we will see also has disturbing overtones. Hosea is called by God to marry and have children by a promiscuous woman, giving these children Hebrew sentence-names that symbolize what God plans to do with Israel, such as "not pitied" and "not my people" (Hos 1:2–9). Then, after the brief insertion of a yet later text reversing this prophecy of judgment (Hos 1:10–2:1), we encounter one of the most powerful passages of the whole book: God's agonized speech to Israel in the wake of Israel's spiritual promiscuity (Hos 2:2–15). In this speech God, not Hosea, is the husband, and the nation of Israel is the wife. God starts with an address to the children of this "Israel," telling them – in effect – that God has divorced their mother:

> Protest to your mother, protest,
>> For she is not my wife
>> And I am not her husband. (Hos 2:2a)

Yet God in Hosea 2 is not as done with this relationship as first appears. God's speech immediately turns toward a plea for the children to get their "mother," their nation, to end her adulterous ways, lest she be subject to the sort of stripping and shaming that wives suspected of adultery had to endure at the hands of their husbands:

> [Tell her to] put away her promiscuity,
>> and remove her adultery from between her breasts.
> Lest I strip her naked,
>> And display her like the day she was born,
> Make her bare as the desert,
>> and make her dry like parched earth,
>> And let her die of thirst. (Hos 2:2b–3)

This Israel, this wife of God, is facing the prospect of drought and famine (the "stripping") because she has gone after "other lovers" in search of love gifts. Yet Yahweh in Hosea's speech insists that she was mistaken about who was providing for her. In actuality, it was really Yahweh, her husband, who was giving her the things a man was to give to his wife: food, clothing, and oil (Hos 2:5, 8).

This list of gifts suggests that Hosea sees Yahweh as betrayed by Israel's worship of other gods, such as Baal (Hos 2:13). According to Hosea, the problem is that Israel sought grain and other benefits from these other gods rather than relying on Yahweh alone. Such worship of multiple gods, of course, was quite common in ancient cultures, and we even see signs (discussed in Chapter 2) that people in earliest Israel worshipped other gods alongside Yahweh. Nevertheless, Hosea proclaims to his people that Yahweh is as offended by such worship of other gods as a husband would be by his wife's adultery. Like a good husband, he provided his wife with good things, and she undermined his manhood by giving her love to others whom she thought could provide better.

In response, Yahweh says that he will block Israel's way to her lovers so that – like the woman of the Song of Songs – she will "seek" her lovers and not "find" them (Hos 2:6–7). Much of the rest of the speech elaborates how Yahweh will devastate the land of Israel for its unfaithfulness. Nevertheless, it concludes not with judgment, but with hope – in this case Yahweh's plan to seduce Israel and bring back the early times when Israel was in the wilderness and fully in love with God:

> Therefore, look, I will seduce her,
>> and I will lead her in the desert,
>> And speak tenderly to her.
> I will give her vineyards from there,
>> and the valley of Achor as a gate of hope.
> She will respond there as in her youthful days,
>> As when she came out of the land of Egypt. (Hos 2:14–15)

In this way, Hosea's image of marriage between Yahweh and Israel is meant to depict not just Yahweh's pain at what Hosea saw as Israel's betrayal, not just Yahweh's intent to bring consequences, but also Yahweh's enduring love, a love which means that God cannot bear to let Israel go for good and aims to bring her back into relationship with him. As if this were not enough, the book further underscores this point through having Hosea himself describe another act of symbolic prophecy. As a symbol of God's intent to take back Israel despite what "she" has done, God tells Hosea to pay a price to hire a woman known for promiscuity and then specify that she not seek any lovers – not even be with Hosea – for a long time (Hos 3:1–5).

The narratives of symbolic prophecy in Hosea 1 and 3 have led many readers to psychologize Hosea's message, believing that his bold new vision of God was prompted by problems in his personal life, perhaps a propensity to end up with the wrong kinds of women. There are clues elsewhere in the book, however, that suggest a more important background: the power politics surrounding Assyrian domination of Israel going all the way back to the time of king Jehu. In Hos 5:8–6:6 we see Hosea's critique of

basics   Book of Hosea

How Hosea was adapted for the south

Hosea himself may have spoken about Judah in the south (one example is 5:8–15), but there are signs that later Judean authors adapted Hosea's sayings so that they included Judah in Hosea's judgment (examples are 5:5; 6:4, 11). Still other additions resemble the conclusion to Amos (Amos 9:11–15). Like that conclusion, they see future hope for destroyed "Israel" being located in a broader "Israel" that is centered in Judah and its Davidic monarchy (1:11; 3:5; 11:12).

Hosea's prophecy for the ages

This adaptation of Hosea was but the first step in having the book's images speak to new communities which Hosea had not addressed. Whatever personal or cultic background there once was to Hosea's marriage and other imagery, it gained a symbolic life of its own. Within the present form of the book, the marriage imagery of Hosea 1–3 introduces Hosea's prophecy more generally and then fades into the background. Later, Hosea quotes Yahweh as saying that "by the hand of the prophets I gave analogies" (Hos 12:10; probably mistranslated in the NRSV). These analogies in Hosea – marriage, parent, covenant – have been applied and reapplied by centuries of later readers.

Israel and Judah's lack of steadfast "love" for Yahweh (6:4). Hosea sees this lovelessness proven when Israel (called "Ephraim" here) pursued "futile" plans (5:11) and even sent away to Assyria to save itself (5:13). In Hos 7:3–7 Hosea condemns as "adultery" (7:4) the constant shifting of kings in Israel, largely in response to the Assyrian threat. In Hos 8:7–10 Hosea likens the kingdom's tribute payments to a case where a prostitute is actually paying her clients ("Ephraim hires its lovers," 8:9). Finally, Hos 9:1–6 mixes images of agricultural plenty and international politics. The prophet tells the people at a harvest festival not to rejoice, because they are like a promiscuous woman who has loved her wages for sex at threshing floor and winepress (9:1–2), and who will soon go into exile in Assyria and Egypt (9:3–6). In these passages, Hosea critiques the multitude of ways that Israel (and Judah) tried to manipulate or buy their way out of oppression by Assyria. According to Hosea, they should have been devoted to and trusted in Yahweh instead of pursuing such power politics.

There may be some critique of Israel's cult practices as well, especially given the frequent references to "Baal" throughout Hosea. The people of Israel had worshipped various

Figure 4.5 Drawing and inscription found at a desert trading post called Kuntillet Adjrud used by eighth-century Israelites. Interpretation of the drawings is disputed, but note the figure playing a lyre on the upper right. The inscription toward the top is understood by many to refer to "Yahweh and his Asherah."

gods alongside Yahweh, long before Hosea's time, and apparently continued to do so. Indeed, scholars have not been able to reconstruct an early period when the tribes of Israel did not worship other gods. Ancient tribal and later sites have yielded female statues that many interpret to be goddess figurines. Early Israelites appear to have born names formed from the names of various deities, including "Baal" and "El." And a couple of early inscriptions from around the time of Hosea feature blessings "by Yahweh and his asherah [or Asherah]" (see Figure 4.5). Though there is debate about how to interpret these blessings, many understand them to imply that Yahweh had taken over Asherah, formerly El's wife, as his own. In all these ways, Hosea faced a much more diverse religious landscape than we often picture for early Israel (see Figure 4.6). What was new was that he argued that this religious diversity, this lack of pure worship of Yahweh, was one reason for Israel's ills. He believed that the religious diversity of his time was a falling away from Israel's past pure devotion to Yahweh in the wilderness. That is how most contemporary readers of the present Bible perceive the matter. Yet his audience probably perceived his calls for pure worship of Yahweh alone as something *new*.

Overall, Hosea's main point seems to be that his people is displaying a massive unfaithfulness – whether in international policy or in religious practice. Such unfaithfulness, for Hosea, is like a wife's unfaithfulness to her husband. Yahweh's response is a mix of emotions typical of wronged husbands: agony and jealous wrath at his wife's

Figure 4.6 Pillar figurines of a sort common in archaeological remains of the eighth century. They indicate to many scholars that some kind of goddess worship continued to prevail in the time of Hosea and Amos.

betrayal combined with a wish to have her back again. In this way Hosea suggests to his fellow Israelites oppressed by Assyria that Yahweh did not fail or abandon Israel; rather Israel abandoned Yahweh first.

Readers over the years have responded differently to Hosea's picture of God and Israel. For many, the book stands as a powerful picture of God's longing for steadfast love and his willingness to go to any length to bring the people back. Yet others are disturbed by ominous parallels between God's behavior in Hosea's prophecy and the cycle of spousal abuse: a husband's anger at his wife and/or jealous accusations of adultery, physical beating and/or sexual humiliation of the wife, and wooing of the wife back. Hosea used the image metaphorically, believing that Israel had actually been spiritually promiscuous and that God was fully in the right to punish her before bringing her back. Many now would reject this image of God as a husband stripping and beating his sinful, human wife (before taking her back again).

There are, however, other images in Hosea that offer alternative ways of envisioning God's agony and passion for reconciliation. Consider, for example, the picture in Hosea 11, where God now is Israel's parent, agonizing over his son's disobedience after God's tender care for him. The chapter starts with God's description of having tenderly cared for Israel as for a child, and Israel's response to such care by sacrificing to other gods and

Hosea and the "Book of the Twelve Prophets"

The book of the Twelve Prophets

Hosea is the first in the **book of the Twelve Prophets**, a collection of 12 shorter prophetic books that is usually placed in bibles after Ezekiel or (Ezekiel and) Daniel. The books are attributed to so-called "**minor prophets**" – Hosea through Malachi. The word "minor" is applied to these prophets not because they are thought to be unimportant, but because the books attributed to them are relatively short. Each of these short books has its own character, but they also show signs of being edited into a larger whole by later scribes.

Hosea 14:9 and prophetic teaching

One possible sign of such editing is the last verse of Hosea, Hos 14:9. It stresses that the "wise" will understand the words of Hosea, and it praises the ways of Yahweh as "right." Such mention of the "wise" is otherwise typical of books such as Proverbs. This verse marks the book of Hosea as a form of prophetic "teaching," much like Solomon's teaching in Proverbs and Ecclesiastes.

At the same time, since Hosea is the first book of the 12 minor prophets, this framing of Hosea's book as a teaching has implications for understanding the 11 books that follow. With this conclusion to Hosea in Hos 14:9, they too stand as prophetic teaching to be understood by the "wise."

going their own way (Hos 11:1–4). At first God responds by announcing the destruction of Israel (11:5–6), but then God starts to relent:

> How can I give you up, oh Ephraim?
> > How can I surrender you, oh Israel? . . .
> I have changed my mind.
> > My compassion is warm and tender.
> I will not act on my wrath,
> > I will not again attack Ephraim.
> For I am God, not a man.
> > I am the holy one in your midst.
> > I will not come in anger. (Hos 11:8–9)

Here Hosea draws on the metaphorical power of the parental relationship, yet clearly distinguishes this picture of God from that of a human "man." God here is deeply hurt by the faithlessness of God's people. Yet God cannot bear to destroy God's own child, Israel. Even if a father could bear to destroy his son, God here is "not a man" (11:9). For Hosea, God's infinite compassion can be imaged, but only partially so, by the powerful compassion a parent feels for his or her child.

Hosea's prophecy proved particularly influential in later biblical writings. We will see elements of his picture of divine–human marriage appear in several other prophets. Moreover, his call for exclusive devotion to Yahweh was foundational for later Israelites. Although the present Bible contains much later narratives that project this call for devotion back into earlier periods of Israel's history (such as Exod 20:1–3), the book of Hosea is our earliest datable witness to this idea, and it probably was not well received at first. Nevertheless, this belief in God's exclusive claims on God's people grew in importance, particularly as Israel and Judah had to grapple with Assyrian and Babylonian oppression, destruction, and exile. The people suffering through these experiences asked themselves what they could learn from them. They looked back to traditions such as Hosea, spoken out of the crucible of imperial oppression, and concluded that they needed to learn to be more faithful to Yahweh and Yahweh alone. They believed they must reject any other lord (human or divine) and choose Yahweh's boundless love instead.

Micah, a Southern Prophet, Predicting Judgment for Judah and Jerusalem

READING
Micah 1–3 and 5–6.

We turn now for a brief look at one of the earliest books containing prophecy from the south, the book of Micah. Here we find, at least in the book's earliest materials, the words of a southern prophet like Amos. Just as Amos spoke to Israel as an outsider from Judah, so Micah spoke to Jerusalem as a Judean refugee coming from an area decimated by Assyria (the town Moresheth). Moreover, both prophets spoke words of judgment to their audiences, attempting to pierce their false sense of security. Yet the differences between these prophets are striking as well, and they point once again to the different traditions held dear by their different audiences. Where Amos undermined northern Israelite ideas of election, Micah attacks southern trust in Zion theology, particularly the idea that Zion/Jerusalem was invulnerable to all attacks, a belief manifest in biblical texts such as Psalm 46: "God is in the midst of the city, it shall not be moved" (Ps 46:5 NRSV).

The book of Micah starts with judgment, as Micah proclaims to the people of Judah that they are not immune from the Assyrian disaster that has hit the north. The first oracle describes an awesome theophany (divine appearance) of Yahweh coming from the Temple (Micah 1:2), yet it quickly becomes clear that this is no cuddly God:

> Yahweh is treading on the sanctuaries of the earth,
> Then the mountains will melt under him,
>   And the valleys will burst open
> Like wax on a fire.
>   Like waters cascading down a slope.

All this, Micah says, is happening because of the "crime of Jacob and the sins of the house of Israel" (1:5). The reader may ask, "What is this crime?" and the text soon answers that it is the capital cities of Samaria and Jerusalem. In a section that sounds much like Hosea, Micah announces that God is about to destroy Samaria, the capital of the northern kingdom, because of its "idols," which he sees as "wages of a prostitute" (1:6–7). But, lest his country-people think they are immune from this disaster, Micah concludes by saying that Judah will be hit by the same destructive power, with the "wound" even reaching the gate of Jerusalem (1:8–9). The next saying, 1:10–12 makes a similar point – tracing the path of the invading Assyrian army as it moves from Gath, town by town, to the gate of Jerusalem.

Obviously Micah, like Hosea, is speaking in the context of Assyrian invasion, but he insists that the impending destruction at Assyrian hands is actually caused by God's judgment of the inner ills of the people of Judah. In a social critique reminiscent of Amos, he pronounces a lament over those who:

> plan evil and acts of evil on their beds,
> When morning comes, they do it,
> Because they have the power to do so,
> They covet fields, and seize them
> Houses, and they take them away.
> They defraud others of their homes
> And people of their land. (2:1–2)

Such critiques continue, as in Micah's attack on those who make women and children homeless (2:9) or in his quote of God's vivid judgment on the leaders who "devour my people's flesh, flay the skin off them, the flesh off their bones, and . . . breaking their bones to bits, chop them up like soup meat in a pot, like flesh in a caldron" (3:2–3).

Apparently, the powers that be in Micah's time did not like this message. He quotes others as telling him "stop preaching . . . that's no way to preach, shame will not overtake us! Is the house of Jacob really condemned? Is God's patience really so short?" (2:6–7). Apparently there were others proclaiming more hopeful messages, and Micah proclaims Yahweh's judgment on those who "cry 'peace' when they have food in their mouths, but launch war on the one who takes food from them" (3:5). In a climactic message, Micah announces an end to all of the leaders who "build Zion with blood and Jerusalem with malice" (3:10):

> [Jerusalem's] leaders administer justice for bribes,
> Her priests give rulings for a fee,
> And her prophets predict the future for pay.
> And then they rely on Yahweh, saying,
> "Isn't Yahweh in our midst?
> No disaster will come on us!" (3:11)

For Micah, these leaders and their trust in ancient Zion theology are bringing about the very disaster they consider unthinkable:

> Therefore, because of you,
> > Zion shall be plowed as a field
> Jerusalem will become heaps of ruins,
> > And the mountain of the house of Yahweh will be a wooded height. (3:12)

Up to this point, Micah sounds a lot like Amos. He maintains that Jerusalem's corruption is so deep that Yahweh will let the Assyrians destroy it. The book so far explains Judah's oppression by Assyria as a result of its deep-seated iniquity.

Nevertheless, much of the rest of the book, including some of its most famous passages, sounds a much more hopeful note. Micah 4 starts with a famous prophecy (4:1–3), also seen in Isaiah 2:2–4, that God will make Zion/Jerusalem the center of world justice, so that – in a reversal of the usual transformation of farmers into fighters (see Joel 3:10) – nations will "hammer swords into plowshares and spears into pruning hooks" (4:3).

basics Book of Micah

Outline: cycles of judgment and salvation – Judah

I   Destruction up to the gates of Jerusalem (1:1–2:11) and prediction of the in-gathering of exiles (2:12–13)

II Destruction of Zion (3:1–12) and its restoration along with the Judean monarchy and people (4:1–5:15)

III Judgment of Israel (6:1–7:7) and prophetic prayer for restoration (7:8–20)

Theme

Whereas the original prophet, Micah, stressed God's impending judgment on Zion, the book now emphasizes salvation on the other side of such judgment. It was addressed to much later Judeans who had experienced many of the disasters that Micah described. The book encouraged them and later communities to have hope for the future. Though God might destroy everything they held dear, God also could restore them.

More information

Micah's words of judgment were not forgotten. A story in the book of Jeremiah, Jeremiah 26, describes how the later, seventh-century prophet Jeremiah was almost executed for proclaiming the destruction of the temple. At this point, the elders reminded the people of Micah's proclamation of Zion's destruction, a prophecy given a century before the time of Jeremiah (Micah 3:12). In addition, they tell a story – not found elsewhere in the Bible – of King Hezekiah listening to Micah's prophecy and repenting (Jer 26:19). Jeremiah's life was spared.

The rest of Micah 4–5 contains prophecies of how Yahweh will redeem "daughter Zion," who has endured pain like a woman in labor, bringing her exiles back to her (4:6–7, 8–10). The book goes on to say that when "[Zion] who is in labor has brought forth" (5:3), a powerful ruler will arise from tiny Bethlehem of Ephratah to reign in glory from Jerusalem (5:2–4). This prophecy, often understood by Christians to be a prophecy of Jesus's birth in Bethlehem, is part of a series of prophecies about how Zion will triumph over the Assyrians and other enemies who dominated her (4:11–5:15).

These words of hope for exiles and promise of victory in Micah 4–5 contrast sharply with the proclamation of absolute doom on Zion in Micah 1–3. Chapters 4 and 5 hardly sound like the words of the prophet who announced that "Zion shall be plowed as a field, and Jerusalem will be heaps of ruins" (3:12). Because of this, most scholars believe that much of Micah 4–5, and possibly 6–7 as well, were added by later – anonymous – prophets to the book of Micah. As discussed in Chapter 3, to copy and expand an earlier work was an ancient way of recognizing its ongoing importance and applying its message to later times. In this case, these prophets had seen Micah's earlier prophecies of destruction come true, had come to treasure his prophecies, and yet addressed an audience in Babylonian exile who needed new words of comfort to balance Micah's words of judgment. These later prophets declared to their exilic (or post-exilic) audience that Yahweh had a grand future for Zion/Jerusalem and for them. These visionary words of hope – both of a glorious ruler (5:2–4) and of a world where people would not "study war any more" (4:1–3) – have been as important or more important to later communities as the earlier words of judgment to which they are now attached.

The rest of the book of Micah, however, is not all words of hope. Micah 6:9–16 accuses Jerusalem of succumbing to the same social ills as its northern neighbor: "You have kept the statutes of Omri and the works of the house of Ahab" (6:16). This may be another saying from the same eighth-century prophet (Micah) who proclaimed that the wound of Israel was coming to the gate of Jerusalem (1:9, 12). Most famous of all is the speech in Micah 6:1–8, which responds to people's complaints that God has burdened them (6:3) by saying that God's requirements are simple: "to do justice, love kindness, and walk wisely with your God" (6:8). Soon afterward, the book insists that "it is true wisdom to fear your [God's] name" (6:9), reflecting the fact that the book of Micah, like Amos and Hosea, is prophetic *teaching* or *wisdom*. It is not clear that Micah 6:2–8 came from the same eighth-century prophet who spoke most of Micah 1–3, but it is quite clear that this saying has served for many as a powerful distillation of the long-term significance of the message of the prophets. The saying in 6:2–8 well exemplifies the way the book of Micah has been enriched over time by multiple voices that could be considered "inspired." As a result, the book of Micah now is a powerful mix of Micah's eighth-century words of judgment and much later prophetic teachings about hope and God's true wishes for God's people.

Isaiah's Vision of Hope for Jerusalem/Zion
Embedded in the Book of Isaiah

READING
Isaiah 1–11
and 28–32.

EXERCISE
Using the Appendix to this chapter, compare and contrast Psalm 46
(a Zion psalm) with two prophecies about Jerusalem/Zion – Isaiah
1:21–6 and Micah 3:9–12. Which is closer to Psalm 46?

The book of Isaiah was one of the first places where scholars recognized this kind of mix of earlier prophecy and later expansion. Isaiah starts with a superscription that identifies what follows as "the vision of Isaiah, son of Amoz, which he saw concerning Judah and Jerusalem during the time of Uzziah, Jotham, Ahaz, and Hezekiah, kings of Judah" (1:1; see also 2:1) – that is, as the revelation given to Isaiah about the southern monarchy during the last few decades of the eighth century. Nevertheless, scholars have found many signs that the book was written over centuries. As early as nine hundred years ago, the Jewish scholar Abraham Ibn Ezra noted that the reference to the Persian king Cyrus in Isa 41:25 seems to indicate that its author not only knew of this king ruling two hundred years after the time of Isaiah (which would be an inspired prophecy), but could describe him to a contemporary audience as one "foretold from the start." Over the last two hundred years, scholars have used these and other observations to distinguish between the words of the eighth-century prophet Isaiah in the book of Isaiah and layer upon layer of prophecies by later writers now in the book as well.

This research has helped scholars see both the complexity and the grandeur of the book of Isaiah. On the one hand, scholars now believe that most sayings actually from "Isaiah ben Amoz" can be found in *parts* of Isaiah 1–11 and 28–32, with most of the rest of the book (and all of Isaiah 36–66) coming from later authors. On the other hand, scholars also have an ever increasing appreciation of the insight and artistry of the entire 66-chapter book, later portions included. Certainly later communities of faith have found inspiration in Isaiah as a whole. Virtually all of the later prophecy in Isaiah 40–66 appears in the cycle of readings used in Jewish synagogues, and the same visions of comfort and restoration have been central to Christianity from the outset. There will be occasion to return to both the design and interpretation of these portions of the book of Isaiah in Chapters 6 and 7 of this *Introduction*.

For now we must emphasize that this is another place where modern presuppositions about authorship and "inspiration" can mislead us in reading the Bible. Often modern interpreters assume that the *real* inspiration can only lie with an original author, a prophet in this case, while all later materials must be corruptions of the original, pure message. What emerges, however, from a look at the book of Isaiah and its history of interpretation, is that Isaiah – the eighth-century prophet – provided a dynamic and complex vision that was only the start of a much bigger process. Ultimately, the power of his vision *increased* as later authors, addressing quite different times, expanded on and adapted it so that it would speak to those times. The result was a grand book of 66 chapters, the first of the three books of the "**major prophets**" (Isaiah, Jeremiah, and Ezekiel).

Let us turn now to take a closer look at the early vision of Isaiah ben Amoz. Much of this vision is focused on Yahweh's message amidst threats related to the Assyrian onslaught. The first such major threat was the attempt by Syria and Israel in 735 to force Ahaz of Judah into joining an anti-Assyrian alliance by laying siege to Jerusalem (the Syro-Ephraimite war). The book of Kings describes Ahaz as responding to the siege by asking for help from Assyria (2 Kgs 16:5–9). As we can see in Isaiah 7–8, Isaiah saw this request by King Ahaz as a fatal failure to trust in Yahweh's protection of Zion. In Isa 7:1–9 Isaiah assures Ahaz that the coalition against Judah will not stand and that Ahaz should "not be afraid." Ahaz in 7:10–17 rejects Isaiah's offer of a sign from Yahweh, and Isaiah announces that the result of this rejection will be an imminent attack by the king of Assyria. Finally, Isa 8:1–8 continues these themes, proclaiming disaster on the attackers from Israel and Syria (8:1–4), but also on the people of Judah for refusing to trust in God's protection of Zion (= "the flowing waters of [Jerusalem's spring] Shiloah," 8:6). Each of these stories features a child with a Hebrew name that signifies the core of Isaiah's message: "a remnant shall return" (7:3), "God with us" (7:14), and "speedy comes the booty" (8:1). In light of the rejection of his message, Isaiah tells in 8:10–18 of Yahweh's command to "seal" his prophetic "teaching" in his "students" (8:16), so that these students can serve as a sign for future generations of "Yahweh who dwells in Zion" (8:18). Perhaps some of these students were Isaiah's own, strangely named children, since literate fathers often taught their own children. In this case, Isaiah is passing on to his children a "teaching" and a "witness" that his own generation would not hear. We probably have this process to thank for the initial preservation of Isaiah's words and the beginnings of the book.

The story of Isaiah's commission in Isaiah 6 reflects his experience of rejection during the time of Ahaz. Many readers are well familiar with the beginning of this text, where Isaiah actually sees Yahweh's terrifying presence in the Jerusalem temple, surrounded by "seraphim" (see Figure 4.7 for more on these) – an Egyptian symbol. Awed by the spectacle, he proclaims a lament, "woe upon me, for I am a man of unclean lips in a people of unclean lips, looking onto the king of kings, Yahweh of armies!" (6:5). One of the winged cobras then burns his lips with a fiery coal, saying that this has removed the prophet's sin and bloodguilt (6:6–7). The rest of the passage then describes how Isaiah's people are about to be subjected to a similar burning process, starting with the prophet's commission to deliver a message that will not be heard:

Figure 4.7 Judean seals from the time of Isaiah and Micah, showing strong Egyptian influence. Note especially the winged cobras, which probably were the referent for the "seraphim" mentioned in Isaiah 6.

Isaiah 6 and the "Call Narrative"

Many scholars would call Isaiah 6 a **prophetic call narrative**." Such a narrative is a story, told in the first person by the prophet ("I," "me"), where he tells of how he was authorized by God to be a prophet and deliver God's message. Other examples are Jer 1:4–10 and Ezekiel 1–3.

Here are the typical parts of a prophetic call narrative, with illustrations from Isaiah 6:

1	A divine appearance	1–4
2	An introductory word by God	5–7
3	The call of the prophet (or leader)	8–10
4	An objection from the prophet	11a
5	A divine reassurance/answer	11b–13
6	A sign reinforcing the answer	[not present]

These prophetic call narratives stand toward the outset of a prophetic book (Jeremiah and Ezekiel) or collection in a prophetic book (the Isaiah memoir in Isaiah 6–8) and emphasize God's authorization of the message in that book. They are as different as the books that they authorize, and some

scholars dispute the application of the term "call narrative" to some of these texts (particularly since the word "call" has its home in later Christian theology). Sometimes they lack one or another part of the typical form. Nevertheless, they share with each other the idea that the prophet's message arose not with him, but with God. The prophet was but a messenger, as signified by the Hebrew word for prophet, *nabi*.

Isaiah 6 probably was written as an introduction to his memoir, insisting on God's role in authorizing his prophecy during the Syro-Ephraimite war even though it was rejected. As this text became part of the larger book of Isaiah, it came to authorize the book as a whole.

Other call narratives: an exercise

Judg 6:11–24 and Exod 3:1–4:17 are call narratives for other figures, Gideon and Moses. Compare these texts with Isa 6:1–13. What is similar and what is different about the form of these texts? What is similar or different about the role they play in the biblical books where they occur?

Go and say to this people:
"Keep listening, but do not comprehend.
　Keep looking, but do not understand."
Make the mind of this people senseless,
　And stop up their ears,
　And shut their eyes,
Lest they see with their eyes,
　And hear with their ears,
　And understand with their mind
And change their ways and be healed. (6:9–10)

Isaiah is understandably upset at receiving this commission and asks "how long?" The answer is that Judah is about to be laid waste – again a probable reference to Assyrian attacks. Only after successive invasions is there any sign of hope. It is a "stump," which Isaiah is told is a "holy seed" (6:13).

We see this image of the "stump" used elsewhere in Isaiah to communicate that there is hope on the other side of apparent absolute destruction: for an apparently dead stump can have a shoot spring forth from it (see Job 14:8–9). At the end of Isaiah 10, Isaiah describes Yahweh as coming through the whole area, cutting down the tallest trees and chopping off their branches (Isa 10:33–4). Since "trees" were an image for royal dynasties, many understand this to be Isaiah's prediction that Yahweh is about to send the Assyrian army through the area, "cutting off" all of the royal dynasties and thus terminating the monarchies of Judah, Israel, and their neighbors. Yet Isaiah sees a future on the other side of this awful event. Though the Davidic dynasty in Jerusalem might seem like a completely dead stump, Isaiah proclaims that a "shoot shall spring forth from the stump of Jesse [David's father]" (Isa 11:1). This "shoot" will be an ideal king:

With social solidarity he will judge the poor,
　And he will rule the oppressed fairly.
He will strike the earth with the rod of his mouth,
　And he will kill the wicked with the breath of his lips. (Isa 11:4)

Although many later interpreters, particularly Christians, now see this text as relating to Jesus, it originally stood as an ancient prophecy that a new king would arise over Judah who would fulfill all the promises of royal theology: a king who judges justly and successfully defends his people. The passage then turns to a grand vision of peace centered in Zion:

The wolf will sojourn with the lamb,
　The leopard will lie down with the calf . . .
They will not hurt or destroy in all my holy mountain,
　For the earth shall be as full of the knowledge of Yahweh
　As waters cover the sea. (Isa 11:6a and 9)

This whole complex of texts (Isa 10:33–11:9) beautifully displays Isaiah's affirmation of the royal and Zion theology that was so important to Judah, even as he proclaims an awesome, forest-felling destruction of its current leadership. His words, both in Isaiah 6 and in Isa 10:33–11:9, helped explain why Judah had undergone such suffering, even as they also offered images of hope that Yahweh eventually would restore Zion and its kingship.

The uniqueness of Isaiah's message is nicely illustrated through comparing Isaiah's words about Zion in Isa 1:21–6 with Micah's proclamation that Zion will be "plowed as a field" (Micah 3:9–12; see the Appendix to this chapter for a side-by-side comparison with Isa 1:21–6). Where Micah presents God as utterly rejecting Zion (/Jerusalem) as having been built "with blood" (3:10), Isaiah's God sounds more like Hosea's, in agony over how his city – envisioned as female – has been corrupted by violent, corrupt leaders:

> How she has become a promiscuous woman,
>   The city that once was faithful!
> She that was full of justice,
>   Social solidarity made its home in her,
>   And now murderers! (Isa 1:21)

To be sure, Isaiah does resemble Micah in his understanding of Jerusalem's ills. He, like Micah, criticizes a loss of "justice" (Isa 1:21; see Mic 3:9) caused by its leaders' robbery (1:23, "companions of thieves"; see Mic 2:2), taking of bribes, and perversion of due process due to the most vulnerable people (Isa 1:23; see Mic 3:11). Yet Isaiah does *not* proclaim a final end to Jerusalem as a result of these misdeeds by its leaders. Instead, in an echo of Isaiah's own burning purification process (Isa 6:6–7), Isaiah announces that God is about to purify Jerusalem as metal alloy is purified in a hot forge (Isa 1:25). Once again, this image of a refining fire is Isaiah's way of announcing grand hope for Zion on the other side of painful judgment:

> I will restore your judges as at the first,
>   And your counselors as at the beginning.
> Then you will be called "city of social solidarity"
>   "The faithful settlement." (Isa 1:26)

Again, Isaiah contrasts here with Micah. Where Isaiah affirms that Yahweh dwells in Zion and will defend and restore it (Isa 8:18), Micah directly attacks its leadership for saying "Isn't Yahweh in our midst? No disaster will come on us!" (Micah 3:11). It is even possible that Micah had prophets such as Isaiah in mind when he blamed Jerusalem's future destruction on those who would affirm Zion theology in this way (Micah 3:12).

Apparently Isaiah's message evolved decades later when he prophesied during the time of King Hezekiah, son of Ahaz. This was the time, described in 2 Kings 18–20// Isaiah 36–9 (and 2 Chronicles 29–32), when Hezekiah joined an anti-Assyrian coalition and barely escaped destruction when the Assyrian army of Sennacherib laid siege to Jerusalem (only to withdraw). The narratives about this event found in Kings and Isaiah depict Hezekiah as a positive contrast to his father Ahaz and Isaiah as more affirming of this later king. Where Ahaz refused the sign offered by Isaiah and failed to trust in Yahweh's care for Zion (Isaiah 7–8), Hezekiah actually consulted with Isaiah, and – as a result – the city was rescued (2 Kgs 18–19//Isaiah 36–7; compare with 2 Chronicles 32). The oracles found in Isaiah 28–31, however, show that Isaiah was more critical in this time than these narratives indicate. He repeatedly announces judgment on leaders like Hezekiah who go to Egypt to form anti-Assyrian alliances (30:1–5; also 28:14–22) and rely on military strength for salvation (30:16). Yet again, Isaiah seems to have experienced rejection, with people telling him to shut up or preach more comfortable words (30:10–11). This is why, he says, God commanded him to write these prophecies down, preserving them in scroll form as a witness against the people of Hezekiah's time (30:8).

The Use and Reuse of Biblical Traditions as Not Limited by Their Original Setting

All this suggests that one major impetus for the initial *writing* of prophecies such as those of Isaiah was the experience of rejection. None of the prophets discussed in this chapter seems to have been a major success in his own time. Yet their words were preserved for a later time by their closest students and/or associates. Moreover, as the words of Isaiah and other prophets (e.g. Hosea, Amos, Micah) appeared to come true over time, the significance of their written prophecies grew. For example, what started as Isaiah's counter-wisdom to the false wisdom of Jerusalem's leaders (see Isa 29:14; 31:1–2) was treasured by later Judeans and expanded in subsequent centuries. Eventually, the smaller groups of sayings seen in Isaiah 1–11, 28–32, and elsewhere grew into the 66-chapter book we now have.

This highlights the multi-layered quality of interpretation of such biblical texts. If the significance of these writings had been exhausted in the time of Amos and Isaiah, we probably would not be reading them now. We have these books because later communities found their sayings so helpful that they copied and expanded them. Moreover, this process of rereading and creative reworking continued in Jewish and Christian communities even after the texts of these prophetic books were fixed. For example, later readers reinterpreted predictions of the imminent arrival of a just Judean monarch (e.g. Micah 5:2–4; Isa 11:1–5) as predictions of a royal messiah who would overcome Rome or some successive oppressive empire. These and other prophecies have retained a lasting significance because problems of injustice and imperial rule did not cease after the Assyrian onslaught in the eighth century.

CHAPTER FOUR REVIEW

1. Know the meaning and significance of the following terms discussed in this chapter:
- Assyria
- book of the Twelve Prophets
- chiasm
- major prophets
- minor prophets
- prophetic call narrative
- Syro-Ephraimite war

2. What are the different sorts of indicators of northern origins in the Jacob story of Genesis on the one hand and in the Moses story on the other?

3. How did Amos and Hosea relate in different ways to the ancient Israelite idea of election?

4. Which chapters in the books of Isaiah and Micah have the largest amounts of material from the eighth-century prophets, and which parts of each book are made up virtually exclusively of texts added by later authors?

5. What differences do you see between the views of these two eighth-century Judean prophets on what is wrong with Jerusalem? What are the main differences in their views of Jerusalem's future? Is either of these identical with Zion theology as seen in Psalm 46?

6. Do you think the eighth-century prophet Isaiah might have been one of the "prophets" whom Micah criticized for "leaning on Yahweh and saying 'Surely Yahweh is with us, nothing will happen to us'" (Micah 3:11)? Why or why not?

RESOURCES FOR FURTHER STUDY

General works on prophecy and all of the prophets

Heschel, Abraham. *The Prophets*. 2 volumes. New York: Harper & Row, 1962.

Koch, Klaus. *The Prophets*. 2 volumes. Philadelphia: Fortress, 1983.

Lindblum, J. *Prophecy in Ancient Israel*. Philadelphia: Muhlenberg, 1962.

Commentaries on all of the 12 minor prophets

Limburg, James. *Hosea – Micah*. Interpretation. Atlanta: John Knox Press, 1988.

Sweeney, Marvin. *The Twelve Prophets*, vols. 1 and 2. Berit Olam. Collegeville, MN: Liturgical, 2000–1.

Hosea

Mays, James Luther. *Hosea: A Commentary*. Old Testament Library. Philadelphia: Westminster Press, 1969.

Amos

Mays, James Luther. *Amos: A Commentary*. Old Testament Library. Philadelphia: Westminster Press, 1969.

Isaiah 1–39

Blenkinsopp, Joseph. *Isaiah: A New Translation and Commentary*, parts 1–3. Anchor Bible. New York: Doubleday, 2000–3.

Childs, Brevard. *The Book of Isaiah: A Commentary*. Old Testament Library. Louisville, KY: Westminster Press, 2001.

Clements, R. E. *Isaiah 1–39*. New Century Bible Commentary. Grand Rapids: Eerdmans, 1980.

The history of interpretation of the (whole) book of Isaiah

Childs, Brevard. *The Struggle to Understand Isaiah as Christian Scripture*. Grand Rapids: Eerdmans, 2004. This forms somewhat of a response to Sawyer (next entry).

Sawyer, John. *The Fifth Gospel: Isaiah in the History of Christianity*. Cambridge: Cambridge University Press, 1996.

Stern, Elsie. "Beyond Nahamu: Strategies of Consolation in the Jewish Lectionary Cycle for the 9th of Av Season."

Pp. 180–204 in *SBL Seminar Papers 1998*. Atlanta: Scholars Press, 1998. If you can find a copy of it, this article provides useful coverage of Jewish interpretation of the book of Isaiah, particularly Isaiah 40–55.

APPENDIX: COMPARISON OF A ZION PSALM (PSALM 46) WITH MICAH 3:9–12 AND ISA 1:21–6

Psalm 46:1–7 (a Zion Psalm)

God is our refuge and strength, a very present help in trouble. Therefore we will not fear though the earth should change, though the mountains shake in the heart of the sea; though its waters roar and foam, though the mountains tremble with its tumult.

There is a river whose streams make glad the city of God, the holy habitation of the Most High. **God is in the midst of her, she shall not be moved**; God will help her right early. The nations rage, the kingdoms totter; God utters God's voice, the earth melts. **Yahweh of armies is with us**; the god of Jacob is our refuge [refrain repeated in verse 11].

Micah 3:9–12	*Isaiah 1:21–6*
Hear this, you heads of the house of Jacob and rulers of the house of Israel,	The faithful city, What a harlot she has become! Zion once full of fair judgment,
who abhor justice and pervert all equity who build Zion with blood and Jerusalem with wrong. Its heads give judgment for a bribe, its priests teach for hire, its prophets divine for money;	Where saving justice used to dwell, but now assassins! Your silver has turned to dross, Your wine is watered. Your princes are rebels, Accomplices of brigands. All of them greedy for presents and eager for bribes,
yet they lean upon the Lord and say, "Is not the Lord in the midst of us? No evil shall come upon us."	They show no justice to the orphan, and the widows' cause never reaches them.
	Hence the Lord Yahweh of armies, the Mighty One of Israel, says this, "I shall get satisfaction from my enemies, I shall avenge myself on my foes.
Therefore, because of you Zion shall be plowed as a field Jerusalem shall become a heap of ruins and the mountain of the house, a wooded height.	I shall turn my hand against you, I shall purge your dross as though with potash, I shall remove your alloy. And I shall restore your judges as at first, Your counselors as in bygone days,
	After which you will be called 'City of Saving Justice' 'Faithful City'."

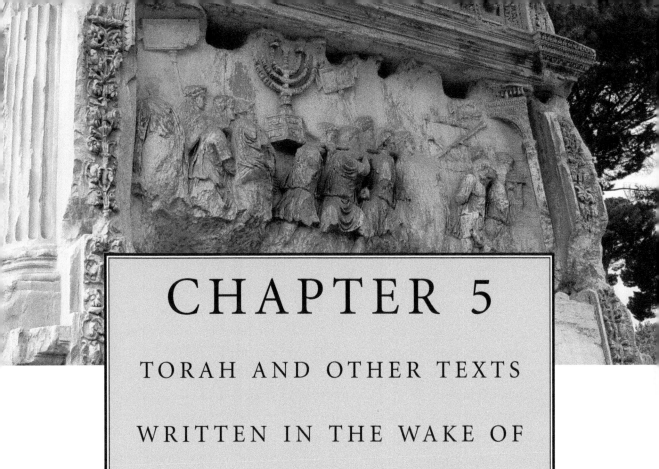

CHAPTER 5

TORAH AND OTHER TEXTS

WRITTEN IN THE WAKE OF

THE ASSYRIAN EMPIRE

Chapter Outline

CHAPTER OVERVIEW

Chapter 4 featured prophecies responding to Assyrian attack in the eighth century, while this one focuses on texts formed in the wake of the collapse of Assyria about seventy years later, in the late seventh century (600s). Foremost among these is the first text to be known as a "Torah of Moses." This first "Torah," however, is not Genesis–Deuteronomy, but rather an earlier, seventh-century edition of the book of Deuteronomy. In this chapter of the textbook we will see how Deuteronomy shows the impact of Assyrian oppression even after the Assyrians had lost control of Judah. The same is true of the books that follow Deuteronomy – Joshua, Judges, Samuel, and Kings. Each of these books reframes earlier traditions about Israel's history in light of Judah's recent experiences of Assyrian oppression. Finally, the prophetic books of Nahum, Zephaniah, and Jeremiah provide a different perspective on the late seventh century, celebrating Assyria's decline and pronouncing God's judgment on the politics and worship of Judah. By the end of this chapter you should see multiple ways in which the central tenets of the Bible and later Judaism – such as the emphasis on law and the importance of worship of God alone – were formed as part of Judah's "hybrid" response to Assyrian oppression and attempt to build a God-centered community, purified of foreign influence, that would not have to undergo another such experience.

Religious and Textual Reform Amidst
the Downfall of Assyria

READING
Nahum 3; Zephaniah 1;
and 2 Kings 21–3.

Your shepherds are asleep [dead],
  Oh, king of Assyria;
  Your nobles slumber.
Your people are scattered on the mountains,
  With no one to gather them.
There is no easing of your [Nineveh's] pain,
  your wound is fatal,
All who hear the report of you,
  Clap their hands in celebration.

For who has escaped your continual cruelty? (Nahum 3:18–19 NRSV modified)
The oracle quoted above concludes a seventh-century book of prophecy, the book of
Nahum. Where eighth-century prophets like Hosea or Micah proclaimed the oncoming
attack by Assyria, this seventh-century prophet proclaims that Assyria itself has been laid
low. Decades of cruelty have come to an end. The Assyrian armies have withdrawn from
Judah and the surrounding countries. And the capital of Assyria, Nineveh itself, was to
fall in 612 BCE, marking the end of Assyria's imperial ambitions. The book of Nahum
celebrates this, proclaiming that Yahweh was the one who brought Assyria down.

basics	Book of Nahum	
Outline: proclamation of the end of Assyrian Nineveh	I Hymn: Yahweh, destroyer of oppressors II Taunt song: destruction of Nineveh	1 2–3
Themes	Though the poem in Nahum 2–3 celebrates the downfall of a specific imperial city, Nineveh, the poem at the outset makes this book into a more general celebration of Yahweh's ability to destroy imperial oppressors and restore the oppressed. For the later revisers of this book, the destruction of Nineveh was but one demonstration of Yahweh's power to destroy oppressive empires.	

This does not mean that everything was fine in Judah. Another seventh-century
prophet, Zephaniah, proclaims Yahweh's irreversible judgment, a "Day of Yahweh," against
Judah and Jerusalem for the kinds of cultic practices that Hosea criticized: worship of

Baal and heavenly objects, swearing by the god of Ammon (Milkom), and failure to seek Yahweh (Zeph 1:4–6). And indeed, archaeological evidence shows that the seventh century was a time when diverse worship practices flourished in Judah, particularly under the 40-year reign of Manasseh, Hezekiah's son (697–642 BCE). In response, Zephaniah proclaims that Yahweh is about to destroy the officials and royalty who promote such impure worship. Echoing the anti-foreign sentiment we also see in Nahum, Zephaniah says that "the officials and king's sons who wear foreign clothes" are about to bear the brunt of Yahweh's judgment. Where others might think of the "Day of Yahweh" as a time when Yahweh comes to rescue the people, Zephaniah 1:7–2:2 – echoing Amos (Amos 5:18–20) – proclaims that this "Day of Yahweh" will be a time of great punishment and sorrow.

basics Book of Zephaniah

Outline: judgment and exhortation to Jerusalem			
I	Announcement: "Day of Yahweh" against Judah		1:2–18
II	Exhortation to repentance		2:1–3:20
	A	Call for repentance amidst judgment of nations	2:1–3:8
	B	Reason for repentance: impending restoration	3:9–20

Seventh-century judgment and later words of hope

This book provides another example of how an earlier prophet's words of judgment (e.g. Zeph 1:2–18) now introduce words of hope written at a later time for later Judeans (e.g. 3:9–20). Thus expanded, the book had a message for generations long after the time of Zephaniah. It taught the need for people in God's holy city, Jerusalem, to repent in light of Yahweh's judgment of other empires.

As long as Manasseh was in power, the religious and political status quo in Judah continued. With his death and the assassination of his son shortly afterwards, however, the people of Judah saw an opportunity. Rather than letting the usual pattern of royal succession continue, the "people of the land" anointed Manasseh's 8-year-old grandson, Josiah, as king of Judah (2 Kgs 21:19–25). This young king would rule for over thirty years (640–609 BCE) and eventually would implement Hosea's (and Zephaniah's) call for religious purity as part of a broader program of national revival in the wake of Assyria's fall. Establishment of religious devotion was one way that Josiah and others believed they could revive the glory of David's kingdom and avoid having to ever experience the kind of foreign oppression they had suffered for decades under Assyria.

The book of 2 Kings tells how, in the eighteenth year of his reign, Josiah funded a renovation of the Temple. At some point in the process the priests told him that "the book of the Torah" had been found there (2 Kgs 22:3–10). When it was read to him, Josiah realized his nation faced curses for disobeying the Torah, and he immediately sent to have its authenticity verified by a prophet, Huldah. She prophesied that the words of the book are true, but that King Josiah would die in peace (2 Kgs 22:14–20). Josiah then had the book read to the elders and the rest of the people, and he led the people in making a "covenant" to follow all the words of the book of the Torah that had just been found (2 Kgs 23:1–3). This then started a process that is often described as "**Josiah's reform**" (623 BCE). Josiah commanded the priests to remove the statue of the goddess Asherah from the Temple in Jerusalem along with all elements related to Baal and other deities other than Yahweh (2 Kgs 23:4, 6–7). He also destroyed all the sanctuaries ("high places") outside Jerusalem and removed their priests (2 Kgs 23:5, 8–14). In an apparent move to restore David and Solomon's united kingdom (see Map 5.1), he even defiled the ancient royal altar at Bethel and destroyed sanctuaries throughout the northern kingdom (2 Kgs 23:15–20). Finally, he commanded a national Passover, now one where the people from the entire kingdom, north and south, must come in pilgrimage to the temple in Jerusalem to celebrate a Passover such as had not been celebrated "from the days of the judges who judged Israel through to the days of the kings of Israel and Judah" (2 Kgs 23:21–3).

This final note indicates that many elements of Josiah's reform were new. Where the Jerusalem Temple had once been the home of worship of multiple divine symbols, now Josiah removed those symbols and dedicated the Temple to worship of Yahweh and Yahweh alone. Where the people of Judah and Israel had worshipped in local sanctuaries since the time of the judges, Josiah destroyed those sanctuaries and had them worship in Jerusalem. And where Passover previously had been a local festival celebrated by clans in their villages, Josiah required all now to come to Jerusalem, the capital city, in a national pilgrimage festival. All this, says 2 Kgs 23:24, was done to implement "the words of the Torah that Hilkiah, the priest, found in the house of Yahweh."

In 1805, about two hundred years ago, the German scholar Wilhelm De Wette noticed that these elements of Josiah's reform are rooted in central elements of the book of Deuteronomy. The laws in Deuteronomy start with a regulation to destroy all non-Yahwistic worship items and local sanctuaries and worship Yahweh in only one place (Deuteronomy 12). This sounds like an authorization for the Temple purification and sanctuary destruction that Josiah implemented. Deuteronomy includes laws for festivals that require all to come to the central worship place (Deuteronomy 16). This sounds like the background for Josiah's Passover. Deuteronomy concludes with curses that will come upon a people that does not follow its stipulations (Deut 28:15–68). This sounds like the curses that Josiah feared would come upon his people for not obeying the Torah found in the Temple (2 Kgs 22:13). Throughout, the book of Deuteronomy refers to itself as the "Torah" or the "scroll of the Torah" and so on (Deut 1:5; 31:9–12, 24–26; etc.), much as 2 Kings refers to the scroll reported by the priest Hilkiah and implemented by Josiah as "the scroll of the Torah" (2 Kgs 22:8, 10, 13, 16; 23:2–3; etc.). In sum, it looks as if the "scroll of the Torah" in Deuteronomy – with its instructions for centralized worship and Passover – is the "Torah" that 2 Kgs 22–3 describes Josiah as reading and implementing in his reform.

This description of Josiah's reign in 2 Kgs 22–3 is not just a fictional glorification of his reign, but reflects actual historical changes that took place during the late monarchy

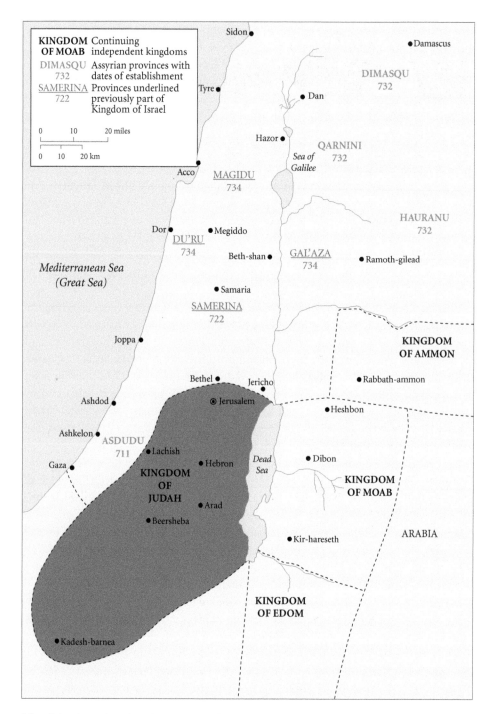

Map 5.1 The Judean kingdom after the fall of the north. Redrawn from Norman Gottwald, *The Hebrew Bible: A Socio-Literary Introduction*. Minneapolis: Fortress, 1985, page 291.

Figure 5.1 Seals and other images from the late seventh century. They well illustrate the decline in use of images in Judah and the rise in importance of texts.

of Judah. Prior to this point, we have tax documents from ancient Samaria and some other early texts that include a significant proportion of deity names other than Yahweh. After this point, the names found in caches of late Judean letters show virtually exclusive devotion to Yahweh. Archaeologists have found a number of sanctuaries that were used for sacrifice outside Jerusalem from the time before Josiah. In the time of Josiah and afterwards, however, the evidence for such sanctuaries diminishes considerably. Finally, there is a massive shift in the diversity of art around the end of the seventh century. In previous chapters we saw examples of female figurines and images, animals, etc. from earlier periods in Israel and Judah's history. Now our archaeological finds – seen in Figure 5.1 – are heavy on text and light on images. The few images that appear are an isolated human or plant. Thus, not only does the Bible testify to a purification and reform, but the archaeological record seems to confirm that this was a time of a radical revolution. A similar revolution in our own setting would mean the elimination of all but one religion in the US and the destruction of all worship places outside Washington, DC, so that all had to travel there to celebrate any major holiday.

What might have caused such a revolution in the religious and political life of ancient Judah? The first thing to affirm is that this reform was built on older roots. For example, the emphasis on pure worship of Yahweh alone and elimination of Baal worship is a major focus in Hosea's prophecy in the northern kingdom of the eighth century, discussed in Chapter 4. In that chapter we also saw signs that Deuteronomy itself, like Hosea, probably originated as a northern text. Judging from this and similar emphases on cultic purity in narratives about the northern prophets, Elijah and Elisha (1 Kings 17–2 Kings 10), it appears that some groups in the Israelite heartland in the north had already strongly advocated pure worship of Yahweh.

Late in the eighth century, the north was destroyed and Judah became the sole place for the preservation of the values and texts of these groups advocating pure worship of Yahweh. As we have seen, Hezekiah was the king in the south then and instituted some cultic centralization and purification while attempting independence from Assyria as well (see 2 Kgs 18:4 and the later descriptions in 2 Chronicles 29–31). This religious reform by Hezekiah is not explained in the biblical narratives, but may have been motivated by Hezekiah's wish to avoid the mistakes of the northern kingdom as identified by Hosea and other northern traditions. Decades later his religious changes were reversed by his successor, Manasseh (2 Kgs 21:3–7//2 Chr 33:3–7), but they were not forgotten. Indeed, Josiah's reform can be seen as a reinstatement of ancient northern emphases on cultic purity and centralization that had already been introduced to Judah, preliminarily, by Josiah's great-grandfather, Hezekiah.

Even as we recognize the precursors to Josiah's reforms, there are also important new elements. First, the biblical reports are more clear in Josiah's case than in Hezekiah's about how Josiah extended his reforms to encompass areas of the former northern kingdom (2 Kgs 23:15–20//2 Chr 34:6–7; compare with 2 Kgs 18:4//2 Chr 31:1 on Hezekiah). By the time of Josiah's reform the Assyrian empire had collapsed. This left a power vacuum in the area of the former northern kingdom where there once had been an Assyrian province. In response, Josiah tried to revive David and Solomon's ancient united monarchy, claiming the north once again as part of a kingdom based in the south. His stress on centralization of worship related to this. Now all, in both north and south, were required to come to Jerusalem for worship at festivals such as Passover.

Josiah's reform is distinguished in another way from Hezekiah's: it appears to be connected to a text, in this case a text sounding much like Deuteronomy. To be sure, there are signs that some kind of reform was already underway before the "scroll of the Torah of Yahweh" was brought to light. Chronicles suggests that Josiah's purification and centralization preceded the discovery of the scroll (2 Chronicles 34), and even 2 Kings implies that Temple renovations were already underway when Josiah was informed about it (2 Kgs 22:3–10). Yet the biblical tradition is clear that this book played an important role in Josiah's reign. This does not necessarily mean that everyone agreed immediately on the authenticity of the book that Josiah put at the center of his reform. Rather, he seems to have felt a need to have the book authenticated (2 Kgs 22:14–20//2 Chr 34:22–8), indicating some doubts about its origins (note also a possible critique of this "Torah" in Jer 8:8–9, discussed below). Indeed, these doubts about the authenticity of Josiah's book have been shared by some contemporary scholars. Nevertheless, whatever the origins of the "scroll" announced by the priest, Hilkiah, it appears to have come to play a pivotal role in Josiah's inauguration of a new era in Judah's monarchy. Let us now take a closer look at Deuteronomy, a probable revision of that ancient scroll.

The Deuteronomic Torah of Moses and the Phenomenon of Hybridity

READING
Deuteronomy 1–3,
6–7, 12, and 17.

The book of Deuteronomy reveals a remarkable blend of ancient Israelite law and radical adaptation of the Assyrian vassal treaty form. To start, the book appears to have ancient roots. Not only does it show signs of northern origins (discussed previously), but many of its laws are revisions of older laws seen in the "Covenant Code" of Exod 20:22–23:33. For example, the altar law in Deuteronomy 12 emphasizes the importance of one altar, while its parallel in Exod 20:24–5 provides instructions for building altars around the land. Similarly, the law about festivals in Deuteronomy

---

basics   Deuteronomy (and the Ten Commandments)

Outline: farewell teaching of vassal treaty with Yahweh

I	Introduction of Yahweh's acts, Ten Commandments, and exhortations	Deut 1:1–11:32
II	Central rules of the treaty with Yahweh (organized by the order of the Ten Commandments)	12:1–26:19
III	Means of remembrance and enforcement of the Treaty with Yahweh	27:1–31:29
IV	Moses's farewell	31:30–34:12

Date(s)

Late pre-exile and exile: Deuteronomy is a combination of an earlier, pre-exilic Deuteronomic lawbook and later, exilic additions to that lawbook. The Deuteronomic lawbook probably includes yet earlier northern materials, but these are impossible to identify precisely.

The Ten Commandments and Deuteronomy

The Ten Commandments in Deut 5:6–21 are classic teaching materials, short and easily memorized by using your fingers. Their form is similar to the "instruction" form found in Proverbs and other teachings. Like such instructions, the Ten Commandments are difficult to date. They almost certainly do not derive from Moses, but do represent many of Israel's deepest shared values.

The importance of these commandments in the book of Deuteronomy is reflected in the fact that the topics at the center of Deuteronomy (Deuteronomy 12–26) follow about the same order as the topics of the Ten Commandments found in Deuteronomy 5. In this sense, the Ten Commandments form the core of the Mosaic "teaching" given in Deuteronomy.

16 parallels the rules about them in Exod 23:14–17, making sure that they are celebrated in only one place. In this way and many others the book of Deuteronomy builds on and revises older legal teachings in Israel, as well as a variety of wisdom teachings in Proverbs (such as Prov 22:28 in Deut 19:14).

That said, Deuteronomy is an example of another, quite remarkable form of revision of a foreign textual form, one originating from Judah's oppressor, Assyria. During the century that Assyria dominated Israel and Judah, it subjugated many nations through a "vassal treaty" form and a related "loyalty oath" insuring the orderly succession of Assyrian rulers. These were like political contracts, in which the subjugated people were required to pronounce curses on themselves if they did not show proper devotion, termed "love" in these treaties, toward their vassal lord, the Assyrian king and his designated successor. Deuteronomy resembles the Assyrian treaties in emphasizing the requirement of allegiance – "love" – that Israel is to offer, but now Israel must offer allegiance to Yahweh "with all [its/your] heart, life strength, and might" (Deut 6:4–6). The laws of Deuteronomy include prohibitions of treason against Yahweh (Deuteronomy 13) that resemble Assyrian prohibitions of treason against the chosen successor of the Assyrian king. Finally, parts of the curses in Deuteronomy 28 are almost exact replicas of curses found at the end of Assyrian loyalty oaths imposed across their empire in the late eighth century. Thus, in the wake of Assyrian oppression, it appears that the authors of the book of Deuteronomy envisioned Israel as in a treaty-like relationship with Yahweh, their God. This was what "covenant" (Hebrew *berit*) with Yahweh meant to them. It was a formal relationship, sealed by blessings and curses. Its core was a requirement of exclusive allegiance to a lord. Yet the authors of Deuteronomy made a revolutionary shift vis-à-vis the vassal treaties and loyalty oaths that they knew: where before Judah had to be exclusively obedient to the Assyrian king, now they were to be exclusively faithful to Yahweh. Where before the Assyrian king was jealous and would tolerate no rivals, now Yahweh is depicted as jealous and intolerant of any rival gods. Before the people feared the invasion of the massive Assyrian army if they were disobedient. Now they faced direct divine punishment, the "curses of the treaty covenant" (Deut 29:20), if they failed to be faithful to the words of Deuteronomy. Thus when Josiah read some form of Deuteronomy to the people and led them in a covenant ceremony based on it (2 Kgs 23:1–3//2 Chr 34:29–31), he was moving them from one vassal relationship to another. Previously they had known subjugation to Assyria. Now Josiah was leading them – by means of an early written edition of Deuteronomy – into a treaty with Yahweh.

We will never know the precise manner in which some yet older form of Deuteronomy was shaped in light of such experiences of Assyrian oppression, but scholars do know analogies to this overall process. In particular, postcolonial theorists have uncovered many examples of writers, artists, and others who appropriate the cultural forms of their former oppressors in the process of trying to develop their own, *post*colonial expressions. For example, even after India achieved independence from Britain in 1947, Indian writers developed a rich tradition of distinctively Indian novels in English. In doing so, they adopted their colonial oppressor's language and an originally non-Indian cultural form, the novel. Yet they used these tools to build a distinctively Indian literature. This is but one example of the way that peoples who must redefine themselves in the wake of oppression often find it helpful to revise and even invert the cultural forms of

Overview: The Covenant Code and Deuteronomy

The laws below cover similar topics, but read a few and see how they treat these topics differently! Though Deuteronomy covers topics not found in the Covenant Code (Exod 20:22–23:33), most topics in the Covenant Code are covered in Deuteronomy. Deuteronomy is thought to be the later of the two. In particular, it makes changes in the Covenant Code laws so that they are consistent with the idea that there should be only one central sanctuary.

Law about altars	Exod 20:22–6	Deut 12:13–28
Slave release laws	Exod 21:1–11	Deut 15:12–18
Cities of asylum	Exod 21:12–14	Deut 19:1–13
Kidnapping	Exod 21:16	Deut 24:7
Consequences of sex with a virgin	Exod 22:16–17	Deut 22:28–9
Penalty for unlawful religious practices	Exod 22:18	Deut 18:9–14
Penalty for sacrifice to other gods	Exod 22:20	Deut 17:2–7
Prohibition of charging interest	Exod 22:25	Deut 23:19–20
Requirement to return a cloak taken as collateral	Exod 22:26–7	Deut 24:10–13
Requirement of first-born sons and livestock	Exod 22:29–30	Deut 15:19–23
Legal justice rules	Exod 23:2–8	Deut 16:18–20
Returning livestock	Exod 23:4–5	Deut 22:1–4
Prohibition of oppressing foreign workers	Exod 23:9	Deut 24:17–18
Sabbath year rules	Exod 23:10–11	Deut 15:1–11
Sabbath command	Exod 23:12	Deut 5:12–15
Pilgrimage festivals	Exod 23:14–17	Deut 16:1–17
Requirement to bring first fruits	Exod 23:19a	Deut 26:1–10
Not boiling a calf in its mother's milk	Exod 23:19b	Deut 14:21b

their former oppressors. Postcolonial theorists refer to this process of adaptation and inversion of oppressors' cultural forms as "hybridity." This concept will come up again in this *Introduction* because it is useful in understanding how many biblical texts were formed in relation to non-biblical textual forms.

For now, it is important to recognize that Deuteronomy, this hybrid vassal treaty with God, presents itself as the most important "teaching" Israel could ever have. It bears the label of "Torah," which is the Hebrew equivalent of "teaching," and the book names numerous ways in which the people of Israel are to insure that this Torah/teaching is foremost on their hearts and minds. They are to memorize this Torah's words (Deut 6:6; 11:18), recite them constantly to their children (Deut 6:7; 11:19), bind

MORE ON METHOD: POSTCOLONIAL CRITICISM

The term "**postcolonial criticism**" embraces a wide range of approaches that look at how texts and their interpretations are interrelated with structures of colonial domination. Within biblical studies it has taken two main forms.

First, many scholars have taken categories developed in earlier postcolonial studies of contemporary literature and used those categories to illuminate the production of ancient biblical literature in relation to imperial domination. This chapter's discussion of Deuteronomy as an example of "hybridity" would be an example of this approach.

Second, other scholars have looked at how the Bible itself has been used as a tool for colonial domination. For more on this approach, see R. S. Sugirtharajah, *Postcolonial Criticism and Biblical Interpretation* (New York: Oxford University Press, 2002).

---

basics   Book of Joshua

Outline: the conquest and settlement of the promised land

I	Exodus-like, holy war conquest	1–12
II	Distribution of the land	13–22
III	Joshua's covenantal farewell	23–4

Date   Late pre-exilic (especially Joshua 1–12) and exilic/post-exilic (13–24).

Theme   Though the book of Joshua starts with an apparent total conquest of the land (Josh 11:23) in fulfillment of Yahweh's command (Deuteronomy 7), chapters 13–22 hint that the conquest was *incomplete* (Josh 13:1–7; 15:63; 16:10; 17:12–13) and show a diversity in the make-up of the people that threatens to split them by the end (Joshua 22). This, then, is the context for Joshua's exhortations to the people in Joshua 23 and 24, where he urges them to avoid the worship practices of the foreign peoples among them (Josh 23:5–13; 24:14–15). Instead, they should, like Joshua, be devoted to Yahweh and the book of the Torah (Josh 23:6; 24:26; compare Josh 1:7–8).

More information: Joshua and Moses   Joshua is Moses's appointed successor in Deuteronomy (Deuteronomy 31), and he is presented in the book of Joshua as a second Moses. Like Moses, he presides over the people crossing water "on dry ground" (Joshua 3–4; compare Exodus 14), and he celebrates a Passover preceded by a circumcision of the new generation of males who were born in the wilderness (Joshua 5; compare Exodus 12). In these and other ways, Joshua is presented as the last semi-Mosaic leader before things fall apart during the time of the judges.

copies of Torah commands on the entryways of their houses and on their bodies (Deut 6:8–9; 11:20), make sure that the king reads and obeys this Torah/teaching constantly (Deut 17:18–20), and carefully copy the Torah and read it aloud to the entire community (Deut 31:11–13). As the Assyrian vassal treaty used some of the same means to instill absolute loyalty to the king of Assyria, so also Deuteronomy uses a yet fuller array of these strategies to insure memorization of this Torah/teaching and loyalty to Yahweh alone.

The Deuteronomistic History (Deuteronomy–2 Kings)

READING

Joshua 1–2, 11; 23–4; Judges 1–2; 1 Samuel 12; 1 Kings 8; 2 Kings 17, 22–3. Review readings from Judges–2 Kings done for earlier chapters. (Note: Deuteronomy is also part of the Deuteronomistic history, but was read in relation to the preceding section.)

EXERCISE

Pick some of the texts above and make a list of the chapters and verses in those texts where you see the following themes (from Deuteronomy) appear: (1) the importance of faithfulness to the LORD (Yahweh) alone; (2) the belief that Yahweh will punish unfaithfulness; (3) the importance of pure worship and sacrifice in only one place; and/or (4) hostility toward foreigners and/or foreign influence.

Most scholars agree that Deuteronomy originally stood at the beginning of a larger history that is termed the "**Deuteronomistic history**" and included the books of Deuteronomy, Joshua, Judges, 1 and 2 Samuel, and 1 and 2 Kings. Though Deuteronomy includes Moses's reviews of stories now in Exodus and Numbers, these reviews are probably there because those books did not yet stand before Deuteronomy as part of a broader Pentateuch. Deuteronomy was the starting point of a larger whole. The rest of that whole is found in the **books of the former prophets:** Joshua, Judges, Samuel, and Kings. These books often refer back to the Torah in Deuteronomy (examples are Josh 1:7–8 and 2 Kgs 23:24–5). Moreover, as you saw in doing the exercise at the outset of this section, these books continue many of the values seen at the heart of Deuteronomy: the importance of faithfulness to Yahweh alone, the belief that Yahweh will punish unfaithfulness, the importance of pure worship and sacrifice in only one place, and hostility toward foreigners and/or foreign influence. These are stipulations of the Deuteronomic vassal treaty with Yahweh. The books of the former prophets describe the extent to which the kings and people of Israel were faithful or unfaithful to these stipulations.

basics Book of Judges

Outline: decline of order/ obedience in the time of judges

I	Prologue: incomplete conquest and overview of disobedience after Joshua	1:1–3:6
II	Specifics on spiraling chaos:	3:7–21:25
	A Worsening judges: Othniel to Samson	3:7–16:31
	B People on their own with no king	17:1–21:25

Date Pre-exilic and exilic/post-exilic.

Theme Though Judges includes older traditions, they have been radically adapted to fit a theological framework that expresses the values of Deuteronomy. The shape of this framework is given in a narrative overview (Judg 2:11–22) that follows the death of Joshua (Josh 2:6–10). We hear in this text of a recurring cycle of punishment and rescue that is repeated in many of the following chapters:

1 Israel disobeys Yahweh and his commands.
2 Yahweh lets them be conquered by a foreign people.
3 They cry out and Yahweh sends a judge to deliver them.
4 The judge dies, and the people start disobeying again.

The stories in Judg 3:7–16:31 roughly follow this framework, but they also diverge in minor ways that show a spiraling decline of order and obedience in Israel. Moreover, the judges progress from unblemished figures, such as Othniel and Deborah, to less impressive leaders, such as Jephthah and Samson. The final chapters, Judges 17–21, show how bad things get when the people are without a king and "do what is right in their own eyes" (Judg 17:6; 21:25).

It is important to realize, however, that the authors of these historical books drew on older traditions in the process of writing a history of Israel's faithfulness and unfaithfulness. The book of Joshua frames older stories of local military victories with new descriptions of total destruction of all Canaanites in the land (Joshua 11–12), certifying that Israel had taken the land just as Yahweh commanded it in Deuteronomy (Deuteronomy 7). The book of Judges radically adapts older texts about the tribes of Israel – such as the song of Deborah – so that they now fit into a cyclical pattern of the people forgetting to be faithful to Yahweh, Yahweh letting them fall into oppression, the people crying out, and Yahweh rescuing them. The books of Samuel contain large blocks of probable older compositions, such as an "ark narrative" (1 Sam 4:1–7:1; 2 Sam 6) and a "succession narrative" (2 Samuel 9–20 along with 1 Kings 1–2) that may

basics Books of Samuel

<table>
<tr><td>Outline: the
beginnings of
the Davidic
monarchy
(1–2 Samuel)</td><td>I</td><td colspan="2">Transitions to kingship</td><td>1 Samuel 1–31</td></tr>
<tr><td></td><td></td><td>A</td><td>Samuel: a judge who anointed kings</td><td>1 Samuel 1–8</td></tr>
<tr><td></td><td></td><td>B</td><td>Samuel to Saul: a failed king</td><td>1 Samuel 9–15</td></tr>
<tr><td></td><td></td><td>C</td><td>Saul to David: the dynastic founder</td><td>1 Samuel 16–31</td></tr>
<tr><td></td><td>II</td><td colspan="2">David's reign as Israel's first king</td><td>2 Samuel 1–24</td></tr>
</table>

Date   Late pre-exile and exile, with some early pre-exilic sources.

Theme   This book spread over two scrolls (1 and 2 Samuel) presents an ambivalent picture of the origins of the monarchy. The reign of David is presented as an improvement on that of Saul. Nevertheless, in episodes such as the affair with Bathsheba and murder of her husband (2 Samuel 11–12), David proves to have flaws of his own. Deuteronomistic speeches at points such as 1 Samuel 12 and 2 Samuel 7 present the move to the Davidic monarchy as a negative development, but one that Yahweh accepted. Such Deuteronomistic speeches reflect the much lower monarchal expectations of scribes looking back at three centuries of Davidic rule.

have been written around the time of David and Solomon. To these and other older traditions the authors of Samuel added their own perspective on the monarchy in 1 Samuel 12, and on parts of the oracle to David in 2 Samuel 7:1–16. Finally, one finds a similar combination of old and new in the books of Kings. Here the authors cite earlier books such as the "Acts of Solomon" (1 Kgs 11:41), the "Annals of the Kings of Israel" (1 Kgs 14:19; 15:31; etc.) and the "Annals of the Kings of Judah" (1 Kgs 14:29; 15:7, 23; etc.). Yet they put their own stamp on the whole, particularly through inserting major theological speeches at important junctures. These speeches concern the dedication of the Temple (1 Kings 8), the theological rationale for the destruction of the northern kingdom (2 Kings 17), and Josiah's reform and attempt to reunite the north and south in a kingdom centered on Jerusalem (2 Kings 22–3). As you saw in the exercise that opened this section, these and other speeches express central values seen in the book of Deuteronomy. Such close links to and dependence on Deuteronomy are what lead scholars to call these materials "**Deuteronomistic.**"

We are discussing these historical books, these books of former prophets, in this chapter because there are signs that they originally concluded with Josiah's reform. If so, then the Deuteronomistic history originally started with the Deuteronomic Torah and ended with Josiah's implementation of Deuteronomy in his reform, Huldah's prediction that he would die in peace, and a praise of him that echoes Deut 6:4–5 (2 Kgs 23:25). As it turned out, Josiah did not die in peace, as we see in a later expansion of

basics Books of Kings

Outline: obedience and sin in the history of the monarchies

I	Solomon's rule: devotion and sin	1 Kings 1–11
II	Divided monarchy: northern sin and southern obedience and sin	1 Kings 12–2 Kings 17
III	Decline of Judah: Hezekiah to exile	2 Kings 18–24

Date

Pre-exilic edition and exilic/post-exilic redaction.

Theme

The books of Kings were divided for space reasons across two scrolls, 1 and 2 Kings, but they tell one story of the rise and fall of the monarchy of Israel, from Solomon to the exile. The story starts with Solomon's building of the Temple in Jerusalem (1 Kings 6–8), which becomes the one place that Israel is allowed to sacrifice, according to the law in Deuteronomy (Deut 12:13–28). The narrative goes on, however, to describe Solomon's fall toward disobedience (1 Kings 11), which is quickly followed by the revolt of the northern tribes and their building of their own altars outside Jerusalem (1 Kings 12).

From then on, each king of Israel and Judah is measured by his faithfulness to the commands in Deuteronomy to worship Yahweh alone and to sacrifice at only one place. The destruction of the Israelite monarchy is explained by the failure of Israel and its kings to follow these rules (2 Kings 17). Despite some ideal leaders, such as Hezekiah and Josiah, most kings in Judah likewise fail. From the perspective of Kings, the final result of such disobedience of Deuteronomic laws is the destruction of Jerusalem and the exile (2 Kings 24).

More information: the pre-exilic and exilic editions of Kings

As we have them now, the books of Kings are late compositions that explain the destruction of the north and exile of the south as resulting from disobedience of the law of Deuteronomy. Yet there are numerous signs that these books are only the latest stage of a long process of revision and growth. An earlier, pre-exilic version of these books may have ended with Josiah, or even Hezekiah. Rather than explaining disaster, such earlier versions would have promoted the initiatives of those kings. Royal narratives elsewhere in the ancient Near East were typically written in the royal court to promote the king. Only later were these royal narratives modified to explain the destruction of the kingship itself.

this history starting in 2 Kgs 23:29. Nevertheless, the major narrative arc of the Deuteronomistic history leads from Deuteronomy on the one end to Josiah's implementation of Deuteronomy on the other. This formed the scope of the pre-exilic edition of the Deuteronomistic history. Only later did editors long after Josiah's time extend this history from Josiah's (violent) death to the destruction of Jerusalem and exile of its inhabitants. This expanded exilic edition of the Deuteronomistic history will be discussed in the next chapter.

In the present context we should view much of Deuteronomy through 2 Kings as (originally) a pre-exilic history of Israel and Judah that was written in the wake of decades of oppression by Assyria. Like Deuteronomy, this history is an example of hybridity. It seems to represent a nationalistic appropriation by Josiah's scribes of a form of history writing that was used in the Assyrian empire to instill pro-royal sympathies in leadership near and far. Starting in the tenth century, both Babylonian and Assyrian educational centers started to rely more and more on epics and narratives that celebrated certain past kings such as Sargon as ideals of kingship, while denigrating others. We also see the increasing use of longer histories of kings, histories that included notes about their major achievements. Some Judean officials probably were required to memorize such royal narratives and histories during the times of Hezekiah and Manasseh. Yet there are crucial differences between those Mesopotamian histories and the Deuteronomistic history in the Bible. Rather than insuring loyalty to a foreign king, the Deuteronomistic history was aimed at insuring loyalty to Yahweh alone. As part of this, it aimed to support Josiah's move from worship of multiple deities at multiple places to pure worship of Yahweh alone in Jerusalem.

This retelling of Judah's story is analogous to the kind of retelling of individual stories that many people do on the other side of a major crisis. A person may tell their own life story one way for a long time, and then something happens – divorce, a near-death experience, struggle with addiction, or another crisis – that makes them realize that some things that they thought were important were not, and other things that they had ignored were very, very important. In light of this experience, that person will tell their life story differently. For example, someone recovering from addiction might find healing through telling others in self-help groups about his or her struggle with addiction, what happened to make him or her seek recovery, and what things are like now. Indeed, many alcoholics and other addicts have found the power to stay free of their addiction by telling and retelling their new stories of addiction and recovery.

Building on this analogy, the Deuteronomistic history might be viewed as ancient Judah's equivalent to this sort of retelling of a personal story. Judah was on the other side of the crisis of Assyrian oppression, and the retelling of its story was aimed at gaining and maintaining freedom from Torah disobedience and oppression by foreign powers. Like someone retelling their own personal story, this retelling of Israel's story incorporates earlier elements, such as the succession narrative or older lists of kings and their years of rule. But the retelling as a whole is now reframed in light of the experience of liberation from Assyria. It is a retelling of the people's history that is completely reoriented toward their new chance to achieve permanent freedom through obedience to Yahweh's Torah.

Each book of the Deuteronomistic history now reflects central themes of that Torah, from hostility to foreign influence to valuing of pure and centralized worship of Yahweh alone. Much like the memorizing of the Torah in Deuteronomy, this retelling of the people's story was aimed at reshaping the communal soul of Israel. Previously, literate Israelites would have memorized other historical traditions (e.g. the succession narrative).

As mentioned before, some officials during the time of Hezekiah and Manasseh may even have learned pro-royal Mesopotamian historical traditions. But this Deuteronomistic history represented a new form of cultural memory, aimed at replacing its predecessors. It grounded Josiah's reform with an overview of life in the land that extended from the Deuteronomic Torah on the one hand to Josiah's reform on the other.

The Conquest and Ancient Holy War

The books of Deuteronomy and Joshua describe Israel as conquering all of Canaan and destroying *all* of its inhabitants (Deuteronomy 7; Joshua 1–11). This is a description of an ancient "holy war" (Hebrew *herem*); that is, a sacred war engaged in not for purposes of gaining booty or wives, but at divine command. biblical rules for the conduct of such sacred wars are found particularly in Deuteronomy 20. One gruesome mark of the "not-for-profit" character of such a war was the destruction of all living beings, human and animal, of the conquered people.

We see this idea outside Israel as well. One example is found in the ninth-century inscription of King Mesha of Moab. He describes a holy war commanded by his god, Chemosh, against a town in Israel called Nebo.

At that time, Chemosh said to me, "Go, take Nebo from Israel." So I deployed my soldiers at night and attacked Nebo from dawn until noon. I won a great victory and I sacrificed seven thousand men, women and children from Nebo to Chemosh as I had vowed I would do. (Translation: *OT Parallels, 168–9*)

One key difference between this inscription and the biblical book of Joshua is that the Mesha text is reporting on a recent killing of people that actually happened. In contrast, Joshua (along with Deuteronomy) draws on the concept of "holy war" to imaginatively depict a conquest centuries before that probably never happened in this way.

All this can give us a new perspective on some of the most troubling parts of the Deuteronomistic history, such as its report of a divine command to eliminate all foreigners in the land (Deuteronomy 7) and description of the Israelites' fulfillment of that command, killing all Canaanites (Josh 10:40–42; 11:16–23). For many people, these are some of the most disturbing texts in the Bible, and they have been used in destructive ways to justify the killing or displacement of Native Americans and others.

Yet as we read these texts in Joshua, we should realize that they are not historically factual reports of the Israelites' total conquest of the land. (The Bible itself contains traditions to the contrary, such as the overview in Judges 1 of non-Israelites still in the land.) Rather, these narratives were designed to help the people of Josiah's time believe in a God who could help them succeed in a battle against all odds. Like the rest of the Deuteronomistic history, the conquest stories were written with the idea that Judah's past oppression was caused by its failure to obey Yahweh's Torah and eliminate foreign influence. Writing from this perspective, the authors of Joshua crafted a narrative that could empower Judah of Josiah's time to eliminate every trace of foreign influence that might cause them to fall back into oppression. Like many disempowered peoples, these authors wanted a God who could fight and fight successfully on their behalf. Perhaps Josiah even trusted the help of such a warrior God in his fatal confrontation with the Egyptian Pharaoh (2 Kgs 23:29–30//2 Chr 35:20–6). In any case, contemporary readers who interpret these texts from a position of privilege should recognize their dangers, but should also note how differently such warlike texts can be perceived by people fighting for liberation against more powerful foes.

Jeremiah's Prophecy of Judgment on Zion

Jeremiah is the second **major prophet**. The book focused on him is a bridge between the time of Josiah's reform and the catastrophic end of Judah: the destruction of Jerusalem, end of the monarchy, and exile of Judah's leaders to Babylon. Jeremiah's earliest prophecy comes from the time of Josiah and his reforms. His prophecy continued with a critique of Josiah's successors. He has a few prophecies directed at Judeans, who were among the first to be forced into Babylonian exile. And these prophecies were shaped and reshaped by exiles and others after the time of Jeremiah, who believed that his words had important lessons for later generations.

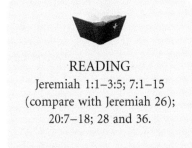

READING
Jeremiah 1:1–3:5; 7:1–15
(compare with Jeremiah 26);
20:7–18; 28 and 36.

In the early part of his career Jeremiah shared Josiah's focus on the importance of pure worship of Yahweh, and some have found affirmations by Jeremiah of Josiah's program of reunification of north and south in passages such as Jer 3:19–23. Yet there is a tantalizing hint in a judgment speech in Jer 8:4–13 that Jeremiah rejected the authenticity of the Deuteronomic Torah that came to stand at the center of Josiah's reform:

> How can you say, "we are wise,
>   And we have the Torah of Yahweh,"
> When, in fact, the false pen of the scribes,
>   has made it into a lie?" (Jer 8:8)

For Jeremiah, the Torah of Moses – probably some form of Deuteronomy – is the product of contemporary authors, "scribes." It does not represent a truly ancient word. Though Jeremiah would later recognize Josiah as a king of justice in comparison with his son, Jehoiakim (Jer 22:15–16), in this central respect – the recognition of the authority of a form of Deuteronomy – he appears not to have been convinced by part of Josiah's reform.

While Jeremiah may have supported parts of Josiah's program, his relationship with Josiah's successors was resolutely bad. A particularly large number of his prophecies are associated with the time of Jehoiakim, who was appointed over Judah by the Egyptians on their way back from their fight with Babylon (2 Kgs 23:34–5). Early during Jehoiakim's reign, Jeremiah delivered a sermon against the Jerusalem Temple that is described twice in the book of Jeremiah, once in Jer 7:1–15 and again in Jeremiah 26. Both versions of this "Temple sermon" feature a frontal attack on Zion theology, especially the idea that Jerusalem and its Temple were invulnerable. To those who continually affirm "this is the temple of Yahweh, the temple of Yahweh, the temple of the Yahweh," Jeremiah proclaims that Yahweh will make it a heap of ruins, much like the ruins of the ancient tribal sanctuary at Shiloh, where the ark of the covenant once was (Jer 7:14//26:6). Such a claim was virtual blasphemy to the people of the time, since the belief in Zion's invulnerability had been reinforced all the more in the wake of the Assyrian king Sennacherib's withdrawal from besieging Jerusalem during the time of Hezekiah. According to Jeremiah 26, the people were ready to kill Jeremiah for speaking such words. Nevertheless, some recalled that Micah had earlier proclaimed that "Zion shall be plowed as a field" (Jer 26:18; see Micah 3:12). Ultimately, Jeremiah was protected by Ahikam, the son of Josiah's former scribe, Shaphan (Jer 26:24).

Another biographical narrative, Jeremiah 36, preserves a fascinating picture of the delivery and writing of Jeremiah's prophecy. It describes how Jeremiah was commissioned by God in Jehoiakim's fourth year to write a scroll containing all of his oracles up to that point in hopes that Judah might hear it and repent (36:1–3). Nevertheless, when the scroll was read to King Jehoiakim, he was not pleased with its contents. As each column of the scroll was read to him, the king cut it off and threw it into the fire. After this, Jeremiah received a commission to write "another scroll." So Baruch, Jeremiah's scribe, produced a new scroll with the words of the original one, along with "many words like them" (Jer 36:27–32). Many scholars believe that much of what is now chapters 1–25 of the book of Jeremiah are the remnants of that new scroll (see Jer 25:13). This scroll, like Isaiah's memoir of rejected prophecies a century earlier (Isa 6:1–8:16) and other prophetic writings, is another example of how the writing of biblical prophecies was prompted by the rejection of those prophecies in the prophet's own time.

Yet Jeremiah, partly because of his long career, appears to have experienced more than his share of rejection. Chapters 26–45 of Jeremiah contain biographical narratives that chronicle Jeremiah's difficult experiences, starting with his brush with execution after the Temple sermon (Jeremiah 26; cf. Jer 7:1–15), and continuing with episodes such as his battle with Hananiah over falsely hopeful prophecy (Jeremiah 28), the burning of his scroll (Jeremiah 36), his imprisonment during the Babylonian siege of Jerusalem as a possible traitor (Jeremiah 37), his being dumped in a cistern to die by opponents (Jeremiah 38), and finally his being carried off into Egypt by rebels against Babylonian rule (Jeremiah 43). Though these narratives about him postdate the prophet, they probably reflect his increasing isolation as he prophesied judgment throughout Judah's long slide from dreams of glory under Josiah to total destruction by the Babylonians.

The difficulty of Jeremiah's career is also reflected in a set of laments in the book where Jeremiah protests to God about the unfair job that God has given him. For example, in the lament assigned for this section, Jer 20:7–20, the prophet describes being "taken advantage of" by God, who has required him to proclaim a harsh message that leads to his own rejection:

> O Yahweh you have seduced me, and I let myself be seduced.
>   You have overpowered me and won.
> I'm a laughingstock all day,
>   Everyone makes fun of me.
> For every time I speak, I cry an alarm.
>   I call out, "Violence and ruin."
> For the word of Yahweh has become for me
>   A cause of embarrassment and criticism all the time. (Jer 20:7–8)

Jeremiah goes on to say that he has no choice, because every time he tries to stop speaking God's message, the word becomes "like a burning fire raging in my bones; I cannot keep holding it in" (Jer 20:9). The lament continues and even reaches a fairly hopeful point, where Jeremiah envisions his eventual restoration and praises Yahweh for it (20:11–13), but then we hear another lament, perhaps originally separate from the one before, where he curses the day he was born and those who announced his birth (20:14–18). These and other laments chronicle the fact that Jeremiah's work was difficult and did not reach a happy ending (see also Jer 11:18–20; 12:1–6; 15:10–21; 17:14–18; 18:18–23).

Though Jeremiah's prophecy was rejected in his own time, his written words became important to later generations of Judeans. His prophecies of disaster appeared in a different light in the wake of the destruction of Jerusalem, removal of the monarchy, and exile of thousands of Judeans to Babylon. Baruch or a later author wrote bio-graphical accounts about Jeremiah, and additional authors enriched the writings about Jeremiah with prose versions of Jeremiah's sayings.

Ultimately, it was writers during the time of exile who put together these diverse materials (poetic prophecy, narratives, and prose prophecies) into a collection much like the one we have now. These exilic authors, working well after the time of Jeremiah, were heavily influenced by the language and ideas of the book of Deuteronomy. That is why so many passages in Jeremiah, such as the version of the Temple sermon found in Jeremiah 7, sound so much like the Deuteronomic Torah. Ironically, though Jeremiah himself appears to have rejected that Torah (Jer 8:8–9), these post-Jeremiah texts quote him as announcing Yahweh's judgment on those who reject God's "Torah" (e.g. Jer 26:4). Such associations with Deuteronomy have led scholars to speak of a "Deuteronomistic redaction" throughout the book. This exilic redaction starts with the description of Jeremiah's call in Jer 1:4–10 (compare with Isaiah 6 and Ezekiel 1–3) and includes many other texts across the rest of the book. We even see the incorporation into the book of Jeremiah (Jer 39:1–10; 40:7–41:18; 52:1–34) of texts also seen in the Deuteronomistic history (2 Kgs 24:18–25:30). In sum, when we look at the book of Jeremiah, much of it reflects the words of Baruch and these exilic Deuteronomistic authors rather than the words of Jeremiah himself.

As in the case of Isaiah, we should not judge that such post-Jeremiah parts of the book of Jeremiah are of little worth. On the contrary, some of the most important texts *basics* Book of Jeremiah

Outline: of
the Masoretic
Jeremiah

I	First scroll: oracles against Judah (and Israel)	1–25
II	Biography: Jeremiah's call for submission and hope	26–45
III	Oracles against foreign nations	46–51
IV	Historical appendix (adapted from 2 Kings)	52

Themes

The book of Jeremiah aims to make sense of the destruction of Jerusalem (described in the historical appendix, Jer 52) through looking back at Jeremiah's once unpopular prophecy of judgment and call for submission to the Babylon empire. In addition, it contains words of judgment on other nations and – particularly in the "book of consolation" in Jeremiah 31–2 – words of hope for Judah.

Documentation
of the growth
of the book
of Jeremiah

Scholars actually have manuscripts of a version of Jeremiah different from *and earlier than* the version translated in most bibles. These ancient manuscripts – both old Hebrew manuscripts found near the Dead Sea (at Qumran) and the ancient Greek translation (Septuagint) of Jeremiah – reflect a version of Jeremiah that was about one-eighth shorter than the standard Hebrew edition of Jeremiah. This earlier (and differently organized) version lacked many phrases and even whole passages (such as Jer 33:14–26 and 39:4–13) that were added by later scribes. We have similar manuscript documentation of earlier versions of the books of Genesis, Exodus, Joshua, Ezekiel, and Proverbs, among others.

for Jewish and Christian communities have been ones that scholars have identified as coming from these later "Deuteronomistic" redactors. For example, Jer 31:31–4 speaks of a "new covenant" that Yahweh is about to make with the house of Israel and the house of Judah. Unlike the covenant of the exodus, Yahweh will put this covenant inside the people, writing it "on their hearts." The prose form of the text and its language mark it as a probable later addition to this part of Jeremiah. Nevertheless, later communities were powerfully affected by its vision of God willing to go to any lengths to make sure the people would be able to obey the covenant that they could not follow before. For example, the Jewish community at Qumran who collected the Dead Sea scrolls saw themselves as a community of the "new covenant" mentioned in Jeremiah. Just a century or two later, the expression "new covenant" came to play a very important role in the early Christian movement as well (see Luke 22:20; 1 Cor 11:25; 2 Cor 3:1–18). Indeed, later Christians applied a derivative of this term, "New Testament," to the scriptures associated with their movement, and they labeled the Jewish scriptures with the corresponding term "Old Testament." In sum, Jer 31:31–4, a probable post-Jeremiah vision of God's salvation, has played a major role in defining multiple movements in Judaism.

Deuteronomy 6:4–9

Having completed an overview, let us turn now to a specific text that exemplifies many of the central dynamics of seventh-century biblical literature, Deut 6:4–9. Many scholars have seen in this text a possible beginning of an early form of Deuteronomy, before later authors added the review of history in Deuteronomy 1–3, the teaching in Deuteronomy 4, and the Ten Commandments in Deuteronomy 5. Whether or not Deut 6:4–9 started an early form of the book, it certainly sums up many of its major themes, along with themes that play a major role in the rest of the Deuteronomistic history and other Deuteronomistic literature, such as the present (post-Jeremiah) form of the book of Jeremiah.

The first sentence is marked off in the Hebrew of the Masoretic text tradition by unusually large final letters at the end of its first and last words. Such letters are often used elsewhere in the Bible to mark the outset of a biblical book (examples are found in Genesis, Proverbs, Chronicles) or an important point in a biblical book. Here they mark the beginning of what is known in Judaism as the "Shema," named after the first Hebrew word in the verse: *shema* – "Hear!" The rest of the sentence can be translated in two ways. One could translate it, "Hear, oh Israel, Yahweh is our God, Yahweh alone." This translation emphasizes that Israel should have one and only one God. The other, equally correct translation (in terms of the Hebrew) is, "Hear, oh Israel, that Yahweh, our God, is one Yahweh." We know from earlier inscriptions that earlier Judeans and Israelites worshipped different forms of Yahweh, "Yahweh from Teman" or "Yahweh from Samaria." According to this translation of Deut 6:4, such local manifestations of Yahweh are false. The Yahweh who belongs to Israel is one and only one deity. This would reinforce Josiah's push to centralize and standardize worship of Yahweh. Both translations link with other traditions in Deuteronomy and the Deuteronomistic history. Perhaps part of the power of this verse was its capacity to express both meanings.

The next verse expresses a core commandment in Deuteronomy and beyond. The people are to "love" God with all that they are and have. The list is often translated as "all your heart, soul and might" (NRSV) or the like, but these English words are a pale reflection of the Hebrew. The first word in the series, *lebab*, is not just the "heart," but also the "mind." For ancient Israel and other ancient Near Eastern peoples, the "heart" and "mind" were connected, not distinct as they so often are in Western culture. The second word that is often translated as "soul," Hebrew *nephesh*, actually refers to the vital life strength that infuses an entire person. It is the power that distinguishes a living person from a corpse, that powers desire, thought, will, and movement. Deut 6:4 calls on all Israel to devote that entire life strength to love of Yahweh. Finally, the word often translated as "might," Hebrew *meod*, refers to power or strength. Most often it appears in the Bible as an adverb, meaning "very." It may serve a similar function in this series in Deut 6:5, emphasizing how very much Israel must "love Yahweh, your God," with all Israel's heart/mind and life strength.

This call to love connects to other texts, both inside and outside the Bible. One of the places in the Bible outside the Deuteronomistic history where we see a similar description of someone "loving" another with their "life strength" (*nephesh*) is the Song of Songs. Several times the woman in the Song of Songs describes her lover as the one whom her "life strength loves" (Song 1:7; 3:1–4). Whether or not one believes that the Song of Songs pre-dates Deuteronomy, the author of this text in Deuteronomy probably expanded on this more general expression for a lover found in ancient love poetry. Where such ancient love poetry spoke of one's love as the one whom one's "life strength" loved, the author of this text speaks of love with one's "whole heart/mind, life strength, and power." Furthermore, similar to Hosea (which also shows possible links to ancient love poetry), this expanded description of love is focused on the people's love of Yahweh, rather than on one human's love for another.

We see this expanded version of the description of love at one other, strategic location in the Deuteronomistic history, the description of Josiah at what would have been the conclusion of a Josianic edition of the Deuteronomistic history:

> Before Josiah there was no king like him who turned to Yahweh with all his heart/mind, all his life strength, and all his power, in accordance with the Torah of Moses, and after him there was never another like him. (2 Kgs 23:25)

This is the highest praise given any king in any part of the Deuteronomistic history. It marks Josiah as the superlative example of a king who followed the law of the king seen in Deut 17:14–20, which specifies that the king must study and follow the "Torah" as he leads his people in faithfulness. Later authors added material after this text to explain why the exile still happened despite Josiah's virtues (2 Kgs 23:26–7), but that does not appear to be in view here. Nor does Josiah's strange and seemingly pointless death at the hands of the Egyptians fit with the preceding materials about him (2 Kgs 23:29–30). Rather, this final evaluation of Josiah's reign in 2 Kgs 23:25 concludes a narrative arc that began with the call to "love" in Deut 6:4–5.

This call to "love" in Deut 6:5 also connects, however, to yet another discourse, and that is the Assyrian requirement that vassal kings and their people "love" the Assyrian king. In this case, the "love" required was far from the sort of passionate love envisioned in love poetry like the Song of Songs. Rather, the "love" – Akkadian *ramu* – required in Assyrian treaties was faithful obedience to the Assyrian king: paying tribute, not joining alliances with other nations against Assyria, reporting traitors and extraditing them to Assyria, etc. As a hybrid response to this experience of Assyrian domination, Deuteronomy 6:5 and the rest of the Deuteronomistic history reflect this dimension of "love" as well. But now Israel is to show faithful obedience to Yahweh and Yahweh alone. The people must not follow other gods (//alliances), and they must report and try prophets who encourage betrayal of Yahweh (//traitors). Thus the "love" envisioned in Deuteronomy is not a passionate or romantic emotion that one feels at one time and might not feel at another. It is a basic attitude of loyalty and devotion to one far more powerful than one's self; in this case, Yahweh, the god of Israel. Deut 6:5 represents a basic reorientation of such loyalty and devotion from the Assyrian king to Yahweh in the wake of the collapse of Assyrian empire.

The rest of the passage, Deut 6:6–9, aims to reinforce that reorientation through making sure that the people internalize the commands of Yahweh that are expressed in the Torah. Wisdom texts, such as the adaptation of the Instruction of Amenemope in Prov 22:17–18 (also Prov 3:3 and 7:3), urged the student to memorize the sayings of the teacher and recite them – "establish them firmly on your lips." The Torah of Moses in Deuteronomy represents a new form of "wisdom," which likewise should be memorized – "put on your heart/mind" (Deut 6:6) – and recited constantly in the presence of one's children, sitting at home, going on one's way, lying down and getting up (Deut 6:7). This constant repetition of the words of the Torah is not just aimed at reinforcing the loyalty of adult Israelites, but it is also intended to teach children the Torah as well, almost like a language that they hear spoken by parents at home. As if this were not enough, the words of Yahweh's commandments are also supposed to be worn on the bodies of Israelites and inscribed on their doorways and gates. Every aspect of their lives is to reflect Yahweh's commands, particularly the call to honor one and only one God, Yahweh, and love Yahweh with all one's heart/mind, life strength, and power (Deut 6:4–5).

Over the long haul, these injunctions appear to have been effective, since this passage ended up being one of the most important texts in both Judaism and Christianity. A version of this command – "you shall love Yahweh, your God, with all your heart, your soul and your mind/energy" – is named as the greatest commandment of all by Jesus in the Christian Gospel of Mark and later parallels to it in Matthew and Luke (Mark 12:28–9//Matt 22:34–7; Luke 10:25–7). This corresponds to the honoring of this command in Judaism as one of the holiest of all. Jews are required to recite this command and then others in Deut 11:13–21 (more on love and memorization) and Num 15:37–41 (on wearing fringes) twice a day, when rising and when going to bed. The great Jewish rabbi Akiba is reputed to have died at the hands of the Romans with the words of the Shema on his lips, and Jewish martyrs in later centuries have followed his example, reciting Deut 6:4 and following while dying during medieval riots associated with the crusades, in the Spanish inquisition, and in Nazi gas chambers. Ironically and tragically, many of these Jewish martyrs have died at Christian hands while reciting what Christians recognized as the "greatest commandment." Deut 6:4–5 has been important in both traditions, but that has not prevented centuries of deplorable Christian persecution of Jews.

Glimmers of the Later Torah and Prophets Collection in the Twilight of Judean Monarchy

Other chapters in this book have included an imaginary overview of the sorts of texts (and some traditions) that were in circulation at a given time in ancient Israel and Judah. Here we conclude with a picture of two different groups of texts that probably were prominent in different groups in late seventh-century Judah. On the one hand, many in ancient Judah continued to study older sorts of texts: proverbs and wisdom instructions, royal and other sorts of psalms, love poetry, creation and flood myths, along with assorted traditions with strong northern connections, such as the story of Jacob in Genesis 25–35 or some form of the exodus–wilderness traditions found (in reshaped form) in Exodus and Numbers. On the other hand, the book of Deuteronomy laid claim to be a new kind of "wisdom." Some, such as Jeremiah, seem to have been skeptical of Deuteronomy's claims to be true Torah wisdom (Jer 8:8–9), and our historical evidence suggests that kings after Josiah did not take the Deuteronomic Torah very seriously. Nevertheless, the book of Deuteronomy lays claim to be a potential replacement of older forms of teaching, and the rest of the Deuteronomistic history retells all of the people's history from that perspective. Though Deuteronomy echoes older wisdom texts, it calls on the people to devote all their time to memorizing Moses's Torah teaching (Deut 6:6–9). There is little room in Deuteronomy or the history that follows it for competing claims or texts.

With Josiah's death, many probably dismissed the claims of Deuteronomy and the rest of the Deuteronomistic history, but at least one family appears to have continued to treasure and expand those writings: the family of Shaphan. Shaphan was Josiah's scribe, and he is described as very involved in the process leading to the introduction of the Deuteronomic Torah to the king and the people (2 Kgs 22:3–10) and the verification of it through the prophet Huldah (2 Kgs 22:14–20). Shaphan may have been involved in the revision of the Deuteronomic Torah at the time of Josiah and the Deuteronomistic reframing of other historical traditions to bolster Josiah's reform. Furthermore, his family played a particular role in later Judean history. His son, Ahikam, sheltered Jeremiah when people wanted to kill him after his Temple sermon (Jer 26:24), and Shaphan's grandson was the first one to hear Jeremiah's scroll of oracles and make sure it was passed on to officials in the palace (Jer 36:10–13). By this point, the family of Shaphan no longer seems to have been part of the Judean inner circle. Yet one of their members, a grandson of Shaphan's named Gedaliah, is put in power by the Babylonians after the last king is removed (2 Kgs 25:22), and he gives a message of cooperation with Babylon that sounds somewhat like Jeremiah's prophecy (2 Kgs 25:23–4//Jer 40:7–12). Gedaliah was soon killed (2 Kgs 25:25//Jer 41:1–3), but his family is the most likely group to have cherished and protected the texts discussed in this chapter. In the twilight of the Judean monarchy, when others may have dismissed texts like Deuteronomy or Jeremiah, they expanded the Deuteronomistic history and revised/expanded Jeremiah's oracles so that the Jeremiah scroll agreed more with the values of that history.

Thus the late seventh century is a time when major traditions in the Bible were introduced, but all these texts still had a journey to make before becoming the biblical texts they now are. They do not seem to have been broadly recognized as important until total disaster struck Jerusalem, with the destruction of the Temple and the monarchy. Moreover, Jeremiah and the Deuteronomistic history were revised in light of this catastrophe, so that the Deuteronomistic history, for example, now extends up through the first part of exile in Babylonia. In the next chapter we will look at the impact of this catastrophe across a broader stretch of biblical traditions. This chapter, however, has traced the introduction in the late seventh century of major building blocks of the future "Torah" and "prophets."

CHAPTER FIVE REVIEW

1. Know the meaning and significance of the following terms discussed in this chapter:
■ books of the former prophets
■ Deuteronomistic
■ Deuteronomistic history
■ Josiah's reform
■ major prophet
■ postcolonial criticism

2. What is postcolonial criticism and what are two different ways in which biblical scholars draw on or engage it? What is an example of the use of postcolonial criticism to analyze Deuteronomy and the Deuteronomistic history?

3. How is the pre-exilic edition of the Deuteronomistic history different from the exilic edition?

4. What is the ancient concept of "holy war"? How does this concept function in the Deuteronomistic history?

5. When did Jeremiah prophesy? How is this time distinguished from the periods in which the book of Jeremiah was formed?

RESOURCES FOR FURTHER STUDY

Discussion of the Deuteronomistic history as a whole

Nelson, Richard D. *The Historical Books*. Interpreting Biblical Texts. Nashville: Abingdon, 1998.

Weinfeld, Moshe. *Deuteronomy and the Deuteronomic History*. Oxford: Clarendon Press, 1972.

Deuteronomy

Mayes, A. D. H. *Deuteronomy*. New Century Bible. Greenwood, SC: Attic Press, 1979.

Miller, Patrick. *Deuteronomy*. Interpretation. Louisville, KY: John Knox Press, 1990.

Tigay, Jeffrey. *Deuteronomy*. Philadelphia: Jewish Publication Society, 1996.

Joshua and Judges

See "Resources for Further Study" in Chapter 2.

1 and 2 Samuel

McCarter, P. Kyle. *I Samuel: A New Translation*; *II Samuel: A New Translation*. Anchor Bible. Garden City: Doubleday, 1980.

1 and 2 Kings

DeVries, Simon. *1 Kings*. Word Biblical Commentary, no. 12. Waco, TX: Word Books, 1985.

Gray, John. *I & II Kings* (2nd revised edition). Old Testament Library. Philadelphia: Westminster Press, 1970.

Nelson, Richard. *First and Second Kings*. Interpretation. Atlanta: John Knox Press, 1987.

Jeremiah

Carroll, Robert. *Jeremiah*. Old Testament Library. London: SCM, 1986.

Clements, R. E. *Jeremiah*. Interpretation. Atlanta: John Knox Press, 1988.

Thompson, John. *The Book of Jeremiah*. New International Commentary on the Old Testament. Grand Rapids: Eerdmans, 1979.

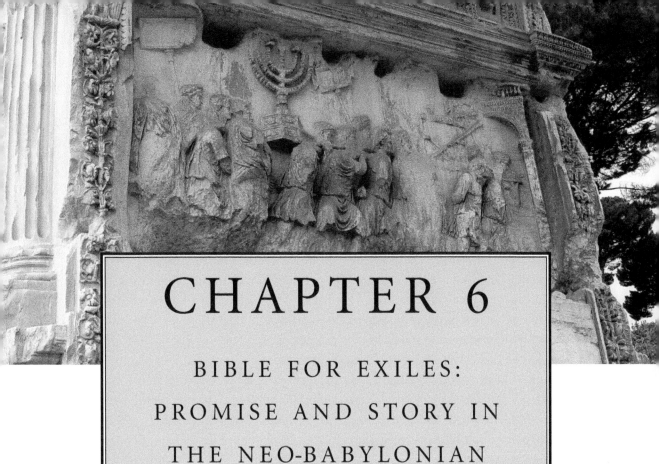

CHAPTER 6

BIBLE FOR EXILES: PROMISE AND STORY IN THE NEO-BABYLONIAN EMPIRE

Chapter Outline

CHAPTER OVERVIEW

The exile is the central point of biblical history, the period around which all others are oriented. Josiah's reform is a crucial turning point in the pre-exilic period, but already that formulation – "pre-exilic" – shows that the period of the exile is more important still. Most discussions of the history of the Hebrew Bible revolve around three periods: the pre-exilic, exilic, and post-exilic. The post-exilic period, as we will see in Chapter 7, is defined particularly by those who returned from exile to Judah. Yet for most others whose families had left Judah, there was no return from "exile" to life in the land, and many "Jews" have lived away from the land of Judah ever since the exile. Thus, the exile of waves of Judeans, first in 597 and then in 586 (and yet another in 582), introduced a new era in the history of the Israelite people and development of the Bible. From this point onward, they had no nation state. In the wake of the exile and destruction of Jerusalem, those scriptures now were scriptures for exiles and returnees living in a land dominated by others. The link between texts and a city-state monarchy was broken. After exile, the Israelites' scriptures never were the same.

This chapter explores the many ways in which the exile shaped the Hebrew Bible we now have. After discussing the exile and general ways that it changed the community, we will look at several texts that are explicitly linked to the exilic experience: laments over the destruction of Jerusalem, the response to exile in the book of Ezekiel and chapters 40–55 of Isaiah ("Second Isaiah"), and the addition – in the exilic period – of some new texts to the Deuteronomistic history that was discussed in the last chapter. These texts provide clues to the increasing importance of Israel's pre-land traditions during the exile and the emphasis in many exilic traditions on Yahweh's promise and ability to work with the people no matter how sinful. The balance of the chapter then shows how our present Pentateuch is an interweaving of two main source documents that reflect these exilic themes of promise: an L Source (or Lay Source) created by lay scribes and leaders, and a slightly later P (Priestly) Source created by priests. In many ways, it is best to think of both of these sources, L and P, as expressions in narrative form of the exilic promise addressed to despairing exiles that we see in prophetic form in the later prophecies of Ezekiel and Second Isaiah. Though the L and P narratives purport to be about ancient figures such as Abraham and Moses, they are stories and laws crafted to address the questions and concerns of exiles. The challenge of this chapter is to see how the concerns of the exiles in Babylon not only are reflected in clearly exilic laments and prophecies, but also played a crucial role in forming how the exiles composed stories about their earlier ancestors, focusing particularly now (in exile) on ancestors such as Abraham, Rachel, or Moses, who, like them, faced living in a land that was not their own.

The Neo-Babylonian Destruction
of Jerusalem and Exile

READING

2 Kgs 23:29–25:30.
Exilic laments: Ps 137;
Lamentations 1;
Isa 63:7–64:12.

EXERCISE

Before reading this section, read the "exilic laments" listed
above and then write down five words that these texts from
the exile evoke for you.

Despite high hopes during the time of Josiah, the kingdom of Judah never achieved an
extended period of independence, nor was its control over the north firm for any length
of time. Instead, Josiah was killed in 609 in an apparently pointless confrontation with
the Egyptian Pharaoh Necho as Necho was traveling through Israel on his way to assist
Assyria in trying to contain a rising military power in Mesopotamia.

That power was the emergent "Neo-Babylonian" state (distinguished from the "Old
Babylonian" empire of the early second millennium), a state ruled by a group of Aramean
people called "Chaldeans." Thus began a period of Judah and its kings struggling under
the shadow of Neo-Babylonian domination. Though the Egyptian Necho appointed
one of Josiah's sons, Jehoiakim, as Josiah's successor, Jehoiakim quickly became a
Babylonian vassal. A few years later, he sought to get out from under Babylonian domination with Egypt's help, but the Babylonian army eventually came and laid siege to
Jerusalem. In an attempt to avert the wrath of the Babylonians, the people of Jerusalem
apparently killed Jehoiakim and replaced him with his son, Jehoiachin, but the Babylonians
still took young Jehoiachin and several thousand elite Judeans into exile (in 597), the first
of several waves of forced resettlement of Judeans in the Babylonian empire. In place
of Jehoiachin, the Babylonians appointed as king his uncle, Zedekiah, a son of Josiah.
Zedekiah ruled for about ten years before he, like his brother Jehoiakim, tried to get
free of Babylon by joining an anti-Babylonian coalition of nations.

This rebellion by Zedekiah was the final straw for the Babylonians. Nebuchadnezzar
marched on Jerusalem in 586 BCE and breached the walls (see Figure 6.1). He destroyed
the Temple that Judah had thought was invulnerable, took yet more of Judah's elite into
exile (though fewer than in 597), and installed Gedaliah, the grandson of Shaphan,
Josiah's scribe, as governor in Mizpah, a town a few miles northwest of Jerusalem. Our
last historical records point to the collapse of power structures in the land. In Judah
things went from very bad to worse. Gedaliah was assassinated, his assassins fled to
Ammon before Gedaliah's forces, and Gedaliah's forces fled to Egypt out of fear of
Babylonian reprisals, forcing Jeremiah to come with them (2 Kgs 25:25–6//Jeremiah
41–2). The last we hear of life in Judah, the Babylonians had attacked again and taken
a third wave of Judeans into exile in 582 BCE (Jer 52:30; see Map 6.1).

Figure 6.1 Ashes and arrowheads left from the Babylonian attack on Jerusalem.

Meanwhile, life went on in Babylonian exile for the thousands of upper-class Judeans who had been forcibly resettled. The books of Kings (and Jeremiah) end with a brief account of how the king, Jehoiachin, was taken out of prison during his thirty-seventh year of exile in Babylon, given a place at the Babylonian king's table, and given rations (2 Kgs 25:27–30; appropriated in Jer 52:31–4; cf. Ezek 1:2). This narrative was written by the exiled authors who extended and expanded the Deuteronomistic history written back in Josiah's time, and is confirmed by a Babylonian list of rations given to Jehoiachin. It shows the sliver of hope that such exiles found in the elevation of their king. Nevertheless, we never hear of Jehoiachin again, and Davidic kings never regained power. The sun had gone down on the Jerusalem monarchy and institutions linked directly with it. The people's future now lay in a life without their own monarch over them.

With no monarchy left to sponsor the writing of any history, we are in the dark about other specific events during the Babylonian exile. Biblical texts only provide indirect information about what life was like in exile. Certainly it was no picnic. The exiles were

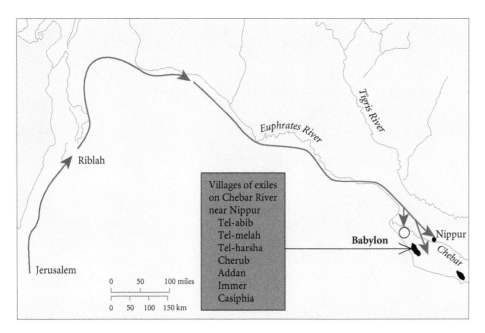

Map 6.1 The journey to Babylon. Redrawn from Yohanan Aharoni and Michael Avi-Yonah (eds.), *The Macmillan Bible Atlas* (revised edition). New York: Macmillan, 1977, map 163.

forcibly resettled into abandoned areas of central Babylonia where they worked and tried to form a viable communal life hundreds of miles from their homeland. Though the exiles were allowed to settle together and were not enslaved, exilic texts refer to Babylonian domination as a "yoke" (Ezek 34:27; Isa 47:6; also Jer 30:8) and Babylonia became a symbol of arch-evil throughout the rest of biblical tradition. Multiple traditions suggest that some exiles were in chains (Jer 40:1; see also Nah 3:10), and exilic texts in Isaiah speak of Jerusalem's time of "forced labor" (Isa 40:2), of being confined in prison (Isa 42:7; 49:9) and robbed (Isa 42:22). Meanwhile, one of Nebuchadnezzar's inscriptions boasts of how he forced people from Judah and elsewhere to rebuild the temple in Babylonia (see the Miscellaneous Box on "Forced Labor for Exiles Under Nebuchadnezzar"). Babylon had become their new Egypt (see Figure 6.2).

Laments and prophetic quotes from this period give a sense of the inner experience of this exile. Psalm 137 speaks of weeping by the rivers of Babylon where the captors of the Judeans mockingly asked them to "sing one of the songs of Zion." The exiles sing of how they will keep Jerusalem in their memory, though they are far from home.

> If I forget you, O Jerusalem,
>   let my right hand wither!
> Let my tongue cling to the roof of my mouth,
>   if I do not remember you,
>   if I do not set Jerusalem above my highest joy. (Ps 137:5–6 NRSV)

Lamentations 1 is an alphabet of suffering, where each stanza begins with a different letter of the Hebrew alphabet. After an initial lament over Zion, she cries forth her suffering herself:

Figure 6.2 Reproduction of part of the magnificent temple of Ishtar located in the heart of the empire of Babylon.

Forced Labor for Exiles Under Nebuchadnezzar

This is an excerpt from a building inscription by Nebuchadnezzar II about his use of peoples from across his empire to build "Etemenanki," the grand temple for Marduk in the heart of Babylon:

the whole of the races, peoples from far places, whom Marduk, my Lord, delivered to me, I put

them to work on the building of Etemenanki. I imposed on them the brick basket. (Translation: D. Smith, "The Politics of Ezra: Sociological Indicators of Postexilic Judaean Society." P. 79 of Philip Davies, ed., *Second Temple Studies, I*, JSOTSup 117. Sheffield: Sheffield Academic Press, 1991)

My crimes have been bound into a yoke,
   my misdeeds braided together by [God's] hand.
They lie on my neck,
   They sap my strength.
The Lord has given me into the hands of
   Those I cannot overcome. (Lam 1:14)

Echoing pre-exilic prophets like Hosea and Jeremiah, this Zion figure says, "I called out to my lovers, but they betrayed me. My priests and elders died in the city while seeking food to survive" (Lam 1:19). Meanwhile, in a lament found in Isa 63:7–64:12, the ancient Judeans cry out to God, "your holy cities have become a wasteland, Zion has become a desert, Jerusalem a heap of ruins" (64:10) and assert to Yahweh, their "father" (64:8), that he has made them "stray from your paths and turn our hearts from fearing you" (64:7). Such laments are part of an ancient literary tradition in Israel of honest crying out to God, even accusing God of being responsible for the people's shortcomings. These laments will be discussed in Chapter 7. For now, it is important to recognize that this type of text, particularly the communal lament, voiced the exiles' mixed feelings of guilt, sadness, fear, and rage as they lived for decades under Neo-Babylonian oppression.

basics	Book of Lamentations	
Outline: five-part (=Torah) cry for restoration of Jerusalem	I Four alphabet poems detailing the suffering of Jerusalem and its people	1–4
	II Final communal plea for restoration	5
Theme and purpose	Other ancient Near Eastern cultures had written and taught laments over the destruction of great cities. These chapters in Lamentations were composed to commemorate the destruction of Jerusalem in 586, particularly on the holiday remembering this event, the Ninth of Av. Over time, however, these poems in Lamentations have come to serve as a cry over Jewish suffering of many kinds, from the destruction of the Second Temple to the genocide of Jews under Hitler and other suffering up to today.	

The dynamics of exile can be illuminated through **social-scientific analysis** of the Bible; that is, analysis that draws on contemporary sociological and anthropological studies to provide a more nuanced picture of ancient Israel. For example, Daniel Smith-Christopher's book *Religion of the Landless* (see this chapter's "Resources for Further Study") draws on ethnographic studies of contemporary groups who have experienced displacement from their homelands to try to reconstruct what the experience of Babylonian exile might have been like. He finds that separation from one's homeland inevitably involves major changes for the displaced group. Continuity is not the norm. Transformation is.

In addition, Smith-Christopher found that communities in exile change in similar ways, reflecting the similar challenges that many such diaspora communities face. Because they must now live as a minority in a majority culture, family and clan traditions often become more important, while other traditions connected with their old life either disappear or are transformed. For example, Judean traditions about the king's blessing may have been adapted in exile so that they now applied to an ancient ancestor's blessing or God's blessing of a foreign deliverer. Meanwhile, in place of the now defunct royal bureaucracy, the sole means of organization of Judean exiles were family units, "houses of the father," which were ruled by a group of "elders." These elders, along with the remnants of the priesthood, were the leaders in the exiled Judean community.

New practices became important for the Judeans in Babylonian exile, practices that preserved communal identity in a hostile cultural environment. It appears that circumcision (which was not practiced by Babylonians) and Sabbath observance grew in importance. Furthermore, exiles like them had to struggle against the tendency to assimilate into the broader culture, particularly through intermarriage. In the face of this, these exiles, like many contemporary communities in exile, sought ways to discourage their children from marrying foreigners. This is but one major way in which peoples in exile, both ancient and contemporary, change in order to survive culturally.

The violence of the exiles' departure may have been yet another factor leading to the transformation of their traditions. Though it is possible that Judean exiles took some scrolls of ancient texts with them into Babylon, it is also quite likely that many did not have a chance to pack much up while Jerusalem burned and the Temple – often a storage place for ancient scrolls – was destroyed. Yet the literate elite who went into exile had memorized ancient texts as part of their education. The Deuteronomic Torah, Proverbs, Song of Songs, and other texts were "written on the tablet of their hearts," as Proverbs would put it (Prov 3:3; 7:3). Once in Babylon, these people could call on their detailed memories of these texts as they produced new copies of them – copies that often reflected the new challenges and hopes of life in exile.

The Exilic Edition of the Deuteronomistic History (and Jeremiah)

READING
Deut 30:1–10 (cf. Deut 30:11–20); 2 Kgs 21:2–16; 23:26–8.

One example of such preservation and change of ancient textual traditions is the exilic revision and extension of the Deuteronomistic history. In Chapter 5 we saw that the pre-exilic version of this history probably reached only as far as the final evaluation of Josiah's reign (2 Kgs 23:25). In this earlier form, this history was meant to provide a historical-theological rationale for Josiah's attempt to reunify northern and southern Israel under centralized worship of Yahweh. Josiah died, however, and Jerusalem, the one legitimate place for sacrificial worship in his kingdom, was destroyed. Later authors had to explain why this happened, and we see this explanation immediately after the positive comments about Josiah's righteousness. The exilic extenders of this history go on to say:

> [Despite Josiah's goodness] the Lord did not turn back from his great anger against Judah and all the awful things that Manasseh [Josiah's predecessor] had done to anger God. The Lord said, "As I banished Israel from my presence, so will I also banish Judah, and I will reject this city that I chose, Jerusalem, and the house where I said my name would live." (2 Kgs 23:26–7)

This is how one group of exiles, those extending the Deuteronomistic history, explained the greatest trauma of the exile: the destruction of the supposedly invulnerable city, Jerusalem, and its sanctuary. The reason they gave was that Manasseh's sin was so grievous that Josiah's virtue could not overcome it. One generation's guilt meant that another generation had to suffer. A proverb quoted by Ezekiel's audience puts it vividly: "the fathers have eaten sour grapes and the children's teeth are set on edge" (Ezek 18:2). As we will see, Ezekiel rejects this idea that a later generation must pay for the sins of their parents. Nevertheless, this passage from 2 Kgs 23:26–7 is a biblical affirmation of this concept. It asserts that later generations of Judah had to suffer the destruction of Judah and Jerusalem because of the sins of Manasseh. Sour grapes indeed.

This is only one example of a range of places where exilic authors seem to have revised or expanded on the pre-exilic edition of the Deuteronomistic history that they had. The readings for this section include one more example, taken from the beginning of the history in Deuteronomy. The speech in Deuteronomy 30:1–10 is shaped for people who have been "exiled to the ends of the world" (30:4), and it reassures them that the Lord will restore them and bring them back to the land if they follow the command of Deut 6:5, loving the Lord "with all your heart and life strength" (30:6). This is a contrast to the threats and promises in Deut 30:11–20, a probable pre-exilic portion of Deuteronomy. The more reassuring message in Deut 30:1–10 was probably added to Deuteronomy by Judean exiles to show a way forward amidst apparent total disaster. Through adding the promises in Deut 30:1–10, these exilic Deuteronomists offered their people hope, a hope based on return to the Lord and the Lord's Torah. Such revisions probably played a key role in insuring that the Deuteronomistic history, including and especially Deuteronomy, became an ever more important text in the exilic and post-exilic periods.

The same could be said for a variety of exilic Deuteronomistic additions in the book of Jeremiah and other prophetic books. In Chapter 4 we discussed how the books of Micah (especially chapters 4–5) and Isaiah (chapters 40–55) contain prophecies of hope for Jerusalem/Zion that probably were written to encourage exiles. The book of Jeremiah was thoroughly revised during the exile through the addition of passages such as God's promise of a new covenant written on the heart (Jer 31:31–4) that was discussed in Chapter 5. We see our first close analogies to this idea of God actually changing the heart of God's people in the next prophet to be discussed, Ezekiel.

Ezekiel's Move from Judgment to
Promise with the Fall of Jerusalem

Ezekiel is the only prophet in the Hebrew Bible whose prophecy can be dated with certainty to the exilic period. He was a priest who went into exile in Babylon with King Jehoiachin and thousands of other exiles in 597. There he lived in a Jewish settlement, Tel-abib, located just a few miles from the ancient Sumerian center of learning at Nippur. Though Zedekiah ruled in Jerusalem from 597 until its destruction in 586, all of Ezekiel's prophecies are dated by the years of Jehoiachin's exile. Apparently his career began six years before Jerusalem was destroyed and then continued another fourteen years after Jerusalem's destruction (see Ezek 1:2; 40:1). Many divide Ezekiel's book into two major parts, corresponding to the two major periods of his prophecy. Ezekiel 1–32 features oracles of judgment dated to the period before Jerusalem's destruction. These judgments by Ezekiel are roughly contemporary with the last phase of Jeremiah's prophecy but are delivered in exile to exiles. Then the tone shifts: once Jerusalem is destroyed and the exiles are in despair about their future with God, Ezekiel develops vivid images of hope, and these are stressed in chapters 33–48 of the book.

READING
Ezekiel 1–3, 8–11, 16, 36–7.

Like the other books of major prophets, the book of Ezekiel prominently features a story of his commissioning by God, in Ezekiel 1–3. Nevertheless, this commissioning is different in ways that mark the uniqueness of Ezekiel's prophecy. It begins, like Isaiah's, with a vision of God and God's attendants (1:4–28), but Ezekiel's vision is more elaborate: with four strange creatures (1:4–14), each associated with a chariot wheel (1:15–25), and a brilliant blue throne overhead on which God is seated, "an appearance of the likeness of the glory of the LORD" (1:28). Moreover, Ezekiel, unlike Isaiah, sees God outside the temple (1:2–28; 3:22–3), and the imagery of the wheels in his call narrative anticipate his later "Temple vision," where he sees God leave the Temple and go into exile (Ezekiel 8–11). This focus on God's presence outside the Temple in both Ezekiel 1–3 and 8–11 is the first mark of the radically new, exilic context of Ezekiel's prophecy.

The message that Ezekiel is commissioned to speak, however, sounds like an extreme version of the message seen in Amos, Isaiah, and other prophets of judgment. God tells him to speak to God's people of "rebels," whether they listen or not (2:1–7). Indeed, God predicts that they will not listen, but will reject his message (3:4–9). Nevertheless, like a sentinel on a watchtower who sees an approaching army, Ezekiel must sound the alarm about God's oncoming judgment and let the people make the decision about whether to respond. Otherwise, the blood of his people will be on his hands (Ezek 3:16–21).

When other prophets faced rejection of their prophecy, they had their oracles written down for other generations (examples: Isa 8:11–18; 30:8–14; Jeremiah 36), and this element of writing is yet more prominent in Ezekiel's call narrative. God offers him a scroll with words of doom written on it and tells Ezekiel to eat it. Ezekiel does eat it, an act signifying his obedient memorization of all that God has told him to prophesy (Ezek 2:8–3:3). Yet the scroll has not lost its purpose. Rather, this narrative implies that its words of doom were included in the book now found in the Hebrew Bible. Though his own generation did not listen, the writing down of his prophecy allowed it to endure and teach future generations.

One central element of Ezekiel's teaching was his proclamation that each generation stood on its own before God: a disobedient generation would be punished for its sins, but if the children of people in that generation were righteous, they would be rewarded. Not everyone agreed on this point. As we saw above, the exilic portions of the Deuteronomistic history blamed the suffering of Ezekiel's generation on the sins of an earlier one, especially the evil of Manasseh (2 Kgs 23:26–7). As we have seen, Ezekiel quotes people of his time saying "the fathers have eaten sour grapes, and the children's teeth are set on edge" (Ezek 18:2), but he decisively rejects that saying. On the contrary, he insists, the fathers will be punished or rewarded for their righteousness, and their children will stand or fall on the basis of their own righteousness as well (Ezekiel 18:3–24). Many who have read this chapter in the contemporary context of emphasis on the individual have seen here the first emergence in the Hebrew Bible of individual responsibility, but this is mistaken. At issue in every example in the chapter is whether or not later generations must pay for the sins of their parents. The point is to get the exiles to stop saying how "unfair" God is for punishing them on the basis of an earlier

basics **Book of Ezekiel**

Outline: judgment and restoration of Jerusalem	I	Sentinel announcement of judgment	1:1–33:20
	II	Restoration of Jerusalem and Temple	33:21–48:35

Date | Early to late exile.

Themes | The judgment and restoration theme is familiar from other prophets, but Ezekiel, a Zadokite priest, adds a different level of spectacle to his visions (e.g. Ezekiel 1–3 and 37) and a new emphasis on purity, and features a particular focus on the Temple (Ezekiel 9–11) and its restoration (Ezekiel 40–8).

More information | Ezekiel is also known for his weird symbolic actions, such as lying on his side for more than a year (Ezek 4:4–8) or not mourning the death of his wife (Ezek 24:15–27). Some in the past have explained these and other aspects of his prophecy as the result of a mental imbalance in Ezekiel. Nevertheless, such attempts to psychologically analyze the prophet on the basis of literature linked to him are extremely risky. Moreover, these approaches miss the emphasis throughout the book on the idea that Ezekiel's words and actions, however unusual, were a message from God for the exiles and later generations.

generation's sins (18:25, 29). Instead, Ezekiel calls on them to repent of their own past crimes, get a "new heart and a new spirit," and live (Ezek 18:31–2).

Ultimately Ezekiel, like other prophetic books, ends with hope, not judgment. After a series of oracles against foreign nations (Ezekiel 25–32), the book returns to a review of major themes from the first part of the book (33:1–20) before moving to prophecies dated to the destruction of the Jerusalem Temple (33:21) or later (40:1). Some of these are words of judgment, such as Ezekiel's oracle against people still in the land who claim Abraham as their ancestor (Ezek 33:23–9) or his condemnation of Judah and Israel's past kings, their "shepherds," for selfishness and injustice (Ezek 34:1–10). Yet these oracles of judgment introduce words of hope to exiles, promising that God will be their shepherd and rescue them from exile and resettle them under a new Davidic king (Ezek 34:11–31). Where Ezekiel prophesied against the mountains of the land in the first part of the book (Ezekiel 6), he offers them hope in this latter part (Ezekiel 36). Where he watched the glory of God leave the Temple before (Ezek 11:22–5), he now sees it returning (Ezek 43:1–6). In one of the most powerful visions of all, he imagines Israel as a valley full of "dry bones," bones which symbolize exiles who are convinced that they are completely finished and hope is lost (Ezek 37:11). God calls on Ezekiel to prophecy to this valley of dry bones, this exiled people, and watch their miraculous resurrection (37:12–14).

The restoration imagined in Ezekiel does not depend on the people finding a way to change themselves. Rather, in this part of the book, Ezekiel reiterates promises given earlier that God will give the people a new heart and new spirit so that they can obey God's laws (Ezek 36:26–7; 37:14; cf. 11:14–21). Though the exiles might despair that God would ever have anything more to do with them after all that they had done wrong, Ezekiel reassures them that god will do all this "for the sake of [God's] holy name" (Ezek 36:22–3, 32). This idea of "holy name" refers to God's reputation. According to Ezekiel, God's reputation among the nations had suffered when God's people was defeated and sent into exile (36:20–1). Now God will redeem God's reputation through bringing the Israelites back into the land in full sight of the nations (36:28–36). In this way, Ezekiel describes a restoration that does not depend on any goodness in the exiles themselves.

The Divine Council

The people of Israel and surrounding countries believed their god had a royal court of divine beings, a "divine council." Just as human kings had counselors and courtiers, so also the divine king had his. We see reflections of this idea of the divine council across the whole Hebrew Bible: Psalm 89:7 refers to Yahweh's "council of the holy ones." Isaiah 6:8, 40:1, and 40:3 feature commands addressed to an unspecified heavenly group. God debates with a group about whether Job is altruistic in Job 1–2. We may even see a pale reflection of this idea in Genesis where God decides to make humanity "in *our* image" (Gen 1:26) and later fears that humans will be "like *us*" (Gen 3:22 and 11:7).

Hope for Exiles in Second Isaiah
(also called "Deutero-Isaiah")

READING
Isaiah 40–55

Very similar themes appear in the other major prophet that is associated with the exile: the anonymous prophet that wrote chapters 40–55 of the book of Isaiah. Chapter 4 of this *Introduction* mentioned biblical scholarship that has identified this section of Isaiah as coming from a later period of Judah's history than the time of the original Isaiah. This part of the textbook examines how these chapters addressed the fears and hopes of exiles a few decades after the time of Ezekiel. By this point in the exile, this **"Second Isaiah"** (or **Deutero-Isaiah**) can proclaim that the LORD has anointed the Persian king Cyrus as God's shepherd, that is, God's king (Isa 44:28–45:1). We know from other historical documents that this Cyrus would eventually bring down the Neo-Babylonian empire in 539 BCE.

This exilic portion of Isaiah opens with a commissioning scene in the **divine council** (Isa 40:1–8) that echoes the scene in the divine council where the earlier prophet, eighth-century Isaiah, was commissioned (6:1–13). The original Hebrew of both texts, Isa 6:1–13 and 40:1–8, indicates that God speaks with other divine attendants, probably members of God's divine council, in the process of deciding who will take God's message to God's people (Isa 6:8; 40:1–5). In Isa 6:8 God asks a group of people, "whom shall I send on our behalf?" while Isa 40:1–2 calls a group to go and tell God's people that the exile, the "time of forced labor," is over:

> Comfort my people, comfort them,
> Says your God.
> Speak tenderly to the heart of Jerusalem,
> And call out to her.
> That her time of forced labor is now over,
> That her bloodguilt has been paid for,
> That she has received from Yahweh double for all her sins. (Isa 40:1–2)

Isaiah 6, the call narrative for Isaiah of the eighth century, stressed his confrontation with his and his people's "bloodguilt" (Isa 6:5). In contrast, this later exilic text emphasizes God's forgiveness. Isaiah 6 described Yahweh's "glory" as filling the whole earth (Isa 6:3), but this exilic text in Isa 40:5 now has the whole earth actually *seeing* Yahweh's "glory" (Isa 40:3–5). Just as Ezekiel had pictured God's reputation being restored through the nations' witnessing God's rescue of God's people (Ezek 36:28–36), so this exilic "Second Isaiah" imagines God's glory being revealed to the whole world in the exiles' departure from Babylon (Isa 40:3–5).

God's announcement of Jerusalem's liberation is followed by the prophet's call and his objection to the call (40:6), an exchange similar to ones in the call narratives for Isaiah (Isa 6:5) and Jeremiah (Jer 1:6). In this case, however, the exilic prophet is worried about despairing exiles, who wither "like grass" when "the breath of Yahweh blows upon it" (40:6–7). He knows that he must address a discouraged people who have heard many false hopes. Yet a divine presence answers his doubts, first by acknowledging their partial truth, "Yes, the grass withers, and the flower fades," then adding the reassurance that "the word of our God endures forever" (40:8). Though the exiles may feel weak and hopeless, God's word of hope and restoration persists and will prevail.

---

basics   ## Second Isaiah/Deutero-Isaiah

| Outline | I | Exhortation to second exodus out of Babylon | 40–8 |
| | II | Announcement of hope and return to Jerusalem | 49–55 |

Date   Late exile.

Themes   This part of Isaiah focuses on giving hope to the hopeless. Though possibly written as a separate prophetic collection, it now links in interesting ways with earlier parts of Isaiah (e.g. Isaiah 40:1–9//Isaiah 6). It is also the part of Isaiah that contains the famous "servant songs" (Isa 42:1–4; 49:1–6; 50:4–11; 52:13–53:12) that have been the subject of much religious and scholarly debate.

The rest of Isaiah 40–55 is divided into two main parts: Isaiah 40–8 and 49–55. The first part, Isaiah 40–8, is a passionate call for the exiles to embrace God's plan to take them out of Babylon. Central to this call is the prophet's reassurance that their God, who might have seemed defeated by other gods in the destruction of Jerusalem, is powerful enough to liberate them. Here "Second Isaiah" invokes creation traditions to affirm that the god who created the world can bring them out of Babylon (Isa 40:12–27). He reminds the exiles of God's care for their ancestors, both Abraham and Jacob and the people of the exodus generation (41:8–9; 44:1–2; also 51:1–2).

It is in the context of these arguments for Yahweh's power that Second Isaiah makes a monotheistic claim that is new in Israelite religion: he asserts that there is no other god anywhere but Yahweh. All other gods are false idols, worthless pieces of wood and metal (40:18–20; 41:7; 44:9–20). In this way Second Isaiah reassures the exiles that other nations' gods are no contest whatsoever for the creator-liberator God of Israel. We have not seen this sort of argument for the non-existence of any other gods in Israelite traditions clearly datable to earlier periods. In Hosea and Deuteronomy we saw calls for Israel not to worship any other gods, yet those calls did not include the assumption that such gods did not exist. Yet here, in the context of Second Isaiah's reassurances to exiles, the prophet argues for just this point of view. Later traditions will take **monotheism** for granted.

Isaiah 40–8, the first half of Second Isaiah, concludes with an argument from prophecy, an argument that only works if it was directly addressed to exiles and not to an earlier audience. God reminds the exiles of earlier prophecies that have come true, "former things" declared through the prophets. Through seeing the past fulfillment of these prophecies, this text insists, God's "stubborn" people should now be able to trust God's announcement of "new things" (Isa 48:4–6), including God's plans to destroy the sixth-century Neo-Babylonian empire (48:14). Even though it is theoretically possible that an eighth-century prophet, Isaiah, could have accurately predicted the demise of the Babylonian empire, he would not have addressed his eighth-century audience as if his prophecies about Judah lay in the past. Nor would Isaiah of the eighth century have called on his audience, still in Judah, to "go out from Babylon, flee from Chaldea, declare with loud shouts . . . 'God has freed God's servant, Jacob'" (Isa 48:20). These are words addressed by an unknown exilic prophet to a later audience of exiles, an audience longing to go home.

The second major section of Second Isaiah, Isaiah 49–55, focuses on the task of resettling and restoring Jerusalem. Like 40–8, these chapters start with a commissioning (49:1–6; cf. 40:1–8). This time, God commissions a "**servant**" who is to gather the exiled Israelites back to the LORD and reveal God's glory to the end of the earth (49:5–6). The identity of the "servant" in this and other passages in Second Isaiah has puzzled readers for centuries (see other "**servant songs**" in Isa 42:1–8; 50:4–9; 52:13–53:12 that likewise focus on a distinctive "servant"). In most of Isaiah 40–8, God addresses the whole people of Israel/Jacob as God's servant (Isa 41:8–9; 43:10; 44:1; 48:20). In other cases, however, the "servant/suffering servant" seems to be separate from the people, serving them (e.g. 49:5–6). Early Christians insisted that the servant of these passages was Jesus Christ. It is highly doubtful, however, that an exilic Judean prophet originally understood himself to be prophesying Jesus Christ. Instead, scholars of the Bible usually

MORE ON METHOD: (STUDY OF) INTERTEXTUALITY

Recent literary criticism has taught biblical scholars to be ever more aware of **intertextuality** in biblical texts. Intertextuality is a word used to refer to the myriad ways different texts can be related to each other. Literary-critical analysis of biblical intertextuality sometimes takes the form of analyzing ways in which biblical texts allude to or build on earlier texts, such as the echo of Lam 5:20 in the lament by Zion in Isa 49:14. Other times, however, such analysis highlights ways that any reading of a biblical text must now consider that text as part of a broader web of texts, many of which it was not originally connected to. For example, in the next section of this chapter we will look at later readings of the poem about the suffering servant in Isa 52:13–53:12 by Christians and Jews that have been influenced by earlier interpretations of the poem in each faith tradition. As Peter Miscall has put it (echoing John Donne), "no text is an island," whether in its original writing or its subsequent interpretation.

For more: Patricia K. Tull, "Rhetorical Criticism and Intertextuality," pp. 156–79 in S. McKenzie and S. Haynes, *To Each Its Own Meaning: An Introduction to Biblical Criticisms and Their Applications* (Louisville, KY: Westminster Press, 1999).

conclude that the "servant" in Second Isaiah was either a now unknown individual in the community of the exiles or stood for the community of Israel as a whole. There are grounds for both positions in Isaiah 40–55.

The servant passage in Isa 49:1–6 is followed by a speech where God addresses Jerusalem, personified once again as a woman. Echoing the book of Lamentations, she cries out that "the LORD has abandoned me, my Lord has forgotten me" (Isa 49:14; compare Lam 5:20). God then answers this lament with a remarkable use of parental imagery:

> Can a woman forget her nursing child,
>   Or her compassion for the child of her womb?
> Even if these ones forget, I will never forget you. (Isa 49:15)

The exilic prophet uses mothers as the ultimate example of compassion and then says that God embodies such compassion and more toward the exiles.

Thus begins a series of speeches in Isaiah 49–55 that alternate between speeches of comfort to female Zion (50:1–3; 51:1–52:12; 54:1–17) and speeches by or about God's "servant" (50:4–11; 52:13–53:12). The climax of the songs about the servant is Isa 52:13–53:12, a poem about the shaming and exaltation of a "servant" who has borne the sicknesses of others. The climax of the songs about female Zion is Isaiah 54, a picture of God's eternal remarriage to Zion after abandoning her "for a brief moment" (54:7). This latter poem is a sharp contrast to Ezekiel's use of marriage imagery earlier in the exile to stress the people's wrongdoing and punishment (Ezekiel 16 and 23). The prophet in Isaiah 54 downplays any past troubles and uses the marriage metaphor to stress God's abiding love for God's beloved city.

The final chapter of Isaiah 40–55 features several distinctive promises to exiles in Babylon. Where once the Davidic monarchy was promised an eternal covenant (2 Sam 7:12–16; 23:5; Pss 89:3–4, 20–1), now – in the wake of the destruction of the monarchy – God promises an eternal, Davidic covenant with the people themselves (55:3). Echoing the earlier affirmation that "the word of our God endures forever" (40:8), this concluding chapter affirms that God's word "will not return to [God] empty" (55:11). As a result, the exiles should "go out in joy and be led back in peace," watching the mountains and hills break forth in song to greet them on their way home (55:12–13). These extravagant promises, made just on the eve of the destruction of the Babylonian empire, were on the minds of many exiles when they returned home with high hopes.

From Promise in the Prophets to Promise in Two Pentateuchal Sources: L and P

In this chapter we have seen a turn toward promise in the two main exilic prophets: Ezekiel and Second Isaiah. In Ezekiel, we could see a contrast between a primary focus on judgment before the destruction of Jerusalem and a primary focus on promise after Jerusalem was gone and the exiles were despairing. In Second Isaiah we see a much more sustained focus on promise addressed to Judeans much later in the exile process.

These promises were addressed to the despair and disorientation that we see in the exilic laments read at the outset of the chapter. The Zion that Judah thought was invulnerable was destroyed. Its leadership was scattered, its monarchy out of power. Many exiles seem to have doubted whether Yahweh would still care about them anymore, sinful as they were. The exiles needed powerful words of promise to maintain hope. The later prophecy of Ezekiel and the entire prophecy of Second Isaiah gave them such words of promise. These words acknowledged that Judah had not done Yahweh's will, but it assured them that Yahweh would liberate them anyway, for the sake of Yahweh's honor and to reveal Yahweh's power.

We turn now to another place where exiles found words of promise and hope: the traditions now found in the Pentateuch (Genesis–Deuteronomy). As we will see, these traditions were not always together as they are now. Instead, during the exile there were two written stories about Israel before the conquest – an L Source created by lay scribes and leaders and a slightly later and parallel P Source created by priests. These sources included blocks of earlier material. Their authors did not write them from scratch. Nevertheless, whatever earlier traditions these two sources contained, the accent of both was on God's promise to Israel's ancestors, a promise with some resemblance to promises seen in prophets such as Ezekiel and Second Isaiah. This promise, however, was expressed differently. Where Ezekiel and Second Isaiah spoke the promise in words of prophecy addressed directly to Judeans, the L and the P sources spoke words of promise to exiles by retelling stories of God's promises to their ancestors. Through revising and combining older traditions about Israel's life before the land, the authors of L and P reassured exiles separated from their land. The L and P sources implied that Yahweh would redeem them, just as Yahweh had redeemed their ancestors.

Promise-centered storytelling in the Lay Pentateuchal Source (L)

We start with what will be termed here the "**Lay Source**" or "**L**." It is given this term because this source appears to have been composed by non-priestly scribes and features the "elders" as the main leadership group of the generation who lived during the time of Moses (indeed, many scholars would refer to this material with the more cumbersome term **non-Priestly** or **non-P**). Note: it is important to realize that though these "lay" leaders do not seem to have been priests, they were hardly everyday people either. On the contrary, they probably were members of the royal leadership (now out of power in exile) and/or other non-priestly elite scholars who drew on their knowledge of older compositions to write a new overall story of their people's life before they possessed the land.

READING
Genesis 12–16, 18–22;
Exod 19:2–24:14
and 32:1–34:35.

The L Source that they produced included the older J primeval history (Gen 2:1–4:26; 6:1–8; 7:1–5, 10, 12 … 8:20–2; 9:18–27), a newly composed story about Abraham (Genesis 12–16, 18–22, 24), a revised form of the northern Jacob and Joseph compositions (most of Genesis 25–50), and a transformed version of older stories about Moses leading Israel out of Egypt to the wilderness. This chapter focuses on the

L Source story of Abraham (Genesis 12–16, 18–22, 24) and the account of covenant making in the wilderness (Exodus 19–24, 32–4). Nevertheless, the source also included other stories about Moses and the Israelites such as the initial account of Israel's oppression in Egypt (Exod 1:8–12, 15–22), the story of Moses's early life and attempts to free Israel (Exod 2:1–22; 3:1–5:1), a strand of the story of the plagues on Egypt and deliverance at the Red Sea, and various stories about Israel in the wilderness (e.g. Exodus 17–18) up through Moses's address to Israel in Deuteronomy just before entry into the land. If you want to imagine this source, try to picture a text that included Pentateuchal stories such as the J primeval history, Genesis 12–16, 18–22, etc., but did not have stories such as the Priestly creation story (Gen 1:1–2:3), the genealogy in Genesis 5, the covenant of circumcision in Genesis 17, etc. We have no manuscript of this separate L Source, but scholars have agreed on its basic contours for over one hundred years.

This L Source was a composite source, a combination of older building blocks and new material, probably created (as a whole) during the exile. An analogy can be seen in some ancient villages found in the hill country of Israel even today. Many buildings in such villages are a combination of old and new. The walls beginning at the ground may come from an older building, but then they are continued with newer materials that extend up to the roof. The yard walls may have an old Greek column built into them or another piece of ancient architecture embedded in newer mortar. So also the L Source was built in part around older literary building blocks such as the J primeval history (see Chapter 3 of this *Introduction*), the covenant code (see Chapter 3), revised forms of the Jacob and Joseph stories originally written in the northern kingdom (see Chapter 4), and a more thoroughly transformed version of the story of Moses written in the early northern kingdom (see Chapter 4). But such building blocks do not make a house. The major shape and emphases of the L Source came from those who used these older literary building blocks to create a broader story of Israel's existence before the land, a story that extended from creation to Moses.

We gain insight into the broader values of the L Source by looking at themes that link its various parts together, binding the primeval history to the stories of the patriarchs and matriarchs and these stories to the Moses–exodus story. As was suggested above, the main theme that unites these various parts of the L Source is the theme of promise to the ancestors. This theme first appears in the Abraham story, when Abraham receives a promise of blessing from Yahweh (Gen 12:1–3) that contrasts with the theme of curse that frequently occurred across the older J primeval history (Gen 3:14, 17; 4:11; 5:29; 8:21; 9:25). The rest of the Abraham story is saturated with this theme of promise. Chapters 12–13 show that Abraham, not Lot, received the promise; chapter 15 stresses that Abraham will indeed have a child to inherit the promise of descendants and land; chapter 16 focuses on an attempt by Abraham to gain such a child through his wife's servant, Hagar; parallel hospitality scenes in Genesis 18–19 again demonstrate Yahweh's preference for Abraham over Lot; and other stories throughout the Abraham narrative show Yahweh's deliverance of family members connected to Abraham on account of the promise (Gen 12:10–20; 20; 21). Finally, in a strange story that has deeply moved Jewish, Christian, and Muslim interpreters (Genesis 22), Yahweh endangers Abraham's son, Isaac, in asking Abraham to burn him as a sacrifice (Gen 22:1–2). When Abraham shows a

The L Source: Terms for It and Pictures of Its Formation

Many scholars would use other terminology for the L or Lay Source discussed here, terminology that reflects a different picture of the formation of this source than that which is presented in this textbook.

An older hypothesis: J ("Yahwistic Source") and E ("Elohistic Source")

Throughout the twentieth century, most bible specialists believed that the material discussed here as L contained two yet earlier sources: a J Source composed in Judah around the time of Solomon and an E Source composed in (northern) Israel sometime in the eighth century. The **J Source** or **Yahwistic Source** was so called because it frequently used the divine name "Yahweh," which, in the German language of those who pioneered this theory, is spelled with an initial "J." The **E Source** or **Elohistic Source** was so called because it more frequently preferred the divine name "Elohim," which means "god" in Hebrew. For example, earlier scholars maintained that the bulk of Genesis 12–16 and 18–19 came from the hypothesized J Source (note the predominance of "LORD" = Yahweh), while parallel stories about Abraham found in Genesis 20–2 were from E (note the predominance of "God" in these chapters).

Problems for the older hypothesis

Many scholars still find this idea of J and E persuasive. Nevertheless, many, if not most, specialists in the study of the Pentateuch have abandoned this approach, for several reasons. First, there are many elements of J and E that link conceptually with later periods of Israel's history, thus making it unlikely that they were early pre-exilic sources. Second, aside from the Abraham story and a handful of other texts, scholars have had a lot of trouble gaining consensus on what might have been the contents of J and E. Third, in cases such as the Abraham story, there are indicators that the hypothesized J texts were shaped in relation to the E texts and vice versa. This suggests that some parts of the Bible divided between J and E were not from separate (written) sources, but from diverse, possibly oral traditions.

Terminology

Scholars who still maintain this older approach would call the texts under discussion here "JE," a term for the combination of the hypothesized J and E documents. Those specialists who no longer believe in J and E often refer to these texts more neutrally as "non-P"; that is, the bulk of texts not assigned to the Priestly Source (to be discussed shortly). This textbook adopts the more positive term L Source or Lay Source to designate these texts, reflecting their links with non-priestly, lay leaders, probably of the exilic period.

willingness to act on Yahweh's request (Gen 22:3–11), Yahweh stops him from sacrificing Isaac and reaffirms the promise to him (Gen 22:12–18). The L Source story of Abraham then concludes with a story of Abraham sending his servant back home to seek a proper wife for Isaac (Genesis 24), a story that likely reflects the increasing emphasis on avoidance of intermarriage that was typical of the exile and later periods.

Indeed, there are many things that lead scholars to suppose that these stories about Abraham were shaped during the Babylonian exile (or later). The exile is the first time we see mention of Abraham as a major figure in datable prophecies – those of Ezekiel (33:24) and Second Isaiah (Isa 41:8; 51:2) – and both exilic prophets show exiles taking comfort from the idea of Yahweh's promise to Abraham. It was during the exile that Abraham became a symbol of Yahweh's promise to Yahweh's people, a symbol that could give hope to exiles who – like Abraham – were small in number and powerless in a country not their own. It was when the Judean exiles themselves lacked a land and felt themselves cursed that they talked about Abraham and referred ever more often to God's promise to him. They focused less on the history of the monarchy and, instead, emphasized stories about their history before entering the land – about their ancestors and Moses – that most closely approximated their current condition. As we will see at the conclusion of this chapter, the L version of the Abrahamic promise in Gen 12:1–3 even takes promises of blessing and fame that once were given to the Judean king and applies them to Abraham, the landless patriarch. This kind of transfer of themes from a past governmental context (in this case, the monarchy) to a new, non-governmental context (in this case, the life of an emigrant) is typical for people undergoing exile. It is one among many signs that these L stories about Abraham were shaped and written down by exiles seeking hope in this promise-centered picture of their ancestor, Abraham.

Yet we have seen that these exiles also were sorely conscious of their shortcomings. They felt Yahweh's anger at them, and many wondered if Yahweh could still live with them after their misdeeds (in their view) had caused the destruction of the Temple and exile into Babylonia. As a result, both Ezekiel and Second Isaiah had to reassure the exiles, who doubted that Yahweh would redeem them, *despite their past and present shortcomings*. Similar themes run through the Lay Source version of the stories of the patriarchs. Like the exiles whom Ezekiel and Second Isaiah addressed, so also the Abraham character in Genesis – the ancestral model of an exile in the L Source – doubts God's promise of protection and lies about Sarah being his wife (Gen 12:10–20; 20:1–18). He also shows doubts concerning God's promise of a son by arranging to have a son through Hagar (Genesis 16). Later on, as a result of the addition of the promise theme to the older Jacob narrative (see the Miscellaneous Box on "The Story of Jacob at Bethel as an Example of the Exilic Addition of Promise to an Older Story"), the stories about Jacob in L now depict him as receiving the promise (Gen 28:13–15) despite having cheated his brother and tricking his father (Genesis 25, 27). Yahweh's promise apparently does not depend on the absolute virtue of its recipients.

The L Source story of Yahweh's covenant with Israel at Sinai (Exodus 19–24, 32–4) provides the clearest illustration of this theme of Yahweh's steadfast love. It stresses Yahweh's forgiveness of Israel even in the wake of Israel's building of the golden calf. This is not an easy forgiveness. The building of the golden calf in Exod 32:1–6 is depicted in the L text as an awful act, one that point by point reverses the covenant that Yahweh just made with Israel. Where Yahweh had just led Israel out of Egypt (Exod 19:4), the people now think Moses did (Exod 32:1); where Yahweh specifically prohibited making "gods of gold and silver" (Exod 20:22–3), the people now feel the need to make a golden calf to lead them in the wilderness (Exod 32:1); and where the previous covenant with

The Story of Jacob at Bethel as an Example of the Exilic Addition of Promise to an Older Story

Many scholars now think that the speech in which God gives Abraham's promise to Jacob in Gen 28:13–15 (along with his reaction in 28:16) was added secondarily into a story about Jacob at Bethel that once only focused on angels going up and down a stairway there. The material in **boldface** below probably was added to an original story about the "gate of heaven." Try reading the story without the boldface elements. How is it different?

> And he [Jacob] dreamed, and, look!, a stairway founded on the earth with its top in heaven. And, behold, divine messengers were going up and down it.
> **And, look!, Yahweh was standing on it and said, "I am Yahweh, the god of Abraham, your father and the god of Isaac. The land on which you are lying I will give to you and your children . . . all clans of the earth shall bless themselves by you and your descendents . . .**

And Jacob woke up from his sleep and said, "Look, Yahweh is in this place, and I did not know it."
And he [Jacob] was afraid and said, "how awesome this place is! It is nothing other than the house of God and the gate of heaven." . . . He called that place Bethel [Hebrew: "house of God/El"]. (Gen 28:12–13, 14b, 16–17, 19a)

Before the exilic, Lay Source addition of the promise theme, the older Jacob Bethel story (in regular type) was addressed to Israelites of the north. It connected the northern kingdom's royal sanctuary at Bethel, "the house of God and gate of heaven," with Jacob, the hero of the Israelites. Now, with the L additions of the promise and Jacob's response to it (the indented, **boldface** section), the new story connects this Jacob to the promise of land and blessing to Abraham (Gen 12:2–3), assuring Judean exiles of God's promise ultimately to them.

Yahweh was sealed with a feast, "whole offerings" and "shared offerings" (Exod 24:5), the very same things seal the new covenant that the Israelites, including Aaron, make with the golden calf (Exod 32:5–6). Faced with this golden calf anti-covenant, Yahweh of this L story is ready to destroy all of the Israelite people and start all over with Moses (Exod 32:7–10). It is only after Moses reminds Yahweh of the promises to the patriarchs and pleads with Yahweh to think about how the Egyptians would perceive such destruction (Exod 32:11–13) that Yahweh changes his mind (Exod 32:14). Punishment still comes. Moses recruits the Levites – who up until this point in the story are just another tribe – and their first act is to kill every Israelite that their sword can reach (Exod 32:26–9). In addition, Yahweh brings a plague on the people (Exod 32:35). Nevertheless, Yahweh eventually comes back near Israel via the "tent of meeting" (Exod 33:7–17), and makes a new covenant with Israel where the essentials of the previous laws are summarized (Exodus 34).

Thus, like the more hopeful prophecies in Ezekiel and Second Isaiah, the L Source stresses Yahweh's ability to work with his people *no matter what they do*. To be sure,

basics (Hypothesized) L Source

Outline: Yahweh's promise-based, unbreakable covenant	I	Gift of ancestral promise-covenant in the wake of repeated primeval problems	Genesis*
		A Problems with creation and post-flood	Genesis 1–11*
		B Gift of promise to Abraham and heirs	Genesis 12–50*
	II	Creation + preservation of Moses-led, covenant people	Exodus*, Numbers*

Date   Exile (building on earlier, pre-exilic compositions).

Themes   If we focus on the later L-Source materials and not their probable pre-exilic sources, the emphasis of the source seems to be on the gift of Yahweh's covenant despite any shortcomings in the recipients. We see this as early as Yahweh's gift and transmission of the covenant to Abraham, Isaac, and Jacob despite their misdeeds and occasional lack of trust. Then, in the Moses story, Yahweh perseveres in giving a covenant to Israel despite their making of the golden calf (Exodus 32) and lack of trust in the promise of conquest (Num 14:11–25), largely on the basis of the earlier promises to the patriarchs.

More information: the gap between ancestors and Moses   Scholars note that the L Source texts in the Pentateuch, aside from a few exceptions such as Genesis 15 or Exodus 32, do not explicitly link the time of the ancestors in Genesis with the time of Moses. This is an indicator to many that writings about the ancestors were not linked with those about Moses until a very late time. Before this time, the stories about Jacob–Joseph, and possibly even those about Abraham and Isaac, stood separately from the Moses story. They were an alternative account of how Israel became related to Yahweh and came into the land.

Thus the exilic link of the primeval, ancestral, and Moses traditions with each other was important. It took what were once competing traditions and put one (the ancestral traditions) before the other (the Moses traditions). Imagine: how would this kind of combination change the meaning of each block of tradition?

the L Source stories and exilic prophecies insist that God gets angry about disobedience and imposes consequences. Nevertheless, as in Ezekiel, Yahweh's ultimate promise to the people does not depend on their virtue. Yahweh saves Israel for the sake of his reputation ("name") and/or his promise to their ancestors. On this basis, the exiles can trust that Yahweh will lead them out of Babylonian bondage and back into their homeland, despite the fact that they have not always lived up to Yahweh's expectations for them, do not do so, and will not do so.

An alternative vision for exiles in the Priestly Pentateuchal Source (P)

Not everyone in the exile, however, would have appreciated the depiction of Israel's early history in the L Source. Alongside the elders, there was another prominent group of exilic leaders – the priests – and they do not come off well in the L Source, especially in the L Source story of the covenant at Sinai. In general, many lower-ranking priests traced their ancestry back to Jacob's son Levi, and the leading priests traced their descent to a particular Levite, Aaron. The L Source does not positively portray either Aaron or the descendants of Levi as a group. Within the L Source Aaron helps the people make the golden calf (Exod 32:1–6) and later challenges the authority of Moses (Numbers 12). Meanwhile, the L Source depicts the founding of the Levitical priesthood as a sad compromise. Yahweh had originally intended that *all* Israel would be a "nation of priests" (Exod 19:6), and this is shown in the fact that

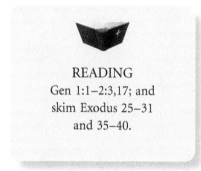

READING
Gen 1:1–2:3,17; and
skim Exodus 25–31
and 35–40.

young men (not special priests) help Moses make the sacrifices that seal the first covenant (Exod 24:5). Only after Aaron had helped make a golden calf does Moses set aside the Levites as a special group, and their first act is to kill every Israelite that they can reach (Exod 32:25–9). In sum, the L Source depicts the priesthood, particularly the Aaronide priesthood, as founded in idolatry and the shedding of Israelite blood – hardly the kind of picture the priests would want to paint of themselves.

These and other concerns probably led the leading Aaronide priests in exile to formulate their own story of Israel's history before it had taken possession of the land, a story aimed at replacing the L Source version of events with a version more favorable to the priests and their concerns. Although the present Pentateuch now has texts from this **P Source** or **Priestly Source** intertwined with the L Source, P probably stood separately from L when it was originally composed in the exilic period. There are too many repeated narrations of events in L and P for one of them to have been created as a supplement to the other, and there are several instances where the original point of a Priestly text is only clear when it is read separately from its Lay Source counterpart. Consider, for example, the divergent accounts in L and P of the reasons for Jacob's departure from Canaan. The L Source version of this story is the old trickster tale about Jacob stealing his father's blessing and fleeing Esau's murderous wrath (Gen 27:1–45). The (later) P version of these events aimed to provide a different reason: Esau had married foreign wives (Gen 26:34–5), those wives had been awful to Rebekah (Gen 27:46), and so Isaac blessed Jacob (on purpose!) and sent him homeward to get a proper wife (Gen 28:1–6). Though they are now separated from one another by the older trickster story (Gen 27:1–45), the P texts that give this alternative explanation connect well together (Gen 26:34–5; 27:46–28:6). They probably originally stood apart from the trickster story in Gen 27:1–45 and were designed to replace it.

Thus, we can learn something about texts from this exilic Priestly Source when we consider them apart from the Lay Source texts with which they are now combined. When the P Source was separate from the L Source, it chronicled God's involvement

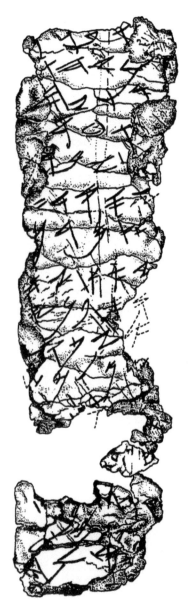

Figure 6.3 Silver amulet, dating to just before the fall of Jerusalem. It contained a version of the priestly blessing found in Num 6:24–6. The inscription proves that some texts now found in the Priestly layer of Genesis (e.g. Num 6:24–6) date to the pre-exilic period. This does not mean, however, that all of the Priestly layer can be dated to that period.

with the world in three major stages: (1) creation, (2) the flood and following covenant with Noah, and (3) the covenant with Abraham and eventual creation at Sinai of Israel out of the heirs to Abraham's promise. The first stage, found in Genesis 1:1–2:3 along with most of Genesis 5, is God's creation of an orderly and peaceful universe, a cosmos crowned by godlike humans who are made in God's image (Gen 1:26–31). The second stage, found in Priestly texts scattered across Genesis 6–9 (such as 6:9–22 and 9:1–17), describes God's actions after this creation was violated by violence: God's destruction of almost all life through a flood, God's rescue of Noah's family and other animals, and God's making of a covenant with Noah and the rest of life not to bring such a flood again. The third and most important stage in P is God's creation of the holy community of Israel. This starts with God's making of a special covenant of circumcision with Abraham (Genesis 17), a covenant in which God gives Abraham and his heirs a special version of the creation blessing given in Genesis 1 (Gen 17:6–8; compare Gen 1:27–8). Other Priestly texts in Genesis show the passing of this blessing on to Jacob (not Esau; Gen 26:34–5; 27:46–28:5; 35:9–15) and trace the genealogies of Abraham's offspring (Gen 25:7–18; 35:22–6; 36:1–43). Jacob in the P Source next goes to Egypt, where his descendants multiply into the people of Israel (Exod 1:1–7) and are oppressed by Pharaoh (Exod 1:13–14; 2:23–5). God then calls Moses and Aaron – in Priestly texts – to lead Israel out of Egypt through plagues and the dividing of the Red Sea (Exod 6:2–7:13; etc.). This prepares for the Priestly story of events and instructions given at Mount Sinai (most of Exodus 25 through Numbers 10). There God works through Moses to build a wilderness sanctuary, a "tabernacle," in which God can dwell (Exod 24:15–31:17; 35:1–40:33) and then instructs Israel (through Moses) on how it can become a holy community gathered round the tabernacle (Leviticus and Num 1:1–10:10). The other main narratives that were part of P focus on God's confirmation of Moses and Aaron's leadership of this new, holy community.

This mass of Priestly material contains some of the oldest texts in the Pentateuch. One Priestly text, the priestly blessing in Num 6:24–6, has been found on an ancient, pre-exilic silver amulet, our earliest copy of a text now in the Bible (see Figure 6.3), and scholars have found signs that other P laws and even some narratives may date from before the exile. Nevertheless, the overall sweep of the Priestly narrative shows several signs of being shaped in the exilic or early post-exilic periods:

- Where Deuteronomy and the rest of the Deuteronomistic history *argue* for the idea that sacrifice to Yahweh can only happen in *basics* (Hypothesized) P Source

Outline   I   Expanded genealogy: creation and promise
            A   Elohim: creation–re-creation   Gen 1:1–2:3; 5:1–9:28*; 11:10–26
            B   El-Shaddai: the Abrahamic covenant   Gen 11:27–50:26*
         II   Yahweh: Moses+Aaron-led pilgrimage
            A   Pilgrimage to Sinai   Exodus 1–19*
            B   Sinai indwelling and instruction   Exodus 20–Numbers 10*
            C   Pilgrimage from Sinai to the land   Numbers 11–36*

Date   Exile into post-exile (with short pre-exilic sources).

Themes: shifts in   As indicated in the outline above, some of the shifts in the Priestly Source correspond
the divine name   to shifts in the divine designation that it uses for God. In the primeval period God
            is known as *Elohim* (Hebrew for "God") and makes with Noah and all life a covenant
            that is marked by a rainbow. During the ancestral period God appears to Abraham
            as *El-Shaddai* (Hebrew for "God Almighty") and makes a covenant with him that
            is marked with circumcision and passed on by Abraham's heirs, Isaac and Jacob.
            In the final period, God appears to Moses and the rest of Israel as Yahweh (see the
            P version of Moses's call in Exod 6:2–8). The centerpoint of this period is Israel's
            stay at Sinai, where the tabernacle is built, the priesthood of Aaron and his sons is
            established, and Yahweh's glory comes down to dwell amidst Israel.

More   The bulk of past and present scholars believe that a shorter form of this Priestly
information: narrative once existed as a separate source, independent of the L texts with which
P as "redaction"   it is now combined. Others, however, believe that the Priestly texts of the Pentateuch
or separate   were written from the outset as an expansion of the L texts and never existed separ-
"source"?   ately. This alternative perspective – P as "redaction" – can make a difference in how
            one understands the structure and themes of the first Priestly Pentateuch. Can you
            imagine how the above survey of P would have to be rewritten if P were an expan-
            sion of the L Source?

one place, the Priestly narratives appear to presuppose this. P does not describe
any sacrifice by Noah or the patriarchs before the establishment of the tabernacle
at Mount Sinai.

■   The P narrative focuses before Sinai on practices that could be carried out in exile
    and were particularly important then, such as circumcision (Genesis 17), an ancient
    form of Passover celebration that was celebrated at home (Exod 12:1–20), and
    Sabbath (Exodus 16).

- Consistent with tendencies of exilic communities to focus on communal boundaries, the P document includes a prominent emphasis on the importance of ethnic purity and the problems with intermarriage, an emphasis seen particularly clearly in the story of Isaac's rejection of Esau because of intermarriage and his sending of Jacob to Haran to get a proper wife (Gen 26:34–5; 27:46–28:9).

basics Book of Leviticus

Outline	I	Establishment of the tabernacle cult	1–10
		A Instructions for sacrifices	1–7
		B Establishment of priesthood subject to instructions	8–10
	II	Establishment of holy people	11–26
		A Purity rules	11–15
		B Holiness Code	16–26

Date Exilic to early post-exilic (building on pre-exilic sources).

Themes Leviticus now stands at the center of the Pentateuch, and it represents the center of Priestly teaching. Though the book starts with specific instructions for priestly sacrifice (Leviticus 1–7), it concludes with rules for creating a holy, priest-like people (Leviticus 16–26). Many eating and purity rules, once meant only for priests, are extended in Leviticus to the whole people of Israel. These cultic rules are not seen as a burden in the book or difficult to follow. Instead, they are an affirmation of the special, particularly holy character of Yahweh's beloved people.

More information: the "Holiness Code" Some past scholars identified Leviticus 17–26 as a "**Holiness Code**" (**H**) that contains distinctive laws, close in perspective to the prophet Ezekiel. This code may have existed before P and been inserted into its present context by a Priestly or later author. Like both the Covenant Code and Deuteronomy, this Holiness Code started with a law about where to sacrifice (Leviticus 17).

Other scholars, such as Israel Knohl (*The Sanctuary of Silence: The Priestly Torah and the Holiness School* [Minneapolis: Fortress, 1995]), see the bulk of Leviticus 17–26 as part of a broader H layer of texts found throughout the Pentateuch. According to Knohl and others, the texts in this H layer are distinguished in language and thought from *earlier*, originally separate Priestly traditions, such as those found in Gen 1:1–2:3 or Exodus 19–25, 35–40.

■   The P document as a whole leads up to the story of God's creation of the wilderness tabernacle with the priests of Aaron at its head. This points to an exilic time when the monarchy is no longer a living institution, and its accoutrements (e.g. a crown; Exod 28:36–8) are assumed by the priests.

The language and concerns of this Priestly document are closest to those of Ezekiel on the one hand and Second Isaiah on the other. Indeed, several scholars have shown that the author(s) of P seem(s) to know Second Isaiah and speak in a similar time period. Like Second Isaiah, the author of the P story encourages exiles to return to the land, in this case through stressing God's power in the exodus, the importance of the land in the promise (see Exod 6:2–8), and God's punishment of those who lack enough belief to embrace God's promise and return (Num 13:32; 14:36–7). In these ways and others, the narratives of P show the impact of the Babylonian exile, along with hopes of return, on the Priestly understanding of Israel's history before the conquest. Though the authors of this P document drew freely on pre-exilic texts of various kinds, the

MORE ON METHOD: INSIGHTS FROM HISTORY OF RELIGIONS

Often we can learn more about the ancient images, metaphors, and ideas in the Bible through looking at other ancient religious ideas and practices studied as part of what is sometimes termed "**history of religions.**" An example is the tantalizing reference to being made "in the image of God" in Gen 1:26–7.

The king as the image of god in the ancient Near East

Texts in both Mesopotamia and Egypt depict the king as an image of god, representing that god on earth much as a divine statue would. For example, one Mesopotamian letter to the king says:

> The father of the king, my lord, was the image of [the god] Bel, and the king, my lord, is likewise the image of Bel.

Similarly, an Egyptian text has the god Amun proclaim about the king:

> You are my beloved son, who came forth out of my love, my image that I set on earth. I let you rule the land in peace.

How this might inform a reading of Gen 1:26–7

These royal ideas are applied to all of humanity in Gen 1:26–7, both the idea of being made in god's image and the idea of this divine image being a mark of authority to rule others.

whole that they put together is a distinctively exilic story for exiles about ancient Israel before the people had a land.

We can see the distinctive mix of older and later materials in the seven-day creation account with which the Bible opens: Gen 1:1–2:3. On the one hand, scholars have found some signs that this chapter was formed out of older materials, and Jeremiah may show knowledge of an older form of this story when he refers to earth as "formless and void" and heaven as "having no light" (Jer 4:23; see Gen 1:1–3). On the other hand, like other texts in P, this story as we have it now links with issues and themes that became particularly prominent in the exile. For example, the whole structure of the text is oriented around a seven-day scheme that climaxes in God's observance of the Sabbath (Gen 2:1–3). We see a similar emphasis on the Sabbath in Ezekiel (Ezek 20:12–24; 22:8, 26; 23:38).

History and Fiction

By this point many readers may be wondering, "But what about what actually happened with Abraham or at Sinai? Does all this just mean that the exiles made all these stories up?" To this, the answer is both "no" and "yes." The answer is "no," because ancient peoples, including ancient Israel, almost always built new stories out of older ones. Especially with respect to stories about people (rather than gods), ancient authors almost always started with a tradition – whether oral or written – about a given person and then built on that tradition. They did not "make them all up." Yet there is also a sense in which the answer to the question is "yes." Ancient authors did make up certain things. Unlike many contemporary historians, these ancient authors felt free to embellish, modify, and extend the traditions given to them. In light of their experience of exile, for example, exilic authors found new, promise-centered ways to tell stories about Jacob and Moses, ways that would never have occurred to them before. They saw these stories through the lens of truths they had learned in exile. As a result, they retold, extended, and connected these stories in light of these truths, in light of what they believed "must have happened."

Now we no longer can untangle later "truths" learned in exile or other periods from the kinds of "historical truth" about Israel's early history that contemporary readers often want to know. Through using both data from archaeology and analysis of non-biblical literature, we can affirm that the traditions in the Pentateuch, both L and P, probably have some kind of historical core. Later storytellers would not have made up characters such as Abraham and Sarah. Certainly, exiles would not have created a deliverer figure like Moses with an Egyptian name and foreign wives. Nevertheless, it appears that the stories as we have them now, including almost all their dialogue and other details, reflect their settings in later periods of Israel's history. As a result, they are more useful as sources for the "truths" learned by Israelites in these later periods than in reconstructing historical "truths" about the times of Abraham and/or Moses. We might wish we knew exactly what Sarah said to God or Moses said to Pharaoh, but the biblical texts about them are not good sources for this. They *can* tell us, however, what later Israelites had to say to each other about their identity as a people and God's intentions toward them.

Let us consider this in relation to a concrete example: the L Source story of covenant at Sinai discussed above (Exodus 19–24, 32–4). Contemporary readers of this story could argue endlessly about whether or not it actually happened. Yet in the end, such arguments miss the larger point of the story. The story that we now have is addressed to Israel of the "thousandth" generation, long after Sinai, an Israel who wonders – as in the laments discussed above – whether God will be eternally angry for past disobedience or will turn and save God's people. The answer given in this story is a decisive affirmation of God's intent to save the people no matter what. This text, with its "yes" to God's mercy, has been absolutely central to Jewish worship and thought, and this affirmation of God's unconditional relationship with Israel can be read by Christians as an anticipation of God's broader unconditional grace toward the world as seen through Jesus Christ. Ultimately, such "truths" about God in Judaism and Christianity are much more central to the ongoing significance of the Bible than specific historical "truths" that could be affirmed or uncovered using modern historical methods. Moreover, these important ideas in ancient biblical texts can be missed if the debates about them all focus on whether or not the events described in them actually happened.

FOCUS
TEXT

Gen 12:1–3

Let us conclude by taking a brief look at God's first speech to Abraham, still called "Abram" at this point, in Gen 12:1–3. This text has two main parts: Yahweh's command to Abram to "go now from your country, your kindred, and your father's house to the land that I will show you" (Gen 12:1), and the following promises that Yahweh will make Abram into "a great nation," make his "name great," and grant him abundant blessing (Gen 12:2–3). These promises echo a more ancient prayer for kings, seen in Ps 72:17, that the king be blessed, have his "name" (reputation) endure forever, and be so fortunate that others "bless themselves by him." This means that the king will be such a paradigm of good luck that others wish on themselves the kind of blessing that the king enjoys (for example, "may God make me as blessed and fortunate as king David of Israel"). Now, in the climactic promise in Gen 12:3, Abram is promised that he, like such kings, will be such an example of blessing that all "clans of the earth" will look to him and bless themselves by him, so that people in other nations might say something like, "may God bless me like Abram and more so."

This promise is echoed in various forms throughout other parts of Genesis (Gen 22:15–18; 26:2–5; 28:13–15), yet Christians and Jews disagree in a basic way on how to interpret the final part about Abram's blessing and other nations: "all the clans of the earth shall . . ." Many Jews follow the lead of Rashi, one of the greatest Jewish commentators on the Bible, who followed a translation much like that given above: that all clans of the earth shall "bless themselves by" Abram; that is, wish on themselves a blessing as good as the one he has. Understood this way, the rest of the Pentateuch following Gen 12:1–3 is a story of God's (partial) fulfillment of the special promises of blessing on Abraham and his offspring, especially God's blessing and protection of

God's chosen people, Israel. In contrast, many Christians follow the lead of Paul in understanding this text as a promise to Abram that "all the gentiles shall be blessed through you" (Gal 3:8), that blessing will flow through Abram – by way of Jesus Christ – to the other nations of the earth. Understood this way, the rest of the Pentateuch following Gen 12:1–3 is not focused on God's blessing and protection of Israel per se, but on the way the people of Israel, Abram's offspring, are a medium of blessing for the other nations of the earth. Thus, these two options for translating the promise in Gen 12:3, both of which are possible in Hebrew, lead to very different understandings of the whole Pentateuch. Rashi's reading remains closest to the emphasis on the people of Israel in the rest of the Hebrew Torah. Paul's reading – reflected in many contemporary translations of Gen 12:3 – reinterprets Abraham's promise in the context of a broader Christian Bible that includes Jesus Christ.

Turning to historical interpretation, Gen 12:1–3 looks quite different depending on whether one thinks it was written by Solomon's scribes or by exilic authors. Some would see Gen 12:1–3 as part of an early continuation of the J primeval history, a continuation written to support and endorse Solomon's kingdom. Read this way, God's promises of greatness and blessing to Abram in Gen 12:1–3 anticipate the time when Israel will "become a great nation" under Solomon, and Solomon will enjoy an immense reputation and fabled blessing. If this is correct, Gen 12:1–3 and the rest of the extended J/Yahwistic document thus provide divine sanction to Solomon's mini-empire. This has led some, such as Walter Brueggemann in his influential book, *The Prophetic Imagination* (Minneapolis: Fortress, 2001), to criticize texts such as Gen 12:1–3 because they see them as J texts endorsing an oppressive empire.

Things look quite different, however, if one understands Gen 12:1–3 and other promise texts to be words of hope to despairing exiles in the wake of the destruction of Jerusalem and loss of the monarchy. Put in this context, Gen 12:1–3 (like Gen 1:1–2:3) is a story where a non-royal figure, Abram, receives promises that were once given to kings. We have seen similar exilic gifts of royal promises to other figures in Second Isaiah – to the Persian Cyrus in Isa 44:28–45:1 and to the people in Isa 55:3. Yet the author of Gen 12:1–3 and surrounding texts tells the Abram/Abraham story in a special way, so that Abraham almost sounds like an exile living long before the Babylonian exile. He is made into someone to whom the exiles can relate. Like them, he lives in Babylon, "Ur of the Chaldees" (Gen 11:28), and, like them, he has been called to go and live as a stranger in a land he does not know (Gen 12:1). In light of this, the promises to Abram become promises of hope to the exiles, much like the prophecies of hope to exiles that we saw in the exilic portions of Isaiah (40–55), Jeremiah, and Ezekiel. Where the exiles longed for a restoration of their nation, they hear in Gen 12:2 that their ancestor Abram, also an exile, was promised that he would "become a great nation." Where we know that the exiles felt "cursed" because of their exile, this text asserts the opposite: they will be so blessed that they will become an example of blessing to other peoples on earth (Gen 12:3). Moreover, there is an additional promise in Gen 12:2–3 that relates specifically to the vulnerability that exiles faced when living as a minority in a larger culture. God reassures Abram of God's protection. God will bless those who bless him, and God will curse those who so much as "treat [him] lightly" (Gen 12:3).

Exiles would have heard this as a promise that God will provide similar protection to them, as Abraham's children, while living in Babylon.

Concluding Reflections on Torah (Pentateuch) and Exile

In sum, it makes a big difference whether you read Gen 12:1–3 and related texts as endorsing Solomon's mini-empire or as reassuring exiles who have been crushed by the Neo-Babylonian empire. This book has followed recent scholarship that dates Gen 12:1–3 and other L promise texts to the exilic period. Yet whatever the date of the L and P texts, it was during the Babylonian exile, when Judean exiles most desperately needed words of hope, that these writings about God's promises to Abraham's children and God's formation of Israel in the wilderness moved to the center of the Hebrew Bible. It was during exile that stories of Israel's history before conquest and monarchy started to become the literary foundation on which everything else in the Bible was based.

Up through the exile, however, this literary foundation, this "Torah of Moses," was split in two: an L narrative (including Deuteronomy) and a quite different P narrative. Each text features different groups, groups probably responsible for preserving each narrative and expanding it. The L narrative features the "elders," a major group of lay leaders in the exilic and post-exilic periods. The P narrative features the Aaronide priests, a priestly group that first achieves dominance in the late exile and post-exilic periods. These groups, and their texts, remained independent throughout the exile. There was no unifying political structure in this period to bring them together; the monarchy was gone. We will not see conditions for unifying these L and P stories until the Persians sponsor the rebuilding of a community of returnee exiles in Jerusalem. We turn next to that important event.

CHAPTER SIX REVIEW

1. Know the meaning and significance of the following terms discussed in this chapter:

- Deutero-Isaiah
- divine council
- E (or Elohistic) Source
- H
- history of religions
- Holiness Code
- intertextuality
- J (or Yahwistic) Source
- L (or Lay) Source
- monotheism
- non-Priestly or non-P
- P (or Priestly) Source
- Second Isaiah
- servant [in Second Isaiah]
- servant songs
- social-scientific analysis

2. What insights can we gain into the experience of ancient Judeans in exile from survey of contemporary social-scientific studies of people living outside their homelands?

3. Where do the exilic edition of the Deuteronomistic history and the book of Ezekiel disagree? Why was this important in this period?

4. Why would the "argument from prophecy" in Isaiah 48 not work as well if it were composed by eighth-century Isaiah?

5. What are two types of "intertextuality" studied by biblical scholars? Give two examples of such study from Second Isaiah. Can you think of other potential examples?

6. What sorts of "history" are best discussed in relation to the Pentateuch? How?

RESOURCES FOR FURTHER STUDY

Sociology of exile

Smith-Christopher, Daniel L. *Religion of the Landless: The Social Context of Babylonian Exile*. Bloomington, IN: Meyer-Stone Books, 1989.

Ezekiel

Blenkinsopp, J. *Ezekiel*. Interpretation. Atlanta: John Knox Press, 1990.
Greenberg, M. *Ezekiel 1–20; Ezekiel 21–37*. Anchor Bible. New York: Doubleday, 1983, 1997.

Second Isaiah

Blenkinsopp, Joseph. *Isaiah 40–55: A New Translation with Introduction and Commentary*. Anchor Bible. New York: Doubleday, 2002.
Muilenburg, James. "Isaiah 40–66: Introduction and Exegesis." Pp. 381–783 in vol. 5 of *The Interpreter's Bible*. Nashville: Abingdon, 1956.

More on the formation of the Pentateuch

Carr, David. *Reading the Fractures of Genesis*. Louisville, KY: Westminster John Knox Press, 1996.

Genesis

Brueggemann, Walter. *Genesis*. Interpretation. Atlanta: John Knox Press, 1982.

Sarna, N. M. *Genesis*. Jewish Publication Society Torah Commentary. Philadelphia: Jewish Publication Society, 1989.

Westermann, Claus. *Genesis: A Practical Commentary*, trans. David Green. Grand Rapids: Eerdmans, 1987.

Exodus

Childs, Brevard. *The Book of Exodus: A Critical Theological Commentary*. Old Testament Library. Philadelphia: Westminster Press, 1974.

Johnstone, William. *Exodus*. Old Testament Guides. Sheffield: Sheffield Academic Press, 1990.

Sarna, Nahum. *Exodus*. JPS Torah Commentary. Philadelphia: Jewish Publication Society, 1991.

Leviticus

Gerstenberger, Erhard S. *Leviticus: A Commentary*. Old Testament Library. Louisville, KY: Westminster John Knox Press, 1996.

Gorman, Frank H. *Divine Presence and Community: A Commentary on the Book of Leviticus*. International Theological Commentary. Grand Rapids: Eerdmans, 1997.

Numbers

Budd, Philip J. *Numbers*. Word Biblical Commentary. Waco, TX: Word, 1984.

Olson, Dennis. *Numbers*. Interpretation. Louisville, KY: Westminster John Knox Press, 1996.

Wenham, Gordon J. *Numbers*. Old Testament Guides. Sheffield: Sheffield Academic Press, 1997.

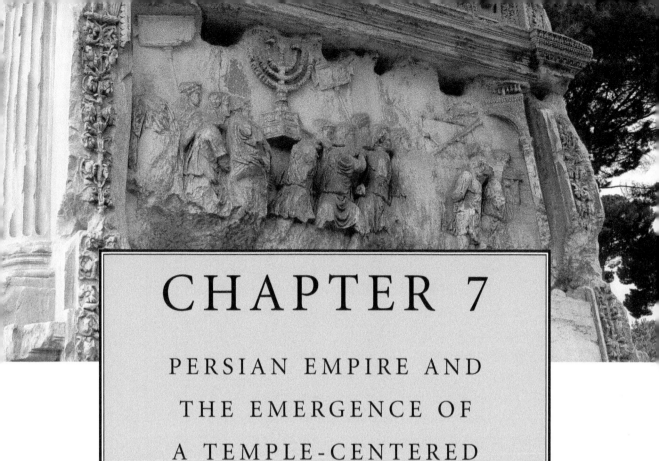

CHAPTER 7

PERSIAN EMPIRE AND THE EMERGENCE OF A TEMPLE-CENTERED JEWISH COMMUNITY

Chapter Outline

CHAPTER OVERVIEW

This chapter traces how central parts of the Hebrew Bible subtly reflect a *positive* relationship between Judeans and the Persian empire inaugurated by Cyrus. We will see how the Persians played a supportive role at several stages in the restoration of Judah, allowing many exiles to return and helping establish a Temple-centered community of returnees in Jerusalem (see Figure 7.1). In significant ways, the present Hebrew Bible, and especially the Torah/Pentateuch, is a collection of Hebrew texts made by former exiles sponsored by the Persian government. The multiple links to Persia help explain why biblical texts criticize the Assyrian and Babylonian empires but adopt a positive tone the few times they mention Persia.

The other major theme of the chapter, however, is diverse perspectives during this period on who was included in this rebuilt community. We will see how some returned exiles, especially Ezra, felt it important to purify the community so that it would never have to undergo exile again. Building on lessons they felt they had learned during exile, these leaders required Judean men to divorce foreign wives and expel them and their children. Meanwhile, other texts, such as chapters 56–66 of Isaiah and the books of Ruth and Jonah, provide an alternative accent on God's mercy toward foreigners and on ways foreigners who were attached to Yahweh (such as Ruth) could be crucially important for the people of Yahweh. Thus, even as the community was uniting around Temple and Torah in this Persian period, we once again encounter multiple biblical voices from a given time speaking quite different words.

Figure 7.1 Relief from the Persian capital of Persepolis. It depicts the many subjects of the Persian empire, dressed in the distinctive dress of each country, bearing tribute to the Persian king. The image well illustrates ways that the Persian empire cultivated the support of diverse cultures for its far-flung empire.

The Persian-Sponsored Building of a Temple- and Torah-Centered Judaism

READING

Zechariah 1 and 4; Haggai 1:1–2:9, the Nehemiah memoir (Neh 1:1–7:4; 13:10–14, 30b–31) and rebuilding/Ezra narrative (Ezra 1–10 and Neh 8; recommended: compare this with 1 Esdras in the Apocrypha); Isaiah 56:1–8 (part of the Persian-period material in Isaiah). Recommended: Jonah, Ruth, and Job 1–5, 38–42.

EXERCISE

Using the parallel below, compare and contrast the Persian king Cyrus's edict about his anointing by the Babylonian gods (Marduk, Bel, and Nabu) with Ezra 1:1–4.

Cyrus cylinder	Ezra 1:1–4
"I am Cyrus, king of the world, great king, mighty king, king of Babylon, king of the land of Sumer and Akkad, king of the four quarters, son of Cambyses . . . whose rule Bel and Nabu cherish, whose kingship they desire for their hearts' pleasures. . . . I did not allow any to terrorize the land of Sumer and Akkad. I kept in view the needs of Babylon and all its sanctuaries to promote their well being. The citizens of Babylon . . . I lifted their unbecoming yoke . . .	1:2 Thus says King Cyrus of Persia:
At my deeds Marduk, the great Lord, rejoiced, and to me, Cyrus, the king who worshipped, and to Cambyses, my son, the offspring of my loins, and to all my troops he graciously gave his blessing, and in good spirit before him we glorified exceedingly his high divinity.	"Yahweh, the God of heaven, has given me
All the kings who sat in the throne rooms, throughout the four quarters, from the Upper to the Lower Sea, those who dwelt in . . . all the kings of the West Country who dwelt in tents, brought me their heavy tribute and kissed my feet in Babylon.	all the kingdoms of the earth,
From . . . to the cities of Ashur and Susa, Agade, Eshnuna, the cities of Zamban, Meurnu, Der, as far as the region of the land of Gutium, the holy cities beyond the Tigris whose sanctuaries had been in ruins over a long period, the gods whose abode is in the midst of them I returned to the places and housed them in lasting abodes.	and he has commanded me to build a house for him in Jerusalem which is in Judah. 1:3 Any of you who are from his people – may his God be with him!
I (also) gathered together all their inhabitants and restored to them their dwellings.	– are now allowed to go to Jerusalem in Judah, and rebuild the house of Yahweh, the God of Israel – he is the God who is in Jerusalem;
The Gods of Sumer and Akkad whom Nabonidus had, to the anger of the Lord of the Gods, brought into Babylon, I, at the bidding of Marduk, the great Lord, made to dwell in peace in their habitations, delightful abodes." (Translation: ANET 316)	1:4 and let all who remain, wherever they live, be supported by the people of their place with silver and gold, with goods and with animals, besides freewill offerings for the house of God in Jerusalem."

Figure 7.2 The Cyrus cylinder.

The **Cyrus cylinder** quoted above (see Figure 7.2) marks another major shift of empires in the Near Eastern world. The Persian king, Cyrus, had just conquered Babylon without a fight, aided in part by disgruntled priests in Babylon who violently disagreed with the religious policies of Nabonidus, the last king of Babylon. Nabonidus had elevated the status of the moon god, Sin, over that of traditional Babylonian gods, and he had removed the divine statues of those gods from their sanctuaries across Babylon. In the Cyrus cylinder, Cyrus uses the Akkadian language and the form of an Akkadian inscription to describe how the Babylonian gods chose him to be king over Babylon and restore the divine statues to their proper places. Apparently, Cyrus's self-promotion was at least partially successful. A Babylonian priest wrote another text around the same time, called "the verse account of Nabonidus," that chronicles the religious crimes of Nabonidus, praises Cyrus's restoration of Babylon's sanctuaries, and concludes by saying that the people of Babylon now have "a joyful heart" and rejoice "to look upon Cyrus as king."

Though Cyrus never mentions Judah in his cylinder, we know from the Bible that the Judean exiles also celebrated this shift in power. Even before Cyrus had conquered Babylon, Second Isaiah had seen him on the horizon and quoted Yahweh as anointing Cyrus to subdue nations and rebuild Jerusalem (Isa 44:28–45:1). Furthermore, similar texts at the end of the books of Chronicles (2 Chr 36:22–3) and beginning of Ezra (Ezra 1:1–4) give a Judean version of Cyrus's proclamation, this time proclaiming that Yahweh has given him rule over all the earth and appointed him to rebuild Jerusalem. Since there is no Persian copy of such an inscription, we do not know if something like this was issued by the Persian government or whether it was created by Judean scribes on analogy with inscriptions like the Cyrus cylinder. In either case, these texts from Second Isaiah and the beginning of Ezra show an important development among the exiles. Where they hated Babylon, many fully supported the Persian empire and endorsed the idea that the Persian king, Cyrus, had been appointed by God to save and restore them.

Our main source for history of Judah in this period, Ezra–Nehemiah, appears to be another example of combination of separate sources, one that ends up focusing on Ezra and another on Nehemiah. Ezra–Nehemiah treats these figures separately, and several early Jewish sources seem to know their stories separately (including, in this case, an old Greek translation of the Ezra source, 1 Esdras). For these reasons, many scholars believe there are two main sources behind the present book of Ezra–Nehemiah: a Nehemiah memoir, which is a first person account by Nehemiah of how he rebuilt Jerusalem and provided for the Levites (Neh 1:1–7:4; parts of Nehemiah 13 and possibly 12), and a rebuilding/Ezra narrative about the rebuilding of Jerusalem and then Ezra's leading of the community to divorce foreign wives and obey the Torah (Ezra 1–10 and Nehemiah 8//1 Esdras). Only later, probably centuries later in the Hellenistic period, did an author interweave these two sources and add new materials, forming a new book where Ezra and Nehemiah overlapped. In the process, this much later author appears to have confused the order of the two figures, not knowing that there were two different Persian kings named "Artaxerxes." He mistakenly placed Nehemiah, who arrived and rebuilt Jerusalem's walls in the twentieth year of Artaxerxes *the first* (445 BCE) *after* Ezra, who found those walls rebuilt and probably arrived in the seventh year of Artaxerxes *the second* (397 BCE).

---

basics | Book of Haggai

Outline: blessing + new rulership after Temple rebuilding	I Oracles around the start of Temple rebuilding	
	A Prophetic-inspired beginning of rebuilding (including promise of blessing for rebuilding 1:2–11)	1:1–14
	B Encouragement: Zerubbabel's future riches	2:1–9
	II Oracles following up on start of rebuilding	
	A Renewed promise of blessing	2:10–19
	B Encouragement: Zerubbabel's future rule	2:20–3

Date   Fifth century BCE (400s, building on prophecies from 520 BCE).

Themes   In his original setting, Haggai promised his discouraged post-exilic community that investing now in rebuilding the Temple would yield returns of agricultural plenty and political independence under Zerubbabel. Amidst the turmoil of Darius's seizure of the throne of Persia in 522 BCE, Haggai may have hoped that Zerubbabel, a descendant of David, would re-establish the Davidic monarchy (2:23). Though this did not happen and the rebuilt Temple was later destroyed by the Romans (70 CE), the book of Haggai still preserves Jewish hope for renewal and restoration on the other side of another Temple rebuilding.

Along with these two main narratives – the Nehemiah memoir and Temple rebuilding/Ezra story – we also have the words of several prophets dated to this time as sources for learning about the period of the post-exilic restoration of the Jerusalem community. These include Haggai, Zechariah (particularly Zechariah 1–8), and post-exilic portions of Isaiah such as "Third Isaiah" in Isaiah 56–66. Using these sources, scholars have identified four main stages of the restoration, each of which seems to have featured some sort of Persian sponsorship: the return of some exiles to Judah, Zerubbabel and Joshua's rebuilding of the Jerusalem Temple, Nehemiah's rebuilding of the walls of Jerusalem, and Ezra's elevation of the Torah of Moses to the center of a Jerusalem community who had just expelled foreign wives and their children. The following paragraphs discuss each stage in turn before briefly considering the situation of Judeans still living abroad in Egypt and Mesopotamia.

basics Book of Zechariah

Outline: from Temple restoration to Yahweh's rule	I Zechariah's visions surrounding Temple rebuilding 1–8 II Later visions of Yahweh's establishment of rule 9–14

Date   Fifth century BCE (400s) for a form of Zechariah 1–8 (earlier oracles). Fourth century BCE (300s) for whole book (note Greeks in Zech 9:13).

Themes   The book of Zechariah is a combination of an earlier book surrounding eight visions attributed to Zechariah (Zechariah 1–8) and so-called "Deutero-Zechariah" (Zechariah 9–14). The earlier book, like Haggai, was associated with Temple rebuilding and the future rule of Zerubbabel and Joshua. Zechariah 9–14, however, lacks the superscriptions and dates of the earlier chapters that link them to Zechariah and the Temple-building process. Divided into two "oracles" (9–11 and 12–14), this latter part of the book envisions Yahweh's dramatic punishment of all Judah's enemies and the lifting up of Jerusalem to be the center of the world.

The biblical account of Cyrus's decree gives permission to exiles to "go up to Jerusalem which is in Judah and build the house of Yahweh, god of Israel, the god who is in Jerusalem" (Ezra 1:3). This introduces the first of a series of returns of exiles from Babylon to Jerusalem. The first wave, probably a tiny fraction of the exiles, returned under Sheshbazzar, a son of the exiled king Jehoiachin, shortly after Cyrus's defeat of the Babylonians in 539 BCE. The book of Ezra asserts that Cyrus even gave Sheshbazzar the Temple implements stolen by the Babylonians so that he could take them back to Jerusalem (Ezra 1:7–11), and Sheshbazzar is reported to have rebuilt the foundation of the Temple (Ezra 5:16). A few years later, around 520 BCE, one of Jehoiachin's grandsons, Zerubbabel, led another group of exiles back to Jerusalem. Still other exiles appear to have returned to Jerusalem under Ezra 120 years later (397 BCE; Ezra 7). In sum, not all exiles came back to Jerusalem, and those that did return came back in several waves. Many, if not most, exiles probably did not want to leave Babylonia. Some, such as Sheshbazzar and Zerubbabel, had assimilated enough to Babylonian culture to have Babylonian names, and we know from later documents of a Jewish family in Babylonia (in the Murashu archive) that some exiles remained there in subsequent centuries. This means that the expression "post-exilic period" is only accurate in indicating the end of *forced* exile, since many Judeans never stopped living away from their homeland.

In addition to allowing some Judeans to return to Judah, the Persians played a major role in the **rebuilding of the Jerusalem Temple** that had been destroyed by the Babylonians. This rebuilding, a centerpiece of Cyrus's decree in Ezra 1:1–4, happened in at least two stages. The first, mentioned above, was Cyrus's giving of the Temple vessels to Sheshbazzar and Sheshbazzar's delivery of these vessels to Jerusalem and laying of the foundations for this **Second Temple** there. This probably occurred shortly after Cyrus's victory over Babylon, around 538 BCE. This initial rebuilding work was not completed, however, until about twenty years later, from 520 to 515 BCE. By this point, Cyrus had died (in 530), his son Cambyses had reigned for eight years (530–522), and Darius, a more distant member of the royal family, had seized power in the wake of Cambyses's death. Darius gained support among peoples of his empire by reversing the harsh policies of Cambyses and rebuilding temples and priesthoods, especially in Egypt (which Cambyses had conquered and subdued). The rebuilding of the Temple in Jerusalem early in Darius's reign probably was part of this broader project. Yet an important shift in Judean leadership seems to have occurred sometime before the Jerusalem Temple was finished. Its rebuilding had begun under both the Davidic leadership of Zerubbabel and the priestly leadership of Joshua. Indeed, certain prophecies by Haggai (2:20–3) and Zechariah (the "branch" in 3:6–10; 6:9–14) indicate that some hoped that Zerubbabel would re-establish the monarchy in Jerusalem, working alongside Joshua. Yet we hear no more of Zerubbabel in traditions after the Temple was completed. No one knows why. From that point forward the Davidic monarchy was completely finished, and the time of Temple-centered Judaism had begun, the time of the Second Temple (515 BCE–70 CE).

The next major step in the restoration that we know much about is Nehemiah's rebuilding of the walls of Jerusalem seventy years later in 445 BCE. According to his memoir, Nehemiah was a cupbearer in the court of Artaxerxes, probably Artaxerxes I, who reigned from 464 to 423 BCE. Having heard reports of the dilapidated state of Jerusalem, Nehemiah convinced Artaxerxes to send him back to Jerusalem to rebuild the city (Neh 1:1–2:8). There he organized the Judean community to rebuild Jerusalem's walls, despite the opposition of neighboring peoples and internal dissenters (Neh 2:17–6:19). His role was that of Persian-appointed "governor" of Judah (Neh 5:14–19), a lay leader alongside the holy leadership of the priests. His biggest achievement was

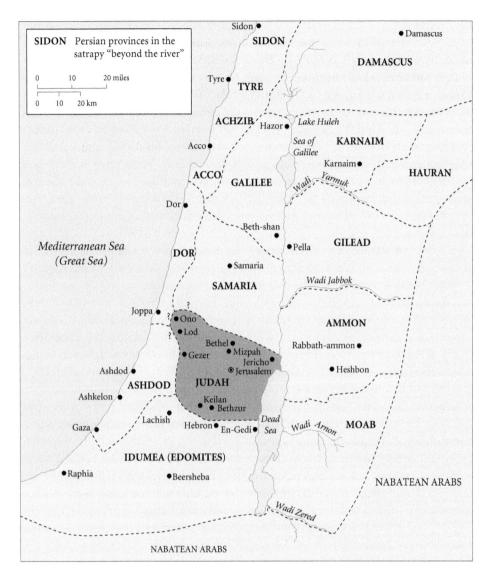

Map 7.1 Judah as a province of the Persian empire. Redrawn from Norman Gottwald, *The Hebrew Bible: A Socio-Literary Introduction*. Minneapolis: Fortress, 1985, page 406.

the re-establishment of Jerusalem as a walled city, an independent political entity (see Map 7.1). Sometime later, perhaps in a second term as governor, Nehemiah may have taken additional measures, such as the purging of the Jerusalem Temple of foreign priests (see Nehemiah 12–13). If so, this was an anticipation of more major purges that were to happen under Ezra.

Ezra took this purging to a new level as part of a more general program of centering Judaism on observance of the Torah of Moses. Like Nehemiah, Ezra was a highly placed Persian official – some sort of secretary in the Persian court. According to Ezra 7, he was commissioned by king Artaxerxes to bring offerings to the Jerusalem Temple and evaluate the extent to which people in the province were obeying "the law of god and the law of the king" (Ezra 7:26). There has been endless debate about what each of these laws contained, but the subsequent narrative of the reading of the "Torah of Moses" in Nehemiah 8 makes clear that something like the present Pentateuch is understood in this narrative to be "the law of god." Nevertheless, on his way to publicly reading and enforcing this holy law, Ezra comes to learn that earlier returnee Judean men have intermarried with foreign women and thus – in his mind – put at risk the whole project of the restoration of the people (Ezra 9:1–3). Many exiles such as Ezra perceived intermarriage with foreigners as a primary reason why Judah had gone into exile in the first place. Seeing this intermarriage among the returnee exiles, Ezra cries out to God:

> God has not forsaken us in our slavery, but has extended to us his steadfast love before the kings of Persia, to give us new life to set up the house of our God, to repair its ruins, and to give us a wall in Judea and Jerusalem.
>
> And now, our God, what shall we say after this? For we have forsaken your commandments, which you commanded by your servants the prophets, saying, . . . do not give your daughters to their sons, neither take their daughters for your sons, and never seek their peace or prosperity, so that you may be strong and eat the good of the land and leave it for an inheritance to your children forever. (Ezra 9:9–12 NRSV)

Ezra sees the whole Persian-sponsored process of the rebuilding of Jerusalem put into question by intermarriage of Judean men with "foreign women," probably a mix of actual non-Israelites and some Judeans who had not gone into exile. In response, Ezra urges all the men of Judah to divorce their foreign wives and expel them along with their children. This description of divorce of foreign wives (and expulsion of their children) is among the most difficult events for students to understand in the history of Israel. This seems to many to be a damaging and excessive way of preventing foreign influence. Within this context it may be helpful to remember three things. First, the documents that report such divorces – particularly the rebuilding/Ezra narrative – are far removed from the events they describe and may not be reliable historical records of those events. Second, insofar as such a divorce of foreign wives occurred, it was part of the returning community's attempt to avoid the mistakes of foreign influence that they believed caused the exile. Third, there are other biblical texts, likely dating from around the Persian period, that offer a different perspective on the role and significance of foreigners in relation to Judah/Israel. For example, the positive picture of Assyrians in the book of Jonah, the account in the book of Ruth of how David had a Moabite grandmother, or the inclusive vision of Israel in what is called "Third Isaiah" (Isaiah 56–66; see especially Isa 56:1–8) all suggest more perspectives on the role of foreigner in Israel (see the Miscellaneous Box on "Alternative Perspectives on Foreigners").

Within the rebuilding/Ezra narrative, the divorce of foreign wives is the prelude to Ezra's climactic reading of the "Torah of Moses" before all of Judah (Nehemiah 8),

basics Book of Isaiah

Outline: exhortation to repentance

I	Introduction: initial exhortation to repentance	1:1–31
II	Elaboration: restoration of Zion after purging judgment on it and the nations	2:1–64:12
III	Concluding paired oracles: consequences for the disobedient (65:1–66:4) and obedient	(66:5–24)

The above outline builds on scholars' observations of an inclusio in Isaiah, where themes appearing together in the exhortation to repentance in Isa 1:1–31 reappear again in the paired divine speeches to the disobedient and obedient in 65:1–66:24. In addition, several parts of the first half of the book, Isaiah 1–33, parallel portions of the second half, Isaiah 34–66:

Isaiah 1–33 (plan for Yahweh's rule from Zion)	*Isaiah 34–66 (initial realization of plan)*
Introduction: call to hear (Isaiah 1)	Call to hear revenge and restoration (Isa 34–5)
Commission of eighth-century Isaiah (Isaiah 6)	
Isaiah-Ahaz materials (Isaiah 7–8)	Isaiah–Hezekiah narratives (Isaiah 36–9) Commission of exilic prophet (40:1–11)
Anti-nations/Babylon (Isaiah 13–27)	Oracle against Babylon (Isaiah 47)
Oracles focused on Zion (Isaiah 28–32)	Oracles on Zion's restoration (49–66)

These and other patterns also bind the book together into a complex unity. It is a chorale of prophetic voices from different centuries, joining in witness to Yahweh, "the holy one of Israel," and his plans for Zion and the nations around it.

Date   Fifth century BCE (400s, building on earlier materials).

Themes   See the discussion in Chapters 4 and 6.

a Torah that seems (at least in this narrative) to be much like the present Pentateuch, with P and L sources combined into a single whole. This enactment of the "Torah of Moses" by Ezra is a major step in the formation of a Torah-centered Judaism. After this, virtually all groups in Judaism, whatever else they may disagree about, agree on at least one thing: the importance of the Torah of Moses.

Alternative Perspectives on Foreigners

History may be written by the winners, but, in the case of post-exilic Judah, the prophets and others got a chance to write a rejoinder. Indeed, several texts in the Hebrew Bible appear to respond to the hostility toward foreigners found in post-exilic traditions such as the Ezra stories. Sometimes the response to the issue takes the form of narrative, as in the story of God's grace toward Assyrians in the book of Jonah, Naomi's evolving attitude toward her Moabite daughter-in-law in the book of Ruth, or the story of an Edomite's unjust suffering in the book of Job. Sometimes, however, the response takes the form of direct prophetic engagement, as in the call in Isaiah 56:3 that the foreigner might not say "Yahweh will separate me from his people," an apparent response to post-exilic efforts to purify Israel through expelling foreigners. Though it is not certain that each of these texts dates from the post-exilic period, they address concerns about foreigners and foreign influence that became prominent in that time.

Much of the significance of all these changes can be seen when comparing Jerusalem of Ezra's time with the situation around the time of Ezra in Elephantine, a Jewish colony of mercenaries (soldiers for hire) settled in the southern Nile area of Egypt. This colony had its own temple, dating from before the rebuilding of the Jerusalem Temple.

Significant Dates in the Persian-Sponsored Restoration of Judah

Cyrus's defeat of Babylon	539 BCE
Wave 1 of returnees to Judah	538 BCE
Another wave of returnees with Sheshbazzar	532 BCE
Return of Temple implements, laying Temple foundation	
Another wave of returnees with Zerubbabel	520 BCE
Rebuilding of Second Temple	520–515 BCE
Nehemiah's return and governorships	445–425 BCE
Rebuilding wall, purification of priesthood	
Another wave of returnees with Ezra	397 BCE
Divorce of foreign wives	
(Combination of L+P?) Elevation of Torah	

The members of the community did correspond with leaders in Jerusalem and Samaria about various cultic matters, such as the celebration of Passover and rebuilding of their local temple, but they do not seem to have known the Torah of Moses advocated by Ezra, or to have followed the more stringent rules against foreign religions seen in the book of Deuteronomy. Only after many years did communities like this either die out or conform to the Torah-centered form of Judaism that arose in Jerusalem. Documents such as the Elephantine archives give us a small taste of the broad diversity of Jewish religion and life in the Persian period, which supplements the biblical accounts given by Jewish returnees to Jerusalem.

The Final Formation of the Torah

The major literary event of the Persian period of Judah's history was the completion of the Torah and its elevation to the center of post-exilic Judaism. This was a work as much or more about combining older texts as it was about the writing of new ones. Building on earlier traditions, Judeans in exile had already written larger stories of Israel's pre-land history in L (including Deuteronomy) and then P. These larger histories probably were separate from one another and cherished by the two major leadership groups in the exile and afterwards: the priesthood descending from Aaron (celebrated in P) and the elders (featured in L). Yet at some point an author combined these L and P sources into one, producing a Pentateuch much like the one we have now. The process of Persian governmental authorization described above may have played some role in this, since it would not have helped someone like Ezra to have the Persians authenticate *two* competing local narrative laws, L and P. Nevertheless, it would be a mistake to see this joining of traditions as a purely political process. Rather, whatever occasion prompted this creation of the combined Lay and Priestly Torah, there is evidence of considerable theological-literary genius in its execution.

READING

Gen 1:1–3:24; 26:34–28:7; Exodus 19–40.

One example of this is the combination of the L and P primeval narratives so that both human possibilities and human limitations are more fully expressed. Genesis starts with the Priestly narrative of creation, where God crowns the cosmos with the creation of humans "in our own image and likeness" (Gen 1:26–7), blesses humanity, and says that the whole creation is "very good." In our present Pentateuch this is now balanced by the garden of Eden story (Gen 2:4–3:24; originally part of the J primeval history and included in L). Now placed after the P creation story (Gen 1:1–2:3), this ancient text tells us more about the sixth "day" on which God created animal and human life (Gen 2:4; cf. 1:24–31). The Eden story ends with curses (Gen 3:14, 17–19) and stresses all of the problems that come from humans' eating the fruit of knowledge and seeking to be "like God" (Gen 3:1–19). In contrast to the P creation story, in which God made humans godlike from the beginning, in this L story God is anxious about humans becoming ever more godlike and expels them from the garden so that they will not gain divine immortality (Gen 3:23–4).

So goes the beginning of the L/P creation and flood story, a story that balances affirmation of human godlikeness (Gen 1:26–7; 5:1–3) and stress on God's care to preserve the divine–human boundary (Gen 6:1–4; 11:1–9). In this way and others, the L and P perspectives are put in a creative tension that is more theologically evocative than either one alone would have been.

We see a similarly majestic combination of sources in the Sinai narrative, where the combined L and P narrative describes God's overcoming of the divine–human boundary that was so carefully protected in the primeval history. As we saw in Chapter 6, the separate L and P sources described events at Sinai quite differently. The L Sinai story

basics **Book of Genesis**

Outline:	I	Story of creation and re-creation of humanity	1–11:26
the transmission	II	Yahweh's response: promise to ancestors	11:27–50:26
of the Abrahamic		A Abraham (and Lot)	11:27–25:11
promise to Jacob		B The next generation: non-heir and heir	25:12–35:39
as an answer to		1 Genealogy of Ishmael, the non-heir	25:12–18
the problems		2 Stories of Isaac's family, the heir	25:19–35:29
of creation		C The next generation: non-heir and heir	36:1–50:26
		1 Genealogy of Esau, the non-heir	36:1–37:1
		2 Stories of Jacob's family, the heir	37:2–50:26

Note: though the above outline focuses on men who inherit or do not inherit the promise, it is women such as Sarah and Rebekkah who play a prominent role in determining who inherits the promise (Isaac, Jacob) and who does not.

Date   Post-exilic (building on earlier sources).

Themes   Genesis is a grand synthesis of Priestly and non-Priestly, Lay texts. The introduction and structure of Genesis come from the Priestly Source. The book starts with the Priestly vision of creation in Genesis 1:1–2:3, and the rest of the book is punctuated with Priestly genealogical headings that now structure the whole (Gen 2:4; 5:1; 6:9; 10:1; 11:10, 27; 25:12, 19; 36:1; 37:2). Much of the substance of Genesis, however, is L, detailing Yahweh's struggles to interact with fallible humans, from Adam and Eve (Gen 2:4–3:24) to Joseph and his brothers (Genesis 37–50). The result of this combination is a book that presents both Yahweh's power to produce order and his struggles to effect his designs with humanity in general and Abraham's family in particular.

stressed God's forgiveness in the face of Israel's building of the golden calf, an act of idolatry that signaled the ultimate rejection of the covenant God had just made with them to make them a kingdom of priests (Exod 19:1–24:11; 32:1–34:35). The "elders" stand at the center of this L narrative (Exod 19:7; 24:1, 9), and God only appoints a special priesthood, the Levites, as a measure to punish the disobedient Israelites (Exod 32:26–8). In contrast, the Priestly story says nothing about any disobedience and focuses instead on God's founding of a wilderness sanctuary run by an Aaronide priesthood (Exod 24:15–31:18; 35:1–40:38; Leviticus; Numbers 1:1–10:10). The emphasis in P is on the creation of a holy people with a sanctuary and proper priesthood to atone for the people's sins.

When these two narratives were combined, the Priestly emphasis on the sanctuary for atonement became part of God's answer to the people's sin that was emphasized in the Lay narrative. Thus, our present combined (L/P) story in Exodus has two simultaneous scenes follow the L story of Yahweh's covenant with the people of Israel (Exod 19:1–24:14). On the mountain (here P material), God gives Moses instructions for creating the sanctuary through which the people can atone for their sin (Exod 24:15–31:18). At the very same time, down below (L material), the people build the golden calf and thus prove their desperate need for such a means of atonement (Exod 32:1–6). In the rest of the L/P Sinai account, the Priestly story of the building of the tabernacle sanctuary (Exod 35:1–40:38) becomes the crowning moment of the L Source story of Yahweh's gradual forgiveness of Israel and willingness to make a new covenant with them (Exod 32:7–34:35). The original L text describes God's new covenant with God's "stiff-necked" people (Exod 34:1–28; L) before the P text tells of how Moses led that people in building a tabernacle sanctuary through which they could atone for their sins (35:1–40:33; P).

This event is a high point of the present Pentateuch, and we see this through parallels between the conclusion of the Priestly creation narrative (Gen 1:1–2:3) and the conclusion of the Priestly tabernacle narrative (Exod 39:42–40:33).

Creation of the cosmos	Construction of the tabernacle
Gen 1:31	*Exod 39:43*
God saw all which God had done And indeed it was very good (Gen 1:31a)	And Moses saw all the work and indeed it was done just as YHWH had commanded (Exod 39:43a)
And the heavens and earth were finished (2:1) And God finished on the seventh day God's work (2:2a) And God blessed the seventh day (2:3a)	And all the work on the tabernacle of the tent of meeting was finished (39:32a) And Moses finished the work (40:33b) And Moses blessed them (39:43b)

These parallels are between parts of the Priestly narrative, but the completion of the tabernacle means yet more in the combined L/P narrative we now have. The story of God coming down to the tabernacle follows L stories in Genesis about how God once worked to preserve the divine–human boundary, expelling humans from

basics   Book of Exodus

Outline: pilgrimage of Moses and of Israel from Egypt to Sinai

(See M. Smith, *The Pilgrimage Pattern in Exodus*, Sheffield: Sheffield Academic Press, 1997.)

I   From Egypt
  A   Oppression and journey of Moses to Midian   1:1–2:25
  B   Two calls and two confrontations   3:1–15:21
II   To Sinai
  A   Provision on wilderness journey to Sinai   15:22–18:27
  B   Two covenants and two sets of tablets   19:1–40:38

Date   Post-exilic (building on earlier sources).

Themes   Many think of the book of Exodus solely in terms of its initial story of Israel's escape from slavery in Egypt. But the climax of the book is Israel's entry into service to a new lord, Yahweh, as a cultic community centered on the wilderness tabernacle (Exodus 19–40). Thus, Exodus is not just a story of getting away. Instead, it is a pilgrimage from painful service to Pharaoh to life-giving service to Yahweh. This Exodus journey by Israel now occurs across the Jewish liturgical year, starting at Passover (Exod 12:2, 39–42), with arrival at Sinai at the feast of weeks (Exod 19:1) and building of the tabernacle at the New Year (Exod 40:2, 17).

More information: whose exodus?   Jon Levenson has criticized some liberationist Christians, such as George Pixley, for their claim that the people of Israel was not the actual historical group to leave Egypt in the exodus. Instead, according to Pixley, the actual exodus group was an impoverished group of slaves that would only later join "Israel." For Levenson, this approach is one more example of an all-too-familiar Christian tendency to try to separate the Old Testament from the Jewish people. He argues that the present, canonical form of the book of Exodus emphasizes the idea that Yahweh rescued Israel not because it was poor, but because it was special to Yahweh. Moreover, this exodus did not mean a rejection of slavery in general, but of Israel's slavery to Pharaoh rather than Yahweh. The *Bible's* story of exodus is *Israel*-centered, not a general endorsement of liberation of the poor.

In response, Pixley and others question whether Christians must focus only on the final form of a book like Exodus. They argue that their historical reconstruction should be evaluated on its historical merits, rather than on its theological implications. For these perspectives, see: Alice Ogden Bellis and Joel Kaminsky (eds.), *Jews, Christians, and the Theology of the Hebrew Scriptures* (Atlanta: Society of Biblical Literature, 2000).

basics Book of Numbers

(For "Book of Leviticus," see Basics Box on p. 174.)

Outline	I Dissolution of the exodus generation	1–25
	A Preparations for departure from Sinai	1:1–10:10
	B Disobedience, death in the wake of Sinai	10:11–25:18
	II Beginning of the conquest generation	26–36

Date   Post-exilic (building on earlier sources).

Themes   Priestly material again provides the introduction (1:1–10:10) and general structure, with the overall book moving from the Priestly counting of the exodus generation (Numbers 1–4) to another Priestly counting of the next generation after their parents have died in the wilderness (Numbers 26). In between, we have P and L stories about rebellion against the authority of Moses and Aaron (11–12, 16–17), the failed expedition to spy out the land (13–14), and a final catastrophic rebellion at Baal Peor (25). These stories help explain the destruction of this exodus generation before their children can enter the land. In the post-exile, this form of the book would have mirrored the experience of most exiled families, in which the vast majority of parents who went into exile did not survive to take their children back to the promised land.

More information: the book of Numbers in context   The focus of Numbers on the transition between generations provides a context for the book of Deuteronomy that follows. Read after Numbers, Deuteronomy is the story of Moses's review of history and law for a generation that did not experience all these events themselves.

---

the garden (Gen 3:22–4), limiting their lifespan after they intermarried with divine beings (6:1–4), and ending their attempt to build a tower up toward heaven in Babel (11:1–9). Within this broader stretch, the Priestly description of the descent of God's glory to dwell in Israel is a crossing of the divine–human boundary described in the J primeval narratives now in L, and a climax of earlier, Lay Source promises that God would "be with" the patriarchs and their descendants (Gen 26:3; 28:15; 46:4; Exod 4:12; L).

Though later authors and editors made some additional changes to the Pentateuch, this combination of L and P narratives was the most significant stage in the formation of the Pentateuch. It was a daring move, taking one narrative (L) and combining it with a narrative (P) that was originally designed to replace it. Turning back to the example of the L and P stories of Jacob's gaining his father's blessing, we see that parts of the P story are placed before (26:34–5; P) and after (27:46–28:7; P) the trickster story they were meant to replace (27:1–45; L). As a result, the P materials provide a new context for Jacob and Rebekah's deceitful actions. In the combined text now in Genesis, Esau marries foreign wives (Gen 26:34–5; P), which provides some justification for Jacob's theft of his father's blessing (Gen 27:1–45; L), which in turn provides a context for Isaac's repeated blessing of Jacob and sending him abroad to get a proper wife (Gen 28:1–5; P). Thus, at this place and others, the post-exilic author who combined L and P balanced the perspectives of both sources without hiding or homogenizing the contrasts. Enough traces of his work were left that scholars could achieve consensus on the basic contents of the L and P sources despite the fact that we have no separate manuscript of either.

The Book of Psalms as a Torah-Centered Collection of More Ancient Psalms

Though the book of Psalms probably contains some of the earliest texts in the Hebrew Bible, its present form shows the rising importance of the Pentateuchal Torah in the Persian and later periods. *As a whole*, the book of Psalms (also known as the **Psalter**) is a collection oriented toward Torah instruction. It opens with a psalm encouraging its readers to "meditate" day and night on the "Torah of Yahweh" (Psalm 1), and its longest psalm is a praise of God's Torah that is 176 verses long, organized into alphabetic stanzas (Psalm 119). The book of Psalms is divided into five parts by a set of similar calls to praise found at Pss 41:13; 72:18–19; 89:52; 106:48; and a concluding psalm of praise in Psalm 150. The focus on praise in these sections helps explain the name of the book of Psalms in Hebrew, *tehillim* – (book of) praises. At the same time, the fivefold division of the book of Psalms (Psalms 3–41, 42–72, 73–89, 90–106, 107–50) mirrors the fivefold division of the Pentateuch (Pentateuch is Greek for "five scrolls"). The focus of the present, five-part book of Psalms is on praises that are grounded in and flow from meditation on and study of God's Torah.

READING
Pss 8 and 104 (hymns of praise), 22 (a lament psalm), 32 (a thanksgiving song). Read and compare Pss 41:13; 72:18–19; 89:52; 106:48; 150.

This focus on Pentateuchal Torah did not always exist in the book of Psalms. Rather, scholars have found clues in the psalm superscriptions that the Psalter is made up of yet older collections of psalms, such as a series of psalms used in pilgrimages (Psalms 120–34), or an "Elohistic" collection of psalms in 42–83 which predominantly uses "Elohim" for God and occasionally duplicates psalms found elsewhere (such as Psalm 53//Psalm 14). Often various psalms reflect the sorts of textual forms used in ancient Israelite worship, such as hymns of praise (e.g. Psalm 8), "laments" praying for help (e.g. Psalm 22), and thanksgivings for God's provision of such help (e.g. Psalm 32). "Form critics" (see the More on Method Box on "Form Criticism and Genre") have uncovered these echoes through comparing

basics   Book of Psalms: Part 2

(For "Book of Psalms: Part 1," see Basics Box on p. 67.)

Outline:
Torah-centered praise of Yahweh's kingship

I	Torah and king introduction		1–2
II	Five-part collection		3–145
	A	Book 1: final individual praise by king	3–41
	B	Book 2: concluding in prayer for king	42–72
	C	Book 3: concluding with lament about destruction of the Judean monarchy (Psalm 89)	73–89
	D	Book 4: moving toward exile (Psalm 106) and stressing Yahweh's kingship (Pss 93, 95–9)	90–106
	E	Book 5: moving toward restoration	107–45
III	Fivefold concluding praise of Yahweh		146–50

Date

Post-exilic (building on earlier sources).

Themes

In addition to the Torah focus mentioned in the main text, scholars have observed ways that the complex collection of psalms now reflects Israel's journey through history, from monarchy to exile and then post-exilic restoration. As indicated in the outline, the concluding psalms in the first four books show a movement from focus on the king (Psalms 3–41) and his role vis-à-vis the people (Psalms 42–72), to the collapse of the monarchy (Psalms 73–89) and rise of Yahweh's kingship in exile (Psalms 90–106). This prepares for the final book, which starts with a psalm focusing on return from exile (Psalms 107–45).

More information: another edition of the book of Psalms

Several psalm scrolls found among the Dead Sea Scrolls at Qumran contain an edition of the book of Psalms that is quite different from the Masoretic edition of Psalms that is used in Jewish tradition and surveyed above. The divergences are particularly striking after Psalm 89. This suggests to some scholars that that Psalms 1–89 (books 1–3 of the Psalter) may have reached their form earlier, while the following Psalms (90–150) may have been organized later into the form we now see them in.

the forms of such biblical psalms with each other and some ancient Near Eastern worship texts. Through this kind of research we can appreciate how the book of Psalms encapsulates within itself the broader history of the formation of the Hebrew Bible, from the writing of early worship texts that often echoed traditions seen in non-Israelite empires (see Chapter 3) up through the increasing focus on the Pentateuchal Torah characteristic of the Persian and later periods of Israelite history.

MORE ON METHOD: FORM CRITICISM AND GENRE

Biblical **form criticism** looks at the characteristics, intention, and social setting of typical categories of psalms, that is, it looks at **genres** in biblical texts. For example, the **lament psalm** is a genre characterized by some or all of the following elements: complaint, plea for help, vow, statement of trust in God's help, and thanksgiving for God's help. One typical intention of such psalms is to gain God's help in a desperate situation. The original social setting for the lament psalm was worship, whether at home, at a local sanctuary, or at the Jerusalem Temple.

Form criticism has achieved many of its greatest results in the study of psalm genres and their social settings, but there have been form-critical studies of many other genres in the Bible as well. Some genres already discussed in this textbook include call narratives (Chapter 7n), and proverbs and instructions (Chapter 5).

As study of form criticism has progressed, scholars have seen more and more complexity, both in the genres and in their links to particular social settings. Many biblical texts are a mix of genres. Moreover, genres can be inverted, as in Amos's use of the lament form to pronounce doom on the nation of Israel. Finally, some genres, such as the Hebrew short story, may be linked to a set of cultural conventions rather than a particular social setting like worship.

For more: Marvin Sweeney, "Form Criticism." Pp. 58–89 in S. McKenzie and S. Haynes (eds.), *To Each Its Own Meaning* (Louisville, KY: Westminster John Knox Press, 1999).

Contemporary readers of psalms now can work with them on multiple levels, depending on their interests and their community. Study of the psalms in relation to their original historical contexts has illuminated their diverse types and possible settings in worship, their roots in older pre-Israelite traditions, and their rich imagery (among other topics). Yet, as in the case of biblical prophets whose words were preserved for later generations, the book of Psalms has survived because the texts in it have transcended their original contexts. Many psalms probably originated in some form during the time of Solomon's first Temple, but that Temple was destroyed and these older psalms (along with newer ones) came down to us as part of a post-exilic, Torah-centered collection. Now, thousands of years later, the book of Psalms is used more consistently in Jewish and Christian worship than almost any other biblical book. Each community places the psalms in a different context. Jews use psalms in a cycle of Torah-oriented worship, while Christians often reread psalms as Christological prophecies. The use and re-use of these ancient, evocative texts, a process already begun in the formation of the book itself, continues even today.

FOCUS
TEXT

The Introduction to Psalms in Psalms 1–2

Psalms 1–2, the introduction to the book of Psalms, illustrate the mix of emphases and materials in the book. They are marked as an introduction by the fact that these two psalms lack any kind of superscription and by the ways in which they introduce major themes that occur across the rest of the book of Psalms. The superscriptions of psalms start in Psalm 3, with a label that places this lament in the context of David's flight from Absalom (see 2 Sam 15:14–17). As discussed in Chapter 3 (see the Miscellaneous Box there on "Labels (e.g. 'Psalm of David'): What They (Don't) Tell Us"), these labels are not historical, but represent an early Jewish attempt to place various "Psalms of David" in the context of his life. Psalms 1–2 lack such a label – there is not even an attribution to David or another figure. Their function lies not in themselves, but in the way they set the other psalms in context. One might view these two psalms as an extended "superscription" to the Psalter as a whole.

Psalm 1 sets the tone for the whole by calling on the readers of Psalms to devotion to Torah. It is a teaching or "wisdom psalm," but one focused particularly on Torah teaching. The expression that begins the Psalm, "happy is the one," is a teaching expression typical of Proverbs, and, like the sayings in Proverbs, this psalm features a sharp contrast between the "way of the wicked" and the "way of the righteous" (Ps 1:1, 6). Unlike Proverbs, however, the thing that distinguishes these two ways is not "fear of Yahweh" in general, but meditation on Torah day and night (Ps 1:2). The psalm draws on the ancient tree imagery central to Proverbs and ancient Israelite religion (the tree associated with the goddess Asherah) to describe the benefits that the Torah devotee will enjoy: that person will be "like a tree planted by the water . . . everything that person does will succeed" (Ps 1:3). In contrast, the wicked, who lack such devotion to Torah, will perish (Ps 1:4–6).

In this way the opening of Psalms links both to the Torah itself and to its immediate aftermath as described in the book of Joshua. At the outset of Joshua, just after Moses has died, Joshua is commanded to do exactly what this psalm calls for: recite Torah constantly and "meditate on it day and night" (Josh 1:8). Through echoing that call here, this psalm calls on its readers to emulate Joshua, the successor to Moses, in constantly keeping before them the teaching of Moses that became ever more central in the post-exilic period.

The introduction to the Psalms does not stop here, however. It also includes Psalm 2. Chapter 3 discussed how parts of this psalm – among several other royal psalms in the Psalter – are good candidates for being among Israel's earliest texts. Royal and Zion psalms like these helped early Israelite people understand how Yahweh was involved in setting up a king in the new capital city, Jerusalem. Now, however, this psalm is linked to Psalm 1 as part of a common introduction to what is now a post-exilic Psalter. The rebellious "conspiring" of the peoples at the beginning of Psalm 2 (2:1 NRSV; Hebrew *hagah*) is the opposite of constant "meditating" on Torah at the outset of Psalm 1 (1:2; again Hebrew *hagah*). Psalm 2 then describes how Yahweh's anointed king at Mount Zion will destroy his opponents (2:4–9) before echoing Psalm 1 again through proclaiming, "*happy are* those who take refuge in Yahweh" (2:12; see 1:1). In sum, within Psalms 1–2 as a whole there are two groups: (1) the "happy" righteous ones who meditate on Torah and take refuge in Yahweh, and (2) "the wicked" – a.k.a. the rebellious nations of Psalm 2 – who meditate or conspire for nothing and will be destroyed by Yahweh's anointed king.

The emphasis both on Torah and on Yahweh's anointed king had a special significance in the Torah-focused, post-monarchic context of the Persian period. After all, there was no anointed Davidic king in this time. Rather, Temple and Torah had risen to take the central place in the existing community that the Davidic monarchy once had. As a result, the returnees in Judah now placed their *hope* in ancient royal traditions. They reread royal psalms such as Psalm 2 not as endorsements of existing power structures, but as *promises* that God, the cosmic king, would anoint an earthly king who would put the empires of the world in their place. This is the expectation of a royal **messiah**, the Hebrew word for "anointed." It is a predominantly post-exilic hope that the empire of God, with a Davidic monarch at its head, would destroy the foreign empires dominating the people of Israel.

In this way the introduction to the Psalter embraces both elements that have been important to centuries of Jewish and Christian interpretation of the Psalms. Psalm 1 anticipates the focus of the rest of the Psalter on the Mosaic Torah. This is a major feature in Jewish exegesis of the Psalms. Psalm 2 anticipates the focus of other parts of the Psalter on kingship – both human and divine – and the expectation that God would establish God's kingship and destroy foreign oppressors. Such hope is still found in Judaism, but the emphasis on God's anointed king in the Psalter has been particularly strong in Christianity, a religion whose name is formed from the Greek word for "anointed" – *Christ*. Psalms 1–2, the introduction to the Psalter, show how such hope for God's *messiah* during the post-exilic period was integrally connected to devotion to the Torah of Moses.

Concluding Reflections on Scriptures In and After the Exile

Ultimately, the Pentateuchal Torah, in combined L and P form, became the scriptural foundation of later Judaism. Other holy texts were increasingly understood in light of this Torah. Not only were ancient collections of psalms organized into a Torah-centered whole, but shorter prophetic books such as Hosea and Zechariah were combined into a collection of 12 books that concludes with a passage that urges constant memory of the "Torah of my servant Moses" (Mal 4:4). And readers of other prophetic texts would have seen this combined L/P Torah in other references to God's "Torah" in Isaiah, Jeremiah, and Ezekiel.

In these and other ways, the Torah that first started to emerge under Josiah and was affirmed – in L and P forms – in the exile became ever more central in the post-exilic Persian period. But this process took time. Some early post-exilic texts, such as Third Isaiah (Isaiah 56–66) and Job, do not yet reflect the dominance of the Mosaic Torah that we see later. The community of Judah evolved significantly from the initial returns of exiles under Davidic descendants (Sheshbazzar, Zerubbabel) to its consolidation around Torah under Ezra the priest. Only toward the end of this period do we see the clear outlines of a Temple- and Torah-centered Judaism that would persist for several centuries of Hellenistic rule. Next we shall turn to look at that chapter in the history of the people and development of the Bible.

CHAPTER SEVEN REVIEW

1. Know the meaning and significance of the following terms discussed in this chapter:
- Cyrus cylinder [know similarities to and differences from Ezra 1:1–4]
- form criticism
- genre
- lament psalm
- messiah
- Psalter
- rebuilding of the Jerusalem Temple [know the date and circumstances]
- Second Temple

2. Why is the Bible's depiction of the Persians so different from its depiction of the Assyrians and Babylonians?

3. Know the four major stages in the post-exilic rebuilding of the Judean community:
- several waves of return;
- rebuilding of the Temple;
- rebuilding of the wall around Jerusalem;
- centering on the Torah.
- Be able to summarize the Persian role in each and other associated circumstances.

4. The expulsion of foreign wives is one of the most difficult events for contemporary readers to deal with. Are there circumstances in which you can imagine supporting a community's wish to insure that their children only marry other members of that community? Or are there other circumstances where you can imagine a community legitimately needing to protect its identity in other ways? Conversely, in what kinds of circumstances can such tendencies be particularly dangerous?

5. What is a way that the documents from the post-exilic Jewish colony at Elephantine are significant?

6. What difference does it make to know that Genesis 1–3 is a combination of the L and P creation stories? What do we learn through realizing that Exodus 19–40 probably is the combination of very different L and P accounts of Sinai?

7. How does the book of Psalms reflect its origins in the Persian period? How does it reflect yet earlier origins?

RESOURCES FOR FURTHER STUDY

Haggai and Zechariah 1–8

Petersen, David. *Haggai and Zechariah 1–8: A Commentary*. Old Testament Library. Philadelphia: Westminster Press, 1984.

Ezra, Nehemiah, and Esther

Blenkinsopp, Joseph. *Ezra–Nehemiah: A Commentary*. Old Testament Library. Philadelphia: Westminster Press, 1988.

Clines, David. *Ezra, Nehemiah, Esther*. New Century Bible Commentary. Grand Rapids: Eerdmans, 1984.

Williamson, H. G. M. *Ezra, Nehemiah*. Word Biblical Commentary 16. Waco, TX: Word Books, 1985.

Psalms

Brown, William. *Seeing the Psalms: A Theology of Metaphor*. Louisville, KY: Westminster John Knox Press, 2002.

Brueggemann, Walter. *Praying the Psalms* (revised edition). Winona, MN: St. Mary's, 1993.

Holladay, William. *The Psalms Through Three Thousand Years: Prayerbook of a Cloud of Witnesses*. Minneapolis: Fortress, 1993. [History of interpretation of Psalms.]

Mays, James L. *Psalms*. Interpretation. Louisville, KY: Westminster John Knox Press, 1994.

Jonah

Lacocque, Andre, and Lacocque, Pierre-Emmanuel. *The Jonah Complex*. Atlanta: John Knox Press, 1981.

Trible, Phyllis. *Rhetorical Criticism: Context, Method, and the Book of Jonah*. Minneapolis: Fortress, 1994.

Ruth

Fewell, Danna Nolan, and Gunn, David Miller. *Compromising Redemption: Relating Characters in the Book of Ruth*. Literary Currents in Biblical Interpretation. Philadelphia: Westminster John Knox Press, 1990.

Kates, Gail Twersky, and Reimer, Judith. *Reading Ruth*. New York: Ballantine Books, 1994, 1996. Excellent collection of contemporary interpretations by Jewish women.

Job

Janzen, J. Gerald. *Job*. Interpretation. Atlanta: John Knox Press, 1985.

Newsom, Carol. "Job." Pp. 319–637 of vol. 4 of the *New Interpreters Bible*. Nashville: Abingdon, 1996.

Isaiah 56–66

Blenkinsopp, Joseph. *Isaiah 56–66: A New Translation with Introduction and Commentary*. Anchor Bible. New York: Doubleday, 2005.

(See also the end of Chapter 6 for commentaries on Isaiah 40–66.)

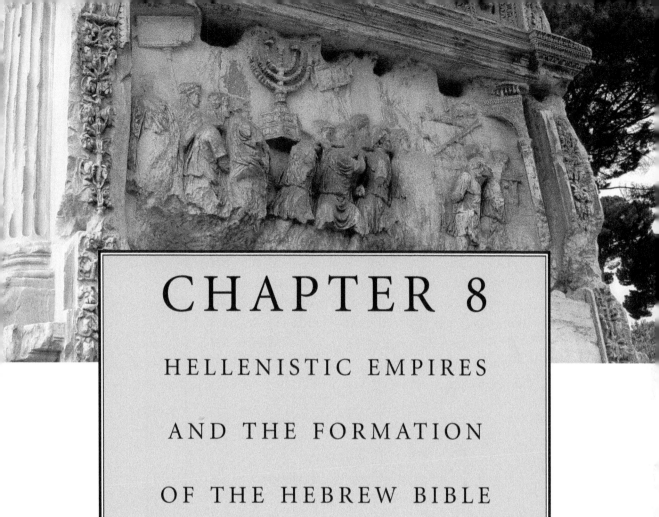

CHAPTER 8

HELLENISTIC EMPIRES

AND THE FORMATION

OF THE HEBREW BIBLE

Chapter Outline

It is hard to come up with a sharper contrast in the experience of empire than that between the Judeans' experience of Persian support and their later near annihilation by the Hellenistic (Greek) king Antiochus Epiphanes IV. Though Hellenistic rule was not a serious problem in the first 157 years after Alexander the Great's conquest of the area (in 332 BCE), a major confrontation occurred in Judah in 174 BCE when Hellenizers sought to take control of Jerusalem and turn it into a Greek city. This led to an attempt to eradicate Judaism by the Hellenistic king, Antiochus IV, a successful rebellion led by a family of provincial priests, the Hasmoneans, and their establishment of a priest-ruled kingdom in Jerusalem that lasted eighty years.

The Emergence of "Judaism"

This is the time when we can start to talk about the emergence of a "Jewish" identity in addition to and distinct from a "Judean" identity. The word "Jew" comes from the Greek word for Judean, *Ioudaios*. Though it encompassed Judeans living in Judah, it also embraced the ever expanding number of Jews living permanently outside Judah. Such Jews still had deep ties to Judah, but they were best known for their distinctive religion and set of practices.

This chapter examines writings composed before and after this confrontation, along with probable finalization of the Hebrew Bible under the Hasmonean rulers. Some writings composed earlier in the Hellenistic period, such as the wisdom of Ben Sira or some apocalypses now in Enoch, were included in the Old Testament collections of the Roman Catholic and/or Orthodox churches, but excluded from the Jewish Tanach (and, as a result, the later Protestant Old Testament). Some later writings composed during or after the Hellenistic confrontation, such as the book of Daniel, were included in the Jewish Tanach (as well as the Old Testament of all churches). Toward its conclusion, this chapter explores the important question of why some texts were included in the Hebrew Bible, while others were left out.

Judaism and Hellenism before the Hellenizing Crisis

READING
Sirach/Ben Sira 1:1–10;
24:1–34; 44–50.

Though early Hellenistic rule was not benign, it was not antagonistic toward the religion and culture of peoples such as the Judeans. From the time of Alexander's conquest (332 BCE) up to initial efforts to Hellenize Jerusalem (174 BCE), Judah was ruled by a succession of Hellenistic rulers without major incident. After Alexander's death in 323 BCE, his kingdom was split among his generals, including Ptolemy in Egypt and Seleucus in Mesopotamia. Judah was ruled first from Egypt by heirs of Ptolemy (323–198 BCE). Then, after a series of major battles, the Seleucids (heirs of Seleucus) took over in 198 BCE and ruled Judah much of the following century. Things were difficult as the two Hellenistic empires struggled for control of the area, but there is no evidence that either the Ptolemaic or Seleucid rulers interfered with the religion of those they ruled or otherwise tried to Hellenize them.

Nevertheless, Greek cities and people who had Greek education received privileges in these kingdoms, while those lacking Greek culture sometimes faced prejudice. For example, a non-Greek camel driver complains in an inscription that he was treated poorly because "I am a barbarian" and "I do not know how to behave like a Greek." An Egyptian priest complains in another inscription that a person whom he is suing "despises me because I am an Egyptian." Within Hellenistic cultures, Greek-educated children of Greek parents were at the top of the social pyramid, followed by Greek-educated children of non-Greek parents, some of whom aspired to be seen as culturally "Greek." Those who lacked any Greek education were disadvantaged even if they – like the Egyptian priest mentioned above – had extensive education in local, non-Greek texts, such as Egyptian classics or Hebrew books.

This meant that societies under Hellenistic rule had a cultural divide. On the one side stood Greek culture, the knowledge of which gave students access to government positions and/or business contacts across the Greek world. On the other side stood the cultures and native texts of peoples in Judah, Egypt, and Mesopotamia. The knowledge of ancient Near Eastern texts was less and less important in the broader Hellenistic culture but was still valued in temple–priestly circles. Therefore, within Judah, the Temple and various priesthoods connected to it became the primary place where people still learned and wrote texts in Hebrew. Otherwise, priests found themselves and their knowledge of ancient texts increasingly marginalized. In earlier times, knowledge of ancient Hebrew texts gave a person privileges in the Hebrew monarchy or Persian empire, but things were different under Hellenism. Now primary political and economic power belonged increasingly to those who could claim on some level to be "Greek."

Judeans and others dealt with this divide in different ways. Some priestly groups in both Egypt and Judah wrote esoteric visionary texts, called "**apocalypses**" after the Greek word for "uncovering." Some of these texts featured detailed tours of heaven ("heavenly apocalypses"), while others reviewed past history and then predicted divine intervention to remove Hellenistic rulers and restore native leaders ("historical apocalypses"). These apocalypses reflected both the broad scholarship of their priestly authors and their alienation from the surrounding Greek-dominated culture. The book of (first) Enoch, revered as scripture in the Ethiopic church, contains some of Judaism's oldest apocalyptic texts, such as the story of God's imminent destruction of bad angels (Enoch 6–11) and Enoch's sermon to the rebellious angels (Enoch 12–16). The meaning of these often obscure apocalyptic texts is unclear initially to most readers. On one level, they elaborate on biblical narratives and feature many unfamiliar characters and scenes, battles between angels and the like. Yet on another level, these apocalypses in Enoch are coded descriptions of battles between Hellenistic rulers (Enoch 6–11) or crises in the Jerusalem priesthood (Enoch 12–16) and God's plan to intervene and set things right. These texts speak to concerns that were present in the third century BCE about Hellenistic domination and the corruption of the Temple, but they claim as their author an ancient, pre-Hellenistic sage, Enoch (see Gen 5:21–4). Such attribution of a later text to an ancient author, termed "**pseudepigraphy**," was particularly common in the Hellenistic age, when ancient authorship determined whether or not a given text would be studied in schools. In this case, however, Hellenistic-style pseudepigraphy was used by Jewish authors to provide extra authority to their predictions of liberation from Hellenistic kings and corrupt leaders.

The book of **Ben Sira** (also known as **Sirach**, its Greek name), originally written in Hebrew by Joshua ben Sira around 200–180 BCE, shows a different way to respond to the divide between local and Hellenistic culture (see Figure 8.1). In a possible critique of esoteric apocalypses such as those in Enoch, Ben Sira discourages speculation about heavenly realms (3:21–4) and rejects dreams as generally misleading (34:1–8). Instead, he writes a wisdom instruction to fit (both) the Torah focus and Hellenistic tenor of

Figure 8.1 Copy of the Hebrew book of Ben Sira found near the Dead Sea.

his present time. Like older instructions in Proverbs, Ben Sira directly addresses his students, encouraging them to live prudently and put wisdom above other values. Like more recent works from the exile and post-exile, Ben Sira portrays the Torah as the ultimate wisdom, now going so far as to identify the Torah of Moses with the female personified wisdom seen in Proverbs and elsewhere (Ben Sira 24; see Proverbs 8).

Yet Ben Sira also shows influence from Hellenistic culture. At various points, his sayings resemble Greek sayings by the sixth-century BCE Greek poet Theognis that were commonly used early in the process of Greek education. Moreover, the Torah takes on a role in Ben Sira that is similar to that of Homer's epics in Greek education. It, like Homer, is the foundation and end point of the rest of the process of education and study. Finally, the book of Ben Sira concludes with a set of praises that share much in common with the Hellenistic genre of *encomium* (work of praise): a praise of "great fathers" that is divided between figures in the Pentateuch (Ben Sira 44–5) and figures found in all of the rest of the Hebrew Bible (46–9), followed by an extended praise of the high priest in Ben Sira's own time, Simon (50:1–21).

Many scholars rightly have seen in this "praise of great fathers" evidence that virtually all of the books in the Hebrew Bible were known and revered by Ben Sira's time (200–180 BCE). Nevertheless, other parts of the book of Ben Sira show that its author was not yet working with an idea of a closed collection of scriptural books. His own description of what a scribe studies includes "the law of the most high" (probably the Torah), wisdom of the ancients, prophecies, sayings of the famous, parables, and proverbs (Sir 39:1–3), as well as foreign wisdom (39:4). The book of Ben Sira, explicitly written in the late second century by a sage of that time, aims to be a new addition to that broader scribal curriculum.

Ben Sira is just one example of a book written in a local language (Hebrew) that reflects Greek learning. But Jews also wrote Greek works and translated originally Hebrew works into Greek. Sometime in the third century the Pentateuch was translated into Greek (the "Septuagint"), and other Hebrew scriptures (including Ben Sira) were translated later on (sometimes the group of these Greek translations is referred to by the term "Septuagint"). New works written by Judeans in Greek often drew deeply on models and values seen in the Greek literature that they had learned. Some of these are found in the deutero-canonical books of the Roman Catholic and other churches, books such as 2 Maccabees, Judith, and the Wisdom of Solomon. For example, the Wisdom of Solomon is a work in Greek that draws deeply and broadly on Stoicism and other parts of Greek philosophy in the process of retelling the story of Solomon's search for wisdom.

When we look across the full range of Jewish texts of this time, it becomes clear that all parts of Judaism were deeply affected by Hellenism and Hellenistic culture, even when they opposed elements of that culture. The apocalypses undergird their messages with Hellenistic-style pseudepigraphy. Ben Sira writes in Hebrew, but draws on sayings, ideas, and forms from Greek education. And the author of the Wisdom of Solomon draws on multiple strands of Greek philosophy in its depictions of wisdom. As a result, there is no clear distinction between "Hellenistic Judaism" and other forms, since all of Judaism was touched by Hellenistic culture and ideas. The main distinction that does appear is between forms of Hellenistic Judaism that were neutral or positive about Hellenism and forms of Hellenistic Judaism that were opposed to it. This distinction emerges particularly in the crisis around the attempt to Hellenize Jerusalem, to which we turn next.

The Crisis over Hellenizing Jerusalem and the Book of Daniel

READING
Narratives about the Maccabean crisis: 2 Maccabees 4–8. Apocalyptic writing: Daniel 7–12.

EXERCISE
After reading this section, try writing a brief historical apocalypse that would empower a contemporary oppressed group. Try to incorporate in your apocalypse the kinds of features (pseudepigraphy, historical review, and projection of divine triumph) that are seen in texts such as Daniel 7 and 10–12, but develop your own coded imagery and attribute the apocalypse to someone other than Daniel. Have a friend read and try to decode it. What is similar and different about your twenty-first-century apocalypse and the one found in Daniel 10–12?

The Seleucids under Antiochus III were initially quite friendly to Jews and Judaism. When Antiochus III took control of Judah from the Ptolemies in 198 BCE, he affirmed more ancient Persian policies toward Judah. He gave tax relief to the city and money for the Temple, and affirmed by royal decree the right of Jews to live "according to [their] ancestral laws." Later on, however, he suffered defeat by the Romans and started to pay heavy tribute to them. He died in the process of trying to raid one of the temples in his kingdom for money, and a similar attempt apparently was made during the reign of his successor, Seleucus IV (see 2 Maccabees 3). By the time Antiochus Epiphanes IV seized the throne from Seleucus in 175 BCE, his kingdom had been humiliated by the Romans, and he needed money to pay them a large annual tribute. At this point, Judah was one of the few Seleucid territories remaining on the Western Mediterranean.

It was under these circumstances that Antiochus IV started to sell the high priesthood in Jerusalem to the highest bidder, a significant move, since the high priest of Jerusalem's Temple functioned at this time as the local ruler and tax-collector for the region. First, Jason, who was a brother of the existing high priest, paid money to Antiochus on the occasion of the latter's accession to the throne for two privileges: (1) the office of high priest and (2) the right to turn Jerusalem into a Greek city, complete with its own gymnasium within sight of the Temple (174 BCE). Three years later, Meneleus, a member of the Tobiad family that once had opposed Nehemiah, outbid Jason, seized the high priesthood, and forced Jason to flee (171 BCE). Meneleus's rule proved highly unpopular, however, and the Seleucids had to intervene twice to restore him to power. The second time, fed up with revolts, Antiochus IV enacted harsh measures aimed at crushing any trace of Jewish culture (in 167 BCE). He imposed the death penalty on Jews for continuing to follow Torah laws such as eating regulations and circumcision, and he set up an altar to Zeus Olympius over the altar to Yahweh in the Jerusalem Temple. What had started as a mild attempt by Jason and other Jerusalemites to gain Greek privileges for Jerusalem and its citizens had turned into a life-and-death struggle for the continuance of Torah observance.

basics Book of Daniel

| Outline: apocalyptic visions with prologue of stories of deliverance | I | Stories about Daniel and other exiles | 1–6 |
| | II | Daniel's four visions | 7–12 |

Language   Several chapters of Daniel are in Aramaic (2–7), others in Hebrew (1, 8–12).

Date   The Aramaic legends in Daniel 4–6 probably date from the late Persian or early Hellenistic period. The book as a whole, including the Hebrew chapters, dates from just before 164 BCE and reflects the crisis of that time.

More information   The Greek translation of Daniel preserves yet other traditions about Daniel and other figures (e.g. Susanna in Daniel 13). In addition, an Aramaic story about Nabonidus was found in the Dead Sea Scrolls at Qumran and represents a different form of the tradition seen in Daniel 4.

The visions in Daniel 7–12 were written to give Judeans hope in this crisis. Like the apocalyptic visions in Enoch, these chapters of Daniel are attributed to an earlier figure, this time the exilic figure of Daniel who is featured in the tales of Daniel 1–6. Moreover, like other historical apocalypses, these visions in Daniel give a coded overview of past history before predicting God's intervention to make things right. We can see an example of this in the vision of four beasts coming out of the sea in Daniel 7. These four beasts correspond to four major world empires leading up to the time of Antiochus IV: the Babylonians who destroyed the Jerusalem temple (7:4), the Medes who domi-nated lands east of Babylonia (7:5), the Persians (7:6), and the Greeks, particularly the

10 rulers – "horns" – of the Seleucid dynasty (7:7), from which a "little horn," Antiochus IV, sprouts (7:8).

After surveying these four empires, the vision moves to the future, predicting the destruction of the fourth, Greek beast and God's gift of eternal dominion to a mysterious "one like a son of man" (7:9–14). Many Christians have read this text in light of gospel accounts where Jesus refers to himself as the "son of man," and have understood Daniel 7 as a prediction of the coming of Jesus. Nevertheless, the details of the text, especially the "interpretation" given to Daniel in 7:15–27, indicate that this chapter was originally intended to give hope to Torah-observant Jews under threat from Antiochus. Antiochus is the one who attempted to end sacrifice and forbid Torah observance, to "change the times and the law" (7:25). In his vision, Daniel is told that God will destroy the kingdom of Antiochus and grant eternal rule to those who have remained faithful to the Torah, "the holy ones of the most High" (7:27).

Things did not work out exactly as this or other visions in Daniel 7–12 predicted, but these visions have continued to give hope to generations of Jews and Christians. Jews have read the text as a prediction of God's establishment of God's rule with the future arrival of the messiah. Christians have read it as a prediction of God's transformation of the world with the second coming of Jesus Christ. In each case, people have found numerous ways to coordinate the obscure symbols of Daniel 7–12 with groups and events of their own time. At their best, such interpretations have given much-needed hope to communities facing oppressors as bad as or worse than Antiochus IV. At their worst, these reinterpretations of Daniel have encouraged people to withdraw from the world and wait for God's imminent intervention on their behalf. Certainly it would be a mistake for any community to suppose that their own understanding of the visions in Daniel is the one and only true way to unlock the code of the book. The persistently strange imagery of the book resists this kind of certainty and is part of what has allowed Daniel to be revered and reinterpreted by communities long after the time of the Hellenistic crisis.

The Hasmonean Kingdom and the Formation of the Hebrew Bible

Ultimately, Antiochus IV was not successful, though not in the ways envisioned in Daniel 7–12. Members of a marginal priestly family in rural Judah, the **Hasmoneans** or **Maccabees**, launched a guerilla war against the Seleucids. They started by destroying pagan altars, killing Jewish collaborators with the Seleucids, and forcibly circumcising males who had been left uncircumcised under Seleucid order. Their effort culminated with the recapture of Jerusalem and purification of the Temple (164 BCE). (Note: **Hanukkah** is the Jewish holiday celebrating this triumph and the purification of the Temple.) In addition, the Hasmoneans were able to negotiate an end to the edict of Antiochus IV against Judaism. Jews were free to observe Torah regulations again, and we hear no more of any attempts to reverse this policy.

Significant Dates in the Rise of the Hasmonean Kingdom

Antiochus IV seizes power over Seleucid empire	175 BCE
Jason buys high priesthood and initiates Hellenizing	174 BCE
Menelaus purchases priesthood	171 BCE
Unpopular rule, uprisings	
Harsh measures by Antiochus IV to eradicate Judaism	167 BCE
Beginning of Maccabean rebellion under Hasmoneans	
Purification/rededication of Temple	164 BCE
End of harsh edicts against Judaism	
Independent Hasmonean rule	142–63 BCE
Beginning of Roman rule of Palestine	63 BCE

All this did not, however, mean an end to Greek domination. Though Antiochus IV died around this time, the Seleucids soon regained control over Judah, killing the leader of the Hasmonean family, Judas Maccabeus ("the hammer"), in battle and forcing the other Hasmoneans and their supporters to flee. Around 152 BCE, however, the Hasmoneans played their cards right in a power struggle over the Seleucid throne, choosing to back the winner of that struggle, Demetrius. In return, Demetrius appointed the Hasmonean Jonathan as high priest and thus ruler of the province of Judah. When Jonathan died about a decade later, his brother Simon declared independence from the Seleucid empire (142 BCE). By then the Seleucids did not have the power to bring Judah back under their control.

Thus Judah was free of direct foreign rule for the first time in hundreds of years. For approximately seven decades (142–63 BCE), the Hasmoneans controlled Jerusalem and the high priesthood. Moreover, they gradually expanded their realm to include not only the old heartland of Judah and Israel but also areas that had few Jews and had not been dominated by Jerusalem for centuries: the Phoenician coastland, Edom and the rest of the Transjordan, and Galilee (see Map 8.1). At the beginning of their activity the Hasmoneans fought for Jewish rights to obey Torah. Now as rulers, they expelled gentiles from some of the areas they conquered, converted others, and imposed (male) circumcision on their subject populations. Their passion for ancient ways is seen in their promotion of the Torah, their advocacy for the Hebrew language in a now Aramaic-speaking populace, and their use of ancient Hebrew script on the new coins that they minted. The book of 1 Maccabees was originally written in Hebrew to celebrate and support the Hasmonean kingdom. It presents the Hasmoneans as true heirs of the Hebrew judges and righteous opponents of the forces of Hellenism.

Nevertheless, the Hasmonean rulers were also influenced in multiple ways by the Hellenistic culture they purported to oppose. The whole practice of issuing coins was

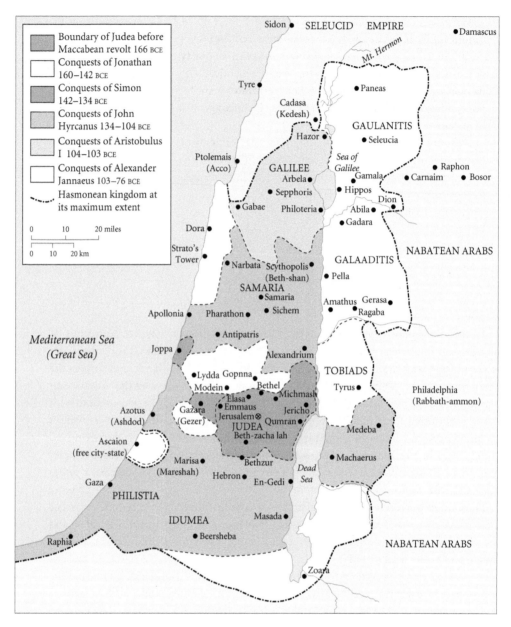

Map 8.1 The expanding kingdom of the Hasmoneans. Redrawn from Norman Gottwald, *The Hebrew Bible: A Socio-Literary Introduction.* Minneapolis: Fortress, 1985, page 407.

a Greek one, and the Hasmonean coins with ancient Hebrew letters also featured images and symbols drawn from older Greek coins of the Ptolemies and Seleucids. In this way, coins, such as the one shown in Figure 8.2, vividly illustrate the kind of cultural hybridity we have seen at other points in Israelite history: the blending of self-determination with elements drawn from the culture of the past oppressor. We see similar hybridity in other cultural products of the Hasmonean period. The Hasmoneans built palaces with Greek columns and friezes but were careful to equip them with baths to preserve ritual purity. Jewish burial tombs from this time are virtually identical with their Greek-pagan counterparts in other countries except for their avoidance of pictorial representation, in obedience to dictates found in Deuteronomy (Deut 4:15–19). The book of 2 Maccabees celebrates heroes who fought for the Torah, using Greek models of heroic martyrs. In these and other ways the Hasmoneans developed a hybrid culture that promoted anti-Hellenism while adapting Hellenistic features.

There are several signs that it was the Hasmoneans who finalized the contents of what we now know as the Hebrew Bible. For example, it is during the time of the Hasmoneans that we first see manuscripts that are close to the later Jewish "Masoretic text" tradition. Moreover, across the whole range of Jewish history after the destruction of Jerusalem and its Temple in 587 BCE, it is the Hasmonean monarchy that most had the power and motivation to establish and promote a standardized set of Jewish texts that could compete with the similarly standardized set of Greek texts valued in the Hellenistic world. These texts then could help unify the Hasmoneans' mini-empire, which expanded into neighboring areas in the late second and early first centuries.

This is the most likely time when it was decided which

Figure 8.2 Coin from the time of the Hasmoneans, combining the Greek practice of coinage (with an image!) with an inscription on the other side in archaic Hebrew lettering.

books were in the Hebrew Bible and which ones were out. Before the Hasmoneans, authors such as Ben Sira knew these texts as a looser collection to which one could still add a book or two. During the Hasmonean period, however, we start to see references in early Jewish texts to a defined collection of scriptures termed the "Torah and Prophets." In addition, the books of Maccabees introduce a new idea of the "end of prophecy," which served to limit which books were understood to be "prophets" (1 Macc 9:27). This boundary included books such as Samuel, Isaiah, or Daniel, since they were attributed to prophets. It even included books such as Psalms and Proverbs, since they were seen as written under the prophetic inspiration of David and Solomon. But the idea of an "end to prophecy" excluded books such as Ben Sira and all Jewish Greek works, since they quite clearly were written in the Hellenistic period. This explains why Ben Sira's grandson felt the need to assert in his prologue to his Greek translation of his grandfather's book that Ben Sira had not only studied and benefited from the "Torah and Prophets," but also studied "other books of our fathers." He was arguing for the ongoing importance of these "other books of our fathers," such as the book of Ben Sira itself, in an environment where many believed that only the "Torah and Prophets" were worth studying.

This does not mean that all Jews everywhere instantly agreed on which books they would consider to be authoritative. The Jews at Qumran who collected the Dead Sea scrolls recognized a broader set of Hebrew texts as scripture, as did the first Christians (who were also Jewish). Nevertheless, the Hasmoneans are the best candidates for producing and initially promoting a clearly defined set of Hebrew scriptures. They had the political authority to establish such a collection, and anti-Hellenistic, pro-Hebrew motives for doing so. For them a clearly defined collection of the "Torah and Prophets" would have served as an authentic Hebrew substitution for the Greek literary texts used in Hellenistic kingdoms like that of the Seleucids. Where youths preparing to work in the Seleucid government once were required to study the Greek curriculum, the Hasmoneans now could have such youths prepare to work in their mini-empire by learning a clearly defined corpus of Hebrew scriptures. These were the texts that the Hasmonean priest-kings preserved and promoted even if other Jewish groups did not agree, and these are the texts that later rabbinic Judaism took as the authoritative Hebrew Bible.

READING
Writings about life in the diaspora: Esther, Daniel 3.

The Hellenistic Period as the Setting for Other Hebrew Bible Texts

Though the Hasmoneans may have intended to create a collection of pre-Hellenistic books, the Hebrew Bible contains several books that probably were written sometime during this Hellenistic period.

basics	Book of Esther

Outline: story of victory behind the holiday of Purim	I	Esther's rise and saving of her people	1–8
	II	Revenge of Jews and beginning of Purim	9–10

Date	Third century BCE (200s).

More information

The book of Esther in Hebrew is distinguished by its lack of mention of God or traditional piety. The Greek translations of Esther include additions which solve this problem by inserting prayers, references to God, etc. These more pious forms of Esther were preserved in the Christian church.

Meanwhile, Esther has become the central reading within Judaism for the raucous holiday of Purim. This holiday, which happens in late February or early March, features dressing up, candy, gifts for the poor, and audience response during the reading of the Esther scroll.

We have already discussed the visions of Daniel, which show clear signs of having been written sometime during the Hellenistic crisis of 169–164 BCE. In addition, the tales about Daniel and other Judeans in the Persian court (Daniel 2–6) probably originate in the late Persian or early Hellenistic period. Most scholars would date the book of Esther to a similar time. And the books of Chronicles and Ezra–Nehemiah, though containing earlier materials, likewise show multiple signs of a Hellenistic period dating.

---

basics Books of Chronicles

Outline: Temple and priest-centered history of Judah's kings	I	Genealogy: Adam to exile	1 Chr 1–9
	II	Reign of David	1 Chr 10–29
	III	Reign of Solomon	2 Chr 1–9
	IV	Judean kingship until exile	2 Chr 10–36

Date   Fourth century BCE (300s).

More information   Though most of the material special to Chronicles is very late, isolated parts may preserve historical materials that are earlier than Samuel–Kings.

Overall, many parts of the Hebrew Bible probably reached their present form in the Hellenistic period. This seems to be the case with books such as the Song of Songs and Ecclesiastes, both of which feature late forms of Hebrew typical of Hellenistic period texts. Though earlier in this textbook we suggested that parts of these books may have been written during the early monarchy (see Chapter 3), they certainly were modified later on. For example, a Hellenistic period scribe appears to have added the following orthodox conclusion to the book of Ecclesiastes:

> The conclusion of the matter:
> All has been heard,
> Fear God and keep God's commandments
> This is the duty of every human.
> For God will bring every deed to judgment
> Even every secret thing, whether good or bad. (Eccl 12:13–14)

This conclusion shows ideas of Torah obedience and final judgment that are common in the Hellenistic period. They contrast strongly with the skepticism of most of the rest of Ecclesiastes, such as "Do not be too righteous and do not be too evil, for why should you be ruined?" (Eccl 7:16). In this way and many others, the present Hebrew Bible/Old Testament, in Ecclesiastes and many other books, is an intricate blend of old and new.

basics Books of Ezra–Nehemiah

Outline: the cultic and political establishment of Torah-centered Judean community

I	Return and rebuilding of Temple	Ezra 1–6
II	Torah+Temple-centered community	
	A Preparations	
	1 Ezra's commission and divorce of foreign wives	Ezra 7–10
	2 Nehemiah's building of politically independent Jerusalem	Nehemiah 1–7
	B Ezra and Nehemiah's creation of Torah-centered community	Nehemiah 8–13

Language Ezra 4:8–6:18 and 7:12–26 are in Aramaic, while the rest is in Hebrew.

Date The present form of the book may date as late as the mid-second century (160–150s BCE).

More information The bulk of the book is probably earlier, particularly the sources for Ezra (Ezra 7–10; Nehemiah 8) and Nehemiah (Neh 1:1–7:4; 13:10–14, 30b–31) that were discussed in Chapter 7.

FOCUS TEXT

Daniel 10–12

The report of a vision in Daniel 10–12 is one of the best examples of a text that is presented as old, but is manifestly new. At the outset we hear that the exilic figure Daniel received this vision in "the third year of king Cyrus of Persia" (Dan 10:1). Nevertheless, the following two chapters make clear that the author knew world history up to the time of the Hellenistic crisis, but not events afterwards. The vision starts with an angelic figure, perhaps Gabriel, appearing to Daniel and anticipating future events in the Hellenistic and Persian periods: Alexander's defeat of the Persian empire (Alexander as "the warrior king" in 11:3), the division of his kingdom among his four generals (11:4), various specific events in the history of the Ptolemies of Egypt ("the king[s] of the south," 11:5–12), the conquest of Judah and Egypt by the Seleucid Antiochus III (11:13–16), the attempt to rob the Jerusalem Temple under his successor, Seleucus IV (11:20), the rise and initial conquests of Antiochus IV (11:21–8), and his profaning of the Temple and persecution of observant Jews (11:29–39). At this point, however, the text diverges from history, inaccurately predicting further conquests by Antiochus IV (11:40–5) and the time when the Temple would be purified and rededicated (12:11–12). Clearly this vision was written after the onset of the Hellenistic crisis in 169 BCE but before its end and the death of Antiochus IV.

This text is particularly important, however, because it concludes with a vision of resurrection that is unique in the Hebrew Bible. Elsewhere, the Hebrew Bible has little place for an idea of afterlife. There is no belief in heaven and hell. Instead, all who died were thought to go to a shadowy existence in "Sheol" that involved neither reward nor punishment. As Proverbs indicates, the main hope for virtuous reward was prosperity in this life, along with children and a good name to continue after death (e.g. Prov 10:4, 7, 27–8; 12:28). This perspective, however, did not provide much comfort amidst a situation like the Hellenistic crisis. There people (and their children) were being killed for staying faithful to the Torah. This text in Daniel promises that this is not the end for them. Instead, those that have been faithful – that is, "the wise ones" – will be resurrected after the death of Antiochus IV and "shine like the brightness of heaven." Meanwhile, those of their persecutors who have died will also be resurrected, but to shame and continual punishment (Dan 12:1–3).

The Greeks had long believed in some kind of individual afterlife (e.g. the kingdom of Hades), but this Hebrew idea of collective afterlife in Daniel now empowered resistance to Greek oppression. It gave people hope to resist Antiochus IV even if opposition to his decree would cost them their lives. Here again we can see how the cultural traditions of the oppressor could be used by the oppressed to enable resistance. Moreover, this idea of afterlife has continued to empower resistance by people facing difficult odds. The belief in a reward during God's final judgment has helped generations of Jews and Christians remain faithful even when facing powerful oppressors capable of killing them.

Two centuries later, these kinds of beliefs in God's (coming) transformation of the world would be common among the Jews of the first century, among whom Jesus and the earliest Christians should be numbered. By then a new powerful empire, that of the Romans, had taken control of Judah. Soon Judah was hammered by crises at least as severe as, if not more so than, the Hellenistic crisis of the second century BCE. Within this context, visions such as Daniel 10–12 gave Jews hope that death at the hands of the Romans was not the final chapter in their lives. Though it might seem to them as if the political powers of evil were triumphing, texts such as Daniel reassured them that God soon would intervene, destroy evil empires, and resurrect the faithful ones to everlasting glory.

CHAPTER EIGHT REVIEW

1. Know the meaning and significance of the following terms discussed in this chapter:
- apocalypse
- Ben Sira/Sirach
- Hanukkah
- Hasmoneans
- Maccabees
- pseudepigraphy

2. What major empires are reflected in the coded visions of Daniel 7 and 10–12? How is the Persian empire viewed in these visions in comparison with the Nehemiah memoir and Temple-rebuilding/Ezra narrative?

3. How was the Hasmonean kingdom different from the ancient Davidic monarchy?

4. How is the phenomenon of hybridity reflected in the works of the Hasmoneans? How might it be reflected in the final formation of the Hebrew Bible?

5. What are other major candidates in the Hebrew Bible to be writings from the Hellenistic period?

6. Should there be a place in the present day and age for the kind of "historical apocalypse" seen in Daniel? If so, why and where? If it should not be reapplied (yet again), why not?

RESOURCES FOR FURTHER STUDY

Jewish writings from the Hellenistic and early Roman periods

Collins, John J. *Jewish Wisdom in the Hellenistic Age*. Old Testament Library. Louisville, KY: Westminster John Knox Press, 1997.

Nickelsburg, George. *Jewish Literature Between the Bible and the Mishnah* (revised edition). Minneapolis: Fortress, 2005.

Daniel

Collins, John J. *Daniel*. Hermeneia. Minneapolis: Fortress, 1993.

Esther

Beal, Timothy. *The Book of Hiding: Gender, Ethnicity, Annihilation, and Esther*. London: Routledge, 1997.

Berlin, Adele. *Esther*. Philadelphia: Jewish Publication Society, 2001.

Chronicles

Japhet, Sara. *1 and 2 Chronicles: A Commentary*. Old Testament Library. Louisville, KY: Westminster John Knox Press, 1993.

The formation of the Hebrew Bible

Carr, David. *Writing on the Tablet of the Heart: Origins of Scripture and Literature*. New York: Oxford University Press, 2005.

CHAPTER 9

STUDYING THE NEW

TESTAMENT IN ITS

ANCIENT CONTEXT

Chapter Outline

CHAPTER OVERVIEW

W̶e turn now to study of the New Testament. In this chapter we come to the last of the imperial powers that influenced the formation of the Christian Bible – Rome. The chapter prepares us for study of the New Testament by examining several different aspects of the ancient context of these writings. You will get a "tour" of ancient Jerusalem as it looked under Rome's rule during the time that Jesus would have traveled there. It may come as a surprise to discover how "Greek" and "Roman" the city had become by the first century BCE. Next the chapter will explore the oral and written traditions that led to the formation of the New Testament writings, especially the gospels. Just as we began with oral traditions in our study of the Old Testament, so too we must consider the role that oral traditions about Jesus played in the growth of the New Testament. The chapter concludes with a discussion of what we can know about the figure that generated the growth of these traditions, namely, the historical Jesus. Although it is difficult to say much with certainty about the historical Jesus (as distinct from the New Testament's various presentations of Jesus), there are some tools that can help. This chapter explains the problems associated with study of the historical Jesus, and the historical methods that New Testament scholars have used in light of these problems. From the evidence available, we will suggest that the theory of Jesus as an apocalyptic thinker is most compelling. First, though, we take another imaginary journey, this time to Jerusalem sometime around 20–30 CE.

Imagining the Jerusalem that Jesus Knew

Chapter 3 took you to the tenth-century BCE Jerusalem of David and Solomon. Here we will travel to this famous city as it stood some thousand years later; we will go to the Jerusalem built by King Herod. Imagine that you are a pilgrim traveling, as Jesus did, to celebrate the Passover festival at the Jerusalem Temple. Approaching the city, you would be able to see the massive Temple mount, foundation for the Temple itself with its surrounding walls and fortified corners (see Figures 9.1 and 9.2). Making your way up under the archways on the wide stone staircase, you might take a stroll on Solomon's porch (Figure 9.3), the beautifully colonnaded walkway on the east side of the Temple. If you were a worldly traveler, this expansive hall atop the outer walls of the Temple mount might bring back memories of your travels in Greece. Indeed, the 182 Corinthian columns were designed to recall the best of Greek architecture. The massive size of the Temple plaza itself would have rivaled any of the finest open civic esplanades in the Roman empire (see Figure 9.4). Adjacent to the Temple mount you would see Herod's imposing Antonia fortress.

Finally, gazing over Jerusalem from the height of the Temple mount, you could look across the city of Jerusalem and see the Greek-styled amphitheatre for the performance of Greek and Roman plays, the hippodrome for chariot races, and of course, the elaborate palace of King Herod with its three enormous fortified towers. To understand the cultural context of the New Testament writings, one must understand why Jerusalem in the first century CE looked like this. How was it that Jerusalem came to be ruled by a king appointed by the Romans and who built Jerusalem to resemble a Greek city? In other words, one must understand Jerusalem in its first century Greco-Roman context.

Figure 9.1 Excavation of outer stairway and arches of the Jerusalem Temple.

Figure 9.2 Model of the Second Temple of Jerusalem, built on the site of Solomon's Temple c. 520 BCE and expanded under Herod in 1 BCE.

Figure 9.3 Model of Solomon's porch on the Temple mount.

Figure 9.4 The Forum of Augustus in Rome. Compare the colonnaded portico to Solomon's porch on the Temple mount.

Rome Comes to Jerusalem

Chapter 8 gave a hint of the growing power of Rome in the second century BCE. By this time, the Roman Republic had taken control of much of the area that is present-day Europe and was pressing eastward. Meanwhile, in spite of the successful Maccabean revolt against Antiochus, Judea did not transition smoothly into independent rule. Instead, the power vacuum left after the revolts was filled with ongoing disputes about who should hold the high priesthood. It was during this time that distinct and often competing groups within Judaism began to take shape, such as the Pharisees, the Sadducees, and the Essenes. More will be said about these different groups in later chapters. For now, it is enough to know that these tensions hastened Rome's entry into Jerusalem, in the person of General Pompey.

In 63 BCE, Judea was embroiled in a civil war between two Hasmonean brothers. At various points in this struggle for power, both brothers sent embassies to Pompey, the Roman general who was then stationed in Syria. Pompey responded by moving his army into Jerusalem to take direct control of the region. Unlike the much earlier invasions by Assyria or Babylon, when the Roman empire seized control of Judea, there was no massive destruction of Jerusalem or its Temple. Nor was there a major deportation of the residents. Instead, Pompey inflicted minimal damage on Jerusalem, ordered the Jewish priests to properly purify the temple after his military advance, and reinstated one of the brothers, Hyrcanus, as high priest.

All of these actions were in keeping with the way that Rome expanded and maintained its empire. The Roman army was never large enough to station garrisons in every part of its expansive empire. Instead, the typical Roman practice was to choose local leaders to rule on their behalf. These **client kings** or procurators, as they were sometimes titled, were typically the elite men of the local communities who stood to benefit from demonstrating their loyalty to Rome. One such local elite man was Herod the Great, who, after carefully working his way into Roman favor, was designated as king of Judea by the Roman Senate in 37 BCE.

Herod, whose reign lasted more than 40 years, is a prime illustration of the cultural complexity that existed in Palestine during this time. Although he identified himself as Jewish, Herod was from Idumea, a region that had been forced to convert to Judaism when the Hasmoneans expanded their kingdom. Given this, local Judeans remained skeptical of his Jewish identity. For his part, Herod understood the need to gain favor both from his Jewish constituents and from his Roman patrons. He therefore began an extensive building program in Jerusalem and throughout Palestine. His Jewish constituents would hardly object to the massive renovation and expansion of the Jerusalem Temple that he funded, nor the construction of roads or aqueducts that improved the infrastructure of Palestine. And his Roman patrons would be impressed with the size and grandeur of his building projects, especially insofar as they competed with the best of Greek architecture elsewhere in the empire.

Indeed, in a paradoxical way, to become Roman during this time was also to become Greek, particularly in the eastern provinces. This is because the Romans themselves were enamored of Greek culture (in spite of Roman claims of superiority). A first-century Roman poet, Horace, put it this way: "Greece, the captive, made her savage victor captive." In other words, although Rome conquered Greece, it was captivated by Greek culture. This is particularly apparent in the way that Roman art and architecture imitated Greek style. The Roman cities that were either newly built or reconstituted across the empire closely resembled the Hellenistic urban centers that were established by Alexander the Great. For this reason, historians often refer to this as the **Greco-Roman period**. Culturally speaking, large swaths of the Roman empire were heavily influenced by an ongoing and even increasing interest in all things Greek. This meant that even the "Jewish" King Herod built cities complete with theaters, agoras, gymnasiums, and so on. If David and Solomon looked to Egyptian and Mesopotamian models for their own emerging kingdom, Herod looked to the Greek-influenced Roman cities as a model for his renovated Jerusalem.

Thus, when Jesus was born in the town of Nazareth in the region of Galilee, he was born into a region which was inhabited predominantly by Jews, ruled by the Romans, and close to cities infused with Greek culture. When he traveled up to Jerusalem to the Temple, it would have been to the grand Temple expanded by Herod. A decade after Jesus's death, when the apostle Paul began his missionary journeys, he would have traveled to cities with Greek-speaking inhabitants. Decades later, when the gospel writers wrote their accounts of Jesus's life and death, they too would write in Greek for a largely Greek-speaking audience. But none of this lessened the fact that politically, all of these regions which concern the New Testament writers were ruled by the Romans. Thus, their stories of Jesus were influenced by their life under Roman occupation. As we turn to examine the earliest traditions about Jesus, we will need to keep in mind this complex cultural and political mix.

The Earliest Christian Traditions

EXERCISE

Read the empty-tomb stories in the four canonical gospels (Mark 16:1–8; Matt 28:1–10; Luke 24:1–12; John 20:1–18). Compare each story, taking notes on who goes to the tomb, who they find there, and what they are told to do.

In the same way we explored the multiple layers of tradition that developed into what we now know as the Old Testament, we must also consider the layered process that lies behind the composition of the New Testament writings, especially the gospels. When you analyzed the four stories of the empty tomb, you may have noticed that, while some details of the story are shared between gospels (Mary Magdalene is present in every case), other details are different. You should also have seen that the stories of Matthew, Mark, and Luke are closer to each other in content than any of them is to John's story.

The type of work that you did in comparing the four gospels was first undertaken seriously in the eighteenth century. The more biblical scholars compared traditions across the four gospels, the more intrigued they became about the literary sources that the authors used to write their stories of Jesus. It soon became clear that Matthew, Mark, and Luke closely resembled each other across major sections of their narratives, while the Gospel of John often had little in common with any of the other three. In fact, Matthew, Mark, and Luke were so similar that they were designated the "**synoptic gospels**." The word "synoptic" means "see together" and indicates the close relationship

Study of the Synoptic Gospels

The gospels of Matthew, Mark, and Luke are known as the synoptic gospels because they are so closely related that one can "see" (optic) them "together" (syn). Scholars who study the synoptic gospels rely on a useful tool called a "synopsis" or gospel parallel. A synopsis of the gospels will align similar gospel texts in parallel columns, so that one can easily compare different versions of a gospel tradition contained in different gospels. Using this tool, scholars have tried to determine how the gospels are related to one another. The question of which of these three gospels was written first and which gospels served as sources for another is known as the "synoptic problem."

between these three gospels. Because they share a great deal of material in common, it is clear there is some sort of source relationship between them. The problem has been to sort out the nature of this relationship. What gospel was written first? What gospel did the other gospel writers have access to? To answer these questions is to solve what scholars have called the **synoptic problem**. Although there are several different solutions that have been suggested, the following has become the consensus view.

First, the Gospel of Mark is widely considered to be earliest canonical gospel. Most scholars date it to sometime near the destruction of the second Temple, 65 to 70 CE. The gospels of Matthew and Luke were written after Mark and incorporate many portions of Mark. Most scholars date Matthew to sometime around 80 to 85 CE, and Luke a bit later, perhaps 85 to 90 CE. The Gospel of John is considered to be the latest of the canonical gospels, dating from around 90 to perhaps as late as 110 CE.

The gospels of Matthew and Luke share additional material that does not appear in the Gospel of Mark. Most of this material contains sayings of Jesus. Because often the same exact wording for these sayings occurs in both gospels, it is likely that the authors had access to another written source, a collection of Jesus's sayings. This hypothetical source is commonly referred to as **Q**, an abbreviation of the German word for source, *Quelle*. In short, most scholars agree that a **two-source theory** provides a convincing solution to the synoptic problem. That is to say that the authors of Matthew and Luke

More on Method: Form Criticism in the New Testament

Scholars have long recognized that the gospel writers relied on oral traditions when they wrote their stories about Jesus. In the early twentieth century, studies of folklore began to influence studies of oral traditions in the Bible. Three scholars in particular, Karl Schmidt, Rudolf Bultmann, and Martin Dibelius, built on these folklore studies to develop a method called **form criticism**. This approach to the text assumes that there are literary units in the gospels that have distinguishable forms that point to their origins in oral tradition. For example, most readers hearing a story that opens with the phrase "once upon a time" and concludes with "happily ever after" recognize the story as a fairy tale. They would not be surprised to find that things happen in sets of three in the story, and that its characters include an evil villain and an innocent protagonist. In the same way, the form critics argued, one could recognize typical features in certain types of Jesus traditions. Healing stories, for example, tend to follow predictable patterns, including a statement of the illness, a reference to complications that prevented healing, and the healing words of Jesus. The form critics suggested that such patterns are signs of an oral stage that predated the written form of these traditions. Such predictable forms made the stories easier to remember and to transmit. Scholarship on the relationship between oral and written traditions has advanced since this early form-critical work, but in recognizing the importance of the oral traditions about Jesus, these scholars helped biblical scholarship take a major step forward.

had two sources that they used for their narrative: Mark and a hypothetical source known as Q. The two-source theory can be illustrated as shown in Figure 9.5.

Note that this two-source solution does not account for all the material in Matthew and Luke. Each of these gospels also contains material that is unique to itself. We will expand the discussion and the diagram in Chapter 12 to account for this material as well. For now, it is enough to recognize that the authors who wrote the gospels of Matthew and Luke were effectively early editors of the Gospel of Mark. Each used the Gospel of Mark as a source, but revised and edited this earlier gospel to suit his own purposes. The same is certainly true for the Q material, but it is more difficult to trace this editorial activity since we have no copy of the Q document.

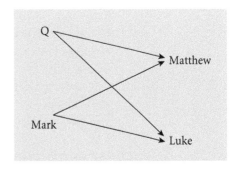

Figure 9.5 Synoptic relationships.

In addition, the diagram tells only one part of the story of the formation of the gospels. It does not take into account the oral transmission of Jesus traditions. As was the case with the earliest stages of the Hebrew scriptural traditions, the traditions about Jesus first developed and circulated in oral form. Because we now live in a digital, rather than oral or even print culture, it takes an active imagination to understand the role of orality in the formation of the New Testament writings. The formation of oral traditions affected the composition of the New Testament at several different stages. First, Jesus himself communicated his teachings in oral form. The gospels all testify that he taught in **parables**; that is, by means of short narratives, or comparative language. The gospel accounts also include various **pronouncements** of Jesus. These are short, direct sayings often designed to best his opponents in a verbal sparring match. Note, for example, the pronouncement that addresses the Pharisees' complaint that Jesus and his disciples are working on the Sabbath: the Sabbath was made for the sake of human beings, not human beings for the sake of the Sabbath (Mark 2:27). The difficulty in appreciating the oral quality of Jesus's ministry is that it has been preserved only in written form. By their very nature, written accounts typically mask the flexibility, fluidity, and repetitiveness that characterize the oral transmission of traditions.

For example, reading the account of Jesus's "Sermon on the Mount" (Matt 5–7), one would no doubt come away with the impression that there was one occasion on which Jesus stood on a mountain and preached this very sermon. But it is far more likely that the contents of this "sermon" are a collection of Jesus's teachings that he used on many occasions in many different places. Similarly, we should imagine Jesus repeating parables and pronouncements on a variety of occasions during the course of his ministry. When he did so, the details likely varied, even as the basic outline of his teachings might have remained the same. These teachings of Jesus comprise the first stage of oral traditions that lie behind the written text of the gospels.

The next stage began some time not long after the death of Jesus when his followers began to retell the stories that Jesus told. These retellings involved the same sort of fluidity and redundancy that were true of the first stage. But now an additional element was added. The followers of Jesus not only passed along his teachings in varying forms, they also began to tell stories *about* Jesus. These stories about Jesus, too, would have been repeated on many occasions in many different places. Again, the telling and retelling of these stories would no doubt vary, while the basic frame of the story would be preserved.

As these stories of Jesus began to spread, there would have been demand for additional stories about Jesus. New believers might have wanted to hear more about the circumstances of his birth, or what he was like as a boy. Although such details may not have been available to the storytellers, there were plenty of cultural models on which they could develop their own versions of Jesus's early days. Stories of "great men" typically included tales of divine omens regarding their birth and their precociousness as children. Similarly, as the emerging community met new challenges, the community may have adapted or created traditions about Jesus that would address their new circumstances. While we might be surprised at the idea of these followers "making up" stories about Jesus, this is because we do not live in an oral culture. Rather than focusing on whether these oral traditions about Jesus are "true" (where "truth" is unhelpfully equated with historical veracity), we should think in terms of what fundamental convictions or "truths" about Jesus these storytellers wanted to convey by means of these stories.

More About the Q Document

The theory that a now lost collection of Jesus's sayings was used as a source for the gospels gained prominence in the early eighteenth century and has continued to be met with scholarly consensus. Evidence that Q was a written rather than oral source comes from the fact that much of this material shared between Matthew and Luke uses identical wording, and is often presented in similar order, something unlikely to be the case if the sayings had been transmitted orally. Also, the fact that these sayings shared between Matthew and Luke, referred to as the **double tradition**, are identical sayings in *Greek* suggests that the source must have been written. Jesus's native tongue would have been Aramaic, making it hard to account for identical Greek renderings of his sayings unless they were written down. In addition, the discovery of the Gospel of Thomas in 1945 lent more evidence to the theory. The Gospel of Thomas, found in Egypt along with a collection of early Christian writings, is a list of sayings of Jesus. While it is not Q, the existence of such a written collection of sayings supports the idea that such collections existed in the early days of the Jesus movement. Some scholars, such as John Kloppenborg (*Excavating Q: The History and Setting of the Sayings Gospel* [Philadelphia: Fortress, 2000]) have posited detailed reconstructions of the hypothetical Q document, but others are skeptical that such a project is possible.

At some stage in this oral process, followers of Jesus also began to use writing to consolidate and spread traditions about Jesus. As mentioned above, one such early written text appears to have been a collection of sayings of Jesus (the Q document). In addition, we have evidence that there may have been similar written collections of miracle stories. But even as these Jesus sayings and miracle stories began to be recorded, there was no sharp break between the oral and written stages of the tradition. Instead, these early written texts remained closely linked with the oral transmission of the Jesus traditions. Written texts would have been learned and memorized as part of the same sort of enculturation process that we saw at work in the memorization of ancient Israelite traditions. On the other hand, even while written texts were produced and circulated (in both written and memorized oral form), early Christians would have continued to tell stories about Jesus that would not find their way into written texts for decades. We see traces of this ongoing process of memorization and recitation both in the types of memory shifts evident in the different versions of Mark or Q present in the synoptic gospels (Mark, Matthew, and Luke), and in the even more basic differences between the synoptic gospels on the one hand and the Gospel of John on the other. In the case of the Gospel of John it appears that its author drew on a stream of oral tradition that was not available to the other gospel writers – perhaps because the oral traditions developed at a later stage, and/or in another geographical location (see Figure 9.6).

Moreover, the gospels that were written in the second and third centuries, gospels that were not included in the New Testament, convey stories about Jesus that are not found in the earlier canonical gospels. For example, the Infancy Gospel of Thomas, a

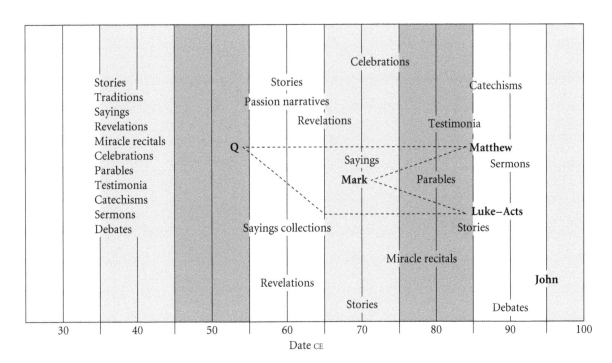

Figure 9.6 Oral and written material that contributed to the development of early Christian traditions. Note that even as some traditions began to be collected and put into written form, the development of oral traditions continued. Redrawn from David L. Barr, *New Testament Story: An Introduction*, 2nd edn., Wadsworth, 1995, p. 203.

second-century text, relates stories of the boyhood of Jesus, presenting him as a temperamental child who initially uses his extraordinary powers to strike down those who are annoying him. Such stories are not eyewitness records from Jesus's contemporaries. Instead, these tales about Jesus are more likely oral traditions about Jesus's boyhood that developed in the ongoing life of the early church alongside its first written texts about Jesus's later career. Thus, when we imagine the transmission of traditions in the emerging Christian communities, we should keep in mind a very active dimension of orality and memorization in early communities, a dimension important for the use both of written and of exclusively oral traditions about Jesus.

By now, it should be apparent that the process by which the gospels were produced was far more complex than you once might have imagined. Rather than a companion of Jesus simply writing down what actually happened during Jesus's life, it turns out that the gospels were a product of the earliest Christian communities. This often leads students to the next obvious question. If these gospels were not written by eyewitnesses, how do we know they are conveying the truth about what Jesus did and said? For that matter, how can we know about what Jesus actually did and said? These are questions about the historical Jesus to which we now turn.

The Jesus of History and the Textual Jesus of Faith

EXERCISE

Read and study the way each of the four canonical gospels describes the baptism of Jesus (Mark 1:9–11; Matt 3:13–17; Luke 3:21–2; John 1:29–34). What details are the same? What differences do you notice? Note also the context for each of these scenes. What comes before and after the baptism in each gospel?

The term "**historical Jesus**" refers to the figure of Jesus that is reconstructed through historical methods, as distinct from the "Jesus" presented in the Bible and other texts. It may be difficult to understand the idea of a "historical Jesus" as distinct from the Jesus that we read about in the New Testament. Unless you have been introduced to New Testament scholarship in another context, you most likely assume that the gospels accurately report on the life of Jesus. But, as we have seen, the process of gospel composition was more complicated than this.

Again, when you examined stories about the empty tomb, you noticed that each gospel has its own version of what happened at the tomb. It is not the case that some stories are simply *more* detailed than others; the details of the stories differ in ways that are irreconcilable. In the Gospel of John, Mary Magdalene goes alone to the tomb. In the Gospel of Mark, the women who go to the tomb include Mary Magdalene, the "other" Mary, and Salome. In the Gospel of Matthew, it is Mary Magdalene and the "other" Mary only. In Luke's gospel, unnamed women find two men in the tomb. The women in Mark's gospel see one young man, while in Matthew's gospel, they encounter an angel. Clearly, it takes a lot of mental gymnastics to try to prove that such differing accounts are all historically accurate. Moreover, it is hardly likely that one of the gospel writers got it right, while the others did not. Instead, the gospel writers all present their own story of Jesus, based on traditions that they have received and their own understanding of Jesus.

This becomes even clearer when we consider questions of dating and authorship of the gospels. As mentioned before, the earliest gospel was likely written around 70 CE. This means that there was a forty-year gap between the death of Jesus and the first written gospel. The other three gospels were written at an even greater distance from the living Jesus. Such a long time gap adds to the difficulty of considering the gospel narratives as reliable historical records. Moreover, despite the titles that were given these gospels, all four of the canonical gospels were originally anonymous. It was only in the second century CE, when the four gospels were published as a collection, that the superscriptions were added to the gospels, attributing authorship to Matthew, Mark, Luke, and John respectively. This is also the time that traditions begin to appear about the authors, claiming that they were either original apostles of Jesus (Matthew and John) or close acquaintances of other well-known apostles (Mark with Peter and Luke with Paul). In spite of these attributions, most scholars do not think any of these men were the original gospel writers. None of the gospels is written in a style that suggests the author was present at the events that are being narrated. Nor is it likely that the disciples of Jesus were able to write in Greek, the language in which the gospels were written. So we are left with the reality that the gospels were written by anonymous Christians decades after the events that they relate. (In the rest of this book, we will refer to the gospels using the traditional names associated with each one, even though we recognize that the gospel writers are unknown.) These authors, whoever they were, believed Jesus to be the long-awaited Jewish messiah and the Son of God, and their writings are an effort to demonstrate the truth of this faith claim. In short, the gospels do not offer the reader clear access to the historical Jesus. They do offer a textual picture of Jesus that grew out of the faith of believing Christians.

In spite of the difficulties in finding objective "history" in these gospels, there has been a centuries-long interest in searching out the historical kernel of the gospels. After all, Jesus was, in fact, a person in history, and it is not unreasonable to expect some traditions about Jesus to be grounded in historical events. This assumption lies behind the so-called "quest for the historical Jesus," a quest that began in earnest during the nineteenth century. A major goal of this quest has been to develop objective scientific methods that one could apply to the gospel accounts in order to construct a historically accurate picture of Jesus. Work on this project has continued in various forms up to the present time. At this point, most scholars who work on this question agree on the following criteria by which to measure the historical authenticity of the traditions about Jesus in the gospels.

- *Multiple attestations from independent sources*: This criterion means that if a tradition about Jesus exists in distinct sources such as Mark, Q, or John it has a greater probability of being historically accurate. Note that the existence of a tradition in Mark, Matthew, and Luke (or some combination of two of these gospels) would count as only one source, since Matthew and Luke both used Mark for their gospels. So, for example, the account of Jesus's action in the Temple during the Passover is present in both the synoptic tradition (Mark 11:15–18, along with parallels in Luke and Matthew) and the Gospel of John (2:13–22), and so is an example of a tradition with double attestation.
- *Dissimilarity*: If a Jesus tradition does not fit in a first-century Jewish milieu, and is not readily explainable as a tradition that might have developed in the emerging church, it is likely to be authentic. For example, one could argue that the reports of Jesus eating with "tax-collectors and sinners" reflect a practice that did not coincide with first-century Jewish practices or developing practices within the Christian community. It is thus potentially a practice unique to the historical Jesus. But note that this criterion only affirms as potentially historical some Jesus traditions that do not fit well with their surrounding context. The criterion cannot confirm or deny the historicity of Jesus traditions that present him conforming to Jewish and/or early Christian norms. Since Jesus probably did do and say many things that fit easily in his milieu, this "criterion of dissimilarity" is not relevant to evaluating a lot of potentially historical traditions about Jesus. Moreover, the criterion also requires us to know what was "normal" for ancient Jewish and Christian communities, and this in itself is a difficult task, since our best evidence suggests that both of these groups varied widely in beliefs and practices during this time.
- *Criterion of embarrassment*: This criterion is related to the previous one, but focuses particularly on traditions that the early church would not likely have developed on its own because they are in tension with the church's confessions about Jesus. The story of Jesus's baptism, discussed below, is one example of a tradition that fits this criterion.
- *Coherence with other already established traditions*: This criterion argues that if a tradition is consistent with another already established tradition, it too may well be authentic. Thus, if one has established that Jesus taught a particular parable about the kingdom of God, one might readily assume that other similar parables could be traced to the historical Jesus.

To see some of these criteria at work, consider the story of Jesus's baptism that you have studied. First, if we read across the gospels, we can see some type of baptism scene attested in two sources: the synoptic tradition (starting with Mark) and the Gospel of John. Thus, this baptism tradition fulfills the criterion of multiple attestations. Second, research into Jewish practices in the first century suggests that John's baptism does not fit easily within the cultural milieu. Although some Jewish communities appear to have used ritual baths for purification, we have no evidence that baptism for the forgiveness of sins was a common practice within first-century Judaism. Thus, John's practice is "dissimilar" to its surrounding culture. Third, a story of Jesus's baptism was unlikely to be a later development in the Christian tradition since the act of being baptized by John suggests that Jesus was a disciple of John. Such apparent dependence of Jesus on John would have been a problem for later Christians. Moreover, John's baptism was for the forgiveness of sins, but the later developing traditions about Jesus claimed that he was without sin. For both reasons, it is unlikely that the church would develop a story about Jesus being baptized by John – the issue of Jesus's baptism would be more of an "embarrassment" to the early church. So, on the basis of several different criteria, it seems likely that Jesus actually was baptized by John.

However, things get more complicated when we look in detail at the accounts of the baptism. Precisely because Jesus's baptism was in tension with emerging ideas about Jesus, each of the four gospels deals differently with the problems posed by the tradition of Jesus's baptism and his interaction with John the Baptist. Thus, while Mark's gospel opens with the baptism scene, Jesus's dependence on John is downplayed by a story of John's prediction of one coming (apparently Jesus) who is more powerful than he is. The Gospel of Matthew deals with the same problem by featuring a conversation in which John objects to the idea of baptizing Jesus, suggesting that Jesus should be the one baptizing him. Luke's gospel literarily distances John from the baptism scene. It reports the arrest and imprisonment of John the Baptist immediately *before* the account of Jesus's baptism (even though John's arrest could only have happened after the baptism of Jesus). It then mentions the baptism only passively, "after Jesus was baptized," giving no explicit statement that John baptized Jesus at all. Finally, as you likely noticed, the Gospel of John never specifically mentions a baptism of Jesus. In this gospel, John, who notably is not called "the Baptist," testifies that he saw the spirit descending on Jesus like a dove. While the dove motif recalls other baptism stories, there is no explicit reference to baptism.

What would account for these differences? The gospel writers were working with the awkward historical fact that Jesus was baptized by John. All the authors present the story in a way that preserves Jesus's superiority to John, in spite of the baptism. In short, the baptism scenes provide a good example of how one might both determine a "historical kernel" in a Jesus tradition and perceive the ways that story is modified by the storytellers. Note that we are not left with the "right" version of the story at the end of our analysis. We can say only that it is likely that Jesus was baptized by John. The historical details of what exactly happened, what was said at the time, and who was a witness to the event are lost to us. What has been preserved are the convictions of believing Christians about Jesus's status and authority vis-à-vis John the Baptist.

Thus, one can see how these basic criteria necessarily fall short in constructing a historically accurate and highly specific figure of Jesus. Indeed, scholars who have contributed to this project have yet to come to a consensus, even though the "quest" has been going on in various forms for about two hundred years. In large part, this lack of agreement about the historical Jesus is due to the limitation of the sources. But to some extent, it is also due to the differing perspectives of the scholars themselves. This phenomenon was famously observed by Albert Schweitzer as early as 1901. In his book *The Quest for the Historical Jesus*, Schweitzer examined the various attempts at constructing the historical figure of Jesus, concluding that:

> each successive epoch of theology found its own thoughts in Jesus; that was, indeed, the only way in which it could make Him live. But it was not only each epoch that found its reflection in Jesus; each individual created Him in accordance with his own character. There is no historical task which so reveals a man's true self as the writing of a Life of Jesus.

Anyone attempting to construct a historically accurate figure of Jesus should be aware of Schweitzer's insight. It is all too tempting to see the Jesus of history just as we would want him to be, rather than what the evidence might suggest. On this point too, Schweitzer had something to say, arguing that "The historical Jesus will be to our time a stranger and an enigma." By this he meant that we must take seriously the temporal, social, and cultural gap between our world and the world of Jesus. If the historical Jesus we imagine seems at home in the twenty-first century, chances are we do not have an accurate historical construction. Instead, as with the stories about Jesus in the early church, our contemporary picture of "Jesus" may well be a projection of our dreams and ideals.

All that said, Schweitzer himself offered his own ideas about the historical Jesus, emphasizing the idea of a thoroughgoing eschatology that motivated Jesus. **Eschatology** means literally "study of the last things." In highlighting the eschatological aspect of Jesus, Schweitzer argued that the historical Jesus, like many other first-century Jews, expected the imminent arrival of the reign of God. According to Schweitzer, Jesus's final pilgrimage to Jerusalem was intended to help usher in the kingdom of God. In more recent years, scholars such as E. P. Sanders, Bart Ehrman, and Paula Fredriksen have followed Schweitzer in highlighting Jesus's identity as an eschatological or, more precisely,

Eschatology versus Apocalypticism

While these two terms are sometimes used interchangeably, for biblical scholarship there is a difference in their meaning. "Eschatology" is a general term that refers to ideas related to the end times. "Apocalypticism," however, refers to a specific worldview that expects God's cosmic intervention to set right the evils of the world. As you saw in Chapter 8, the term "apocalypse" literally means "uncovering," and historical apocalypses typically convey revealed knowledge of how God's intervention is going to occur. We should recall, however, that as a literary genre, not all apocalypses are of the historical type. The heavenly apocalypses described in Chapter 8 may have little to do with the end times.

an **apocalyptic** prophet. By using the term "apocalyptic," these scholars are suggesting that Jesus had a particular expectation of God's direct intervention in human affairs – one that we have already seen introduced in Daniel. In this case, **apocalypticism** indicates a belief that divine intervention will inaugurate a glorious new age for those who have remained faithful and just. Meanwhile, the evil powers that have been in control of the world will be judged and punished.

As we will see in the chapters that follow, apocalypticism is a consistent strand that runs through much of the early Christian literature, beginning with the letters of Paul. And, as we have already seen, Jesus most likely was a follower of John the Baptist, who proclaimed an apocalyptic message of preparation for the coming judgment of God. According to the Gospel of Mark, Jesus's own preaching focused on the coming of the reign of God, and many of his parables were about the coming kingdom. All of this suggests that Jesus was one of many apocalyptic Jewish thinkers living in the first century CE.

In addition to recognizing the apocalyptic worldview of Jesus, any historical construction of Jesus must take into account the fact that Jesus was crucified by the Romans. For this to have occurred, his words or activities must have threatened the Roman regime in some way. To be sure, the gospel narratives are clear that Jesus was in conflict with various leaders in the Jewish community. But it was not the typical practice of Roman rulers to execute men over intellectual and/or religious disagreements with their contemporaries. Jesus's dispute may well have been with the religious leaders of his time, but his activities also gained the attention of the Roman authorities.

One clue may lie in the report provided by all of the gospels that Jesus was crucified under the charge that he was calling himself "king of the Jews." The title appears in various accounts of Jesus's trial before Pilate (Mark 15:2; John 18:33) and is also in accounts of an inscription that was hung on the cross with Jesus (Matt 27:37; Luke 23:38; John 19:19–21). "King of the Jews" is not a title that his followers appeared to use. In fact, in John's gospel, there may be deliberate avoidance of the title, as Jesus is called king of Israel (John 1:49). In any case, if this was the charge that was brought to the Roman authorities, it may well have been the reason for his death at the hands of the Romans. Roman authorities would have viewed such a claim as treason against the emperor and thus cause for execution.

Apart from this charge, the Gospel of Mark suggests that Jesus's actions in the Temple were a decisive factor leading to his arrest and crucifixion (Mark 11:18; see also Luke 19:47). The so-called "cleansing" of the Temple is attested by multiple witnesses (Mark 11:15–17; John 2:14–16). Moreover, if Jesus did engage in this act of protest, he would not have been alone in his critique of Temple leadership and practices. We have already learned about disputes among different Jewish groups during the Maccabean period. There is additional evidence from the first century CE for ongoing disputes about the Temple. For instance, the writings discovered in the desert caves at Qumran suggest that a Jewish group had retreated to the Judean desert in protest over the Temple leadership. The group, which many scholars identify as the Essenes, rejected the authority of "the wicked priest" and lived under the leadership of a figure described as the "teacher of righteousness." Several of these writings suggest that the group was waiting for the restoration of the proper family to the Temple priesthood. Given this general time of unrest, it is thus quite conceivable that the historical Jesus also engaged in a critique of the Temple leadership and practices. Perhaps he predicted the Temple's destruction (see Mark 14:58), and symbolically enacted this destruction by causing a disturbance in the Temple precincts. As we saw in our study of the prophets, this sort of symbolic enactment was common in the prophetic tradition. More to the point, this type of civil disruption might well have triggered a strong reaction from the Roman authorities.

In the end, we can only speculate about the historical realities that lie behind the narratives of Jesus as we find them in the gospels and other New Testament writings. The discussion in the coming chapters will focus more on the different depictions of Jesus that come to us from the New Testament texts. This is the Jesus known by early Christians living in the midst of the Roman empire. It is this Jesus that lived on in the cultural memory of the early Christians and was transmitted in oral and written form for later generations.

CHAPTER NINE REVIEW

1. Know the meaning and significance of the following terms discussed in this chapter:
- apocalyptic
- apocalypticism
- client kings
- double tradition
- eschatology
- form criticism
- Greco-Roman period
- historical Jesus
- parables
- pronouncements
- Q
- synoptic gospels
- synoptic problem
- two-source theory

2. What was the role of both oral and written sources in the composition of the gospels?

3. What is the difference between the historical Jesus and the textual Jesus? What problems do scholars encounter in researching the historical Jesus? What methods do they use for their work?

4. Students are often troubled to learn that some of the gospel stories of Jesus may not have actually happened just as they are reported. The question that seems to follow is, "Are the stories true?" Can you think of examples of stories that communicate something that you think to be "true" even if the stories did not really happen? What does this suggest about using historicity as the ultimate measure of "truth"?

RESOURCES FOR FURTHER STUDY

General gospel studies

Aland, Kurt. *Synopsis of the Four Gospels.* United Bible Societies, 1985.

Kelber, Werner. *The Oral and the Written Gospel: The Hermeneutics of Speaking and Writing in the Synoptic Tradition, Mark, Paul, and Q* (2nd edition). Bloomington/Indianapolis: Indiana University Press, 1997.

Perkins, Pheme. *Introduction to the Synoptic Gospels.* Grand Rapids, MI: Eerdmans, 2007.

Powell, Mark Allan. *Fortress Introduction to the Gospels.* Philadelphia: Augsburg Fortress, 1998.

Studies of the social and historical context of the New Testament

Barrett, C. K. *The New Testament Background: Selected Documents: Revised and Expanded Edition.* San Francisco: HarperOne, 1995.

Cartlidge, David R., and Dungan, David L., eds. *Documents for the Study of the Gospels* (revised edition). Philadelphia: Fortress, 1994.

Ferguson, Everett. *Backgrounds of Early Christianity* (3rd edition). Grand Rapids, MI: Eerdmans, 2003.

Levine, A. J., Allison, Jr., Dale C., and Crossan, John Dominic, eds. *The Historical Jesus in Context.* Princeton, NJ: Princeton University Press, 2006.

Malina, Bruce. *The New Testament World: Insights from Cultural Anthropology* (3rd edition). Louisville, KY: Westminster John Knox Press, 2001.

Historical Jesus studies

Dunn, James D. G., and McKnight, Scot, eds. *The Historical Jesus in Recent Research.* Winona Lake, IN: Eisenbrauns, 2005.

Ehrman, Bart. *Jesus of Nazareth: Apocalyptic Prophet for the New Millennium.* New York: Oxford University Press, 1999.

Fredriksen, Paula. *From Jesus to Christ: The Origins of the New Testament Images of Jesus.* New Haven: Yale University Press, 1988.

Schweitzer, Albert. *The Quest for the Historical Jesus.* London: SCM, 2001.

Sanders, E. P. *The Historical Figure of Jesus.* New York: Penguin, 1995.

Theissen, Gerd. *In the Shadow of the Galilean: The Quest for the Historical Jesus in Narrative Form.* Minneapolis: Fortress, 2003.

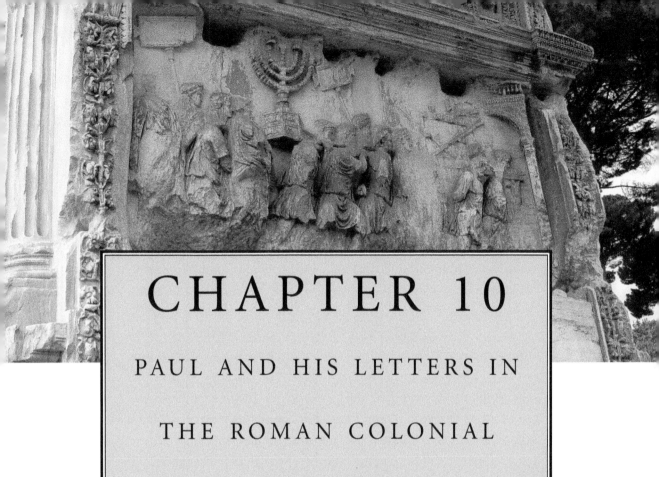

CHAPTER 10

PAUL AND HIS LETTERS IN

THE ROMAN COLONIAL

CONTEXT

Chapter Outline

CHAPTER OVERVIEW

This chapter will introduce you to the apostle Paul and to a group of letters that are attributed to him. While we have looked at the ways that imperial forces have helped to shape the biblical text, Paul provides an interesting example of how imperial forces helped to shape one's personal identity. Paul is the product of multiple cultural influences – Jewish, Greek, and Roman. As we will see, the influence of imperialization is stamped on his personal identity, and affects the way he views the world. Studying the Pauline letters also provides an opportunity to explore the urban settings in which early Christianity took root and spread across the Roman empire. The chapter will show that along with Paul's success in convincing gentiles to worship the God of Israel and to believe in his son Jesus Christ came a number of problems. These new converts had strong opinions about life issues such as sexuality, marriage, eating practices, and ritual practices that Paul did not always share. His letters provide a glimpse into the earliest days of emerging Christianity as these believers worked out their new identity in the midst of the larger culture. Although we cannot examine all of Paul's letters in detail, we will discuss issues in three of his major letters: 1 Corinthians, Galatians, and Romans. Finally, the chapter will discuss the disputed letters. These are letters that are attributed to Paul, but whose authorship is disputed by many scholars.

Paul's Travels and Letter Collection

Imagine that you discover a collection of letters written by someone who lived two thousand years ago. The letters are written to communities in several different cities, or in some cases to particular individuals. While the letters share some ideas, they appear to address different issues, and the tone of the letters ranges from joyous to angry. Your task, upon finding these letters, is to learn as much as you can about who wrote the letters, why they were written, and what they were intended to mean to the communities who received them. This is one of the central tasks in studying the letters of Paul.

Perhaps it seems unusual to begin the study of the New Testament with this letter collection, since the gospels and the Acts of the Apostles appear earlier in the New Testament. But, in fact, Paul's letters were likely written at least ten years before the first canonical gospel was written. When he addressed these fledgling Christian communities, neither they, nor he, could have read any of the gospels because they did not yet exist. In short, there was no "New Testament" for these earliest Christians. Beginning our study with Paul gives us a glimpse of the real-life issues that concerned these earliest Christians as they began to forge a new identity in the midst of the Roman empire.

We begin with a brief look at the cities in which Paul concentrated his missionary efforts. By the first half of the first century CE, Rome had conquered vast amounts of land, reaching the peak of its power in the early second century (see Map 10.1). This expansion was made possible not only by Rome's military strength, but also by the impressive system of roads that was developed, maintained, and protected by Rome. These roads, which moved Roman armies across the empire, also made possible the spread of Christianity. The use of these roads by Paul (and by his followers who delivered his letters) is one concrete example of the influence of Rome on the New Testament writings. In fact, if you were traveling with Paul on his missionary journeys, you would have traveled on a major Roman thoroughfare called the Via Egnatia, or the Egnation Way (see Figure 10.1). This road was built to connect a series of Roman colonies, one of which was Philippi. This small Greek city was named after its founder, Philip of Macedon, the father of Alexander the Great. Arriving there with Paul, a decade or so after the death of Jesus, you would have entered a city that had been colonized by Rome for more than one hundred years, and settled by Roman war veterans and their descendents. Latin inscriptions would mark the civic buildings and imperial statues, although a sizeable portion of the inhabitants would be Greek speaking.

If you continued on the Via Egnatia you would also come to Thessalonica, a major trading hub between Europe and Asia, located at the crossroads of the east–west Via Egnatia and the road running between the Danube River in the north and the Aegean Sea in the south. In Paul's time, Thessalonica was the large capital city of a Roman province. It had a cosmopolitan population, and, unlike Philippi, remained a Greek city under Roman rule, with Greek inscriptions outnumbering Latin ones.

Another major city on Paul's missionary route was Corinth, located to the south on two harbors. Like Philippi, Corinth had been reconstituted as a Roman colony and thus had a strong Latin presence. Like Thessalonica, it served as the capital of a Roman province, Achaia, which included southern Greece. Given its control of two harbors, it was a major center of trade. In Paul's time, the city would have been bustling with life and a diverse group of inhabitants (see Figure 10.2). And all of these cities would have

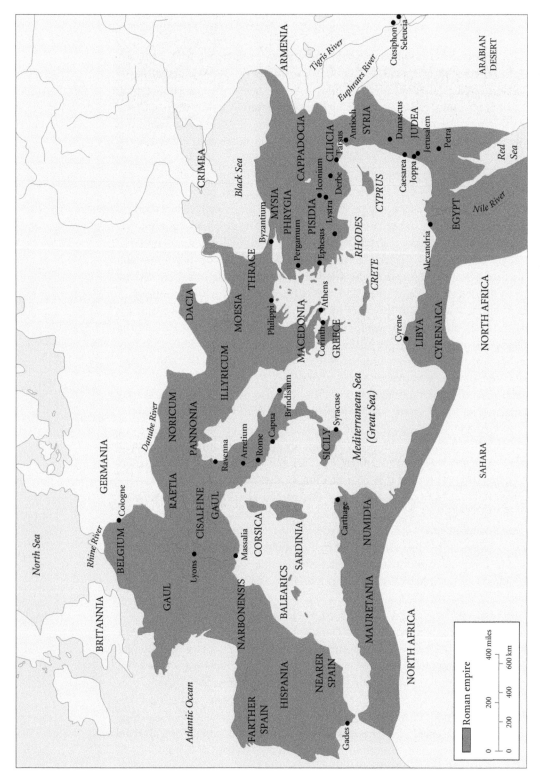

Map 10.1 The Roman Empire c.30 BCE. Redrawn from Steven L. Harris, *Understanding the Bible* (6th edition). McGraw Hill, 2003, page 352.

Figure 10.1 Remains of the Via Egnatia, Rome's primary artery to the east. Paul would have traveled along this road to Philippi and Thessalonica.

Figure 10.2 Doorways of shops in ancient Corinth.

Figure 10.3 Statue of Augustus showing him wearing the veil of the *pontifex maximus.* the highest priestly position in the Roman state religion.

shared elements common to the Greco-Roman cities of this period: large amphitheaters, temples devoted to various deities, an agora or outdoor assembly place, a gymnasium, and a colonnade leading to important buildings such as the forum for civic affairs.

Moreover, all of these cities would convey the power of Rome in various forms. Statues of the emperor would proclaim him as the bringer of peace and savior of the people. Inscriptions on public pillars would celebrate military achievements, or honor imperial officials. One famous example is the Priene inscription discovered in modern-day Turkey. Dating from 9 BCE, the inscription marks the institution of a new calendar "for good luck and salvation" based on the birthday of Augustus (see Figure 10.3). The decree announces the reign of the emperor as "the beginning of the good news for the world" and describes the emperor as "a savior, who brought an end to war and established peace." (See "The Priene Calendar Inscription," p. 318.)Other marble reliefs conveyed the important priestly role of the emperor as one who mediated between the people and the gods, thus ensuring divine favor toward the empire.

When we consider Paul's mission and the communities to whom he wrote, we should imagine him in these urban settings. Paul worked among people who were immersed in diverse urban populations that had long been under the reign of Rome. The issues that concerned them in their new religious identity often grew out of their urban environment. But what about the apostle Paul? What more can we know about the man who traveled thousands of miles across the empire to preach the gospel in these Greco-Roman cities?

Who Was Paul?

READING
Rom 9:1–5;
Galatians 1–2;
Phil 3:1–11.

EXERCISE
What clues about Paul's identity do you find in these passages? How did Paul regard himself? Who does he mean by the phrase "my own people" (Rom 9:3)?

The apostle Paul represents the sort of person that imperialism and its aftermath tend to produce: one shaped by multiple and sometimes competing cultural influences.

By the first century CE, the many instances of imperial domination across the Mediterranean made the existence of a "pure" cultural identity virtually impossible. So we see in Paul a blend of identities working together to produce a fascinating and complex personality. To be sure, Paul claims for himself a solid Jewish identity: he is a "Hebrew of Hebrews," circumcised on the eighth day, a Pharisee who is blameless in matters of the law (Phil. 3:5–6, see also 2 Cor 11:22). He speaks of the Israelites as his own people, his kindred according to the flesh (Rom 9:3–4). He claims that he was more advanced than his peers in the traditions of the ancestors (Gal 1:14), suggesting an education based on the Torah and the oral traditions of the Pharisees. Still, it is clear that Paul is also thoroughly Hellenized, writing in Greek with a rhetorical style that could only have been learned through a Greek education. Moreover, his letters demonstrate that he knew proper Greco-Roman letter form, a further indication of his education. In this way, Paul is a product of both the Hellenistic empire that introduced the standard of a Greek education across the Mediterranean, and the Roman empire that reinforced the importance of this education for successful Roman citizens.

The Structure of Paul's Letters

You know how to properly begin and end different letter styles, whether a formal letter of application, or a note to your friend. So too Paul followed the first-century cultural conventions of letter writing, with some modifications. Greco-Roman letters typically adopted the following structure:

- salutation: identification of letter writer and the addressee(s);
- health wish;
- body of letter (adopting standard rhetorical conventions depending on the purpose of the letter);
- greetings to particular people associated with the addressee(s);
- closing.

Paul follows this same basic form with two modifications. Rather than the health wish, he typically substituted a thanksgiving section in which he includes praise of the community for their acceptance of and work on behalf of the gospel (see, for example, 1 Thess 1:2–10; Phil 1:3–11). Similarly, instead of standard words of closing, Paul uses a blessing at the end of these letters (for example, 1 Thess 5:28; Phil 4:23). In the body of his letters, Paul frequently uses rhetorical patterns that he would have learned as a youth, such as deliberative (persuading his audience to take a particular course), judicial (defending his actions), or epideictic (praise and blame of others).

This brings us to the last aspect of Paul's cultural identity. For, in addition to this mix of Jewish and Greek identities, the Acts of the Apostles also portrays Paul as a Roman citizen. Paul himself never says he is a citizen in his surviving letters, so it is difficult to gauge the accuracy of this claim. Still, because Roman citizenship could be granted any number of ways, there is no strong reason to doubt the tradition. One could be born into citizenship (which is what the author of Acts has Paul claim for himself in Acts 22:28), or citizenship could be granted to all the inhabitants of a foreign city, to the aristocratic class of a Roman provincial city, or to an individual as a reward for service to Rome. In sum, if Paul was a Roman citizen, then he was a Hellenized Jewish Pharisee with Roman citizenship who had aligned himself with a group that confessed Jesus to be the promised Jewish messiah. Quite a blend of identities! Understanding this range of influences that shaped the identity of Paul will help us interpret his letters.

A major issue that confronts a student who wants to learn about Paul is the problem of sources. On the one hand, we have the advantage of both primary and secondary sources upon which to draw to construct a life of Paul. On the other hand, both types of sources raise difficult questions. The primary sources, Paul's letters, raise questions of authorship. Although there are 13 letters in the New Testament that are attributed to Paul, there are good reasons to doubt that Paul wrote all of them. (Note that Hebrews has no internal author attribution, although some ancient manuscripts credited the writing to Paul. See Chapter 15 for additional discussion.) Most scholars agree that 7 of the 13 Pauline letters are authentic, that is, were written by Paul. These **undisputed letters** (because no one disputes their authorship) are Romans, 1 and 2 Corinthians, Galatians, Philippians, 1 Thessalonians, and Philemon. They share a common style and vocabulary. Moreover, the letters all seem to fit within a span of about ten years beginning around 49–50 CE. It is more difficult to make such claims for the remaining six letters – the **disputed letters**. For various reasons, the authorship of 2 Thessalonians, Ephesians, Colossians, 1 and 2 Timothy, and Titus is debated, with many scholars arguing that later followers of Paul wrote these letters in his name. We will return to these disputed letters later. For now, it is important to understand that scholars must make an assessment about the authorship of these letters before they can rely on them as a primary source.

The Undisputed and Disputed Letters of Paul

The undisputed letters are:

Romans
1 Corinthians
2 Corinthians
Galatians
Philippians
1 Thessalonians
Philemon

The disputed letters are:

Ephesians
Colossians
2 Thessalonians
1 Timothy
2 Timothy
Titus

The main secondary source, the Acts of the Apostles, is also problematic for use in reconstructing Paul's life. Although much of this canonical work narrates Paul's missionary journeys and his conflicts with Jewish and Roman authorities, it is often difficult to reconcile with Paul's own letters. As we have already seen, Acts provides details that Paul never mentions in his own letters, such as his birthplace in Tarsus in Cilicia (Acts 22:3), his Roman citizenship, and three different accounts of his encounter with the resurrected Jesus (compare 9:3–22; 22:3–13; 26:4–18). More problematic are details about Paul that conflict with what Paul himself writes. Whereas the Paul in Acts reports several trips to Jerusalem, including one immediately following his time in Damascus (e.g., Acts 9:26; 15:2; 21:17), Paul writes that he did *not* go to Jerusalem until three years after his time in Damascus (Gal 1:15–19). Indeed, one gets the impression he visited Jerusalem only twice, and was planning on one more visit before heading west to Spain. Similarly, whereas the Paul in Acts begins his teaching in the synagogues, turning to the gentiles only after he has been rejected by the synagogue leaders, he states in his letters that he was called to be an apostle to the "uncircumcised" while others will go to the "circumcised." Such differences suggest that we cannot rely uncritically on the Acts of the Apostles for historical information about Paul.

Given this, most scholars focus on the undisputed letters as a starting place for understanding Paul. This is the approach we take in this chapter. In the next section, we will pay particular attention to Paul's statements of self-definition in these undisputed letters. These are things that Paul wants others to know about him, and such statements give us insight into what Paul thinks is important about his own identity and mission.

Apostle to the gentiles

If we proceed on this basis, several aspects of Paul begin to emerge. Foremost, as already mentioned above, Paul speaks of himself as an apostle who has been called by God to bring the gospel to the gentiles. Beginning with his earliest surviving letter, 1 Thessalonians, Paul indicates that he is writing primarily to gentiles and celebrating their turn to faith in God (1 Thess 1:9). In Gal 1:15–16, Paul expresses his God-given mission to the gentiles most clearly:

> But when God, who had set me apart from my mother's womb and called me through his grace, was pleased to reveal his Son to me, so that I might bring the good news of him to the gentiles . . .

Later in this same letter, Paul describes a meeting with the leaders in the Jerusalem church at which they are convinced that God has entrusted him with the gospel to the gentiles, and agree that he should continue that work (Gal 2:1–10). The letter to the Romans conveys similar ideas. There, too, Paul writes of being called by God, and set apart for the gospel in order to bring about obedience of faith among all the gentiles (Rom 1:1–6; see also 1 Cor 1:1).

The Swedish scholar Krister Stendahl in *Paul among Jews and Gentiles and Other Essays* has helpfully brought to our attention what Paul does *not* say in relation to his identity. While Paul speaks regularly of his *call* to apostleship, he does not speak about a *conversion* to a new religion. Paul never suggests that he has given up his Jewishness for a new religion called Christianity. Rather, he has gained a radically new understanding of how the God of Israel relates to gentiles, and he believes that God has called him to communicate God's message to the gentiles. Key to his new understanding is that gentiles, too, can now be heirs to the promises that God gave to Israel. Also key to his understanding is that this status is gained not through adherence to the requirements of the law, but through faith. What precisely this means for Paul is a point to which we will return.

Although the Acts of the Apostles relates a story of Paul's revelation on the road to Damascus, Paul does not write of this episode in his letters. Using the third person, he speaks rather mysteriously about "knowing a man" who experienced "visions and revelations from the Lord," was transported to the "third heaven," and heard things that "no mortal is permitted to speak" (2 Cor 12:2–4). Such a description recalls the heavenly journeys of the apocalyptic literature that was popular among certain Jewish groups. This brings us to another significant aspect of Paul's identity.

Paul's apocalypticism

In the first century CE, the **apocalyptic worldview**, first reflected in the literary apocalypses of the third and second centuries BCE (see Chapter 8), had gained in popularity among certain Jewish communities. One such community, commonly referred to as the Essenes, lived in the Judean desert awaiting the coming of both a priestly and a royal messiah who together would usher in a golden age. Apocalyptic literature from this period shared the view that the world was currently in the grip of evil forces, but that God would intervene in a decisive, cosmic way, to punish the evildoers and reward the righteous. Unlike most contemporary expressions of apocalypticism, the idea was not that the world would come to a catastrophic end, but that the reigning evil and injustice would end as God ushered in a glorious new age of peace and justice. Those who endured oppression and suffering (which was expected to get worse as God's intervention drew near) would be rewarded. The point of this view of reality was not to frighten people into obedience with the threat of destruction. Instead, it was meant to give hope to those who felt persecuted, and to give meaning to their suffering. In this way, the apocalyptic worldview was directly related to the experience of imperial domination. In situations where one feels powerless against a much stronger force, the hope and expectation of a supernatural intervention that will set things right can be particularly appealing. Paul's and others' embracing of the apocalyptic worldview in the first century CE suggests that this way of seeing the world continued to be attractive to those living under Roman domination.

Like other apocalyptic thinkers, Paul thought that the world in which he lived was ruled by evil powers that God would defeat. But Paul's experience of the risen Christ led him to reshape the traditional Jewish apocalyptic worldview in particular ways. For Paul (along with other early followers of Jesus), God's defeat of these evil forces was no longer a future event. Rather, God already had intervened decisively in the world

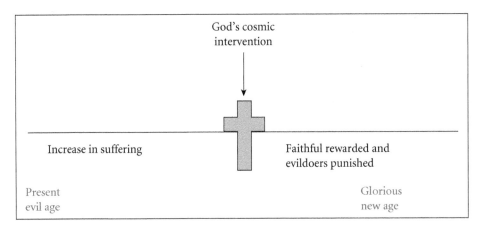

Figure 10.4 Paul's apocalyptic worldview.

through the death and resurrection of Jesus. Thus we find Paul writing of how Jesus "gave himself" to set believers free from the present evil age (Gal 1:4). This was God's cosmic intervention (see Figure 10.4).

Of course, this modified apocalyptic view presented a problem. If God intervened in the world through the death and resurrection of Christ, where was the promised glorious new age? It is clear from Paul's letters that he and the communities to whom he wrote were still experiencing suffering. Paul deals with this reality by speaking of Christ's resurrection as the "first fruits" of God's saving work in the world (see, for example, 1 Cor 15:20–3). Believers, according to Paul, must wait for the return of Christ that will bring God's saving intervention to completion. This second coming (or *parousia*, Greek for "presence") will also bring God's final judgment, which Paul refers to as the "wrath."

Here we find the link between two major aspects of Paul's identity: his mission to the gentiles and his apocalyptic worldview. In a number of other places in his letters, Paul suggests that his mission to the gentiles is directly connected to his expectation of God's judgment over godless people. Thus, in 1 Thessalonians, he praises the faith of the Thessalonian community who "turned toward God, away from idols, to serve a living and true God and to wait for his son from heaven whom he raised from the dead – Jesus, the one who rescues us from the coming wrath" (1 Thess 1:9–10). Similarly, Paul refers to the Corinthians as waiting for the revealing (the Greek word is *apocalypse*) of Jesus Christ. Paul further reassures them that God will strengthen them "to the end," so that they will be found blameless on "the day of our Lord Jesus," that is, on the day of judgment (1 Cor. 1:7–8).

Especially notable is Paul's view that this second coming of Christ will happen during his lifetime. This is clear in his reassurances to the Thessalonians, who apparently were so convinced of Paul's teaching that they were worried about the fate of those among them who had died before Jesus returned. Paul, for his part, reassures the Thessalonians that those who have died will not be forgotten. In fact, Jesus will come to them first.

For this we say to you with the word of the Lord, that we who are living, who are left behind until the Lord's coming, will definitely not go before those who have died. Because the Lord himself, with a shout of command, with an archangel's voice and the sound of God's trumpet, will come down from heaven, and the dead in Christ will rise first. Then we who are living and who are left behind, will be carried off together with them in the clouds to meet the Lord in the air. And so we will be with the Lord always. (1 Thess 4:15–17)

In Paul's letter to the Romans, the cosmic nature of his apocalypticism is particularly evident, as is the interpretation of suffering in relation to future glory.

I think that the sufferings of this present time are not comparable to the glory about to be revealed to us. For the creation eagerly expects the revealing of the sons of God; . . . For we know that all of creation together has been groaning and suffering labor pains until now. (Rom 8:18–19, 22)

Paul's expectation of this imminent and cosmic event affects the way he teaches his communities to live. He sees no point in changing one's position or status in life since soon everything will be changed. Thus, Paul exhorts his readers to "each live in the way

Paul and Slavery

One troubling aspect of Paul's letters is that he nowhere condemns the practice of slavery. In 1 Corinthians he urges the slaves in the community *not* to seek freedom. "Were you a slave when you were called? Do not be concerned about it. Even if you can gain your freedom, make use of your present condition now more than ever" (1 Cor 7:21). Similarly, as discussed later in the chapter, the Deutero-Pauline letters explicitly exhort slaves to obey their masters with sincere hearts (Col 3:22; Eph 6:5). A more ambiguous position on slavery is found in Paul's letter to Philemon. Many believe that the letter concerns a situation in which Paul is sending a runaway slave, Onesimus, back to his owner, Philemon. The purpose of the letter is to urge Philemon to receive Onesimus without penalty. Philemon is to welcome him "no longer as a slave, but more than a slave, as a beloved brother" (16). But Paul's letter is so filled with innuendo that it is difficult to know his intent with any certainty. This ambiguity is reflected in the fact that in the southern states of the US before the civil war Paul's letters, including Philemon, were used not only to justify slavery, but also to teach slaves that it was their Christian duty to obey their masters. Meanwhile, northern abolitionists argued that in principle Paul's letter to Philemon supported an end to the institution of slavery. From our twenty-first-century perspective, it is easy to see that slavery was and is a violation of the basic rights of every human being. But the example of the issue of Paul and slavery provides reason to consider how the Bible is deployed in other, more contemporary cultural debates.

that the Lord assigned, each as God called" (1 Cor 7:17). According to Paul, this is his command "in all the churches." The rule, according to Paul, applies to the "circumcised" versus "uncircumcised," slaves versus free, married versus unmarried, and virgins. They should stay as they are "in view of the present crisis" (1 Cor 7:26). In other words, according to Paul, one's personal status will soon be irrelevant because "the time is short" and "the form of this world is passing away" (1 Cor 7:29, 31).

To summarize so far: to understand Paul means to be attuned to his complex identity as a self-described Jewish Pharisee, immersed in the Greco-Roman culture, and convinced that God had called him to be apostle to the gentiles. It also means understanding his thoroughgoing belief that the world will soon undergo a radical change in which God, through the return of Jesus Christ, would come to judge the evildoers and reward the righteous. These fundamental aspects of Paul's identity help explain much of what we find in his letters, including places where he appears to be thoroughly inconsistent in his message to his readers.

Three Undisputed Letters of Paul: 1 Corinthians, Galatians, and Romans

While it is not possible to discuss all of Paul's letters in depth in the space of this chapter, we will explore three of them briefly. Our aim will be to see how Paul approached three quite different situations on the basis of his fundamental convictions. Our foray into these letters will also provide an opportunity to see Christianity under construction, so to speak, as these communities, with Paul's help, sort out what their new life means in relation to their cultural context.

The First Letter to the Corinthians

READING

1 Corinthians 1–10.

EXERCISE

Make a list of the different issues that Paul addresses in these chapters that are causing tensions in the community. Note how Paul responds to each of these issues.

Paul's correspondence with the Corinthian community gives us a fascinating glimpse of him working with newly converted gentiles. Several letters passed between Paul and this community, and it is likely that fragments of these have been combined in the two letters that we now have in the New Testament. In what we know as "first" Corinthians,

Paul refers to a letter that he had already written to them (1 Cor 5:9) and also indicates that he is responding to a letter that they wrote to him (1 Cor 7:1). In what we label "second" Corinthians, Paul mentions yet another letter that he wrote out of distress and "with many tears" (2 Cor 2:3–4, 7:8). Some argue that this "tearful letter" is 2 Corinthians 10–12, since these chapters take on a particularly anguished tone. In any case, the references to this ongoing correspondence suggest that Paul's relationship with this group was a rocky one, culminating in a challenge to his leadership which seems to have resolved in his favor (2 Cor 7:9).

basics 1 Corinthians

Outline:	I	Salutation and thanksgiving	1:1–9
negotiating life	II	Body of the letter: conflicts in Corinth	1:10–16:12
as new believers		A Divisions and Paul's authority	1:10–4:20
		B Issues of sexuality and marriage	5:1–7:39
		C Eating food sacrificed to idols	8–10
		D Problems with rituals and worship	11–14
		E Disagreements over resurrection	15:1–58
	III	Concluding matters and greetings	16:1–21

Date and audience Paul started the Corinthian community in 50/51–2 CE. This letter, which is not actually Paul's first to the community, was probably written about 55 or 56 CE. The Corinthians were a mixed community of both Jews and gentiles, as well as of differing social status. This diversity likely led to some of the divisions and conflicts addressed in the letter.

The evidence from 1 Corinthians suggests that the community was made up of a variety of groups with differing perspectives, no doubt reflecting the cosmopolitan nature of the city itself. The letter itself indicates that there were existing factions, seemingly on the basis of alignment with different leaders (1 Cor 1:12–13). But there are clues in the letters suggesting that differences in social status may also have been an issue. Addressing the Corinthians, Paul claims "not many of you were wise by human standards, not many of you were powerful, not many of you were of noble birth" (1:26). In other words, not many, but some, were of high social standing. Later in the letter, he admonishes some in the community who are apparently eating a full meal in the context of the Lord's supper, while others go hungry (11:21–2). Again, Paul's description suggests a difference in socio-economic class among members of the group. Some had enough food for a lavish meal, while others had none.

Conflicting opinions are also evident about basic life issues such as sexuality, law suits, married life, diet, and ritual practices. For example, with regard to sexuality, at least some in the community adopted a lifestyle of self-denial, arguing that "it is good for a man not to touch a woman" (1 Cor 7:1). Others in the community were not so ascetically inclined, as is clear from Paul's sharp criticism of their sexual practices (5:1–2; 6:16). Some insisted that there was nothing wrong with eating food that had been sacrificed in pagan temples, while Paul felt the practice was potentially problematic (1 Cor 8–10). Some in the community appeared to elevate the gift of speaking in tongues, while Paul insists that the gift is useful only insofar as there are interpreters to make sense of what is being said for the rest of the community (1 Cor 12–14).

From Paul's perspective, there is a general attitude of arrogance that underlies many of these issues. Indeed, the theme of arrogance shows up several times in 1 Corinthians (1 Cor 4:6–8; 4:18–19; 5:2; 8:1). It may be that the Corinthians understood themselves to have achieved a higher status in their new life in Christ that gave them certain liberties. Perhaps when Paul brought his apocalyptic message to them (God has already intervened through Jesus Christ to bring about salvation for the gentiles), they did not fully grasp the second part (Christ will return for a day of judgment). Thus, on the matter of sexuality, some among the Corinthians apparently thought that what they did with their bodies was irrelevant, given their newly achieved superior spiritual existence. Such claims as "all things are possible for me" and "the food is for the stomach and the stomach is for food" (1 Cor 6:12–13) are euphemistic ways of saying that the body is meant for sex and anything goes. Paul rejects this argument about sexuality, and insists that what the Corinthians do with their bodies *is* directly relevant to their spiritual state. In fact, since Paul understands the Holy Spirit to dwell within the believer, he consider the body to be a temple for the Spirit (1 Cor 6:19).

Another issue that shows up in this community concerns food. Chapters 8–10 of 1 Corinthians address the issue of eating meat that was sacrificed to Greco-Roman deities. The issue here is not just one of diet or religious practice, but also one of basic social relations. To flourish and have important contacts in an urban center such as Corinth, one needed to be a member of a **voluntary association**, perhaps a trade guild, or a cult devoted to a particular deity. A prominent part of such associations was gathering for meals which often included meat that had been offered to a deity. Paul's converts had to decide whether it was acceptable to eat such food. Their decision had implications for their participation in the broader culture of their city. The Corinthians' position on this issue again reflects their self-confidence: "We all have knowledge," they argue (1 Cor 8:1). This "knowledge" is apparently what Paul taught them about their former religious practices and their newly adopted one, namely, "there is no idol in the world," and that "there is no God except one" (1 Cor 8:4). In other words, if there are no other real gods besides the one true God, then the sacrificial nature of the food is insignificant. The Corinthians suggest that there is no harm in eating the meat, or presumably in participating in the social events connected to the meal. As they argue, "Food will not make us present to God. We will not lose an advantage if we do not eat, nor gain one if we do" (1 Cor 8:8). Paul, however, remains critical. While he agrees with their position in principle, he is concerned about what it might mean in practice.

It may cause some who are less certain of their new belief in only one god to return to the idea of sacrificing to many gods (I Cor 8:10).

In sum, in dealing with the members of the Corinthian community, Paul must address basic issues of daily life for these newly converted gentiles: what they do with their bodies, what they eat, to whom they may relate, whether they should get married, and so on. In the midst of this range of social issues, Paul pushes back against expressions of freedom or confidence that he sees as immoral and/or destructive to the community. "See that this liberty of yours," he argues "does not cause the weak to stumble" (1 Cor 8:9).

The Letter to the Galatians

READING
Paul's letter to the Galatians.

EXERCISE
What tone does this letter have? What are the Galatians doing that disturbs Paul? Why do you think this issue is so upsetting to him?

Galatia was not a city, like Corinth or Thessalonica, but a Roman province. Paul apparently traveled throughout this region and sent his letter to the "churches of Galatia" (Gal 1:1). The situation that he faced in Galatia was quite different than in Corinth. Whereas Paul had to caution the Corinthians about misunderstandings of the freedom in Christ, he had to remind the Galatians of their freedom from the law: "For freedom Christ has made us free. Stand firm, therefore, and do not be subject to a yoke of slavery again" (Gal 5:1).

From the beginning of his letter, it is clear that Paul is particularly agitated by the situation in Galatia. He omits altogether the thanksgiving section that typically opens his letters. Instead, Paul admonishes the Galatians for "deserting" him and calls curses down on those who are confusing and perverting the gospel of Christ (1:6–9). And with this, Paul is just getting warmed up! Later in the letter he calls the Galatians ignorant (3:1) and wishes that those who are leading them astray would castrate themselves (5:12). In short, the letter to the Galatians presents a striking example of the passion and vigor with which Paul could argue his point and defend his position against opposing views.

The issue that so disturbs Paul concerns circumcision. There are some in Galatia who have urged gentile believers to become circumcised. We do not have more details about this group. Paul refers to them only as "those of the circumcision" (Gal 2:12). Most likely this "circumcision faction," as the NRSV translates this, were Jewish Christians who thought it necessary that gentile converts be circumcised. In this letter, it is not

basics Galatians

Outline: defining
identity in Christ
for the gentiles

I	Salutation and invocation of curse	1:1–10
II	Body of the letter: the problem of circumcision for the gentiles	1:11–6:10
	A Establishment of Paul's authority	1:11–2:14
	B Argument against circumcision	2:15–4:31
	C Instructions for a life of freedom in Christ	5:1–6:10
III	Closing	6:11–18

Date and
audience

The letter to the Galatians was likely written in the mid-50s CE. Who is meant by the "Galatians" is not clear, since Galatia was a large Roman province in Asia Minor. Scholars debate whether the letter was intended for cities in the southern part of the province (Antioch, Iconium, Lystra, Derbe), inhabited by a Hellenized population, or for the northern part of the province in which ethnic Galatians lived (descendents of the Gauls who invaded the territory in the third century BCE).

The Question of Circumcision

The question of whether circumcision was required for gentiles interested in the Jewish traditions was not limited to early Christian communities. According to the Jewish historian Josephus, a Jewish merchant named Ananias persuaded the Mesopotamian king Izates to "worship god according to the Jewish religion." When Izates also sought circumcision, Ananias assured him that he could worship God without being circumcised. God would forgive this omission, Ananias argued, because if Izates were to be circumcised his subjects might reject him due to his fondness of foreign rites. When a second Jewish teacher, a certain Eleazar from Galilee, came to the palace and found the king reading the Torah, he offered an opposing opinion. Eleazar, "who was esteemed skillful in the learning of his country," argued that it was not enough to read the law, the king must also practice it. "How long will you continue uncircumcised?" he asked Izates. "But if you have not yet read the law about circumcision, and do not know how great impiety you are guilty of by neglecting it, read it now." At this, the king sent for a surgeon, and "did what he was commanded to do" (Josephus, *Antiquities* 20.3–4).

clear exactly *why* Paul feels so vehemently opposed to circumcision for the gentiles, only *that* he is. His passionate objections are more assertions than argument: "if you are circumcised, Christ will not benefit you" (5:2). Or, as Paul graphically puts it, for the gentiles to be circumcised would be to "cut" themselves off from Christ (5:4).

Throughout Paul's argument in the letter, he uses references to the Jewish law (Torah) to make his case that the law regarding circumcision does not apply to the gentiles. Clearly, for Paul, the issue is not one of the legitimacy of the law. Rather it is one of understanding *how* the law relates to gentiles. Paul makes the case that the gentiles in Galatia are descendents of Abraham, the father of Judaism, not by way of adherence to the law, but through Christ.

First, Paul argues that God entered into a relationship with Abraham on the basis of Abraham's belief. In his words,

> Just as Abraham "had faith in God, and it counted as righteousness for him," so, you know, those who have faith are the sons of Abraham. And the scriptures, foreseeing that God would justify the gentiles on the basis of faith, announced the good news to Abraham in advance, saying, "All the gentiles shall be blessed in you." For this reason, those who have faith are blessed with Abraham who had faith. (Gal 3:6–9)

Paul's example of Abraham's faith and God's response comes from Gen 15:6. What is significant for Paul is that God's announcement to Abraham occurs before the covenant of circumcision that is described in Genesis 17:10–14. In other words, Paul is arguing that Abraham entered into a relationship with God *before* he was circumcised.

Having established this, Paul makes an interesting move. Using a typical Jewish method of interpretation, he pays special attention to grammatical form, noting that God made promises to Abraham and to his "offspring" (*sperma*, Gal 3:16). Since the Greek word *sperma* (seed, or offspring) is singular rather than plural, Paul argues that it must refer to one person only, namely Christ. Here is a good illustration of the way early Christians reread the Jewish scriptures and traditions to link them to their experience of Jesus. In this case, Paul connects Abraham to Christ so that the promises that God made to Abraham extend through his "offspring," Jesus. For Paul, those original divine promises to Abraham are still critically important, even as he now understands God to be working through the person of Christ. Finally, Paul makes the deciding link between Christ and the gentiles. Since the gentiles have "clothed themselves" with Christ and "belong" to Christ, they are also heirs to Abraham, and thus, children of God (Gal 3:29). Paul has reread the Genesis text to show the Galatians that they are included in the promises of God without being circumcised.

But Paul may also be appealing to the Galatians on another level – that of social status. There are several aspects of his rhetoric that seem designed to convince the Galatians that faith in Christ will help them to be more "manly." Knowing how to be a true man and avoiding behaviors that would mark one as "unmanly" were key values in Greco-Roman culture. So, for instance, on one level, Paul's reference to being clothed with Christ is probably quite literal. Descriptions of early Christian baptism include putting on a white cloth as part of the ritual. But on another level, Paul may also be using this language to evoke a much more widespread cultural tradition. J. Albert Harrill has suggested that the Galatians, who lived in a region in which "Romanization" was quite successful, may have heard Paul's rhetoric of being "clothed in Christ" in light of the Roman toga ceremony. The donning of the white toga was an important Roman tradition that marked an adolescent boy's transition to manhood. If Paul is alluding to the toga ceremony, it would be to convince the Galatians that their newfound freedom in Christ made them "manly" in the broader culture of the Roman world.

Along the same line, the letter to the Galatians includes rhetoric about children, guardians, and heirs of the household (see 4:1–7), all terms that relate to the transition to adulthood symbolized in the toga ritual. In Latin literature, references to this ritual include admonitions for the boy to live into his new manly identity, assuming the proper conduct as heir to the household. Paul's exhortations to the Galatians contain similar language. For example, he contrasts freedom with slavery, recalling the free male citizen's status in contrast to the slaves of the household (5:1). The use of vice-and-virtue lists (5:19–23), and Paul's reminder that those who "belong to Christ" have "crucified the flesh with its passions and desires" (5:24), are also in keeping with how "manly" behavior was defined among the Roman elite. To be a true man meant exhibiting self-control and not giving in to one's passions. Arguing against the circumcision faction, Paul urges the Galatians not to sacrifice their Christ-won freedom (and its associated manliness) by submitting to circumcision. To understand why he was so opposed to the idea of circumcision for the gentiles, we need to turn to Paul's letter to the Romans.

The Letter to the Romans

READING
Romans 1–4, 9–11.

EXERCISE
Try to follow the course of Paul's argument in these sections of Romans. What issues are involved? How does he describe God's relationship with the Jews? How do the gentiles fit into God's plan for salvation?

If 1 Corinthians allows a glimpse of the social issues facing newly converted gentiles, and Galatians reveals a point of conflict in the forging of a new community of Jews and gentiles, Romans provides the fullest insight into Paul's understanding of the gospel. Paul writes to the Romans in preparation for his pending journey to Rome (1:10–11; 15:23). Although he has never visited the Roman church, he seeks their support as he moves his mission further westward to Spain (1:13; 15:24). His letter serves, in part, as an introduction of his gospel for this community (see Figure 10.5). The first eight chapters, especially, seem to serve this purpose. Here Paul returns to the themes of his

Figure 10.5 Artist's reconstruction of ancient Rome, depicting the emperor's palace in the background as well as the home of the vestal virgins directly in front of it. Note also the Arch of Titus in the lower left. One should imagine other major Greco-Roman cities as similarly majestic, though on a smaller scale.

letter to the Galatians: being in relationship with God on the basis of faith, the example of Abraham as one faithful to God, the problem of the law, and life in the spirit. Coupled with Galatians, these chapters provide insight into Paul's objections against circumcision for the gentiles. They also reveal a tension between Paul's idea of universal salvation and his insistence on the particular place of Israel and the Jewish people in God's plan. This last point comes to a climax in chapters 9–11, which will be the focus text for this chapter.

Before looking more closely at those chapters, it is important to understand Paul's basic theological conviction. Perhaps its clearest expression is found in Rom 3:28–30. There Paul states:

> For we maintain that a person is put into right relations [with God] on the basis of faith apart from works of the law. Or is God the God of Jews only? Is he not the God of gentiles also? Yes, of gentiles also, since there is one God who puts into right relationship the circumcised on the basis of faith and the uncircumcised through that same faith.

The importance of this statement is best recognized by considering the inverse of Paul's logic. If a person's right relationship with God was *not* distinct from works of the law, then God would be God of the Jews only. But "since there is one God," that is, because Paul is a monotheist, that same God must be in relationship with everyone – Jews and gentiles.

basics Romans

Outline: Paul's letter of introduction to the Romans			
	I	Salutation and thanksgiving	1:1–15
	II	Body of the letter: Paul's gospel	1:16–15:13
		A God's impartiality to Jews and gentiles	1:16–4:25
		B The role of Christ, sin, law, and spirit	5–8
		C The problem of Israel and the place of the gentiles	9–11
		D Instructions for life as a community of believers	12–14
	III	Concluding matters with extended greetings	15:14–16:27

Date and audience This is the latest of the letters of Paul, written toward the end of the 50s CE. It is also written to a community that he did not found and had not yet visited. Thus, the purpose for the letter is, in part, an introduction of his gospel to a community who had not yet heard him preach. The letter suggests that its intended audience was a mixed community of Jews and gentiles, perhaps living in some tension, given Paul's concerns that gentiles "not boast" over the Jews (Rom 11:17–21).

In some ways, this theology is an extension of developments seen earlier in Second Isaiah (Isaiah 40–55). Recall how during and after the exilic period, after extensive engagements with foreign nations, the exiles in Babylon reconceived their local God of Israel in universal terms – as the *only* God that existed anywhere. Moreover, this one and only universal God welcomed foreigners who observed the Sabbath and sacrificed in the Jerusalem Temple (Isa 56:6–7). Paul takes this argument a step further. Far more radical than affirming that God welcomes foreigners who observe Torah and sacrifice in the Temple, Paul argues that God shows no partiality between Jews and gentiles (Rom 2:6–11). Again, he argues that what is required of the gentiles is not observance of Jewish traditions (e.g. circumcision), but only sharing the same faith in God that Abraham had (Rom 4:1–25).

What complicates this argument about faith, for Paul, is the question of the Jewish law. If, as we have seen, Paul considers himself a "Hebrew of Hebrews" (Phil 3:5), if he can state that he was blameless with respect to the law (Phil 3:6), if he can recognize the law as a gift from God (Rom 9:4), how can he also state that the law brings wrath (Rom 4:15)? Or how can he say, as he does to the Galatians, that those who adhere to the law are under a curse (Gal 3:10)? From these negative statements, one might reasonably assume, as many readers of Paul have, that he is opposed to the law. But if we consider that he also states that the law is holy, and the commandment is holy, just, and good (Rom 7:12), things do not seem so clear.

One way to sort out these conflicting statements is to consider that Paul's primary audience for his statements *against* the law are gentiles. When he speaks of the law bringing judgment (or wrath) he has in mind the law's function in relation to the gentiles. Jews of Paul's time tended to see the law as something that privileged Jews and judged gentiles. Yes, from Paul's perspective, the law brings a curse to anyone who does not obey it (namely, gentiles) (Gal 3:10). But for Paul, the solution to this problem was not to insist that gentiles obey the law (that is, be circumcised). In essence, that would mean that the gentiles would need to become Jewish. To put this demand on the gentiles would be to return to the idea of God being the local God of Jews only. For Paul, this way of thinking diminishes God.

Moreover, Paul also makes clear that those who obey the law (the Jews) are not excluded. The promise is still for them and they remain heirs to Abraham. Paul's argument is that the promise is to them, *and also* to those who share the same faith in God shown by Abraham (Rom 4:16–17). In short, what Paul achieves in Romans is a radical statement of God's (and Abraham's) universality. As Paul affirms, Abraham is the father of "all of us."

In spite of this universal perspective, Paul cannot entirely dismiss the long tradition of God's particular election of Israel that was at the heart of Israelite and Jewish tradition. On the one hand, he can insist on God's impartiality (2:11). On the other hand, he can ask, "Then what is the special advantage of the Jew? Or what is the usefulness of circumcision?" and respond "much in every way" (3:1–2). This tension between universality and particularity reflects the lived experience of a Hellenistic Jew such as Paul. Whereas Hellenism encouraged cross-cultural interaction and produced widely varied communities, the Jewish tradition emphasized the maintenance of a cultural identity distinct from all others. Paul finds himself balancing between these two points as he tries to articulate God's work among both Jews and gentiles.

FOCUS
TEXT

The Problem of Israel and the Place of the Gentiles (Romans 9–11)

Romans 9–11 is a poignant text that gives evidence of Paul's complex identity and his deep theological convictions about God's salvific work with both Jews and gentiles. Some argue that this section is actually the climax of the whole letter, addressing the fundamental question of how God works to bring about salvation for all people. There are troubling aspects of Paul's language as he works toward his grand conclusion in chapter 11, and we will point to some of the difficulties along the way. We will also highlight Paul's extensive and creative rereading of scripture to make his case. These chapters provide further evidence of the way Paul and other early Christians reinterpreted their scriptural traditions in light of their belief in Jesus as the messiah.

Romans chapter 9 opens with an intensely personal expression of Paul's feelings. The preceding section of his letter concludes with soaring words of praise (8:38–9). But as chapter 9 begins, Paul abruptly changes tone and speaks of his great sorrow and unceasing anguish on behalf of his own people. Affirming their status before God, he claims,

"They are Israelites, and to them belong the adoption, the glory, the covenants, the lawgiving, the rituals, and the promises; to them belong the ancestors, and from them is the Christ according to the flesh" (9:4–5). These Israelites, according to Paul, are "his kin according to the flesh," and he goes so far as to wish that he himself would be cut off from Christ for their sake (9:3).

As Paul thinks of his fellow Jews who have not recognized Jesus as the messiah from God, he is troubled by two things: their lack of conviction and what their rejection of the gospel says about God's broader plans. If God promised to be their God, and if they reject the messiah sent from God while the gentiles did not, did God somehow make a mistake? In fact, Paul has anticipated this problem already in chapter 3. There, while listing the advantages of the Jewish people, he raised the question, "What if some do not believe? Will their unbelief put an end to the faithfulness of God?" (Rom 3:3). Chapters 9–11 are Paul's answer to this question, arguing that God's promises and justice remain steadfast. He asserts from the beginning, "But it is not as if the word of God had failed" (9:6).

To make this point, Paul introduces several different ideas and draws on a wide range of Hebrew scriptures. In 9:6–13, his argument is based on the concept of election. This idea that God chooses his people, which was so central to the Deuteronomistic history, now becomes the key to Paul's explanation of why some Jews believe in Jesus and some do not. Paul points out that the promise did not go to *all* of Abraham's children (9:7), but only to a particular line of descendents. According to Paul, this idea of election applies also to God's mercy. God has mercy on whomever he chooses and hardens the heart of whomever he chooses (9:15). In other words, Paul explains the lack of belief of some of this people by claiming that God has hardened their hearts (9:18).

Next Paul anticipates objections to this argument. You may already have thought of some of these yourself. If God is choosing mercy for some and not for others, how can anyone be blamed for their lack of faith? And how can it be fair for God to choose some and not others? In responding to such objections, Paul alludes to the traditions of Job (Job 9:12) and Isaiah (Isa 29:16; 45:9), both of which point to the inappropriateness of a mere mortal's questioning of the creator God. While this may not be entirely satisfying, Paul is not ultimately concerned here about questions of predetermination or even about an individual's standing before God. He is not thinking about individual salvation at all, but rather of the place of Israel as a people in God's plan and how Israel stands in relation to the gentiles. This is clear as Paul continues his reading of the prophets. Indeed, in a creative "misreading" of the prophet Hosea, Paul finds scriptural warrant for the inclusion of the gentiles in two modified quotations from the prophet.

> I will call "not my people," "my people" and "not beloved," "beloved." And in the place where it was said to them. "You are not my people," there they will be called "sons of the living God." (Rom 9:25–6; see Hos 1:10; 2:23)

In Hosea, these words refer to the estranged people of Israel with whom God restores a relationship. But Paul reinterprets Hosea's words to apply to God's inclusion of the gentiles. Similarly, he draws on Isaiah to introduce the concept of a "remnant" among Israel that God will save (Rom 9:27; cf. Isa 10:22).

Still, Paul is not content with only a remnant being saved. This is not the end of his argument. In fact, the climax of the argument comes in chapter 11, which begins with a direct question: "I ask then, has God rejected his people?" Paul quickly and firmly rejects the idea, using himself as an example – he is an Israelite and God has not rejected him! (11:1). At this point, Paul begins a new argument that intricately links the role of the Jewish "stumblers" with the fate of the gentiles (11:11–12). The grand conclusion that Paul arrives at in chapter 11 is that God is working with *both* groups in ways that will bring about salvation to all. It is God's initial hardening of some of Israel that has allowed salvation to come to the gentiles. In fact, the rejection of Jesus by some Jews has led, Paul thinks, to "the reconciliation of the world" (11:15).

Finally, Paul shifts the argument to address the gentiles directly. He warns them not to become proud or feel superior because they are Christ's followers while others are not. The gentiles are but a wild olive branch that, because of God's kindness, has been grafted on to the rich root that is Israel (Rom 11:17–20). In concluding his argument this way, it is clear that Paul can no more condemn his people than he could give up on his own belief in Jesus. The centuries of scholarship that have understood Paul as anti-law and anti-Jewish failed to take this climactic portion of Romans into account. To be sure, one can quibble with the weakness of Paul's argument. He clearly is struggling with a reality that he does not fully understand. In fact, the solution at which he arrives is described as "a mystery" (11:25). What Paul reveals in Romans 9–11 is his firm conviction that the promises of God that were extended to Israel in the past remain steadfast, "for the gifts and the calling of God cannot be changed" (11:29).

The Disputed Letters

So far in our discussion of Paul, we have focused on three of the undisputed epistles (1 Corinthians, Galatians, and Romans). But the Pauline letter collection also includes letters attributed to Paul that likely were not written by him. Three of these letters – 2 Thessalonians, Colossians, and Ephesians – are typically referred to as **Deutero-Pauline** ("secondary to Paul") because they stand apart from the undisputed letters in style, vocabulary, and basic ideas. For instance, 2 Thessalonians sounds much like 1 Thessalonians on the surface, but its view of the end times, its **eschatology**, is quite different from what Paul wrote in 1 Thessalonians. In 1 Thessalonians, as we saw earlier, Paul expects "the day of the Lord" to come during his lifetime. The community is to be vigilant because Jesus could return at any moment. But in 2 Thessalonians, the author suggests that they not be too anxious about its arrival and assures the readers that the day of the Lord will not come until other events take place (2 Thess 2:1–12). Notably, the author of 2 Thessalonians prefaces his discussion with a warning that the audience not be deceived by a letter "as though from us" (2:2). Calling attention to the possibility of **pseudonymous** writers (those writing under a false name) was actually a common practice of pseudonymous texts during this period! These aspects of the letter have led many scholars to believe that 2 Thessalonians was probably written in the later half of the first century, when concerns were growing about lack of the delay of Christ's second coming.

Two other Deutero-Pauline letters, Ephesians and Colossians, have a writing style that is quite different from what we find in the undisputed epistles. The sentence structure is more complex and the vocabulary is quite different as well. Once again, the letters appear to reflect a later period. For instance, whereas Paul speaks about Christ as the foundation for the community (1 Cor 3:11), Ephesians adds another layer of authority so that "household of God" is built upon the foundation of the apostles and the prophets, with Christ as the cornerstone (Eph 2:20). The ideas about Christ also reflect more development. The author of Colossians describes Christ as "the image of the individual God, the firstborn of creation," who "is before all things, and in him all things hold together" (Col 1:15–16). This is a more cosmic conception of Christ than one finds in the undisputed letters.

Ephesians and Colossians are also distinctive in their inclusion of **household codes**; that is, instructions for proper conduct of various members of the household (Col 3:18–4:1; Eph 5:21–6:9). The codes urge all members of the household – husbands, wives, children, and slaves – to maintain their proper positions in the household hierarchy. Such codes are not unique to these letters; they were standard fare in Greco-Roman moral philosophy. What is significant here is that the author of the epistles calls for behavior that is aligned with the cultural values of the Roman empire. It may be that, by the time these post-Pauline letters were written, Christians were increasingly recognized as a distinct group. In response, the authors of these letters advocated traditional family structures that matched the values of the broader Greco-Roman culture. At a time when new cultic practices were regarded with suspicion, embracing traditional cultural values would make the early Christian communities less threatening to others.

The last three of the disputed epistles, 1 and 2 Timothy and Titus, are often referred to as the **Pastoral Epistles** because they are written in the form of instructions regarding pastoral duties. Whereas there is still debate regarding the Pauline authorship of 2 Thessalonians, Colossians, and Ephesians, the large majority of scholars agree that the pastoral letters were not written by Paul. Rather they were written by someone in the second century, using Paul's name to lend authority to the instructions. For example, 1 Timothy assumes a level of organization in the church that did not exist when Paul was forming his churches. It lists proper qualifications for bishops and deacons in a way that suggests these are established positions in the church (1 Tim 3:1–13; see also Titus 1:7). Paul's undisputed letters, written during the formative stages of these communities, do not reflect this level of church structure.

Finally, the position regarding women that is reflected in the Pastoral Epistles is considerably different than Paul's attitude toward women in the undisputed epistles. The general tone of Paul's undisputed letters suggests that he considers women to be active members of the community, including in positions of leadership and authority. For example, in his long list of greetings at the end of the letter to the Romans, nine of them are directed toward women, with several receiving high praise from Paul. Prisca is a co-worker of Paul's who risked her life for him. Junia is outstanding among the apostles. Mary, Trypehna, Tryphosa, and Persis all work hard in the Lord. Such greetings suggest that Paul recognizes and welcomes these women as co-workers. In his letter to the Corinthians, Paul gives further evidence of his acceptance of the active role of women: receiving reports from "Chloe's people" (1 Cor 1:11), accepting that women pray and prophesy (in spite of his concern about their hair covering) (1 Cor 11:5), and recognizing the advantages of a life of celibacy for women in a culture that emphasized marriage and childbearing (1 Cor 7:34).

There is one place in 1 Corinthians where Paul's tone shifts dramatically. In 1 Cor 14:34–6, Paul states that women are not permitted to speak in church. If they have questions, they should wait until they are home to ask their husbands. Since he has already recognized that women pray and prophesy (1 Cor 11:5), this passage seems out of place. Some scholars have argued that this material must be a later, non-Pauline addition, since it is so different from Paul's attitude toward women elsewhere in these letters. Others suggest that Paul may be dealing with a conflict relating particularly to the Corinthian women. They may have been experiencing a freedom in Christ that pushed the cultural boundaries beyond Paul's comfort level. In any case, even though it appears to be an exception to Paul's typical attitude toward women in the church, this passage in 1 Corinthians provides an opening to the direction in which the Pastoral Epistles will take the Pauline tradition.

Compared to most of Paul's own positions, the Pastoral Epistles are narrow in their perception of women's roles in the church. Rather than promoting celibacy, the "Paul" behind these letters claims that women will be saved through childbearing (1 Tim 2:15). Rather than recognizing the contributions of women to the work of the church, these letters portray women as "silly," and "overwhelmed by their sins and all kinds of desires" (2 Tim 3:6). In the Pastoral Epistles no woman is permitted to teach or have authority over a man; "she is to keep silent" (1 Tim 2:12). To bolster the point, the author evokes the story of Adam and Eve, contributing to a long and distorted history of interpretation that places the blame for transgression on Eve alone (1 Tim 2:13–14; cf. 1 Cor 5:12). Such extensive departure from the undisputed epistles suggests that this author has taken on a decidedly more restrictive approach to women than Paul himself did.

Conclusion: From Letters to Scripture

At some point in the early second century, Paul's letters were published together as a collection. Paul himself might have gathered some of his letters together for publication, since letter writers frequently had their secretaries make copies of their own letters before the original was sent. Later, followers of Paul added to the collection until all 13 of the letters that are now in the New Testament were published together. Once they were published as a whole, interest in the particular situations that Paul addressed faded into the background in favor of interpretations that focused more generally on Paul's theology and Christology. In other words, Paul's ideas about the meaning and significance of God and God's work in the person of Jesus Christ became the central concern for later readers. Paul may well have approved of this development, especially insofar as it built up the community of believers, both Jews and gentiles, for whom he cared so much. But we do well to continue also to explore Paul's perspective before it was made to conform to the questions and concerns of the later church. Doing so helps us understand Paul better and gives us fascinating insights into the early years of a movement that would eventually grow into a world religion.

CHAPTER TEN REVIEW

1. Know the meaning and significance of the following terms used in this chapter:

- apocalyptic worldview
- Deutero-Pauline
- eschatology
- household codes
- Pastoral Epistles
- pseudonymous
- undisputed and disputed letters
- voluntary association

2. In what way did the interests of the Roman empire contribute to Paul's missionary efforts?

3. What are some essential aspects of Paul's identity?

4. What issues were at stake in Paul's correspondence with the Corinthians?

5. What was the major issue confronting Paul in the churches of Galatia? How did he respond to this issue?

6. In what ways do you think Paul's own hybrid identity affected his understanding of the relationship of Jews and gentiles in the letter to the Romans?

7. On what basis do some scholars dispute the authorship of some of the Pauline letters?

RESOURCES FOR FURTHER STUDY

Gager, John G. *Reinventing Paul*. Oxford and New York: Oxford University Press, 2000.

Harrill, J. Albert. "Coming of Age and Putting on Christ: The Toga Virilis Ceremony, its Paraenesis, and Paul's Language of Baptism in Galatians," *Novum Testamentum* 44 (2002): 251–77.

Meeks, Wayne. *The First Urban Christians: The Social World of the Apostle Paul*. New Haven: Yale University Press, 1983.

Roetzel, Calvin. *The Letters of Paul: Conversations in Context* (4th edition). Louisville, KY: Westminster John Knox Press, 1998.

Stendahl, Krister. *Paul among Jews and Gentiles and Other Essays*. Philadelphia: Fortress, 1976.

Twomey, Jay. *The Pastoral Epistles through the Centuries*. Chichester and Malden, MA: Wiley-Blackwell, 2009.

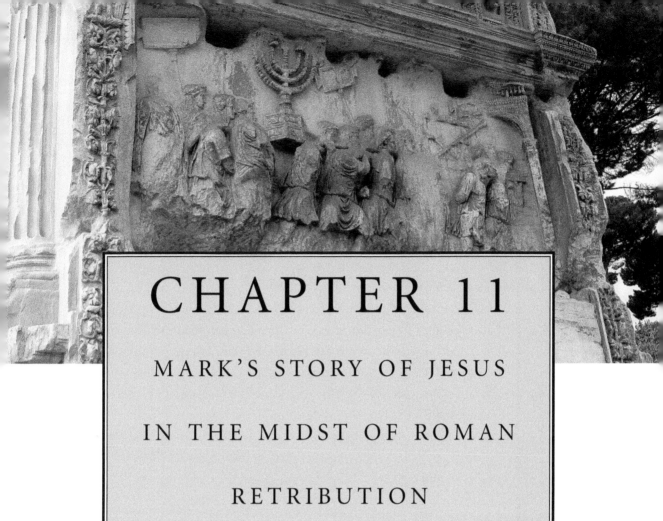

CHAPTER 11

MARK'S STORY OF JESUS IN THE MIDST OF ROMAN RETRIBUTION

Chapter Outline

CHAPTER OVERVIEW

This chapter begins with an overview of a watershed event in the history of Judaism and emerging Christianity: the Jewish War and the destruction of the Jerusalem Temple by Rome. There are indications in the Gospel of Mark that it was written soon after this event. Students who are new to critical study of the gospels often regard them as eye-witness news reports of Jesus's ministry. In the case of the Gospel of Mark, it is more accurate to view it as a story about Jesus's life written several decades after Jesus's death, in the immediate aftermath of the Jewish War and the destruction of the Second Temple. The depictions of Jesus's life and death would no doubt have been influenced by such historic and catastrophic events. This chapter will explore the themes of the gospel and the presentation of Jesus in light of the conflict with Rome. The Gospel of Mark tells the story of a messiah who must be rejected, suffer, and die. It also suggests that those who would follow this messiah should expect to follow him in suffering as well. Surprisingly, the very disciples who follow the Markan Jesus seem unable to understand or accept this idea. By the end of this chapter, you should be able to see the Gospel of Mark not as a modern-style historical account of Jesus's life, but as a set of stories about Jesus shaped to address Christians in a situation of instability and crisis in the wake of the destruction of the Temple.

The Jewish War (66–70 CE)

As we saw in Chapter 9, toward the end of the first century BCE, Herod engaged in a massive building program designed to gain favor from his subjects and from his Roman benefactors. A tour of Jerusalem during this time would have offered much to impress the traveler. But a traveler to Jerusalem toward the end of the first century CE would have encountered a very different sight. Instead of the glowing achievements of Herod, after 70 CE the traveler would have found broken city walls, the Jerusalem Temple looted and ravaged by fire, and much of the city destroyed by war. All of this would have been the result of the **Jewish War** – the Jewish revolt against Rome that began in 66 CE, an event that changed the history of the Jewish people forever (see Figure 11.1).

As you may recall, the end of Jewish independent rule came with the invasion of Palestine by the Roman general Pompey in 63 BCE. By 6 CE, Judea and the surrounding regions were reorganized by Rome into a larger Roman province. This change to provincial status meant that Rome now had direct rule over the region through "prefects" or governors that were

Figure 11.1 Silver shekel minted about 67 CE during the Jewish revolt. The inscription in archaic Hebrew recalls the Zion theology of the ancient past, stating "Jerusalem the Holy."

appointed by the Roman Senate. These prefects, including the Pontius Pilate of the gospels, were notorious for both their incompetence and their brutality. Such incompetence led to increasing unrest among the local Jewish community, which culminated in an armed revolt against Rome in 66 CE.

Although the Jewish rebels had some initial successes, by the spring of 70 CE, the Roman army had Jerusalem in the grip of what would become a protracted siege. According to the Jewish historian Josephus, this was a time of great suffering for the inhabitants of Jerusalem, with widespread starvation and deadly struggles for what food remained. Those who left the city in search of food were soon captured by the Romans and crucified outside the city walls. Of these, Josephus states, "so great was their number, that space could not be found for the crosses nor crosses for the bodies" (*Jewish War* 5.451). In 70 CE, under General Titus, the Roman army breached the walls of Jerusalem and burned down most of the city, including the Temple (Figure 11.2).

READING
Mark 13.

EXERCISE
What events does the Markan Jesus describe in this chapter? Which ones fit the historical events described above?

Figure 11.2 Pillaging of the Jerusalem Temple depicted on the Arch of Titus, which still stands in Rome, commemorating Titus's triumph over the Jewish revolt.

Figure 11.3 "Judaea Capta" coin minted by Rome to commemorate victory over the Jewish rebels. The seated woman represents conquered Judea. Depicting a defeated opponent as a woman was a common means of humiliation in the Roman world.

For the Jewish people, this was a devastating end to their rebellion against Roman imperial rule. With the city and Temple destroyed and large numbers of the population either dead or scattered to other regions, it may well have seemed like the end to the Jewish people altogether (see Figure 11.3).

Pointers to the Dating and Context of the Gospel of Mark

Although it is unlikely that the Gospel of Mark was written in Jerusalem, there are indications that the tragic events that occurred in the city from 66 to 70 CE helped shape this particular story of Jesus. From your reading of Mark 13, it should be clear why scholars have linked certain predictions in this chapter with the events of the Jewish War. Jesus's description of war, famine, and betrayal would have recalled the experience of those besieged within the walls of Jerusalem. Indeed, it is this chapter in particular that leads most scholars to date the Gospel of Mark to sometime close to 70 CE. Particularly notable is the reference to "the desolating sacrilege set up where it ought not to be" (Mark 13:14). This is an allusion to Dan 11:31 and an evocation of an earlier time when the Temple was violated by a foreign presence, the Seleucid king Antiochus IV. The Markan narrative is interrupted at this point by a direct address to the reader ("let the reader understand"), suggesting that the audience of the gospel should recognize the allusion in relation to current events.

basics Gospel of Mark

Outline: Mark's story of Jesus as the suffering messiah

I	Rising popularity of Jesus and rising conflict with authorities	1:1–8:21
II	Transition: passion predictions and instructions about the demands of discipleship	8:22–10:52
III	Predictions fulfilled: the suffering messiah	11:1–16:8

Location and audience

There is no certainty about who wrote the gospel or where it was written. Church tradition has associated the gospel with Peter, claiming that Mark was Peter's "interpreter" and suggesting that Peter related these stories to Mark while he was in Rome. Many have questioned this traditional association, noting little evidence for a story told from Peter's point of view. Some have theorized that the gospel was written somewhere closer to Jerusalem, perhaps in northern Galilee or Syria. At points, the narrative seems to assume a lack of familiarity with Jewish customs (7:3–4), leading some to argue that the author had primarily a gentile audience in mind.

The reference to Daniel also highlights the strong apocalyptic flavor of Mark 13. Like Paul, the gospel writer saw the world through an apocalyptic framework. Here too, we find an understanding of increased suffering culminating in divine intervention that will reward the faithful who have endured (Mark 13:13). Note that the reference to suffering includes not only war and famine, but also persecution from synagogue and governmental authorities, and hatred because of Jesus's name (Mark 13: 9, 13). While there is no evidence of widespread persecution of Christians as early as 70 CE, we do have reports of isolated incidents. The best-known of these is the report by the first-century CE Roman historian Tacitus of Nero's persecution of Christians in Rome. According to this account, Nero used the Christians as a scapegoat for a devastating fire that swept through Rome in 64 CE. The references to persecution in the Gospel of Mark may allude to this, or to a more general increase in tensions toward the followers of Jesus as their growing numbers drew more attention from local authorities.

Overview of the Gospel

With this evidence for the dating and context of Mark in mind, we turn now to discussion of the narrative. The structure of the Markan narrative can be seen as two parts with a transition section that links them together. The first part of the gospel (Mark 1:1–8:21) tells a story of Jesus's miracle-working ministry, resulting in his ever rising popularity among the crowds. This is juxtaposed with increasing opposition from authorities from Jerusalem. The transition section (Mark 8:22–10:52) features Jesus traveling to Jerusalem with his disciples, preparing them for his impending trial and crucifixion, and instructing them in the ways of discipleship. For their part, the disciples continue a pattern of misunderstanding Jesus that had already been introduced in the first section (Mark 1:1–8:21). The transition or teaching section (Mark 8:22–10:52) prepares the gospel audience for a shift from the miracle-working Jesus of the first section to the stark picture of the suffering messiah featured in the second part of the gospel. This second part of the book focuses on Jesus's final days in Jerusalem, during which his predictions of his suffering and death are fulfilled (Mark 11:1–16:8).

Rising popularity of Jesus and rising conflict with
the authorities (Mark 1:1–8:21)

READING
Mark 1–4, 8:1–21.

EXERCISE
What does Jesus do and say in these chapters and to whom? Note the response of the crowd to Jesus in these opening chapters of the story. Where do you see signs of conflict between Jesus and the authorities?

The first eight chapters of the gospel tell the story of the rapidly rising popularity of Jesus juxtaposed with the increasing conflict between Jesus and the Jewish authorities. The first words of the Markan Jesus take the form of proclamation: "The time is fulfilled, and the kingdom of God has come near, repent and believe in the good news" (Mark 1:15). The first chapter of the gospel then depicts Jesus in the full range of activities that will make up his ministry: calling disciples (Mark 1:16–20), teaching (Mark 1:21–2), casting out demons (Mark 1:23–6, 32–4, 39), and healing the sick (Mark 1:29–34, 40–2). Jesus seems to move quickly through these activities, especially because of the frequent use of the Greek word *euthus*, "immediately." This word occurs so often in this chapter, and in the first half of the gospel more generally, that English translations typically find different ways to render the term to avoid repetitiveness (see, for example, 1.10, 12, 18, 20, 21, 23, 28, 29, 30, 42, 43; also 2:8, 12; 3:6; 4:5; 4:15, etc.). While the frequent use of the term may indicate the author's limited Greek skills, it nevertheless creates an impression of fast-paced activity on the part of Jesus which corresponds to his rapidly increasing fame. One reason given for Jesus's appeal is that he speaks with authority or power (Greek *exousia*), in contrast to the scribes (Mark 1:22, 27). By the end of the chapter, Jesus is so popular that "he was no longer able to go into a town openly . . . and people came to him from all directions" (Mark 1:45).

Mark 2 introduces the other dynamic at work in the first section of the gospel: the increasing hostility on the part of the authorities toward Jesus. The story of the paralytic (Mark 2:1–12) begins as a healing story that again highlights the popularity of Jesus.

MORE ON METHOD: NARRATIVE CRITICISM OF THE GOSPELS

Until the 1970s, study of the gospels was heavily influenced by questions of source and redaction. Scholars were interested in what the authors used to compose their gospels and how they edited their material. Much of this work concentrated on establishing the early layers of authentic Jesus material and later editorial layers of the gospel writers or other redactors. (For redaction criticism, see p. 295.) It was common to view the author of Mark as little more than a compiler of tradition who linked different Jesus stories together like beads on a string. A change in this view of the author occurred when biblical scholars became interested in the literary aspects of the gospel narratives. The Gospel of Mark was among the first to be studied from the perspective of **narrative criticism**. This method examines the gospels as literature, attending to such literary aspects as plot, characters, setting, point of view, and narrator. The insights gained by this approach have had a strong influence on gospel studies. With the turn toward narrative criticism in the latter part of the twentieth century, the evangelists were no longer viewed as mere compilers of tradition, but as authors who actually crafted a narrative to articulate a particular story about Jesus.

For more on narrative criticism of the Gospel of Mark, see David Rhodes and Donald Michie, *Mark as Story: An Introduction to the Narrative of a Gospel* (Philadelphia: Fortress, 1982).

The only way to get near to Jesus is by lowering the paralytic down through the thatched roof of the house he is in (Mark 2:3–4). But the healing story soon hints at the conflict to come as the scribes appear on the scene for the first time, "questioning in their hearts" and accusing Jesus of blasphemy (Mark 2:6–7). By chapter 3, the two themes are closely linked. After Jesus performs another healing, this time on the Sabbath, the Pharisees conspire with the Herodians about how to destroy him (Mark 3:6). The very next scene shows Jesus so overwhelmed by crowds from all over Palestine that he must get into a boat on the lake to avoid being crushed (Mark 3:7–8). The juxtaposition of these two themes in the early part of the gospel produces an image of the fervent expectations around this miracle-working healer on the one hand, and the lurking and dangerous threat from his opponents on the other.

An Exorcism of Rome?

Another allusion to Roman power (and its imagined demise) may be found in the story of the demon-possessed man in Gerasene (Mark 5:1–20). In the story, Jesus arrives by boat in "the region of the Gerasenes" and encounters a demon-possessed man living among the tombs. Unlike other exorcism stories in the gospel, in this one Jesus demands to know the name of the demon. The response, "My name is Legion," is the first clue that this exorcism may be more than a healing story (5:9). "Legion" is the term for a Roman cohort of soldiers. Caesar's tenth legion, which took part in the Jewish War and was then stationed in Jerusalem, had an image of a boar on its standards. The story contains other military terms as well. For example, the Greek term for "herd" which refers to the group of pigs is a term that was used to refer to military recruits. Two verbs from the story, *epetrepsen* (he permitted) and *hormāsen* (they charged), are both typically used in a military context. These are subtle allusions and not every scholar is convinced that the author had Rome in mind. To be sure, the story serves equally well as an example of Jesus's battle with Satan at the ushering in of God's reign on earth. But for the ancient readers, these two interpretations would not be mutually exclusive.

Here it is worth pausing over the identity of Jesus's opponents in this gospel. They are typically identified as the scribes, Pharisees, and chief priests (e.g. Mark 2:6; 3:22; 7:1; 8:31; 10:33; 11:27). Past scholarship has often assumed that these were legalistic "experts" on the written and oral religious traditions of Judaism whom Jesus challenges in the interest of a more spiritual and humane interpretation of tradition. More recently, scholars have also recognized the political implications of these opponents. As discussed in Chapter 9 of this *Introduction*, Roman imperial structures of authority operated primarily through local elite men. Even Rome's military strength was not large enough to keep its vast empire under control. Instead, Roman commanders enlisted the support of local leaders who stood to benefit from cooperating with Rome. This is how the Jerusalem scribes would have functioned toward the end of the Second Temple period. They would have either worked in the Temple or been employed in the government administration. In either case, they would have been perceived as working closely with Roman authorities.

To be sure, the gospel narrative suggests that the role of the scribes involved interpretation of the scriptural and religious traditions (Mark 9:11; 12:32–3), but notice that the Markan Jesus paints a different picture. He warns his followers to beware of the scribes, describing them as men who love public recognition and prestige, but are vicious toward the disadvantaged (Mark 12:38). Note also that these opponents are repeatedly described as coming from Jerusalem, the seat of Roman power for Judea. Given that, it is intriguing that in Mark's gospel, Jesus's ministry begins in Galilee (which, incidentally, was also the place where the Jewish revolt against Rome began) and ends with an exhortation for the disciples to return to Galilee to find the risen

Jesus. In this gospel, Jerusalem is the place of Jesus's opposition, the place where he is crucified. Galilee, the point of origin for the revolt, is also the point of origin for Jesus, and the place (according to the gospel) where he will appear to his disciples after he has been raised from the dead. The critique of Jerusalem and its leaders will be evident throughout the gospel. Most likely, the critique was not only about religious leadership, but also concerned the associations with Rome that these leaders depended on for their power.

Another theme that emerges quite early in the gospel concerns the identity of Jesus, an aspect in the gospel that scholars have labeled "the messianic secret." Although the most striking examples of this theme will occur in the transition section (Mark 8:22–10:52), the secrecy theme is already evident in some of the early healing and exorcism stories in Mark 1–7. For example, on several occasions, Jesus urges those he has healed not to speak to anyone about it (Mark 1:43–4; 5:43; 7:36, see also 8:26). Similarly, Jesus silences the demons "because they knew him" (Mark 1:34; 3:11–12). We will return to this puzzling aspect of the gospel in the next section.

Related to the theme of Jesus's identity is the characterization of the disciples as followers who repeatedly misunderstand Jesus and his teaching. The first indication of the disciples' lack of comprehension appears in Mark 4. There Jesus answers a question about why he teaches in parables with this surprising statement,

> To you has been given the mystery of the kingdom of God, but for the ones on the outside, everything comes in parables; in order that "seeing, they may see but not perceive, and hearing, they may indeed hear, but not understand; so that they may never turn and be forgiven." (Mark 4:11–12)

The reason that the Markan Jesus gives for teaching in parables is startling in itself. Most contemporary readers do not expect Jesus to explain that he teaches in parables so that outsiders will be kept on the outside and have no chance of forgiveness. But given Jesus's explanation, it is even more surprising that the disciples themselves do not understand Jesus's parables (Mark 4:13). The audience is left to wonder whether the disciples are on the outside. Although Jesus goes on to explain the parable to the disciples (Mark 4:14–20), and the narrator claims that Jesus "privately explained everything to his own disciples" (Mark 4:34), they do not seem to benefit from these explanations. Instead, the narrative soon turns again to the disciples' lack of understanding and the claim that their "hearts were hardened" (Mark 6:52). One familiar with the Hebrew scriptures might well associate this phrase with the hardening of Pharaoh's heart against the works of God in the exodus tradition (see, e.g., Exod 4:21; 7:3, 13; 8:15; 9:12; Mark 4:21; 7:3, 13–14, 22; 8:15, 19). Moreover, in a later scene Jesus links the disciples' hardened hearts with the same condition that he used to describe those on the "outside" in chapter 4.

> And he ordered them, saying, "Look! Watch out for the yeast of the Pharisees and the yeast of Herod." They discussed it together, saying, "We have no bread." And perceiving it, Jesus said to them, "Why are you discussing that you have no bread?

Do you not yet perceive or comprehend? Have your hearts been hardened? Having eyes, do you not see? Having ears, do you not hear?" (Mark 8:15–18; cf. 4:12)

The scene ends with a final question from Jesus that is left unanswered: "Do you still not understand?" (Mark 8:21). The question may also echo in the ear of the reader, who by this stage in the narrative may be confused about Jesus. And this may be the point. In the wake of the destruction of the Second Temple, the author of this gospel was addressing followers of Jesus who may have been thoroughly confused about what to think about Jesus. Initially, their confessed belief in him as the Jewish messiah was probably accompanied by an expectation of the imminent restoration of Israel. But instead Rome destroyed the Temple, the central symbol of Judaism. Certainly, this would have raised major questions about whether Jesus could really have been the longed-for Jewish messiah.

Teaching and more misunderstanding on the way
(Mark 8:22–10:52)

READING
Mark 8:22–10:52.

EXERCISE
What are some general themes of Jesus's teaching in this section? What does he teach about himself? What does he teach about discipleship? How do the disciples respond?

The central section of the gospel seems designed to respond to such confusion. From 8:22 to 10:52, the rapid pace of the beginning of the gospel slows down and the focus shifts to Jesus's instructions to his disciples while they are on the way to Jerusalem. The journey begins when they are at the furthest point north in their travels: Caesarea Philippi, located at the source of the Jordan River (Mark 8:27). Jesus's teaching involves both what awaits him in Jerusalem and what it means to be his disciple. In this sense, the transition section continues themes that emerged in the first part of the gospel regarding Jesus's identity and mission, and the portrayal of the disciples. The author's creative use of healing stories to frame this teaching section suggests that understanding Jesus may be a gradual and initially difficult process both for the disciples and for the audience of the gospel. The first healing story, Mark 8:22–6, is unusual because Jesus must try twice to successfully heal the blind man. After the first attempt, the man reports that he has limited vision: "I see people, but I see them as trees that are walking" (Mark 8:24). It is only after Jesus's second try that the man can see clearly (Mark 8:25). The fact that this story follows Jesus's sharp questioning of the disciples, and comes immediately before the extended section of instruction to them, suggests its symbolic importance. The disciples are like the blind man – it will take a determined effort on Jesus's part to help them see clearly.

The Messianic Secret

"The **messianic secret**" emerged as a scholarly problem with the 1901 publication of William Wrede's book of the same title. Wrede noticed a number of elements in Mark's narrative that contributed to a theme of secrecy around Jesus's messianic identity, such as Jesus's silencing of the demons, his commands to silence about his healings, and with respect to the disciples' claim of his messianic identity. Wrede's major contribution was to identify and link these various aspects of the text, but there is much that remains unclear about the secrecy motif. One debate concerns the origin of the motif. Most scholars do not think that the commands to secrecy and silence came from the historical Jesus. Wrede suggested that the tradition developed in early stories about Jesus as a way of explaining why people did not recognize Jesus as the messiah during his lifetime.

Others see the theme as a literary element added by the author of the gospel. From this perspective, the author may have been underscoring that Jesus's messianic identity can only be fully understood once the necessity of his suffering and death is accepted.

But the puzzle of the messianic secret is not easy to solve. One problem is that the Markan Jesus is not consistent in his commands to secrecy (see Mark 5:19–20). Sometimes the point seems to be that the secret *cannot* be kept in spite of Jesus's commands to silence (see, for example, 1:40–5). To date, no single explanation has been offered that accounts for all of the elements of the gospel that have been grouped under the idea of "the messianic secret." In fact, some have argued that the idea of a "messianic secret" is more scholarly construction than literary reality. What do you think?

It is also at this point that the theme of the "messianic secret" becomes most evident. In a climactic moment in the narrative, Jesus asks his disciples, "Who do you say that I am?" (Mark 8:27). Peter responds to Jesus's question about his identity with the statement, "You are the Christ" (Mark 8:29). This is the first time in the gospel that anyone has attributed this title to Jesus, and he responds quite forcefully: "He strongly warned them to tell no one about him" (Mark 8:30). There is no explanation as to why Jesus says this, but the warning recalls other commands to silence that appear earlier in the narrative (see e.g. Mark 1:43–4; 3:11–12; 5:43). Moreover, something similar occurs in Mark 9. Following a revelation of Jesus in shining glory to a select group of disciples, they are strictly ordered "not to describe what they had seen to anyone, except when the Son of Man had been raised from the dead" (Mark 9:9). This verse seems to be the most significant clue to the meaning of the secrecy theme. It suggests that before one can know or fully understand Jesus's messianic identity, one must first witness his suffering and death.

Jesus the "Son of Man"

Among the various titles attributed to Jesus in the New Testament, the "Son of Man" is particularly intriguing since it appears only in sayings *of* Jesus, never in sayings *about* Jesus. This has led scholars to believe that the historical Jesus used the phrase in reference to himself, rather than seeing the title as one the early church applied to Jesus as ideas about him developed in later tradition. Even if one sees this as a title used by Jesus, what he intended by its use remains a point of debate. In other Jewish literature, the phrase can be used simply to mean "human" or "self." The phrase appears throughout Ezekiel, for example, where it is used by God as a reference to the prophet. The NRSV translates the phrase as "mortal one" (see Ezek 2:1ff). Other texts, such as 1 Enoch, use "son of man" to refer to an apocalyptic judge. A similar use appears in Dan 7:13, where the "son of man" comes with the clouds of heaven ("like a human being" in the NRSV). Whether one thinks the historical Jesus had this use in mind in using the title as a self-reference depends on whether one thinks the historical Jesus has an apocalyptic worldview.

This idea is reinforced throughout the teaching section. As Jesus travels from Caesarea Philippi to Jerusalem (see Map 11.1), the narrative reports several conversations between him and his disciples that occur "on the way." This phrase indicates both the final journey to Jesus's deadly confrontation with the authorities, and "the way" of disciple-ship that Jesus teaches. As with the issue of Jesus's identity, the misunderstanding of the disciples becomes even more accentuated in this section.

In fact, a pattern is repeated three times throughout this section. Three times Jesus predicts his coming suffering, death, and resurrection (Mark 8:31; 9:31; 10:33–4). Each of these **passion predictions** (see next section on the passion narrative) is followed by an example of misunderstanding on the part of the disciples. In the first instance, Peter rebukes Jesus (a verb used elsewhere only for Jesus's "rebuking" of the demons). Jesus rebukes Peter in return, exclaiming, "Get behind me, Satan! You're not thinking of the things of God, but of the things of humans" (Mark 8:33). The implication is that Peter is not willing to hear of Jesus's suffering and death, something that Jesus describes as the "things of God." The second passion prediction is followed by a report of an argu-ment among the disciples about who among them is the greatest (Mark 9:33–4). The third prediction is followed by a request from James and John that they be given seats of honor beside Jesus "in his glory" (Mark 10:35–7). In each case, Jesus's description of his suffering and death is put aside in favor of misguided visions of greatness and glory on the part of the disciples. All three times, the disciples' misunderstanding pro-vides Jesus with an opportunity to instruct them in the ways of discipleship. Each time, in different ways, Jesus informs his companions that to follow him means to put aside greatness in favor of suffering and service (Mark 8:34–5; 9:35; 10:42–5).

Finally, at the end of the teaching section, another healing takes place. This time a blind beggar from the roadside calls to Jesus asking to see again (Mark 10:47–8). Jesus

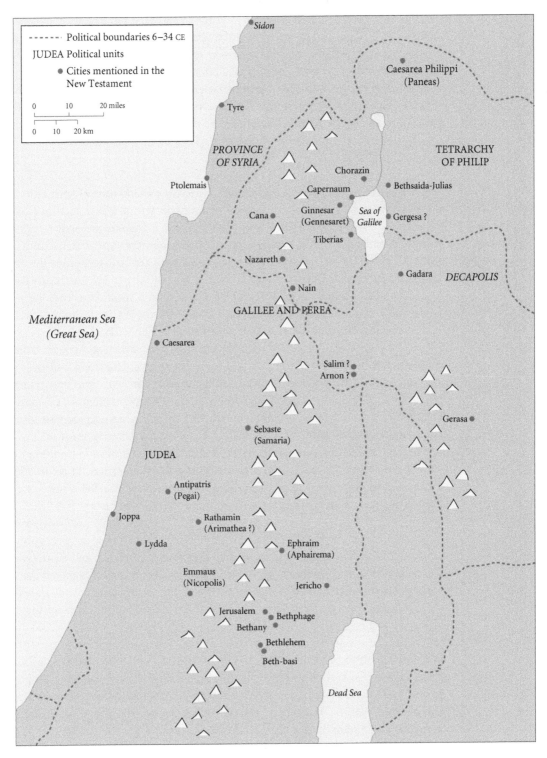

Map 11.1 Palestine in the first century CE. Redrawn from Bart Ehrman, *The New Testament: A Historical Introduction to the Early Christian Writings* (3rd edition). Oxford: Oxford University Press, 2004, page 73.

tells him that his faith has healed him, and significantly, the restored man follows Jesus "on the way." In other words, at the end of this transition section, the narrative provides an example of a new disciple with his vision fully intact. To be sure, as the story continues, those closest to Jesus may not exhibit such clear vision – there is still betrayal and denial to come. But for the ancient audience of the gospel, the teaching section may have opened their eyes to the idea of a suffering messiah. The conclusion to the gospel puts the image of such a messiah directly before them.

The suffering messiah (Mark 11:1–16:8)

The last section of the gospel is traditionally called the **passion narrative**, since it relates the story of Jesus's suffering or "passion" (from Latin *passus*, a past participle of *pati*, "to suffer"). The passion narrative in Mark's gospel represents the earliest surviving written narrative about Jesus's trial and crucifixion. Because it is presented as a more sustained account compared to the episodic quality of the first section of the gospel, some have hypothesized that the author used an already written account of the passion as a source. But whether the source was written or oral, it seems clear that the author was relying on traditional interpretations of the last days of Jesus in writing his account. A close reading of the Markan passion narrative shows how thoroughly the story was shaped by certain texts from the Hebrew scriptures, in particular passages from the prophets and the psalms. Early believers were intent on interpreting and telling the story of Jesus's suffering and death as fulfillment of their own scriptural traditions. In addition, this final section of the gospel continues the themes that we saw in earlier sections such as the growing conflict with the Jerusalem authorities, the disciples' failure to understand Jesus, and especially, the idea of the suffering messiah.

The link between the passion narrative and the Hebrew prophetic tradition begins early in the section. Jesus's "triumphal" entry into Jerusalem on a colt secured by his disciples (Mark 11:1–10) appears to be an enactment of the following text from Zechariah:

> Rejoice greatly, O daughter Zion! Proclaim, O daughter Jerusalem! See, your king comes to you. He is just and one who saves, showing clemency and mounted on a donkey, that is, on a new colt. He will cut off the chariot from Ephraim and the horse from Jerusalem; and the bow shall be destroyed, and he shall command peace to the nations. He will rule from sea to sea, and from the river to the ends of the earth. (Zech 9.9–10)

In Zechariah, the oracle concerns God's defeat of Israel's enemies, followed by a royal procession of the victorious king into the capital city, Jerusalem. In the gospel, the crowd lays a royal processional way for Jesus, welcoming him as a king with words evoking Ps 118:25–6. "Hosanna! Blessed is the one coming in the name of the Lord! Blessed is the coming kingdom of our father David! Hosanna in the highest!" (Mark 11:9–10). Clearly, the gospel describes the people as symbolically welcoming Jesus into Jerusalem as the anointed king who will bring peace to the city. Given this, Jesus's entry into the Jerusalem Temple is anti-climatic. He simply goes in, looks around, and then leaves, because, as the text explains, it was already late (Mark 11:11). After the long trip to Jerusalem, Jesus and his disciples do not stay in the city, but go back to the village of Bethany to spend the night. Perhaps this is a way for the author to distance Jesus from Jerusalem and the Temple – he will not even stay inside the city walls. This idea is confirmed by Jesus's actions in the Temple on the following day.

Mark 11:12–21 is an example of Markan intercalation (see the Miscellaneous Box on "Intercalation or the Markan 'Sandwich'"). In this rather odd account, Jesus curses a fig tree because he is hungry and it has no fruit on it. He then re-enters the Temple and causes a disturbance, overturning tables and driving out those who are buying and selling animals for Temple sacrifices. By way of explanation, the Markan Jesus cites a passage from Isaiah: "Is it not written, 'My house will be called a house of prayer for all the nations?' But you have made it a cave of bandits" (Mark 11:17; see Isa 56:7). The implication is that the Temple is infested with corrupt practices and Jesus's actions are a critique of this corruption. Upon Jesus's leaving the Temple, the fig tree is once again the focus, when the disciples notice that it has withered. This combination of fig tree and Temple seems to make little sense. Why would Jesus curse a tree for not having fruit when it is not the season for fruit? And what does a fig tree have to do with Temple corruption? As with the entry into Jerusalem, the key to understanding this scene may be found in the prophetic literature. We have already seen the way the eighth-century prophets linked corruption with the downfall of Israel and Judah. Now the same type of prophetic critique is reintroduced at a time when Jerusalem is again suffering through the aftermath of a war with a dominant foreign power. In this case, Hos 9:10–16 is particularly suggestive as a backdrop for Jesus's actions. In the Hosea text, Israel is first identified as "the first fruit on the fig tree, in its first season" (Hos 9:10). As the text continues, it describes Israel's corruption and the resulting judgment from God: "Because of the evilness of their deeds, I will throw them out of my house" (Hos 9:15). The oracle closes with a description of the stricken Israel: "the root is dried out. It will no

Intercalation or the Markan "Sandwich"

One sign of the author's literary sensitivity is found in the way he often inserts one story into another story. Scholars have called this literary device **intercalation**, or more descriptively, Mark's "sandwich" structure. The fig tree/Temple episode is one example of Markan intercalation, but there are others. Mark 5:22–3 relates two healing stories – a request for healing by a synagogue leader's daughter framing the account of a lone woman's surreptitious seeking of Jesus's healing power. In this case, the intercalation increases narrative tension because the diversion created by the older woman allows enough narrative time to pass for the daughter to die. Other examples of the sandwich structure include Mark 3:21–35; 6:7–30; 14:53–72. Read these and note how the interwoven stories comment on each other.

longer bear fruit" (Hos 9:16). In other words, the book of Hosea and the Gospel of Mark feature the same pattern to express judgment – a fig tree with reference to its season, an expulsion from the Temple, and a reference to a barren fruit tree. Through evoking the figure of the corrupted and rejected fig tree/people in Hosea, the gospel writer places Jesus's confrontation with later authorities in the context of God's longer-term judgment of God's people.

In addition to these examples, other details of the passion narrative are clearly influenced by the Hebrew scriptures, especially Isaiah and the Psalms. For instance, Jesus's silence during much of his trial recalls the servant songs of Isaiah (Mark 14:61; 15:4–5; cf. Isa 53:7). In particular, the writer of the Markan passion narrative seems to have used elements from Psalms 69 and 22 to fill out the description of Jesus's suffering. Just as Ps 69:4 speaks of false accusations, the writer describes the opponents of Jesus bearing false witness against him (Mark 14:56). So also the gospel describes bystanders giving Jesus sour wine (Mark 15:36), an echo of the psalmist being given vinegar to drink (Ps 69:21). When the soldiers in the Markan narrative are described casting lots for Jesus's clothes (Mark 15:24), it is a recollection of the psalmist's experience in Psalm 22 (Ps 22:18), and the bystanders' mockery of Jesus (Mark 15:31–2) recalls the mockery of the psalmist by others (Ps 22:7–8).

A Glimpse of Life under Roman Occupation

One Markan conflict story is especially revealing in light of the reality of Roman occupation and the difficulties it posed for local residents of Judea. In this case, the Pharisees and Herodians come to trap Jesus with a question concerning the Roman tax. "Is it lawful to pay taxes to the emperor, or is it not?" (Mark 12:14). The tax in question was first imposed on the region when it became a province of Rome in 6 CE. At that time, resistance to the tax was mounted by a certain Judas (not the disciple of Jesus), who called on others to refuse payment of the tax (see Josephus, *Jewish War* 2.8.1 §117–18). Some sixty years later, during the time of the revolt, the issue of paying tribute to Rome was again a pressing question. Although one point of the conflict is to show the cleverness of the Markan Jesus in besting his opponents, the story also illustrates life under Roman occupation. The question of paying tribute to Caesar is another iteration of the centuries-long dilemma of Israel's paying tribute to a foreign nation when doing so was understood as paying tribute to a foreign god. The telling of this story around 70 CE would no doubt tap into the deep tensions of a colonized people. As Christianity spread across the empire, paying tribute to the emperor would emerge as a particularly pressing question.

Finally, the Markan Jesus will quote Psalm 22 directly at the moment of his death (Mark 15:34), a point to which we will return.

In addition to the idea of scripture fulfillment, the story of Jesus's arrest, trial, and crucifixion is also shaped by themes introduced earlier in the gospel. Indeed, two themes that emerged in the early part of the gospel – the growing popularity of Jesus and his increasingly deadly opposition – move toward a climax. We have already noted the way Jesus is welcomed by crowds into the city of Jerusalem. But this kingly procession is followed by a series of conflict stories between Jesus and the Jerusalem authorities, who are trying to "trap him in what he said" (Mark 12:13). The relationship between the two themes is evident in the dilemma expressed by Jesus's opposition: "The chief priests and the scribes were looking for a way to arrest Jesus by stealth and kill him; for they said, 'Not during the festival, or there may be a riot among the people'" (Mark 14:1–2).

What gives way, in the gospel story, is Jesus's popularity. As the narrative counts down days until the Passover (and Jesus's crucifixion), the adoring crowd that flocked to Jesus in Galilee, as well as the "many" who laid cloaks on the ground as he entered Jerusalem, fade from view. Instead, the last reference to the crowd in the gospel shows it clamoring for Jesus's crucifixion (Mark 15:11–14).

Even worse, the Markan Jesus's own disciples fail him miserably in his time of need, continuing the theme of the disciples' misunderstanding and failure that emerged in the first half of the narrative. As Jesus approaches his death, he indicates the impending betrayal of one of his disciples (Mark 14:18–21), the abandonment of all of them (Mark 14:27), and the denial of Peter (Mark 14:30). Despite the disciples' vehement protests against his predictions, all of them come to fruition (Mark 14:44–5, 50, 66–72). In his way, a major aspect of the suffering of Jesus in the gospel is that of abandonment. This gospel makes clear that none of his followers or family is present in this final hour – the closest they come seems to be the women followers who were watching from far away (Mark 15:40). Most telling, however, are Jesus's final words, a quote from Psalm 22: "My God, my God, why have you abandoned me?" (Mark 15:34). In the Gospel of Mark, there is no answer to Jesus's question.

Mark's Enigmatic Ending

A final enigmatic aspect of the gospel concerns its closing scene. The Gospel of Mark has no stories of Jesus's appearance after his resurrection from the dead. Instead, Mark 16:1–8 relates the story of the empty tomb. To be sure, this story is intended to convey to the reader that Jesus "has been raised," as the young man in white reports to the women. What is puzzling is the women's response to his words. Although they are asked to go and tell the others to meet the risen Jesus in Galilee, the narrator reports that the women say nothing to anyone, for they are terrified (Mark 16:8). At this point, according to all of the oldest surviving manuscripts of the gospel, the gospel ends.

Therein lies the problem. Why would a gospel writer end his story with the failure of devoted, yet terrified women? The scribal activity around Mark's ending suggests that at least some early Christians were troubled by this abrupt ending. There were two different endings added to the gospel by later scribes. One, the "shorter ending," has the women fulfilling the command, then concludes with language unfamiliar to the Gospel of Mark about Jesus's "sacred and imperishable proclamation of eternal salvation." Another scribe added a series of resurrection appearances, some of which are found in other canonical gospels. But adding more endings to the gospel, as these two early Christian scribes did, still leaves us with the question of the gospel's original ending. Some scholars have argued Mark's abrupt end was *not* the original ending, but that a more complete ending was lost when some of the original manuscript broke off. But many readers of Mark think that this is precisely how the author intended the gospel to end. They focus on the potential impact of the ending on the audience. Perhaps the fear of the women matches the audience's own fear in a time of political turmoil. The ending may be a way of empathizing with this emotion. At the same time, the silent women may act as literary foils for the audience, presenting a negative example of discipleship that the audience can surpass if they boldly spread the gospel to others. Here is a case where the narrative form of the gospel allows for multiple interpretations. The end of the gospel is truly open-ended.

FOCUS
TEXT

Mark 12:1–12

We conclude with a closer look at a parable in the gospel: the parable of the vineyard in Mark 12:1–12, which conveys a number of the themes that we have seen in the gospel. In fact, Mary Ann Tolbert in *Sowing the Gospel* has called this parable a "plot synopsis" for the gospel. It is a sharp indictment of the Jerusalem leaders. The context for the parable is yet another challenge to Jesus's authority in which the chief priest, scribes, and elders have asked Jesus directly, "By what authority are you doing these things? Who gave you this authority to do them?" (Mark 11:28). Jesus first responds with a question concerning the authority of John the Baptist that the authorities are at a loss to answer (Mark 11:29–33). He then tells the parable.

It begins with clear allusions to Isa 5:1–7, another parable of judgment, but the focus of God's wrath is different in Mark. Both texts begin with careful preparation of a vineyard, which is Israel. In Isaiah 5, the vineyard/Israel yields wild grapes instead of cultivated ones, thus incurring God's judgment. In the Markan parable, the vineyard is put in the care of tenants, who kill multiple slaves who are sent to collect produce from the tenants. Since the parable has begun with an allusion to Israel, it is likely that these "slaves" represent the line of prophets who have been rejected. The tension of the parable rises as the vineyard owner decides to send his "beloved son," assuming they would not dare to kill him. The "beloved son" is an obvious reference to Jesus (see Mark 1:11; 9:7). In the parable, the tenants do not hesitate to kill him so that they will gain the inheritance. So too in the broader Gospel of Mark, the Jerusalem authorities plan for the death of Jesus. In this way, the parable of the vineyard serves as a prediction of Jesus's death and also an indictment of the authorities who seek to kill him. Note that the parable elicits sympathy for the vineyard owner, the one who wields power, rather than for the tenant workers who rebel against his authority. Indeed, in this version of the parable, the audience is intended to approve of the punitive actions of the vineyard owner, who "will come and destroy the tenants, and give the vineyard to others" (Mark 12:9).

Here is a reappropriation of the original Isaiah text that works on multiple levels in the political and religious context of the gospel. In Isaiah's vineyard story, it is God who brings destruction upon Israel, the vineyard. In the gospel parable, the vineyard owner/

God is coming to destroy not the vineyard itself, but the tenants of the vineyard, who in the larger context of the parable are understood to be the Jewish elite. What actually happened historically, of course, is that Rome brought destruction on Jerusalem, decimating its leaders and devastating what was once the center of power in the region. In this way, the gospel alludes to Rome as the agent of God's wrath that carries out God's judgment against the elite men (the chief priests, scribes, and elders) responsible for the death of Jesus. Indeed, the parable suggests that the destruction of Jerusalem and the Temple, and the resulting loss of authority for the priests and scribes associated with the Temple, is God's just punishment for their unjust behavior. The parable goes on to suggest that, as part of this divine intervention, the vineyard will be given to others.

Past interpretations of the parable, influenced by supersessionist interpretations of Christianity, saw these "others" as the gentile church of emerging Christianity. In this misreading of the parable, Judaism was destroyed and "Israel" – that is, the people of God – were now the new gentile Christian church. However, as we have seen, it is not Israel/the vineyard that is destroyed in Mark's version, but the leaders/tenants. The "others" in the parable represent the new, faithful leaders emerging from the followers of Jesus who will replace the unfaithful ones (who were in power, in part, because of collaboration with Rome). One possible reading of the Markan parable, then, is that God is working in mysterious ways, using Rome to destroy the Temple (which had been corrupted by economic exploitation) and the Temple authorities (who cooperated with Rome). This destruction has made possible the emergence of a new leadership of a renewed Israel, a community that will be a place of prayer for all the nations.

Such a mixed portrayal of Rome in the gospel as both oppressive enemy and agent of God is yet another example of the ambivalent attitude that often results between the colonizer and the colonized. Rome is the ever present dominant power, whether seen as political oppressors or deliverers of divine justice against other, more localized opponents.

The parable concludes with a scripture citation, this time by way of direct quotation by the Markan Jesus. He asks, "Have you not read this scripture: 'The stone that the builders rejected has become the cornerstone; this was the Lord's doing, and it is amazing in our eyes'?" (Mark 12:10–11; see Ps 118:22–3). The link between Jesus and various "stone sayings" was already well established in early Christianity (see Rom 9:32–3; Eph 2.20; Acts 4:11; 1 Pet 2:4–8). The gospel writer draws on the stone tradition here to shift the focus from judgment of Jesus's opponents to vindication of God's "beloved son." In this way, the parable tells the whole story of God's work in Jesus Christ: the sending of the son, his rejection and crucifixion, and eventually – with this stone saying – the resurrection by which he will become the "cornerstone" of the new community of believers.

Finally, note that in this case, "those outside" have no difficulty understanding that the parable is told against them (Mark 12:12). In this way, the parable differs from the earlier explanation about why Jesus teaches in parables. The opponents of Jesus *do* hear and understand this parable. So, too, perhaps the ancient audience is meant to understand that in spite of the present dismal circumstances, God is still working in the world, in the midst of Roman occupation and perhaps even *through* Roman occupation, to restore the people of God.

CHAPTER ELEVEN REVIEW

1. Know the meaning and significance of the following terms:
- intercalation
- Jewish War
- messianic secret
- narrative criticism
- passion narrative
- passion predictions

2. Why do scholars typically date the Gospel of Mark to around 70 CE?

3. What are some possible reasons why the author portrayed the disciples as repeatedly misunderstanding Jesus?

4. How does the presentation of Jesus in the Gospel of Mark fit with the historical circumstances at the time the gospel was written?

RESOURCES FOR FURTHER STUDY

Boring, M. Eugene. *Mark: A Commentary*. Louisville, KY: Westminster John Knox Press, 2006.

Collins, Adela Yarbro. *Mark: A Commentary*. Philadelphia: Fortress, 2007.

Iersel, Vas van. *Reading Mark*. Edinburgh: T & T Clark, 1989.

Tolbert, Mary Ann. *Sowing the Gospel: Mark's World in Literary-Historical Perspective*. Minneapolis: Fortress, 1989.

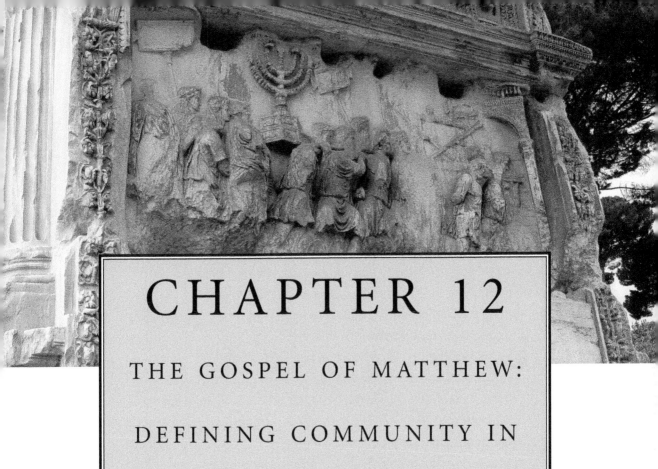

CHAPTER 12

THE GOSPEL OF MATTHEW: DEFINING COMMUNITY IN THE WAKE OF DESTRUCTION

Chapter Outline

CHAPTER OVERVIEW

The phrase "post-9/11 world" has become a common expression to define American life on the other side of the tragic events of September 11, 2001. In a similar way, we can consider all of the gospels to be written in a "post-Temple world." All of the gospel writers are telling a story of Jesus, a Jewish messiah, on the other side of the destruction of the Jerusalem Temple, a powerful show of Roman force. Whereas the Gospel of Mark reflects the suffering, fear, and uncertainty in the immediate aftermath of this event, the Gospel of Matthew addresses the early stages of post-Temple community rebuilding and redefinition.

Most scholars date the Gospel of Matthew a decade or so later than Mark, around 80 to 85 CE. The author was writing at a time when the Jewish community was once again wrestling with questions of its identity and survival following the disastrous results of the rebellion against Rome. The Gospel of Matthew addresses the question of identity in several different ways. It uses familiar Jewish symbols in new ways, so that followers of Jesus can associate themselves with the long and rich history of the Jewish people. It defines this new community of believers by providing instructions for how they are to live in relation to each other and the broader world. It also draws sharp boundaries for the community, marking the lines between those inside and those outside by vilifying its opponents. By the end of this chapter, you will see how these strategies help to shape the emerging Christian community a decade or so after the destruction of the Temple. We will see how the gospel links Jesus explicitly to a central Jewish symbol, the Torah of Moses. It presents Jesus as a teacher and lord instructing the new community of believers in the ways of righteousness. At the same time, it defines the community following Jesus over against the "hypocritical" Pharisees and the Jewish people more generally.

The Sources and Structure of the Gospel of Matthew

Before moving to discussion of these themes, we need a general understanding of how the gospel was written. Unlike the Gospel of Mark, this gospel begins with a genealogy of Jesus, followed by the story of his birth. In addition, this gospel concludes with a series of appearances of the resurrected Jesus. These scenes are all unique to the Gospel of Matthew – when we study the Gospel of Luke in the next chapter we will see that the Lukan stories of Jesus's birth and resurrection are different from the Matthean stories. Given this, we can now add to our original discussion of the two-source theory.

As you already know from Chapter 9, the author of Matthew drew on both the Gospel of Mark and Q in writing his gospel. But he apparently drew on yet another source, one reflected in material unique to this gospel. It is difficult to know whether this unique material came from an oral or a written source. And it is possible that some of this unique material was created by the author. Indeed, all three of these options are possible depending on the material. Because of this uncertainty, scholars have simply labeled this unique Matthean material **(M)**, with the parentheses indicating the uncertainty about the origins of material. Looking ahead, the same will be true for the Gospel of Luke. It too will have material that is found only in the Gospel of Luke, which scholars have labeled **(L)** material. Thus, we can add to Figure 9.5 in Chapter 9 as shown in Figure 12.1.

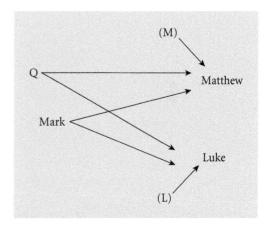

Figure 12.1 The four-source theory.

Taken together these sources are the basis for the **four-source theory**, which identifies the Gospel of Mark, Q, (M), and (L) as four different sources that were used in different combinations for writing the synoptic gospels. The four-source hypothesis is the most commonly accepted solution to the synoptic problem.

Equally important to identifying the sources of the gospel is understanding how the author uses them to structure his gospel. The author of Matthew clustered the Q material (primarily sayings of Jesus) into five major sections of the gospel. The result is a gospel built on an alternating pattern of discourses and narrative. Each of the discourses is clearly marked by a concluding formula: "when Jesus had finished . . ." (Matt 7:28; 11:1; 13:53; 19:1; 26:1). Given the emphasis we will see on Jesus's relationship to the Torah (which has five books), the fact that there are five discourses is suggestive. Perhaps the author had in mind the five books of the Torah as he gathered the sayings traditions of Jesus into five distinct discourses.

As we will see, the author of Luke puts these sayings traditions together in a different way. Because these two authors make different and creative use of the sayings source, it seems clear that neither one is preserving entire sermons of Jesus just as they were delivered. Instead, the author of Matthew has clustered together sayings more or less thematically. In so doing, he constructs a story of Jesus that includes large sections of instruction on topics that would be relevant to life in the community of believers.

292 GOSPEL OF MATTHEW

basics Gospel of Matthew

Outline:
Matthew's
retelling of the
story of Jesus

The following illustrates the five-part alternation of narrative and discourse. The narrative sections are often a loose collection of traditions about Jesus, while the discourse material collects sayings of similar types.

I	Introduction: Jesus's birth narrative			1–2
II	Five-part alternation of narrative and discourse			3–25
	A	Part 1	The beginning of Jesus's ministry	3–7
			Narrative: baptism, temptation, and gathering of disciples	3–4
			Discourse: Sermon on the Mount	5–7
	B	Part 2	Ministry in Galilee	8–10
			Narrative: the healing ministry of Jesus	8–9
			Discourse: instructions for the twelve disciples	10
	C	Part 3	Opposition to and conflict with Jesus	11–13
			Narrative: stories of conflict	11–12
			Discourse: parables of the kingdom	13
	D	Part 4	The power of Christ and life in the church	14–18
			Narrative: nature miracle traditions, passion predictions	14–17
			Discourse: parables and instruction on life in the community	18
	E	Part 5	Journey and teaching in Jerusalem	19–25
			Narrative: testing of Jesus	19–22
			Discourse: "woes" and teaching on the coming judgment	23–5
III	Passion narrative/resurrection accounts			26–8

Location
and author

The gospel was likely written in Antioch of Syria. It is cited frequently in the letters of Ignatius, bishop of Antioch in the second century. Another early Christian text that was used in Syria, the Didache, also makes frequent use of the gospel. In Matt 4:24, the author adds a reference to his Markan source, stating that Jesus's fame "spread throughout all of Syria."

As with all the gospels, we know little about the author. Church tradition associated the gospel with Matthew, though it is unclear why this particular association was made. Perhaps someone with the name of Matthew had prominence in the early Christian communities that read this gospel. The interest in portraying Jesus in relation to the Jewish Torah and tradition and the ambivalent references to gentiles (Matt 5:47; 6:7, 32; 10:5) suggest a Jewish author.

He also constructs an image of Jesus that emphasizes his role as an authoritative teacher and "Lord" of this new community.

MORE ON METHOD: REDACTION CRITICISM

A primary method for studying the gospels is to examine how the authors edited or "redacted" their sources to emphasize particular themes that were important to them. Editorial activity might involve additions, omissions, rearrangement, or rewording of a source. **Redaction criticism** thus focuses on the theological interests of the evangelist and his motivations for editing his sources in particular ways. A helpful tool for redaction criticism is a gospel synopsis or parallel, a resource that arranges similar gospel passages (also known as pericopes) in parallel columns for the sake of comparison.

See also Norman Perrin, *What is Redaction Criticism?* (Philadelphia: Fortress, 1969).

Here we should note that Matthew's gospel is the only one of the four canonical gospels that actually uses the Greek work *ekklesia*, meaning gathering or assembly, but typically translated "church." The most significant occurrence of the word is in the Matthean redaction of the scene at Caesarea Philippi. If you compare the Matthean version of this scene (Matt 16:13–20) with the Markan one (Mark 8:27–30), you will see that the author of Matthew has added to the tradition that he knew from the Gospel of Mark to include a focus on Peter as the "rock" on which Jesus will build his *ekklesia* (Matt 16:17–19). Thus we see an emphasis both on Peter's leadership and on the establishment of a particular group. A reference to this *ekklesia* is also found in 18:17, which says that this "*ekklesia*" should intervene in the case of a "brother" who sins. Both of these references suggest that the author of the gospel envisions a distinct community that operates on a different set of principles than its surrounding culture.

The Matthean Jesus and the Torah of Moses

READING
Matthew 1–2, 5–7.

EXERCISE
Where do you see references to Moses or to the law in these chapters? (Hint: of whom does Herod remind you?) How does the Matthean Jesus regard the law? What do these chapters suggest about how the author viewed Jesus in relation to the Torah?

The last time we considered issues of community rebuilding and self-definition was during the post-exilic period. Two key events in the lives of the returning exiles were the rebuilding of the Jerusalem Temple and the establishment of the Torah of Moses as central to Judaism. Now, some five hundred years later, the Temple had been destroyed once again. What remained was the Torah. In the years following the Second Temple's destruction, Jewish leaders would eventually turn with renewed vigor toward focused study of the Torah as a way of defining and solidifying the post-Temple Jewish community. Indeed, the form of Judaism that has survived to this day traces its origins to the Jewish leadership that gathered the community around the study of the Torah during this time. It is in this context that we should read the emphasis on the Torah that is in the Gospel of Matthew. The author of the Gospel of Matthew recognizes the centrality of the Torah, but presents an image of Jesus that suggests devotion to the Torah can be accomplished through devotion and obedience to Jesus. This is a form of reappropriation – an old symbol is put to use in a new way. To examine this reappropriation in more detail, we begin with the Matthean birth narrative.

Gender and Matthew's Genealogy

Amidst the patrilineal line that is traced in this genealogy, four women are mentioned. This is unusual for a genealogy from the Jewish tradition, and many have puzzled over why these four particular women are mentioned. Some readings have highlighted the marginal status of Tamar, Rahab, Ruth, and the wife of Uriah (they were understood to be sexually suspect and/or foreigners). Mary is placed in the same line of tradition as these women with whom God worked in unconventional ways. Some feminist readings of the gospel have interpreted the women's presence in the genealogy as subverting the patrilineal tradition. Such readings point especially to the conclusion of the genealogy, which ends not with Joseph "begetting" Jesus, as is customary in the Hebrew tradition, but with Mary, "of whom Jesus was born" (Matt 1:16). While it may be empowering to women in our contemporary setting to understand this text as subversive, it is doubtful that an ancient reader would understand Matthew's genealogy as a strike against patriarchy. On the contrary, a major point of the genealogy is to place Jesus within a line of honorable masculine ancestry that links him both to the founding father of Judaism and to the royal Davidic line precisely through Joseph. So even though it is the Holy Spirit and not Joseph who is responsible for the conception of Jesus (Matt 1:18–20), the author uses the genealogy to connect Jesus to Joseph's ancestral line.

As mentioned earlier, the birth narrative in Matthew's gospel is (M) material, meaning it is unique to this gospel. The gospel begins with a genealogy that points to the author's interest in linking Jesus to King David and to Abraham (see Matt 1:1). Once this line is established, the gospel moves to the story of Jesus's conception and birth. As the story of Mary's conception and the angelic announcement to Joseph unfolds, another link between Jesus and the Hebrew scriptures is introduced:

All this came about in order to fulfill what had been said by the Lord through the prophet: "Look, the virgin shall conceive and bear a son, and they shall name him Emmanuel," which means, "God is with us." (Matt 1:22–3)

This is the first example of many **fulfillment citations** that occur in the Gospel of Matthew. The author uses some variation of the formula "this was to fulfill" throughout the gospel to show that the life of Jesus was completely in line with the Torah and especially the prophets (see, for example, Matt 2:15, 17, 23; 4:14; 5:17; 8:17; 12:17, etc.).

The birth narrative links Jesus to the Torah in another, more subtle way. Several of the details of the birth narrative are allusions to the story of Moses. Just as Pharaoh ordered the slaughter of all the sons born to Hebrew women (Exod 1:15–16), the Gospel of Matthew says that Herod ordered the killing of all the boys less than two years of age in order to eliminate the threat that Jesus poses to him (Matt 2:16). In case this allusion is missed, the gospel links directly to Egypt, describing Joseph's flight there to save his family from Herod (Matt 2:13–14). Thus, from the beginning of the narrative, the Gospel of Matthew tells the story of Jesus in a way that recalls the figure of Moses. The reasons for this become clear in the first extended discourse of the gospel.

We should also not forget that the Herod depicted in this gospel is the same client king of Rome described in Chapter 9 of this *Introduction*. Although there is no evidence external to this gospel for the "massacre of the innocents," as it has been called in church tradition, the brutality of the act certainly captures the reign of Herod, who had several of his own children executed during his rule. In having the story of Jesus begin with his escape from this client king of the Romans, not only does the gospel begin with a link between Jesus and the figure of Moses, it also begins with a story of resistance to Roman imperial power. Here we should note too how closely the Jewish leaders are linked with Herod in this story. Herod assembles the chief priest and scribes to gather information about the birth of the messiah, which they readily supply (Matt 2:3–6). Thus, the gospel opens with a scene of the Jewish elite cooperating with Roman authority.

The link between Jesus and Moses is found not only in Matthew's opening narrative, but also in the opening discourse. In Matthew 5–7 Jesus delivers the so-called **Sermon on the Mount**. Note, however, that only this gospel portrays Jesus as actually ascending a mountain before he begins teaching (cf. Luke 6:17, which locates Jesus in a level place). Since much of the first part of this discourse concerns interpretation of the law, the author no doubt intended once again to recall the figure of Moses giving instructions regarding the law to the ancient Israelites. The Matthean Jesus openly asserts that he has come to fulfill the law: "Do not assume that I have come to destroy the law or the prophets; I have come not to destroy but to fulfill. For truly I tell you, until heaven and earth pass away, not one letter, not one stroke of a letter, will pass away from the law until all things take place" (Matt 5:17–18). He then goes on to teach about the law using a formula that emphasizes not only fulfillment but also reinterpretation: "You have heard that it was said . . . but I say to you . . ." (Matt 5:21, 27, 31, 33, 38, 43). In each case, Jesus intensifies the law and also challenges his audience to exceed the scribes and Pharisees in righteousness (Matt 5:20). They are to "be perfect" as their "heavenly Father is perfect" (Matt 5:48). The combination of the echoes of Moses in the opening infancy narrative and reinterpretation of the law in this opening discourse suggest that Jesus is one who surpasses Moses in authority.

The Matthean Jesus is linked to the Torah in still another way. In the early Christian tradition there already was an association between Jesus and the personified Wisdom figure of Jewish wisdom literature. This gospel draws on a Q saying that has Jesus defending himself against his opponents with the statement that "Wisdom is justified by her deeds" (Matt 11:19; Luke 7:35). The author of the gospel takes the association of Jesus with Wisdom still further with the following saying of Jesus:

> Come to me, all those who are weary and burdened, and I will give you rest. Take my yoke upon you, and learn from me; for I am lenient and humble in heart, and you will find rest for your souls. For my yoke is easy to bear, and my burden is light. (Matt 11:28–30)

Compare this to the words of personified Wisdom in Sirach:

> Come to me, those who desire me, and be filled from my harvest. (Sirach 24:19)

> Put your neck under the yoke, and let your soul welcome instruction; it is close by to find. (Sirach 51:26)

Matthew's Jesus is speaking Wisdom's words! To be sure, this saying of the Matthean Jesus does not quote personified Wisdom exactly, but there is enough overlap for an audience familiar with the tradition to hear Jesus speaking as God's Wisdom. What is most significant to our discussion of Jesus in relation to the Torah, however, is the claim made by Sirach following a speech by personified Wisdom: "all these things are the book of the covenant of the most High God, which is the law that Moses commanded us" (Sirach 24:23). In other words, for Sirach, God's Wisdom and God's law are synonymous. Thus this allusion to Jesus as God's Wisdom was another away of associating him with the Torah.

In short, the Gospel of Matthew links Jesus with the Torah in multiple ways – fulfilling Torah, interpreting Torah, speaking as Wisdom/Torah. One of the sayings of the Matthean Jesus expresses this close association most clearly. In Matt 18:20, Jesus says, "For where two or three are gathered in my name, I am there among them." We should not be surprised to find that a very similar tradition is found in the Mishnah, a collection of early rabbinic teachings: "But two who are sitting, and words of Torah pass between them – the Presence is with them" (*Abot* 3.2, Neusner translation). Whereas the study of the Torah was understood by some early Jewish groups as mediating the presence of God, the Matthean Jesus teaches the new community that gathering "in his name" will be a means to experience his presence.

Instructions for Life in the New Community

Another way that this gospel works to form a new Christian identity is by structuring the gospel to present Jesus as the teacher instructing the new community of believers. We have already seen how the author worked with his sources to create long discourse sections that feature Jesus teaching his disciples and the crowd who follow him. A comparison with one scene in the Gospel of Mark illustrates the point. The author of Mark reports in the first chapter of the gospel that Jesus "went into the synagogue and was teaching" (Mark 1:21). The response from the crowd is astonishment because "he taught them as one having authority and not as the scribes" (Mark 1:22). The Gospel of Matthew uses this same saying from Mark, but with a major difference: it comes after three chapters in which Jesus is featured as actually teaching (Matt 7:28–9). In other words, whereas the Gospel of Mark reports *that* Jesus taught, the Gospel of Matthew reports *what* he taught.

So how are the members of this new community to live with one another? We have already discussed the content of some of Jesus's teaching in the previous section. The Matthean Jesus expects his followers to *exceed* the Pharisees in their righteousness. The notion of being "righteous" runs throughout the gospel. Some form of the Greek word *dikaios* shows up over twenty-five times in the text. The word has a range of meanings that include being just, doing what God requires, and being in right relationship with others. Joseph, for example, is described as *dikaios* and therefore not wanting to publicly humiliate Mary (Matt 1:19). The idea of righteousness is present also at the inauguration of Jesus's ministry. When John the Baptist resists the idea of baptizing Jesus, Jesus responds, "Let it be for now; for it is fitting for us to fulfill all righteousness" (Matt 3:15). While the meaning of this statement to John is not altogether apparent, it is clear that the Matthean Jesus begins his ministry by modeling a concern for righteousness.

The Matthean Jesus's first teaching discourse continues the focus on righteousness by acknowledging the privileged place of those who "hunger and thirst for righteousness" and who "are persecuted for righteousness' sake" (Matt 5:6, 10). Followers of Jesus are not to worry about food or clothing, but are to "seek first for the kingdom of God and its righteousness" (Matt 6:33). Elsewhere in the gospel there are indications that such seeking means doing the will of God. As the Matthean Jesus puts it, "Not all who say to me, 'Lord, Lord,' will enter the kingdom of heaven, but the one who does the will of my Father in heaven" (Matt 7:21). As we will see in the next section, in Matthew's gospel, the promise of reward is often balanced with the threat of punishment. Such exhortations reinforce group identity both positively and negatively.

Matthew's Parables of the Kingdom

READING
Matthew 13, 18.

EXERCISE
Note the places where Jesus describes the kingdom of heaven. What similar themes run through the teachings about the kingdom? Who gains entry to the kingdom? Who does not? Why not?

The Matthean Jesus spends far more time teaching in parables about the kingdom of heaven than does the Markan Jesus. In fact, many of the kingdom parables come from the Q source, as we can tell from their appearance also in the Gospel of Luke. But the Matthean parables, even when they come from another source, have their own accent – especially the theme of separation of the evildoers and the eternal punishment that accompanies visions of the kingdom and eternal life. The Matthean versions of the parables construct an image of a God who rewards the righteous, and harshly punishes the "evildoers." In fact, each of the five discourses of the Matthean Jesus ends with an anticipation of rewards and punishments (Matt 7:13–27; 10:29–42; 13:36–52; 18:23–35; 25:31–46). For example, chapter 10 describes the rewards to come for those who welcome a disciple or a "righteous one," or give a cup of water to a "little one" (Matt 10:40–2). The discourse in chapter 13 concludes with images such as the separation of weeds from good seed (Matt 13:37–40), or good fish from bad (Matt 13:47–8), to distinguish those who will enter the kingdom from those who will be eternally punished. It also describes the Son of Man sending his angels to "pluck out of his kingdom all those who cause sin and all lawless ones, and they will throw them into the fiery furnace, where there will be weeping and gnashing of teeth. Then the righteous will shine forth like the sun in the kingdom of their Father" (Matt 13:41–3). Chapter 18 features one of the more disturbing parables of the gospel, which tells of an angry master handing over his slave to be tortured because he had not shown mercy to a fellow slave. The parable concludes with the claim, "So will my heavenly father do to you, if you each do not forgive your brother from your hearts" (Matt 18:35). While the Matthean Jesus assures the gospel audience that the merciful will receive mercy (Matt 5:7), he also makes clear that the unforgiving will be harshly punished.

We should take special note of this depiction of divine judgment and punishment in the New Testament because there is a common tendency to distinguish the "wrathful" God of the Old Testament from the "loving" God of the New Testament. But the fact is that a close reading of the Old Testament often uncovers a God with unrelenting love for God's people, while a close reading of the New Testament, including a number of passages from Matthew, uncovers images of God as a harsh judge. Indeed, the language of judgment and condemnation in the Gospel of Matthew has much in common with the prophetic messages of Amos or Micah. As you recall, both of those eighth-century prophets conveyed an image of God as one who would severely punish leaders who had exploited others. So too in Matthew, God is imaged as one who balances the lavish rewards of eternal life for the righteous with eternal fire and damnation for the unrighteous. Not only does this language recall the prophets, it is also very much part of the gospel's apocalyptic perspective. Indeed, the image of the righteous "shining" in God's kingdom echoes similar language from Daniel (Dan 12: 3).

This use of both prophetic and apocalyptic language in the Gospel of Matthew suggests that the gospel writer's experience under Roman domination in the first century CE had something in common with earlier times when the people of Israel experienced imperial force. While we may find the language of burning fire, gnashing of teeth, and eternal punishment problematic, it would have been cathartic for a people who knew the ability of Rome to punish with fire and destruction. The gospel's depiction of the coming kingdom implies coming punishment for the enemies of the *ekklesia*.

Indeed, in addition to considering the image of God in these parables, we should also consider how "kingdom" language would sound to the audience of the gospel. Their lived reality was colonization under the "kingdom" or reign of the Roman emperors. In the face of that reality, the Gospel of Matthew speaks of a kingdom that is like a hidden treasure or a merchant of fine pearls (13:44–5). It is ruled not by the Roman emperor, but by God, who has given the resurrected Jesus reigning authority. From our perspective, we might not recognize the subversion in Jesus's closing claim that "all authority on heaven and earth" has been given to him (Matt 28:18). But from Rome's perspective, only the emperor had all authority on earth, and heavenly authority was reserved for the gods (see Figure 12.2). Thus, the first-century BCE to first-century CE Roman poet Ovid writes:

Figure 12.2 Roman coin depicting Augustus subduing and ruling the earth, to indicate his sole power.

> Jupiter controls the heights of heaven and the kingdom
>   of the triformed universe;
> But the earth is under Augustus's sway. Each is both sire
>   and ruler. (*Metamorphoses* 15:858–60)

To conclude the gospel with the claim of the resurrected Jesus's authority over both heaven and earth places him above even imperial authority and puts him on a par with the gods.

Notice also that this alternative kingdom of God as described in the gospel will be inhabited by the "righteous." Those chosen to enter will be those who respond appropriately to God's invitation (22:1–14). Their righteousness can be recognized by their acts of forgiveness (18:21–35) and generosity (20:1–16). Again, this image of the "good" ones being welcomed into an alternative kingdom, and the "wicked" ones being excluded, may have encouraged those who felt defeated in the midst of the current political reality.

Defining Community by Vilifying Opponents: Matthew's Polemic against "the Jews"

READING
Matthew 23, 26–28.

EXERCISE
Of what are the scribes and Pharisees accused? Who is to blame for the death of Jesus? For what reason is a guard placed at the tomb of Jesus?

Like the Gospel of Mark, this gospel depicts the chief priests and Pharisees as plotting to put Jesus to death (Matt 21:46; 26:3–5, 14–15). But the animosity in the Gospel of Matthew is not one directional. The Matthean Jesus matches the aggression of the Jewish leaders with harsh attacks against them. In chapter 23, the author draws on Q material to include a series of "woes" against the scribes and the Pharisees. This chapter (and its parallel in Luke 20) presents a caricatured image of the "hypocritical" scribes and Pharisees who concern themselves with outward appearances (Matt 23:27–8) and legal regulations (Matt 23:23, 25), but in reality are greedy and self-indulgent (Matt 23:25), caring nothing about justice, mercy, and faith (Matt 23:23). Far from affirming that the kingdom of heaven is accessible to the poor in spirit (Matt 5:3), these leaders – according to Matthew – "shut the kingdom of heaven in front of people and do not permit them to go in" (Matt 23:13). The series of woes ends in judgment and condemnation, not just for the scribes and Pharisees but for "all of this generation" (Matt 23:36). Indeed, the Gospel of Matthew goes further still in its oppositional rhetoric. Not only does it blame the Jewish leadership for the death of Jesus, not only does it engage in extensive attacks on the scribes and the Pharisees, but it stands alone in the gospel tradition in transferring the blame for Jesus's crucifixion to the Jewish people themselves. The gospel depicts the Roman governor, Pilate, absolving himself from Jesus's death. He washes his hands before the crowd, stating, "I am innocent of this man's blood; see to it yourselves." To this *all* of the people respond, "His blood be on us and our children!" (Matt 27:25). In the time of the writing of Matthew's gospel, its earliest audience could have viewed this curse as coming to fruition in the next generation. The gospel encourages a reading of the events of 70 CE as divine punishment – the children of those who put Jesus to death were punished in 70 CE with the destruction of Jerusalem and its Temple. We saw a similar theme in the Gospel of Mark, but there the judgment was restricted to the Jewish leaders, the "tenants" of the vineyard. In Matthew's gospel, *all* of the Jewish people are implicated in the death of Jesus and the destruction of Jerusalem. Both the chief priests and the "Jews" are implicated at the end of the gospel as well. In this case, the narrative moves outside of the story time to refer directly to the later time of the gospel's composition. The narrator claims that "to this day" a story fabricated by the chief priests to explain Jesus's missing body is still told among "the Jews" (Matt 28:15). What is remarkable about such references to the Jews, and the reason the term is here put in parentheses, is that the author of the gospel was almost certainly Jewish himself.

Indeed, from a twenty-first-century perspective we might wonder how a gospel so concerned to associate Jesus with the Torah of Moses and the lineage of Abraham and David could so harshly condemn the Jewish people and their leaders. But if you consider political debates between differing parties of one nation, or debates on social issues between different Christian groups, you are moving closer to the sort of polemic we see in the Gospel of Matthew. Particularly when opposing groups share a common identity, say Americans or Christians, they often define themselves ever more sharply against those whose positions they oppose. In the ancient world, such self-definitions often included polemic against the "other" group. The Gospel of Matthew represents one Jewish movement defining itself over against another Jewish group, and in so doing, vilifying its opposition, and distancing itself from "the Jews." Or, as the biblical scholar

Who Were the Pharisees?

The earliest references to the Pharisees suggest that they began as a political party during the Maccabean period (167–63 BCE). They aligned themselves with certain Jewish leaders, and opposed others. During Herod's reign they counseled the people to accept him as their leader, according to the Jewish historian Josephus. He portrays them as having "the complete confidence of the masses" over against the Sadducees, who were supported by "the people of highest standing," or the aristocracy (Josephus, *Antiquities*, 13.13.5 §401). The political influence is last attested in the early stages of the Jewish revolt against Rome of 66 to 70 CE, when the Pharisees joined the "principal citizens" in opposing the Jewish revolutions, speaking out against starting a war against Rome that they could not win.

Our sources are limited in describing the beliefs and practices of the Pharisees except for the following: in contrast to the Sadducees, the Pharisees followed the "traditions of the ancestors," an oral tradition that rabbinic tradition claims was given to Moses at Sinai, along with the written law. They believed in a resurrection from the dead (again in contrast to the Sadducees). And they were concerned that the same purity regulations that were practiced by the priests be extended to the common people, presumably so that the people could stand in the same relationship to God as did the priests. As noted above, the group was apparently very popular. Josephus claims that they are "extremely influential among the masses; and all prayers and sacred rites of divine worship are performed according to their exposition." Josephus writes his history well after the destruction of the Temple, and by then the Pharisees had secured their place as the dominant group among the Jews. Precisely such popularity would elicit strong polemical rhetoric from a competing group.

Shaye Cohen put it, "these charges are the unverified and unverifiable attacks of one Jewish group against its major rival" (*From the Maccabees to the Mishnah*, 2nd edition [Philadelphia: Westminster John Knox Press, 2006], p. 149).

Finally, one thing we learn from postcolonial criticism concerns the ways that colonization and imperial power create internal tensions within, and rivalries between, indigenous groups of a particular culture. Unable to confront the actual source of their oppression, these groups often turn against one another to express their frustrations. We will never know how the Jesus movement might have developed in relation to other expressions of Judaism apart from the events of 70 CE, and without the pressures of living under Roman domination. What we do know is that after the destruction of the Temple, the surviving Jewish communities – both the followers of Jesus and those aligned with emerging rabbinic Judaism – contended bitterly between themselves over issues of identity and belief.

Matt 25:31–46

FOCUS
TEXT

The focus text for this chapter is often called "the Last Judgment." The passage is (M) material; that is, it is a text found only in the Gospel of Matthew. The theme of the passage – acts of charity as a basis for God's judgment – was a familiar one within Judaism. Prov 14:31 and 19:17 convey the idea that caring for the poor honors God and will be rewarded. Similarly, Deut 15:7–10 instructs the Israelites to give willingly to the needy, with the assurance that God will bless their efforts. The call to feed and clothe the needy and give hospitality to the traveler also occurs in the prophets (Ezek 18:7, 16; Isa 58:7) and another wisdom text, Job 31:32. Thus, the idea spans the Hebrew scriptures and fits well within a first-century Jewish setting. The author is drawing on a well-known tradition of care for the other, reinterpreting it in light of a new belief in Jesus as the messiah and apocalyptic Son of Man. Indeed, the author's own distinctive interests are evident in several ways in which he uses the judgment tradition. Note that he placed the passage at the end of Jesus's last discourse in the gospel. In this position, Matt 25:31–46 is the culmination of a series of instructions and parables concerning watchfulness and judgment about the end time that begins at chapter 24. The passage thus stands as the final instructions of Jesus before the passion narrative begins in chapter 26, suggesting that this account of judgment held particular significance for the author. Note also that the designation of "the righteous" for those who are rewarded (Matt 25:37, 46), and the threat of "eternal fire" (Matt 25:41, 46), link with earlier teachings in the gospel about the righteous and the condemned.

The passage begins with apocalyptic imagery that is familiar to us from the Gospel of Mark – the Son of Man coming in glory with his angels (see Mark 8:38). But in Matthew's gospel this image is used as a jumping-off point for a scene that fits well with the Matthean interest in judgment. Here the Son of Man sits on his throne and "the nations" or "the gentiles" (Greek *ethnē*) come before him for judgment (Matt 25:31–2). Since the Greek word *ethnē* can be translated either way, as "the nations" or "the gentiles," it is not completely clear who the author understands to be included in the judgment scene. We will return to this point below. This image of the Son of Man executing judgment from a heavenly throne is distinctive in Matthew's gospel. In Mark 14:62, the Son of Man is seated at the "right hand of the ruling power." But in Matthew's text the Son of Man himself executes judgment from his own throne. More than an eschatological figure ushering in the reign of God, he assumes the role of ruling authority and heavenly judge. Perhaps for this reason, the image of the Son of Man shifts from that of a shepherd separating sheep to his right and goats to his left (Matt 25:32–3) to that of "king" (Matt 25:34). The author may have gotten this image from Dan 7:13, which describes a "Son of Man" who is given "dominion and glory and kingship." The image of the resurrected Jesus as king links with the earlier association between Jesus and kingship in the gospel (Matt 13:41; 20:21). And, of course, the scene anticipates the conclusion to the gospel, where, as we have seen, the resurrected Jesus announces that he has been given "all authority on heaven and on earth" (Matt 28:18).

As the scene unfolds, those on the king's right hand are invited to "inherit the kingdom" on the basis of their acts of mercy – providing food, drink, and clothing to those in need, caring for the sick, providing hospitality to strangers, and visiting the imprisoned (Matt 25:35–40). Such actions recall the gospel's earlier emphasis on righteousness and mercy. As we have already seen, the merciful are promised mercy (Matt 5:7), while the unmerciful are condemned to eternal punishment (Matt 18:8). Given this, it is no surprise that those who have shown mercy are referred to as "the righteous" (Matt 25:37). Significantly, the righteous are not even aware of when they cared for the king. The passage suggests that it is not enough to be motivated to serve someone of higher rank (perhaps hoping to gain from doing so). Instead, the reward comes to those who extend care in spite of rank or status – "to one of the least significant of these brothers of mine" (Matt 25:40). If the righteous are rewarded for their care of these members, we can then anticipate the plight of the "goats." They also are unaware of their lack of care for the "Lord," but then, they had not cared for even one of the least significant (Matt 25:41–6).

Just as it is unclear who is included in the phrase "the nations," so also the identity of these least significant brothers is uncertain. Does the passage refer to the needy in general? Or are the "needy" only those who are members of the community of believers? Past readings of this passage differ with respect both to who is included in the final judgment and to who is meant by the reference to the "least." The early reading of the text, from Christian interpreters in the third century CE, tended to have *only* the Christian community in view. Thus, these interpreters understood the "least of these" to be members of the Christian community, and the "nations" as Christians who provided for them. With this reading, the point of the passage was understood to be moral instruction motivating believers to do acts of mercy for needy Christians.

By the eighteenth century, new cultural conditions elicited a different interpretation focused on the treatment of Christians by non-believers. In this case, "the nations" was understood as "all non-Christians," while the "least of these" was interpreted as "all Christians." This view of the passage meant that all non-Christians would be judged on the basis of their treatment of Christians. This shift in meaning came during a time when many Christian groups were involved in foreign missionary work, often as part of the Western colonization of Africa and India. Reading Matt 25:31–46 in this way could have offered comfort to missionaries who felt oppressed and persecuted, suggesting that those who mistreated them would ultimately be punished. From another angle, movement into these "foreign" lands meant a growing awareness of the numbers of non-Christians in the world and the realization that many of these people would remain non-Christians. A reading that portrayed non-Christians receiving rewards on the basis of their charity toward Christians made room for the salvation of non-Christians. Although many people today, including Christians, would be troubled by the idea of a final judgment of non-Christians only, especially one that was contingent only on treatment of Christians, at the time it may have been a way of introducing the notion of heavenly reward apart from conversion.

We should also note that in both the early church and later readings up until the twentieth century, one finds an even more troubling and persistent interpretation of the passage, in which the "goats" are assumed to be the Jews that did not accept Christ. Aside from the fact that there is nothing in the passage to identify the goats with the Jewish people, such a reading clearly ignores the Jewish orientation of the gospel as a whole. It also ignores the basic intent of the passage, which says nothing about doctrinal belief or confessions of faith as conditions for judgment, but focuses only on acts of mercy.

Along this line, the twentieth century brought yet another reading, far more universal than most earlier interpretations. In this reading, "the nations" has been understood as *all* peoples coming under judgment, and "the least of these" as *anyone* that is in need, regardless of their religious convictions. This reading has been particularly important for liberation theologians, who lift up God's concern for the poor as a central theological claim. This interpretation emphasizes the undogmatic aspects of the passage and promotes the idea of a "practical" Christianity that is grounded in acts of love toward other human beings. It recalls an earlier saying of the Matthean Jesus: "Not all who say to me 'Lord, Lord' will enter the kingdom of heaven, but the one who does the will of my father in heaven" (Matt 7:21).

Given these diverse interpretations, is there anything we can say about the author's original intention? If we look to the broader themes of the gospel, we may find some clues. This is a gospel with a strong missionary emphasis – the Matthean Jesus sends out his disciples "like sheep in the midst of wolves" (Matt 10:16). They are to expect persecution and betrayal (Matt 10:21–3), and as we have seen, those who welcome the disciples and provide hospitality will be rewarded (Matt 10:40). Similarly, the Matthean Jesus's last instructions to the disciples are to go "make disciples of all nations" (*ethnē*), the very same group that is called before the throne in Matt 25:32. Moreover, the reference to "these brothers of mine" suggests a reference to those within the community, rather than needy persons in general. It may well be that in speaking of "the least of these brothers of mine," the gospel writer is acknowledging that the traveling missionaries of this new Jesus movement do not rank very high in the broader Roman culture and may not be well received as they travel from town to town. In this sense, the passage would serve to encourage hospitality to these traveling missionaries among other believers.

Still, these diverse readings provide another example of how a text is not limited to its original meaning as it is reread across time and space. As we have seen repeatedly in the course of our study, new readers of the Bible are continually finding new meaning for their own life experience. In this case, as we reflect on these different readings of the text, we may well find some of them offensive. Certainly, few would advocate an anti-Semitic interpretation in which all Jewish people will be condemned. Nor would many advocate a reading that elevates the treatment of needy Christians as the central criterion for heavenly reward. Indeed, in our current cultural context, even if we understand the original missionary focus of the text, we may now choose to emphasize a more universal interpretation, one that recognizes the value of all people and the necessity of caring for anyone in need regardless of their religious practice.

CHAPTER TWELVE REVIEW

1. Know the meaning and significance of the following terms:
- *ekklesia*
- four-source theory
- fulfillment citations
- (L)
- (M)
- redaction criticism
- Sermon on the Mount

2. What sources did the author of Matthew's gospel use for writing his story of Jesus?

3. How does the structure of the Gospel of Mark differ from the structure of the Gospel of Matthew?

4. What effect does this different structure have on the presentation of Jesus?

5. How and why does the Gospel of Matthew relate Jesus to the Torah?

6. How does the theme of judgment relate to the gospel's historical and cultural setting?

7. In what ways is the Gospel of Matthew even more critical of Jesus's opponents than the Gospel of Mark? Why is this so?

RESOURCES FOR FURTHER STUDY

Allison, Jr., Dale C., ed. *Matthew: A Shorter Commentary*. London and New York: T & T Clark International, 2004.

Carter, Warren. *Matthew and Empire: Initial Explorations*. Harrisburg, PA: Trinity Press International, 2001.

Clarke, Howard. *The Gospel of Matthew and Its Readers: A Historical Introduction to the First Gospel*. Bloomington: Indiana University Press, 2003.

Harrington, Daniel. *The Gospel of Matthew*. Sacra Pagina. Collegeville, MN: Liturgical Press, 1991.

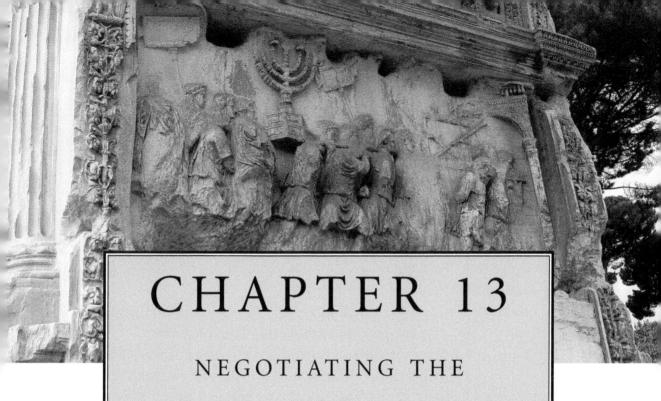

CHAPTER 13

NEGOTIATING THE EMPIRE IN LUKE–ACTS

Chapter Outline

CHAPTER OVERVIEW

If your name was Theophilus and you lived toward the end of the first century CE, you might be the esteemed patron of a major, two-volume account of the life of Jesus and the growth of the early church. Both the Gospel of Luke and the Acts of the Apostles begin with prologues in which the author writes directly to a certain "most excellent" Theophilus (see Luke 1:1–4; Acts 1:1–5). Because of this, and because of the many thematic links between these two works, it is clear that the same author wrote both the gospel and Acts. In this chapter we will focus on the links between these two volumes (typically referred to as Luke–Acts) and the story that they tell about Jesus and his earliest followers. Part of this story involves linking Jesus and his followers to the past history of Israel. Doing so enables the author to assert one of his main theological claims: that Jesus and the community of believers are instrumental to God's universal plan for salvation. But, as we will see, the author is as much concerned with situating the Jesus movement in the Roman present as he is with linking it to Israel's past. The chapter will illustrate how the Lukan Jesus and his followers are presented in ways that are consistent with the cultural values of the educated elite of the Roman empire. Together, these two aspects of the narrative – continuity with Israel's past and accommodation to the Roman present – serve to legitimate and affirm the significance of the emerging church in the late first century CE. To begin, we take a look at the prologues of the gospel and Acts, which provide strong evidence of the common authorship of these two works and tell us something of the author himself.

The Lukan Prologues

READING
Luke 1:1–4; Acts 1:1–5.

EXERCISE
Why is the author writing the gospel? What method did he use for writing it?

As with all the canonical gospels, we do not know precisely who wrote Luke–Acts. But the openings of both books offer some intriguing details. First, the prologues situate the author among the literary elite of the Greco-Roman culture. They are similar to other literary prologues found in works by figures such as the famous Greek historians Herodotus and Thucydides and by more contemporary historians, such as Josephus. The author of Luke–Acts was clearly aware of this literary convention and may have used it to position his two volumes alongside other respected literary works, thereby elevating its status. Moreover, the prologues suggest a relationship between the author and Theophilus as one of sophisticated client writing on behalf of wealthy patron (Luke 1:3). Whether Theophilus actually existed is debated. He may have been a recent wealthy convert who commissioned the author to write the two-volume work. But because Theophilus means "friend of God" or "God-lover," it is also possible that the figure is a literary construct intended to refer to believers in general. In either case, the effect of the reference to the "most excellent Theophilus" remains the same; it situates the author and his work in a setting of high social status. As we will see, the narrative of Luke–Acts does the same thing for Jesus and the apostles. By the end of the story, they too will come into contact with various men of high status.

The prologue of the gospel tells us yet more about the author and how he wrote the gospel. He acknowledges that "many" have tried to write orderly accounts, implying that they have not been entirely successful. And what is he including in the reference to "many"? It is a tantalizing detail that leaves us wondering about how many such accounts were available. Is he referring to the Gospel of Mark and the sayings source, Q? Or were there other accounts of the life of Jesus that have been long lost to us? Notice also that the author makes clear that he is *not* an eyewitness, but is using accounts that have been handed down by eyewitnesses to put together his own orderly narrative.

Beyond highlighting the links between the volumes and the author's literary prowess, the prologues raise the question of genre. How should we classify this two-volume work within its ancient literary context? Because there is a second volume that tells of the growth and spread of the church after Jesus's lifetime, the most obvious answer may be to consider Luke–Acts as a work of history. The minute we assert this, however, we are left with more questions. What would constitute history writing in the first-century *basics* Books of Luke–Acts

Outline:
Luke's story of
Jesus and the
expanding
Christian
movement

I	Luke: from Galilee to Jerusalem	
	Prologue: introduction to the two volumes	1:1–4
	A Birth narrative and preparation for ministry	1:5–4:13
	B Jesus's ministry in Galilee	4:14–9:50
	C Journey to Jerusalem	9:51–19:27
	D Entry to Jerusalem and teaching in the Temple	19:28–21:38
	E Passion, resurrection, and ascension in Jerusalem	22:1–24:53
II	Acts: From Jerusalem to Rome	
	Prologue: introduction to the second volume	1:1–5
	A Apostolic mission in Jerusalem	1:6–7:60
	B Spread of mission beyond Jerusalem	8:1–12:25
	1 Spread of the mission in Palestine and Paul's conversion	8:1–9:43
	2 Initial mission to the gentiles as far as Antioch	10:1–12:25
	C Paul's journeys	13:1–28:31
	1 The mission from Antioch to Asia Minor and Greece	13:1–19:20
	2 The journey, by way of Jerusalem, to Rome	19:21–28:31

Date and
authorship

The author of Luke was traditionally identified as the traveling companion of Paul, likely based on the passages in Acts that use the first person plural (Acts 16:10–17; 20:5–15; 21:1–18; 27:1–28:16). This alone is not compelling evidence, however, since other ancient travel narratives also switch to the first person plural, seemingly for dramatic effect. Moreover, much of what is narrated about Paul in Acts does not cohere with what Paul himself claims in his letters. As with all of the gospels, we can only infer some things about the author from the work itself, and attempts to identify him must remain speculative. Similarly, there is little evidence to help us site the composition of this gospel in a particular place or time. Since the author used the Gospel of Mark as a source, we can guess, as with the Gospel of Matthew, that it was written sometime around 80 to 85 CE. The second volume, Acts, need not have been written at the same time, but could have been composed as much as a decade later.

Greco-Roman context? How should we understand the relationship between the type of history that the author writes and the various truth claims that are made in the narrative? These are weighty questions and worthy of more discussion than we can give them here. But we can at least say that the concept of history and of the purpose of history writing was quite different than most of our contemporary understandings of history. Much like ancient orators, ancient history writers were more concerned to shape model citizens for the city-state than to give an objective account of particular events. Indeed, whereas we would expect a detailed report of what actually happened, ancient histories were far more likely to construct dialogues and speeches from major figures based on what they thought these people must have said.

In a sense, it is more accurate to consider ancient history writing as the author's view of what *must* have happened, rather than an attempt to discover what actually *did* happen. By communicating what must have happened, the historians shaped the account in a particular way, writing a persuasive narrative of events rather than an objective "historical" report. If we are to call Luke–Acts history, we should consider it this type of historical writing. The author of Luke–Acts writes of what must have happened based on his understanding of the significance of Jesus and the earliest believers. In so doing, he helps to shape Christian self-identity for the future generations of believers. As we will see in the next section, part of this self-identity involves seeing the church as growing out of the long and rich history of Israel's past.

Continuity with Israel's Past in Luke–Acts

READING
Luke 1–4, 24; Acts
1:1–7:60, 10

EXERCISE
Note the ways that these narratives evoke ideas from Israel's past and how they focus on the Temple and Jerusalem. Pay special attention to Peter's speech and to the introduction of a new character, Stephen. Who is he and what happens to him?

Throughout Luke–Acts, the author links Jesus and the growing community of believers with the past history of Israel. Immediately after the prologue, the narrative actually "sounds" like the Hebrew scriptures, or more accurately, like the Septuagint, the Greek version of the scriptures. For example, the story begins with a description of the righteous priest Zechariah and his wife Elizabeth, who both live blamelessly "according to the commandments and ordinances." Those familiar with the stories of the ancestors in Genesis would recognize the theme of Elizabeth's barrenness and also Zechariah's assumption that the couple is too old to conceive a child (1:18). And this is just one example. The author also has his characters "speak" biblically in the birth narrative. For example, Mary's song of praise (1:46–55) sounds like Hannah's song from 1 Sam 2:1–10. Moreover, both Mary and Zechariah speak of the blessings and mercy of God on Israel, and God's promise to the ancestors (1:55, 72–5). In this way, the birth of Jesus is established in the context of God's promises to Israel.

The Lukan Jesus himself is cast in the role of one of the prophets of Israel, who, like earlier prophets of Israel, is rejected by the people. The first detailed account of Jesus's teaching in a synagogue features him in the role of prophet and ends in violent rejection by the people (Luke 4:16–30). This important scene will be studied in more detail later as the focus text for this chapter. Later in the gospel, the author includes a Q saying that is a lament over Jerusalem, "the city that kills the prophets and stones those who are sent to it" (Luke 13:34). In the Gospel of Matthew, this saying occurs in the context of woes against the Pharisees and refers to a list of past prophets that have been killed (Matt 23:34–7). In the Gospel of Luke, the saying occurs after some Pharisees warn Jesus about Herod's plans to kill him (Luke 13:31). Not only does this different context illustrate the author's more favorable depiction of the Pharisees in Luke's gospel than in Matthew's, it also suggests that Jesus is among the prophets that Jerusalem will kill. In Acts, Jesus is again put in the line of rejected prophets in Stephen's speech, when Stephen relates the way that Moses was rejected, and quotes Moses as saying, "God will raise up a prophet for you from your own people as he raised me up" (Acts 7:35–41). In the same speech, Stephen rails against the people who, by killing Jesus, have done just what the ancestors did to prophets before him (Acts 7:51).

The focus on Jerusalem and the Temple creates another important link between Jesus, the apostles, and Israel in Luke–Acts. Only this gospel relates scenes from Jesus's infancy and childhood that feature his connection with the Temple. The first of these comes when the family brings Jesus, a first-born male, along with a sacrificial offering to the Jerusalem Temple (2:22–32). The second occurs when Jesus is 12 years old and the family travels to Jerusalem for Passover. As Jesus's parents travel home, they discover he has gone missing. He is found back in Jerusalem, sitting with teachers in the Temple, displaying his precocious learning abilities (2:41–51). These early links with the Temple foreshadow the importance that Jerusalem and the Temple will have later in the narrative.

Additional emphasis on Jerusalem comes at the end of the gospel and the beginning of Acts. Only the Gospel of Luke has the risen Jesus instructing the disciples to stay in the city of Jerusalem to wait for "power from on high" (Luke 24:49). Even more striking, the gospel concludes with the disciples "continually in the Temple blessing God" (Luke 24:53). When the second volume opens, this is precisely where the apostles are – waiting in Jerusalem to receive the Holy Spirit. But even after receiving the Spirit, the early followers are in the Temple "day by day" (Acts 2:46). Later, when the apostles are imprisoned by Temple authorities, an angel rescues them and commands them to "Go, and stand in the Temple, speaking to the people all the message of this life" (Acts 5:20). In spite of conflict with the authorities, "every day in the Temple they did not stop teaching and proclaiming about Jesus Christ" (Acts 5:42). This emphasis on the link between the community of believers and the Temple is the author's way of connecting the Jesus movement with the central symbol of Judaism.

Since most scholars think the author probably was a gentile, one might well wonder why Jerusalem and the Temple are important to him. There are likely several different reasons. One may have been a very practical reason. By the first century CE, the Roman imperial rhetoric focused on restoring the traditional cultural values, including honoring the traditional Roman deities. Indeed, one of Caesar Augustus's major programs was to restore the traditional temples and reinvigorate the traditional Roman rites. This came at a time when many people were interested in more individually focused cults such as devotion to Isis (a goddess tradition originating in Egypt) or to the god Mithras (another Eastern tradition). Both of these cults required a personal initiation rite and promised benefits to the individual who devoted himself or herself to the deity. In this context, followers of Jesus might also be viewed with suspicion if Jesus were understood as another new god from the East. Showing Jesus's connection with Israel and the long-established and familiar tradition of Judaism may have served to alleviate suspicions about this new movement. But, since Luke–Acts is directed toward believers, this concern for appearances was not likely the main reason for the focus on Israel and the Temple.

Another reason for this focus on links to Jewish tradition may be connected to the author's previous attraction to Judaism, even before he became a believer. As we saw from Josephus's story of King Izates (see the Miscellanous Box on "The Question of Circumcision" in Chapter 10), there were gentiles who were interested in the Jewish tradition. Indeed, it is likely that the first gentile converts to the Jesus movement were those who were already attracted to Judaism and already listening to the Septuagint in local synagogues. In fact, the author features one such gentile at a key point in the narrative. Cornelius is a Roman centurion of the Italian cohort who "revered God with his entire household" and "prayed all the time" to God (Acts 10:2). If the author came from a similar background, he not only would be familiar with the Hebrew scriptures, but would understand the significance of Jesus precisely through the history of the Jewish tradition and its expectation of a coming messiah.

But most significantly, the focus on Israel and the prophetic role of Jesus is a key part of Luke–Acts' theological emphasis on God's universal plan for salvation. In this sense, what happens next with the character of Cornelius is revealing. As the story continues, the Jewish believer Peter and the God-fearing Roman centurion Cornelius both experience divine interventions that lead them to each other (Acts 10:3–33). What Peter comes to understand through his vision and encounter with Cornelius is that "God is not prejudiced, but in every nation, anyone who fears him and acts justly is pleasing to him" (Acts 10:34–5). Peter then preaches to those gathered with Cornelius in Caesarea just as he earlier preached to the Jews in Jerusalem, with similar results – the spirit falls upon all who hear the word (Acts 10:34–44; cf. Acts 2:14–48). Notably, the Jewish believers with Peter are "astonished that the Holy Spirit has been poured out also on the gentiles" (Acts 10:44–5).

Those who have attended to the narrative from the very beginning will not be surprised. The author has laid out God's universal plan of salvation from early in the gospel. The righteous and devout Simeon, upon seeing the infant Jesus in the Temple, declares "My eyes have seen your salvation which you prepared in the presence of all people, a light for revelation to the gentiles and glory for your people Israel" (2:30–32). In this way, the Lukan Jesus is predicted to be the bearer of salvation for all. Continuing the theme at the end of the gospel and linking it to the next volume, the risen Jesus declares that the "repentance and forgiveness of sins must be preached to all nations" (24:47).

Notably, in the infancy narrative, Simeon also prophesies that Jesus will be the cause of opposition and "appointed for the falling and rising of many in Israel" (2:34). And this is what comes to pass in the narrative. Some Jews come to believe in Jesus, and some do not. In Acts, when Paul's preaching of the gospel is rejected by the synagogue communities, it gives him cause to turn to the gentiles (see, for example, Acts 13:42–51; 14:1–7; 17:1–15; 19:8–9; 28:17–28). Thus, this pattern of rejection becomes a crucial part of the theology of Luke–Acts – Jewish rejection leads to gentile inclusion.

At this point, it may be helpful to recall again that the author is presenting a particular version of "history" that makes sense for him in light of his understanding of Jesus and the believing community. Early believers had to account for the fact that many among them did not join their belief in Jesus as the long-awaited messiah. The author of Luke–Acts makes sense of their rejection (much as the apostle Paul did in Romans 9–11) by putting it in the context of God's larger plan for the eventual salvation of both Israel and the gentiles (see Acts 26:22–3).

Situating the Jesus Movement in the Roman Present

READING
Review Luke 1–3 and read Acts 21–8.

EXERCISE
What authorities does Paul encounter in these chapters of Acts? How is he portrayed in relation to these various authorities?

In addition to connecting the story of Jesus with the story of Israel, Luke–Acts also links Jesus with the politics and culture of the Roman present. This occurs in a number of ways ranging from regular mention of Roman rulers to depicting the Lukan Jesus and the apostles in Acts as displaying the traits of admirable Roman elite males. The following section explores how and why the author presents Jesus and his earliest followers in sync with the basic cultural values of Rome.

On a basic level, the author takes care to place the birth and ministry of Jesus in the context of Roman ruling authority. For example, in this gospel, Joseph and Mary must travel to Bethlehem because of a decree of the emperor Augustus, which is also identified in Luke as taking place during the time when Quirinius was governor of Syria (2:1–2). Neither of these claims is historically accurate – there is no record of such a decree from Augustus outside of this gospel, and Quirinius was not governor, but a military

More on Method: Social-Scientific Approaches to the New Testament

Those who study the New Testament using a social-scientific approach begin with the basic understanding that the ancient world was very different than our own. They argue that we cannot simply transport our own particular society's values and categories back to the ancient text and assume that we understand the text in the same way its ancient audience would have. Rather, to fully understand the implicit meanings of a work like Luke–Acts, readers need to know common cultural values of first-century Mediterranean society, what basic institutions structured the society, how its economic system worked, what sort of class systems existed, how rituals and public ceremonies contributed to the social fabric, and so on. Social-scientific studies often use a comparative approach to construct models of typical social patterning of a particular type of social group. Those models are then used by social-scientific students of the Bible to analyze what they see in the biblical text.

One example of a social-scientific approach to Luke–Acts would be to analyze the text through the lens of the ancient Mediterranean cultural value of **honor** vs. shame. This is a complex value system that infused many aspects of life in the ancient Mediterranean, but here one illustration will suffice. Honor could be achieved in many ways, but the most basic was through honorable blood lines. The Lukan birth narrative takes pains to show the excellent lineage of Jesus – he came from both priestly and royal blood lines on both Mary's and Joseph's sides. Also unique to the Gospel of Luke is the portrayal of John the Baptist as a blood relative of Jesus. As we saw in Chapter 9 of this *Introduction*, all of the gospel writers had to deal with the popularity of John the Baptist, who, as a potential competitor, could threaten the honor of Jesus. By presenting John as a blood relative of Jesus, and narrating parallel scenes of annunciations and birth stories, the author accentuates the reputation of Jesus, who actually gains in honor by the tribute paid to John because they are blood relatives.

For more on this approach to the New Testament see Richard L. Rohrbaugh, *The Social Sciences and New Testament Interpretation* (Peabody, MA: Hendrickson, 2004).

appointee of Augustus. But such historical inaccuracy only underscores that the aim in Luke is to tell the story of Jesus with the backdrop of powerful Roman figures. Note how the announcement of Jesus by John the Baptist is prefaced with a list of no fewer than five Roman rulers and two high priests (3:1–2). This interest in placing the early Jesus movement in the context of Roman rule is further reinforced in the Acts of the Apostles, where Paul is repeatedly called before various Roman authorities to make his case (Acts 18:12–13; 24–6). The Paul of Acts even demands a trial before the emperor's tribunal (Acts 25:10–12), resulting in a journey to Rome, where the narrative concludes (though with no account of a trial) (Acts 28:30). These multiple links between Jesus, his early followers, and Roman imperial authority were likely meant to impress upon the reader the importance and significance of the growing movement.

Not only does the author mention various Roman rulers, he also draws on imperial rhetoric to describe the importance of Jesus. Indeed, for the ancient audience, the same narratives that connect the story of Jesus's birth to the history of Israel also define Jesus's saving work in terms typically used for the emperor. To call Jesus a "savior" in the first-century context would be as much a political claim as a religious one (Luke 1:69–71). Similarly, to speak of Jesus directing people toward the way of peace (1:79) would resonate with one of the fundamental claims of Rome – that the empire has brought peace to a war-torn world. The Gospel of Luke counters that Roman claim with the idea that it is Jesus, not the emperor, who is savior and bringer of peace.

The Priene Calendar Inscription

The following inscription, dating from 9 BCE, was found in ancient Priene, located in modern-day Turkey. It marks the institution of a new calendar "for good luck and salvation" based on the birthday of Augustus. The inscription illustrates the rhetoric typically used to describe the emperor. When similar claims were made about Jesus by early Christians, this type of imperial rhetoric would be the most immediate frame of reference. Note also the idea of Augustus as a gift from Providence who is deeply invested in humankind.

It seemed good to the Greeks of Asia, in the opinion of the high priest Apollonius of Menophilus Azanitus: "Since Providence, which has ordered all things and is deeply interested in our life, has set in most perfect order by giving us Augustus, whom for the benefit of humankind she has filled with virtue, as if for us and for those after us she bestowed a savior, who brought an end to war and established peace . . . and since he, Caesar, by his appearance (excelled even our anticipations), surpassing all previous bene-factors, and not even leaving to posterity any hope of surpassing what he has done, and since the birthday of the god Augustus was the beginning of the good tidings for the world that came by reason of him which Asia resolved in Smyrna . . .

Just as the birth narratives draw on imperial rhetoric to present Jesus as a powerful saving figure, so also the ascension scene at the end of the gospel (Luke 24:50–2) and also at the beginning of Acts (Acts 1:6–11) makes an implicit connection with Roman imperial status. The Lukan Jesus gives final words of instruction to his disciples and then is "lifted up" into heaven. Such heavenly transport sounds unusual to us, but an ancient Greco-Roman audience would associate the scene with one more familiar to them – that of imperial **apotheosis**, or deification (see Figure 13.1).

Beginning with the death of Julius Caesar, the Roman Senate began a tradition of honoring a deceased emperor with the status of a god. The deification of Caesar Augustus in 14 CE was celebrated across the empire and commemorated with coins, temple dedications, and the establishment of priesthoods and cult rituals. In other words, for a first-century audience, the ascension scenes in the gospel and Acts would be a way of

Figure 13.1 Relief from the Belvedere altar in Rome. Though the identification of the figures depicted is uncertain, it may depict the apotheosis of Julius Caesar (top right), observed by Venus and Augustus's heirs on the right and Augustus himself on the left.

making explicit Jesus's divine status and authority and putting him on the level of the most powerful position in the known world, the Roman emperor (see Figures 13.2 and 13.3). Interestingly, at one point in the narrative, the author even has opponents to the believers articulate this challenge to imperial authority. They are accused of "turning the world upside down" and "acting contrary to the decrees of the emperor, saying that there is another king named Jesus" (Acts 17: 6–7).

Of course, the fact that Jesus was executed by the Roman empire complicated this claim of authority. Far from a display of power, the crucifixion of Jesus would appear to most as the utterly shameful death of a convicted criminal. The Lukan narrative deals with this problem by stressing the innocence of Jesus. In the Lukan trial scene, Pilate explicitly states that he can find no reason to charge Jesus with a crime (23:4, 14, 22). Only Luke's account includes a separate trial before Herod, governor of Galilee (23:8–16), who also does not charge him with a crime (23:15). Most striking is the way the author adapts the Roman centurion's statement at the death of Jesus. In the Markan version, the centurion at the cross declares, "Truly, this man was a son of God" (Mark 15:39). In the Lukan account, the centurion declares, "Truly, this man was innocent"

Figure 13.2 Book cover dating to the fifth century CE and depicting the heavenly ascent of an emperor. That such images could still be found in the Christian empire of the fifth century illustrates how deeply the idea of a divine emperor was embedded in Roman culture.

(23:47). Such a claim of innocence would reassure believers that Jesus was an honorable figure in spite of the way he died.

In fact, the narrative of Luke–Acts goes even farther in making the case that Jesus and his followers have qualities that define them as highly respectable members of society. Their characters illustrate several basic values of the educated elite men of the Roman empire. We have already seen the way the prologues to Luke and Acts signal to the reader that the work itself should be viewed as one on a par with literary Greek and Roman histories. The author also depicts his characters in ways that show their intellect and education. For instance, the story of Jesus learning from the rabbis in the Temple is a way to show his keen intellect. Only this gospel explicitly presents Jesus as literate (Luke 4:16). Similarly, the narrative calls attention to the frank and bold public speech (*parrēsia*) of Peter and John, a skill they have achieved even without a formal education (Acts 4:13). Such rhetorical skill was regarded highly in the Greco-Roman culture, and it is no coincidence that the narrative calls attention to it. Notably, in the Lukan narrative, it is this confident speaking ability that enables others to recognize Peter and John as those who were with Jesus.

Another important quality for the Roman man was described as *pietas*. While this Latin word is often translated as piety, it means something closer to duty or loyalty to the gods, as well as to one's family and country. The first-century BCE poet Vergil regularly described Aeneas, the hero of his epic poem about the founding of Rome, as "*pius Aeneas*," as dutiful or "pious" Aeneas. So too Luke–Acts illustrates the piety of Jesus and the apostles. One way is to show them in close connection with the Jerusalem Temple. Although we have already discussed the emphasis on the Temple in relation to links with Israel, from a Greco-Roman perspective, close association with the Temple would also indicate the *pietas* and thereby the high standing of Jesus and his followers. The same would be true for the author's regular references to Jesus and his followers praying, another distinctive feature of Luke–Acts (see, for example, Luke 3:21; 5:16; 6:12; 9:18; Acts 1:14; 2:42; 4:31; 6:4; 7:59; 10:30; 11:5).

One more fundamental trait that was highly valued in the Greco-Roman culture, particularly as a sign of masculinity, was self-control. Many of the practical philosophers at this time provided instruction on how to live a life of virtue that included control over the passions – anger, lust, and so on. As

Figure 13.3 Base of an honorific column in Rome showing the apotheosis of a second-century CE emperor and his wife.

we saw earlier, the apostle Paul writes regularly in his exhortations that the community should live a life of self-control. And in this work, too, we find the idea that being a believer can help one achieve manly self-control. Perhaps the best example is the way the Paul of Acts speaks of his early life and the type of transformation that occurred once he became a follower of Jesus. He speaks of his early life when he persecuted "many of the saints" and was "furiously enraged at them, pursuing them to other cities" (26:11). This is a picture of a man out of control, and thus "unmanly" in the Roman culture. At the end of Paul's account, the Roman governor Festus claims as much, saying that Paul has lost his mind (26:24). Paul denies it, asserting on the contrary that he speaks truth and moderation (*sōphrosunē*) (26:25). In other words, whereas he formerly was a man out of control, now that he is a believer he speaks truthfully and with the self-control that was so highly esteemed in the culture.

In sum, Luke–Acts tells the story of the early Christians in a way that suggests that being a Christian would actually help one attain a life of virtue, and thus be seen as a manly and respectable member of the society. Jesus and his followers are presented as self-controlled, educated, pious – in short, as civilized men.

Possessions and the Poor: A Lukan Puzzle

Scholars have long struggled to understand the attention given to the theme of the poor and possessions in Luke–Acts. On the one hand, it seems clear that the author has a vision of how God relates to the poor and of the place of possessions in the community of believers. On the other hand, there is no consistent message about possessions that is woven all the way through the narrative, so that we are left with a puzzle as to what the author intended. For example, Mary's song (1:46–56) describes a God of reversal, one who exalts the lowly and brings down the rich and powerful. The Lukan Jesus suggests that he has been chosen to "announce good news to the poor and release to the prisoner" (Luke 4:18), and the Lukan version of the beatitudes reads simply "Blessed are the poor" rather than "Blessed are the poor in spirit" as in Matthew's version (Luke 6:20; cf. Matt 5:3). In addition, several parables that are unique to Luke highlight God's care for the poor and castigation of the rich (Luke 12:16–21; 16:19–31). The rich young man is told that he must sell all that he has and distribute the money to the poor in order to inherit eternal life (18:22).

Still, this message of status reversal and concern for the poor is not sustained through the two volumes. Zacchaeus, for example, is a rich man who is granted salvation because he pledges to give *half* of his possessions to the poor (Luke 19:1–9). Moreover, Acts 4:32–7 describes the Jerusalem community of believers as a group with no private ownership of possessions. They do not sell their possessions to give the money to the poor. Instead, the proceeds are distributed among the community on the basis of need. A couple who violates this process by holding some private money in reserve is struck down dead (Acts 5:1–11). After this scene, the theme of possessions disappears from the rest of the narrative. In fact, the word for "poor" never occurs in Acts. And, as we have seen, the author also seems interested in appealing to the status-conscious members of his audience, portraying the followers of Jesus as civilized men associated with other men of high status.

Although scholars have proposed a range of different solutions to this interpretive puzzle, there is no scholarly consensus regarding the poor and possessions in Luke–Acts. Nevertheless, the gospel's message about God's liberation of the poor and oppressed has played a central role in **liberation theology**. Originating in poor communities in Latin America, liberation theology promotes the idea that God has a "preferential option for the poor," and the work of the church should be politically active on behalf of the poor to liberate them from unjust social structures.

The Holy Spirit in Luke–Acts: Linking Past, Present, and Future

Just prior to the Lukan Jesus's heavenly ascent, he gives instructions that provide a clue as to how the author understood the connection between Israel's past, the present reality of Jesus's crucifixion and resurrection, and the future growth of the church:

Then he said to them, "These are my words that I spoke to you while I was with you, that it was necessary that all the scriptures concerning me in the law of Moses, the prophets and the psalms be fulfilled." Then he opened their minds to understand the scriptures. And he said to them, "Thus it is written, that the Christ will suffer and be raised from the dead on the third day, and repentance for forgiveness of sins is to be proclaimed in his name to all nations, starting with Jerusalem. You are witnesses of these things. Look, I am sending the promise of my Father on you. So you are to stay in the city until you have been clothed with power from on high." (24:44–9, modified from NRSV)

Three key ideas appear in these closing words of the risen Jesus in Luke: the notion of the fulfillment of the Hebrew scriptures, the proclamation of repentance and forgiveness, and the importance of the Holy Spirit, here expressed as "power from on high" (Luke 24:49). All three of these themes serve to connect the past history of Israel to the present movement of the church.

We have seen the fulfillment theme before, especially in the Gospel of Matthew. But the author of Luke–Acts does something new with this theme. Because this is a two-volume work, the author extends the idea of fulfillment of the Hebrew scriptures to the fulfillment of Jesus's own words. Thus, not only is it written "that the Christ is to suffer and to rise from the dead on the third day," but also – and this is the particularly Lukan theme – "repentance and forgiveness of sins is to be proclaimed in his name to all the nations starting from Jerusalem." This is precisely what the apostles do as the narrative continues in Acts, beginning with Peter's speech at Pentecost (Acts 2:38–39). From there, the apostles take the message of repentance to the Jews (3:19; 5:30–1), but also to the gentiles (11:18; 17:30–1). In this way, they fulfill the Lukan Jesus's command to preach repentance and forgiveness to all the nations.

Notably, at some early point in the gospel's transmission process, this theme of forgiveness was added to the crucifixion scene itself in Luke 23:34a. Here Jesus speaks directly to God, saying, "Father, forgive them because they do not know what they are doing." This verse does not appear in many early manuscripts; it appears to have been added at a fairly early stage, perhaps to have Jesus initiate this theme of forgiveness in a radical way from the cross.

The carrying out of this universal mission could not take place without the "power from on high," that is the Holy Spirit (24:49). The figure of the Holy Spirit takes a leading role from the very beginning of the gospel. The opening chapter relates parallel stories of Elizabeth and Mary conceiving and giving birth to John and Jesus. In both stories, the Holy Spirit drives the events of the narrative. An angelic announcement foretells that John will be filled with the Holy Spirit even before his birth, and both Elizabeth and Mary are reported to be filled with the Spirit (1:35; 1:41). In Mary's case, it is the Holy Spirit that is responsible for her conception. Zechariah and Simeon are also Spirit-filled, causing them to prophesy about John (1:67–79) and Jesus (2:27–32) respectively. These references to the work of the Spirit and Spirit-filled prophecy are, for Luke, an indication of the last days and God's saving work. Indeed, the author makes this explicit with Peter's quote of the prophet Joel in Acts:

This is what was said through the prophet Joel: "And it will be in the last days, God says, 'I will pour out from my Spirit on all flesh, and your sons and your daughters will prophesy, and your young men will see visions, and your old men will dream dreams. And also on my male slaves and on my female slaves in the last days, I will pour out from my Spirit; and they shall prophesy. And I give wonders in the heaven above and signs on the earth below – blood and fire and smoky vapors. The sun will be turned to darkness and the moon to blood, before the coming of the great and glorious day of the Lord.'" (Acts 2:16–20, modified from the NRSV)

The prophet Isaiah also lies behind Luke's use of the Holy Spirit. There, too, the pouring out of the spirit is associated with God's saving work (Isa 32:14–15; 44:3), and God's saving figures are filled with God's spirit (Isa 11:2; 42:1; 61:1).

We should not be surprised, then, to find that the Holy Spirit is also prominent in the ministry of the Lukan Jesus. The Spirit descends on Jesus at his baptism in all of the gospels, but only in Luke's gospel do we find repeated references to Jesus being filled with the Holy Spirit. For instance, Jesus is "full of the Holy Spirit" as he is led by the Spirit into the wilderness to be tempted (4:1–2). He then begins his Galilean ministry, "with the power of the spirit" (4:14). Only in Luke's gospel does Jesus "hand over his spirit" at the time of his death (23:46). And only in Luke's gospel does the resurrected Jesus instruct the disciples to stay in Jerusalem until they are "clothed in power from on high" (24:49). This opens the way for the role of the Holy Spirit to continue in Acts, and in fact, it becomes even more prominent.

When the second volume resumes the narrative, the promise that the followers of Jesus will receive the Holy Spirit is twice repeated (Acts 1:5, 8) and then comes to fruition (2:4). Once this occurs, the disciples follow Jesus in preaching and teaching as they are "filled with the Holy Spirit" (see, for example, 4:8; 4:31; 6:3; 7:55; 13:9). But, the author appears to take this idea even further than the spirit-filled prophecy from Isaiah and Joel. In Acts, the Holy Spirit seems to take on the role of a character in the narrative, speaking to other characters (8:29; 11:12; 13:2; 16:6) and moving them from place to place (8:39; 13:4). At times, the apostles are even forbidden by the Spirit to travel to certain places (Acts 16:6–7). In this way, the narrative of Luke–Acts shows the prominent role of the Holy Spirit in the past history of Israel, as well as its ongoing role in the present and future development of the early church.

FOCUS
TEXT

Jesus's Sermon in Nazareth (Luke 4:14–30)

Luke 4:14–30 is a programmatic text for the Gospel of Luke, and points ahead to the narrative of Acts. The author builds on a tradition of Jesus's rejection in his hometown to convey several central ideas in the two-volume work. First, the author moves the tradition earlier in his narrative so that the story relates the Lukan Jesus's first reported public teaching. In the Lukan narrative, Jesus returns to Galilee after the temptation in the wilderness. As we would expect, he is "filled with the power of the Spirit" (Luke 4:14), and quickly gains recognition and praise as he teaches in the synagogues. It is not until he comes to his hometown that the content of his teaching is reported. The scene unfolds in two parts. In the first part, Luke 4:16–22, his words gain high praise from his hometown audience. In the second part, Luke 4:23–30, things turn in a radically different direction.

As noted earlier, only this gospel writer portrays Jesus as reading from a scroll (4:16). While to us, this detail is unremarkable, in the ancient world it would have been an indicator of the Lukan Jesus's literacy, and thus, his status as an educated man. Beyond the fact *that* Jesus reads, however, is *what* he reads:

> The Spirit of the Lord is upon me, because he has anointed me to bring good news to the poor. He has sent me to proclaim release to the captives and recovery of sight to the blind, to let the oppressed go free, to proclaim the year of the Lord's favor. (4:18–19, NRSV)

In his first public statement of the narrative, the Lukan Jesus reads a text from Isaiah that coincides with several major themes of the gospel: the identification of Jesus with the prophets of Israel, the role of the Holy Spirit, and the Lukan Jesus's attention to the poor and oppressed. All of these themes were introduced in the birth narrative, and now this opening statement of Jesus reaffirms their importance to the gospel. The story builds tension as the narrator reports in detail Jesus rolling the scroll back up, handing it to the synagogue attendant, and then sitting down to comment on the scripture. The Lukan Jesus's announcement that the scripture has been fulfilled in their hearing brings words of praise from the synagogue members. Here is another sign that this author has a particular story to tell that differs from his source, the Gospel of Mark. In the Markan version people question Jesus's origins in a way that criticizes his presumptuousness. "From where is he getting these things? . . . Isn't this the carpenter, the son of Mary, and the brother of James and Joses and Judah and Simon? And aren't his sisters here with us? And they were offended by him" (Mark 6:2–3). In the Gospel of Luke, this line of questioning is changed into words of praise: "And all were impressed with him and amazed at the gracious words that came from his mouth, saying, 'Isn't this Joseph's son?'" (Luke 4:22). They are proud of the hometown boy.

But at this point, the scene shifts in tone. The author juxtaposes two different proverbs, first having the Lukan Jesus anticipate the skepticism of the crowd and their demand for working wonders, then responding with a prediction of his rejection. Again, the author draws on a saying from Mark: "no prophet is acceptable in his own country." In the Markan version, the saying is a fitting conclusion to the offense the crowd has shown; in Luke's version, the people have shown no rejection of Jesus at this point. Instead, another expansion of the Markan version will take the scene in a different direction. Luke's account prefaces the statement about rejection with another saying that anticipates a demand for miracles from the community. Together the two sayings function as a prediction of what is to follow rather than a response to what has taken place so far. The Lukan Jesus then begins a series of examples about how God worked (or not) with ancient Israel in the time of earlier prophets – Elisha and Elijah. This evocation of early prophets is another means of connecting Jesus with the prophetic tradition of Israel. But it does more than that. By the time the Lukan Jesus has finished, just as he predicted, the synagogue has decided he is not acceptable. Indeed, they become so enraged with his words that they are determined to throw him off a cliff and kill him.

What has caused this sudden change in mood? The examples that the Lukan Jesus provides are both cases when God helped out a non-Israelite rather than an Israelite in a time of need. In so doing, the gospel continues the theme already introduced in the birth narrative that God will save both Israel and the gentiles. Thus, this programmatic passage introduces a major theological claim of Luke–Acts: that God's saving acts are universal. The reaction of the crowd also anticipates the narrative pattern discussed earlier in the chapter: the rejection of Jesus (or preaching about Jesus) by the synagogue community. Although Luke–Acts has a more open attitude in general toward the Jewish community (many repent and believe in Jesus), as we have seen, the author also links the spread of the Jesus movement to the gentiles with the rejection by the synagogue. The theme of universal salvation is so important that the two-volume work ends on just this note. As Paul is under house arrest in Rome, he meets with the local Jewish community and tries to convince them about Jesus "both from the law of Moses and the prophets" (Acts 28:23). As has been the case throughout the work, some are convinced but others refuse to believe. In response, Paul quotes a passage from the prophet Isaiah, one used regularly in the New Testament writings to explain why not all Jews believed in Jesus (Isaiah 6:9–10, cf. Mark 4:12; Matt 13:14–15; John 12:40; and recall the ideas in Romans 9–11). The Paul of Acts then concludes with the statement, "Let it be known to you then that this salvation of God has been sent to the gentiles; they will listen" (28:28).

CHAPTER THIRTEEN REVIEW

1. Know the meaning and significance of the following terms:
- apotheosis
- honor [vs. shame]
- liberation theology

2. What are the different ways that the author of Luke–Acts connects Jesus to the story of Israel in the Old Testament? List as many as you can.

3. How and why does Luke–Acts situate the Jesus movement in relationship to the Roman empire and Roman values?

4. What are three characteristics of the masculine ideal in Roman culture, and how and why does Luke–Acts stress ways that Jesus and his followers exemplify these characteristics?

5. How does the author of Luke–Acts emphasize the role of the Holy Spirit? What importance does the Spirit have in the early church?

6. How does the story of Jesus's sermon at Nazareth in Luke 4:14–30 illustrate central themes of Luke–Acts, such as emphasis on links to the story of Israel, the aim of universal salvation, and Jesus's status vis-à-vis Roman masculinity?

RESOURCES FOR FURTHER STUDY

Parsons, Mikeal, C. *Luke: Storyteller, Interpreter, Evangelist.* Peabody, MA: Hendrickson, 2007.

Neyrey, Jerome H., ed. *The Social World of Luke–Acts: Models for Interpretation.* Peabody, MA: Hendrickson, 1991.

Shillington, V. George. *An Introduction to the Study of Luke–Acts.* T & T Clark Approaches to Biblical Studies. London: T & T Clark, 2007.

Tannehill, Robert C. *The Narrative Unity of Luke–Acts: A Literary Interpretation.* Foundations and Facets. Philadelphia: Fortress, 1986–90.

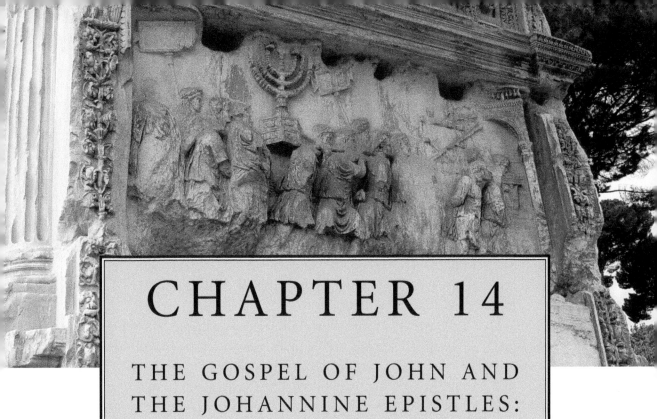

CHAPTER 14

THE GOSPEL OF JOHN AND THE JOHANNINE EPISTLES: TURNING INWARD AS A STRATEGY FOR LIFE IN THE EMPIRE

Chapter Outline

CHAPTER OVERVIEW

From the opening lines of the Gospel of John, it is clear that we are entering a different narrative world than that of the synoptic gospels. In this world, there is little talk of the kingdom of God, no talk at all of miracles, but plenty of talk of signs, the hour, glory, and Jesus as one who was sent into the world by the Father. There are also significant chronological differences between the synoptic gospels and the Gospel of John, as well as different characters and events. And, far from urging secrecy about his identity, the Johannine Jesus speaks in bold, self-descriptive, "I am" statements. These distinctive features of the Gospel of John have intrigued readers for centuries. Scholars have long debated the origins and composition of the gospel and how it relates to the synoptic tradition. For example, a second-century bishop known as Clement of Alexandria famously argued that because the author knew that the other gospels had "set out the outward facts" about Jesus, he composed a "spiritual gospel." While this suggestion likely helped the Gospel of John secure a place in the canon alongside the synoptic gospels, it has led to misconceptions about both John and the other gospels. There is no shortage of spirituality in the synoptic gospels, and certain aspects of the Gospel of John may be more "factual" (within the limits of our ability to know "facts" from this time) than the synoptic traditions.

Rather than labeling John as more "spiritual" or arguing that the gospel writer wants to show Jesus's divinity (another common claim for this gospel), the focus in this chapter will be on how the Gospel of John represents another early Christian response to life under Roman occupation. We have seen how the other gospel traditions responded to Rome in various ways – sometimes challenging its power, sometimes imitating it, sometimes accommodating to it through various depictions of Jesus. The language of this gospel works to strengthen the identity and cohesion of the believers by turning inward, creating a community that insulates and protects itself from its enemies and from "the world." The gospel paints an oppositional world of light and dark, above and below, from God and not from God, belief and unbelief. And the text makes clear which side of this dualistic world one should be on. Moreover, the Johannine Jesus is emphatically depicted as one who is not of the world, but rather sent into the world to draw believers to him and give them power to become children of God (John 1:12). One especially troubling aspect of the gospel is its vitriolic characterization of "the Jews." While we have seen this tendency to vilify "the Jews" in the Gospel of Matthew, in the Gospel of John the anti-Jewish rhetoric is even stronger. We will discuss possible reasons for this strong language and the implications of its presence in the Christian canon.

The Other-Worldly Jesus of John's Gospel

READING

John 1:1–18;
3:16–17; 15:18–19.

EXERCISE

How is the world portrayed in these passages? What is Jesus's relationship to the world? What is the relationship of the believers to the world? What is Jesus's relationship to God?

The Jesus that comes to the reader from this gospel is decidedly alien to the world. This idea permeates the gospel, but is stated most directly by the Johannine Jesus when he says, "I am not of this world" (John 8:23). The gospel narrative tells of Jesus coming into the world for a limited time from another place and then returning to that place. Again, as the Johannine Jesus states, "I came from the Father and have come into the world; again, I am leaving the world and I am going to the Father" (16:28). In this sense there is both a temporal and spatial dimension to the **incarnation**, the divine becoming human in the person of Jesus. The opening verses of the gospel already indicate the other-worldly aspect of the Johannine Jesus. Rather than with a birth narrative, the Gospel of John opens with a poetic prologue that reaches back to the "beginning" to answer the question of the Johannine Jesus's origin. Whereas the Gospel of Matthew traces Jesus's genealogy to Abraham, and the Gospel of Luke takes it back to Adam, John's gospel links Jesus to the timeless *logos* or "word" that existed alongside God before the created world. Indeed, the *logos* is active in creation with God, bringing life and light into being (1:3–4). It is this pre-existent aspect of the divine that is made flesh in Jesus (1:14). With the incarnation, the infinite becomes finite. Thus, there is a temporal dimension to the presence of Jesus, the incarnate *logos* in the world.

Along with this temporal dimension, the Johannine Jesus's entry into the world is also conceived in a spatial way. He is one who came "from above" or "from the Father" or from heaven (e.g., 3:31; 6:51; 8:23; 16:28). Even more frequently throughout the narrative, the Johannine Jesus is described as one who was sent into the world by God (see, for example, John 3:17; 5:23, 36–7; 6:44, 57; 7:29; 8:18, 42; 12:49; 14:24; 17:18). In chapter 11, Martha's confession of who Jesus is includes both the traditional titles "the messiah, the Son of God," and also "the one coming into the world" (11:27). And at his trial before Pilate, the Johannine Jesus asserts that his kingdom "is not of this world" (18:36).

In John's gospel, the crucifixion is directly linked to both temporal and spatial dimensions of Jesus's journey to "this world." For example, from the beginning of his ministry to his crucifixion, the term "the hour" is used as a reference both to the time the Johannine Jesus will depart from the world (2:4; 7:30; 12:23, 27; 13:1) and to his crucifixion (8:20; 12:27). Moreover, the crucifixion is not so much suffering and death

basics | Gospel of John

Outline: the sojourn of the word in the world

The gospel has two main sections. The first part focuses on the signs of Jesus and is patterned around the Jewish festivals. A clear break is indicated at 13:1, where Jesus "knows" that his hour has come to depart and return to the Father. John 11 and 12 serve as a transition to the second section, narrating the final sign (11:1–44) and foreshadowing Jesus's death and glorification (11:45–12:8; 12:27–36), which will be narrated in the second section.

I	Signs of the Johannine Jesus	1–12
	A Prologue: the word coming into the world	1:1–18
	B Belief and unbelief in response to the signs	1:19–11:44
	C Transition: the final sign and foreshadowing of the hour	11:45–12:50
II	Jesus's departure from the world	13–20
	A Farewell meal with the disciples	13
	B Farewell discourse and prayer	14–17
	C The hour of glorification	18–20
III	Epilogue: Jesus's last meeting with his disciples	21

Date and authorship

The question of authorship of the gospel attracts even more scholarly attention than that of the authorship of the synoptic gospels because of the mysterious figure of the "beloved disciple" (13:23; 19:26; 20:2; 21:7, 20), a figure some have taken to be the author. Aside from the fact that there is nothing in the gospel itself to indicate that this figure should be understood as the author, there is also no indication in the gospel of the identity of the beloved disciple. Scholars have posited dozens of possibilities ranging from the resurrected Lazarus to Mary Magdalene. Church tradition has identified the author as John, the son of Zebedee, who is said to have written the gospel in his old age in Ephesus, but once again, there is no certainty about who wrote the gospel or where it was written.

There are indications that the Gospel of John went through several editorial revisions before it reached its current form. The clearest evidence of this is at John 20:30–1. These verses appear to be a conclusion to the gospel, but it continues with chapter 21. This final chapter looks like an epilogue to the original ending, which resolves issues of Peter's status after his denial of Jesus (21:15–19) as well as rumors about the beloved disciple (21:20–3). Chapters 15–17 may also have been added to an earlier form of the gospel. Note the way 14:31 concludes the discourse of Jesus, only to have it continue for three more chapters. Whether or not these speculations about its earlier formation are correct, we can say that the gospel in its present form is the latest of the canonical gospels, probably undergoing a final editing sometime between 95 CE and 125 CE, or perhaps even later in the second century (see Figure 14.1).

(as in the synoptic tradition) but a "lifting up" (3:14; 8:28; 12:32) and a glorification (12:23, 27–8; 13:31; 17:1). In other words, in the Gospel of John, the death of Jesus is interpreted not as a sacrificial death for others, but, together with the resurrection, as a mark of Jesus's departure from the world back to his divine origins. It is the ultimate sign of his glory, which in turn, reflects the glory of God (17:4–5).

Notably, believers also take on this other-worldly existence in this gospel. The prologue declares that believers are born "not from blood, nor from the will of the flesh, nor from the will of man, but from God" (1:13). In chapter 3, the Johannine Jesus explains this birth to a confused Nicodemus. One must be born "from above" (*anothen*) to enter into the kingdom (3:3). The Greek word *anothen* produces a word play, since it has a double meaning: it can mean either "from above" or "again." Nicodemus misunderstands and thinks Jesus means again (3:4) when the Johannine Jesus means "from above" (see the use of *anothen* in 3:31, where it clearly means one who comes "from above"). The point is that, like Jesus, believers must come from another place, that is "from above." This is made even clearer later in the gospel. In chapter 15, Jesus claims that his followers are not of the world. Rather, Jesus has chosen them out of the world (15:19).

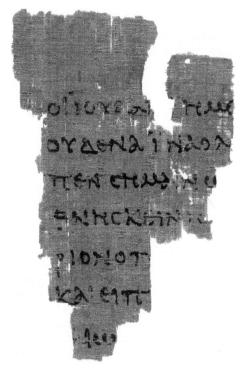

Figure 14.1 Papyrus codex with lines from the Gospel of John. Although this text has typically been dated to the first half of the second century, one recent re-examination of the paleography suggests it may be as late as the third century.

Knowing and Believing in the Johannine Jesus

Coming to know and believe in this other-worldly Jesus is the most central theme of the Gospel of John. For this reason, much of the gospel is focused on the identity of this Jesus one is to believe in – who he is and where he is from. The author reveals Jesus's identity through the reporting of "signs" that he performs, through what the Johannine Jesus says about himself and to other characters in the narrative, and by describing the different ways that characters respond to him.

A major way that characters in the gospel come to belief is on the basis of "signs" performed by Jesus. These are a distinctive feature of the Gospel of John. They serve as pointers to the identity of Jesus and reveal his glory. For example, the first sign – the changing of water into wine at the wedding at Cana – reveals Jesus's glory so that his disciples believe in him (2:11). Similarly, toward the end of the gospel, the audience is told that the signs have been written down so that they "may believe that Jesus is the Christ, the Son of God" (20:30). Some scholars posit that the multiple references to signs in the gospel may indicate that it contains an earlier **signs source**. This would have been a list of the signs of Jesus somewhat comparable to the sayings source that was used by Matthew and Luke. Other evidence for such a source includes the counting of

The *Logos* and Divine Wisdom in the Gospel of John

The Greek term that lies behind the "word" that was in the beginning and became flesh (1:1, 14) is *logos*. In the first century, *logos* was a term with multiple meanings that was used in a variety of contexts. In Hellenistic philosophy, particularly the philosophy known as Stoicism, *logos* referred to the notion of a universal rational principle that gave order to the cosmos. By the time this gospel was written, the notion of the divine *logos* as universal reason or mind was a pervasive element of Greco-Roman moral philosophy. The term also finds its way into Hellenistic Judaism. Philo of Alexandria, a Hellenistic Jewish philosopher, used *logos* to indicate the divine mediator of God's activity in the world.

Most relevant is Philo's association of the *logos* with divine wisdom. The gospel writer also seems to have linked *logos* to wisdom, as is seen in the many parallels between *logos*, Jesus, and personified Wisdom in the gospel. For example, like the *logos*, God's wisdom is understood to be present with God from the beginning (Prov 8:23–4; Sirach 24:9; Wisdom 6:22) and to participate in the divine act of creation (Prov. 8:30; Sirach 1:9–10; Wisdom 7:22; 9:2–3). Wisdom is commanded by God to "pitch a tent" in Israel; so too the *logos* in the Gospel of John "becomes flesh" and "pitches a tent" (Greek *eskēnosen*; "dwells among us" in the NRSV) (Sirach 24:8; John 1:14). Wisdom urges followers to accept her commandments; so does Jesus in the gospel (Prov 2:1–5; 3:1; John 15:10, 14). As Wisdom is rejected by her people, so too is the Johannine Jesus (Prov 1:24–5; Baruch 3:12; John 1:11; 6:66; 10:25). As disciples of Wisdom become friends of God, so do disciples of Jesus in the gospel become his friends (Wisdom 7:14, 27; John 15:14).

signs in 2:11 and 4:54. Note that although John 4:54 announces that "this was the second sign that Jesus did," this comes after an earlier report that many in Jerusalem believed in Jesus because they saw the signs that he was doing (2:23). If the author was drawing on a list of signs, he may have incorporated the listing of the "second sign" despite the earlier mention of signs. Seven signs are detailed in the gospel, though there is no explicit counting of signs beyond the second one (2:1–11; 4:46–54; 5:1–9; 6:1–14, 16–21; 9:1–41; 11:1–44). What is most important about Johannine signs is the way they become occasions for conversation and interpretation about the identity of Jesus.

The two primary examples of this are the story of the healing of the blind man and the raising of Lazarus. In both cases, the healing itself takes up relatively few verses in the narrative (9:1–7; 11:38–44). But these brief healing stories are part of much longer accounts that shape the meanings of these stories in particular ways. The healing of the man born blind, for instance, becomes an occasion to display the "blindness" of the Pharisees to the identity of Jesus (9:39–41) and the gradual coming to belief of the formerly blind man. He moves from calling Jesus a man (9:11), to a prophet (9:17), to one who is from God (9:33), to a direct confession of belief in and worship of Jesus (9:38–9). Similarly, the raising of Lazarus is preceded by a discussion between Jesus and Martha that prepares the reader to understand the raising of Lazarus as an indication that Jesus is "the resurrection and the life" (11:25). The conversation also elicits Martha's full confession of faith before the sign even occurs (11:25–7).

MORE ON METHOD: FEMINIST CRITICISM AND GENDER CRITICISM

Feminist criticism of the Bible can take several forms. It may work to uncover the role and significance of women in the biblical tradition by focusing on texts that feature women. It may also unmask the ways that the ancient patriarchal culture influenced biblical writings. Feminist biblical criticism typically has a political aspect to it, promoting equal treatment for women by reading through a hermeneutic of liberation. So for example, feminist criticism of the Gospel of John focuses on the prominent role of women in the narrative – the mother of Jesus, the Samaritan woman, Mary and Martha of Bethany, Mary Magdalene – as conversation partners and witnesses to Jesus. This prominence is seen as an indication that women held significant roles in early Christian communities, and should also hold significant leadership roles in contemporary society.

In contrast, **gender criticism** does not focus on women, but instead explores the way that a particular culture communicates what is "normal" or "ideal" for gender identities. A gender-critical approach sees sex and gender not so much as biological categories, but rather as the product of complex ideological forces. For the study of the New Testament, gender criticism would involve analyzing evidence from the first-century Greco-Roman culture to understand how it defined and valued what it meant to be a man or woman. Gender-critical studies of the Gospel of John have focused on the way it presents Jesus as an ideal man with respect to the cultural definition of masculinity. So, for example, the Johannine Jesus is always presented as one in complete control of himself, which in the Greco-Roman culture was a key indicator of one's masculine status. Note that he takes charge of his own arrest (18:1–11) and trial. In fact, the Johannine Jesus makes clear that he even lays down his own life. In presenting the crucifixion in this way, the author transforms what would be a humiliating and emasculating death into a noble self-sacrifice and therefore a manly death.

For feminist- and gender-critical work on John see Amy-Jill Levine and Marianne Blickenstaff, eds., *The Feminist Companion to John* (London and New York: Sheffield Academic Press, 2003).

These two examples make clear that, for this gospel, belief in the Johannine Jesus is the criterion for eternal life and salvation (3:16–18). This may not seem particularly remarkable until we recall that not all the gospel writers make this point in this way. For example, Matthew's gospel had a different emphasis. In that gospel, one entered the kingdom of heaven because one obeyed and did the will of the Father. But as the Gospel of John unfolds, characters are portrayed in relation to the question of belief or lack of belief in the other-worldly Jesus. We find this contrast already in the prologue – those who "believe in his name" receive power to become children of God, in contrast to those who do not receive him (1:10–12). Only in this gospel are characters asked directly about their belief in Jesus. The blind man healed by the Johannine Jesus is asked by him, "Do you believe?" (9:35–8). Martha, too, is directly asked whether she believes in Jesus as one who gives life (11:25–6). By the end, even the reader is directly confronted with the issue of belief (20:31).

The gospel includes many long discourses by the Johannine Jesus about himself. In contrast to the commands to secrecy in the Gospel of Mark, the Johannine Jesus speaks openly about his identity throughout the narrative, often referring to himself by means of the Greek phrase *ego eimi* ("I am"). He describes himself as the bread of life (6:35, 48), the living bread that comes down from heaven (6:51), the light of the world (8:12), the gate for the sheep (10:7), the good shepherd (10:11), the resurrection and life (11:25), the way, truth, and life (14:16), and the true vine (15:1). Such self-descriptive statements are unique to the Gospel of John and offer a rich array of images alongside the traditional titles that are applied to Jesus in the synoptic gospels. The use of this metaphorical language suggests that, for this gospel writer, the identity of Jesus cannot be fully expressed in traditional leadership titles like messiah or king. Instead, the "I am" statements of the Gospel of John evoke the life-giving significance of Jesus through basic images of sustenance.

In seven instances, the "I am" phrase stands on its own (8:24, 28, 58; 13:13, 19; 18:6, 8). In English translations, this is often rendered "I am he." While grammatically correct, this translation dilutes the force of the phrase. In the Septuagint, especially in the oracles of Isaiah, "I am" is divine, self-revelatory speech (Isa 43:10, 25; see also Exod 3:14). In the Gospel of John, Jesus's use of "I am" carries similar weight. Note, for example, the reaction of the soldiers who have come out to arrest Jesus (John 18:6). When Jesus says "I am," they fall to the ground as if stunned by a divine revelation. Does this mean that Jesus is equal to God, according to the author? Are Jesus and God one and the same? The answer this gospel gives is a paradoxical yes and no.

As we have already seen, the Johannine Jesus is portrayed as one sent by God. If we examine additional statements in the gospel about the relationship between God and Jesus, or Father and Son, as they are often called, it is clear that Jesus acts as God's representative in the world. As such, Jesus is united with the Father and can say "The Father and I are one" (10:30; 17:22). Nevertheless, as God's representative, or agent in the world, Jesus also indicates his subordination to the Father. The Son can do nothing on his own (5:19, 30; 8:28). The Father is greater than Jesus is (14:28), and Jesus speaks as instructed by the Father (8:28) and does what the Father commands (14:31). Because Jesus is God's agent, those who know him also know the Father (14:7), and those who honor him also honor the Father (5:22–3).

Opposition from the World

READING
John 14–17.

EXERCISE
How is the relationship between Jesus and his disciples described? How does the Johannine Jesus speak of the world in these chapters?

One of the claims of the gospel is that the Johannine Jesus was sent by God to save the world (John 3:16–17). This is also the conclusion reached by the Samaritans who declare that Jesus is "truly, the savior of the world!" (4:42). But, in spite of these claims, the rest of the gospel suggests that "the world" is decidedly hostile toward the Johannine Jesus and his followers. This is conveyed particularly strongly in the **farewell discourse**, the common designation for the Johannine Jesus's parting words to his disciples before his departure, found in chapters 14–16 of the gospel. In this discourse, Jesus acknowledges to his followers that the world hates him, and therefore may hate them also (15:18). He explains how he will reveal himself to his followers but not to the world (14:22–3), and he asserts that in the world his followers have trouble, or more literally "pressure" (16:33). As we have seen above, the Johannine Jesus has chosen his followers out of the world and instead of loving the world, he loves "his own who were in the world" (13:1). Similarly, believers are given a new commandment to love one another (13:34). Compared to the synoptic command to love one's enemies (Matt 5:44//Luke 6:27), this represents a decided focus on the internal community.

Along with being "hated" by the world, the Johannine Jesus is also in conflict with "the ruler" of this world. The Johannine Jesus claims that "the ruler of this world" will be driven out (12:31), but also that he will no longer be able to speak with the disciples because the ruler of the world is "coming." Nevertheless, Jesus asserts that this "ruler" has no control of him (14:30), and that the ruler has been condemned (16:11). Indeed, the Johannine Jesus proclaims that he has conquered the world (16:33). On one level, the "ruler of the world" likely refers to Satan (although this designation explicitly appears only once in the gospel, at 13:27). On another level, the ancient audience would also, and perhaps primarily, associate the phrase with the Roman emperor, who was in fact "the ruler of this world." In either case, the audience is urged to believe that (appearances notwithstanding) the Johannine Jesus has gained a victory over the present earthly authority and therefore conquered the world. Maintaining such a belief would be both a catharsis and a challenge in a world in which the Romans exerted their power at will in the lands they occupied.

As suggested at the outset of this chapter, the rhetoric of alienation and opposition in relation to "the world" may be another strategy to cope with the political reality of alienation and powerlessness that results from imperial occupation. Turning inward and drawing strength and personal identity from your own group might help to counter the humiliating experience of being ruled over by a foreign power. This would be especially true for a community gathered around a divine figure who claimed to have conquered the world and its evil ruler, as we see in the Gospel of John. Such a community could draw comfort from these claims and from the expression of unity and love for one another. In fact, the Johannine Jesus makes the offer of comfort explicit in his farewell discourse with a promise of sending a **Paraclete** to the believers after his departure. This Greek term can mean comforter, advocate, intercessor, and counselor (literally, "one who is called beside to help"). This full range of meanings is lost when one opts for one translation over another, which is why some English versions simply transliterate the Greek word "Paraclete" rather than translating it. The presence of this figure further encourages group identity and solidarity. In addition to being a "comforter" or "advocate," the Paraclete will bear witness on behalf of the departed Jesus (15:26; 16:8), guide and instruct the believers (16:13–14), and remind them of Jesus's words (14:26). This last point is particularly interesting with respect to the canonical development of the New Testament writings. The Gospel of John is the first of the canonical gospels to highlight the words of Jesus as having ongoing significance in the life of the community. Indeed, there is some indication earlier in the gospel that the words of Jesus were already being put alongside "the scripture" as authoritative (2:22).

The Problem of the Jews in the Gospel of John

READING
John 6, 8–9.

EXERCISE
How are the Jews portrayed in these chapters? What is the Johannine Jesus's attitude toward the Jews?

In addition to a general opposition from the world, the Johannine Jesus encounters opposition from a group identified as "the Jews." We have already seen the negative portrayal of scribes, Pharisees, and chief priests in the synoptic traditions, but only in the Gospel of John do we find the frequent use of the term "Jews" to refer to opponents of Jesus. From the beginning of the gospel, this group persecutes Jesus (5:16), seeks to kill him (5:18; 7:1, 25), complains about him (6:41), claims that he is demon-possessed (8:48, 52), tries to stone him (10:31), and insists over Pilate's protests that Jesus must die (19:7). During the trial of Jesus, the narrative aligns these "Jews" with the Roman emperor. They hint to Pilate that releasing Jesus would be treasonous, and they openly claim that they have no king but Caesar (19:12, 15). "The Jews" cause fear in others in this gospel. The parents of the formerly blind man will not speak to the authorities about Jesus because they are afraid they will be expelled from the synagogue (9:22). This fear is reiterated later in the gospel when some Pharisees keep their belief in Jesus a secret, again, because of the fear of expulsion (12:42).

This negative portrayal of "the Jews" is reinforced by fiercely antagonistic rhetoric directed at the Jews by the Johannine Jesus. The Jews are from "below" and are "of this world" (8:23). He wonders why he bothers speaking with them, and has much to condemn about them (8:25–6). Most troubling, the Johannine Jesus denies their assertion that they are children of Abraham (a foundational truth for Jewish identity) and insists instead that their father is the devil, "a murderer from the beginning" and "the father of lies" (8:44). The Johannine Jesus also prepares his followers for expulsion from the synagogue and death at the hands of his opponents (16:2).

Finally, the Gospel of John creates distance from Jewish traditions in general. In speaking to "the Jews," the Johannine Jesus refers to "your law" (8:17; 10:34; 18:31), as if it is not also his law. When we recall that the Matthean Jesus insisted that he came to *fulfill* the law, the difference in John's gospel is all the more apparent. A similar distancing from the Jewish traditions is seen in the gospel references to "the festival of the Jews" or the "Passover of the Jews" (2:13; 5:1; 6:4; 11:55), as though the author and audience no longer viewed these festivals as their own.

Understanding who is intended by the use of the term "the Jews" and the reasons for this strongly negative portrayal has been one of the most vexing problems of Johannine scholarship in the past decades. The issue became particularly pressing in the aftermath of World War II, when the genocide perpetrated on European Jews was revealed. Many Christians began to examine Christian complicity, not just in the Holocaust, but also its role in promoting a centuries-long history of anti-Semitism. Reconsidering the portrayal of the Jews and Judaism in the New Testament, particularly the Gospel of John, has been part of that process.

A first step in contending with the anti-Jewish rhetoric in the Gospel of John is to view the gospel as a reflection of the author's situation, rather than as an accurate account of the time of Jesus, just as we have been doing all through our study of the Bible. Here is a place where the distinction between the historical Jesus and the textual Jesus is particularly important to maintain. Indeed, there is widespread agreement among biblical critics that the historical Jesus would not have distanced himself from the Jewish tradition in the way he is described as doing in this gospel.

But, with the Gospel of John, it has not been enough to simply shift the focus to the time of the gospel's composition if the goal is to alleviate the effects of its anti-Jewish rhetoric. This is because many interpreters still have taken the gospel as an accurate account of Jewish misdeeds, merely transposing the misdeeds to the level of Jewish persecution of early Christians. Indeed, the dominant academic reading of the Gospel of John for the past few decades has held that the gospel reflects a time when Jewish Christians were being driven out of their local synagogues because of their belief in Jesus. According to this theory, the Johannine Jesus's strong invectives against the Jews actually represent the Christian community's reaction to being persecuted by the local synagogue leaders. From here it is a short step to viewing the victimized church as superior to the synagogue (see Figure 14.2).

This dominant theory about John and the Jewish persecution of early Christians has some serious limitations. While it is clear that the gospel reflects a time when the followers of Jesus viewed themselves as distinct from the Jewish synagogue community, it is likely that animosity went both ways. The gospel reflects a one-sided view of this heated conflict in which Jewish opponents are cast in the worst possible light. Anyone who has ever had a bitter argument with a once-close friend should be wary of taking the depiction of "the Jews" in the Gospel of John at face value, whether in the time of Jesus, or in the late first/early second century CE. Unfortunately, the historical details of this ancient argument and the eventual break that it led to are lost to us. There is

Figure 14.2 Early Christian image of the church preferred over the synagogue. The angel under Christ's arm on the left ushers in the church, while the angel under Christ's arm on the right violently drives out the synagogue, who is blindfolded and has lost her crown.

some evidence to suggest that in the second century the problem for Christians was people *returning* to the synagogue, not being *driven from* it. As we will see, it is possible that the Johannine epistles reflect this phenomenon. If this was the case at the time of the gospel's composition, it would make sense of the gospel's strong emphasis on belief in Jesus. The gospel's picture of confessing Christians being rejected by the synagogue may have been a way of discouraging a move back to the synagogue. Another possibility may be that the author and audience of the Gospel of John were not in the midst of a debate with the synagogue, but were already separate. If this is the case, the depiction of Jesus and "the Jews" in John's gospel may serve an explanatory role. It tells how their current division came to be, reading it back into the life of Jesus. It would not be the first time that we have seen traditional stories (in this case, the story of Jesus) retold to provide a meaningful foundation for a later community.

Postcolonial theory offers yet another way to understand the dynamics of the Gospel of John. Once again, we should consider the ways that the Roman presence created and exacerbated tensions between different Jewish groups. As we saw in our study of the Gospel of Matthew, the destruction of Jerusalem by Rome opened the way for different Jewish movements to compete for power and the allegiance of the Jewish people. And our study of the Gospel of Mark suggested that the conflict of Jesus with the scribes and Pharisees from Jerusalem may reflect political as well as religious conflict between Christians and collaborators with Rome. Both of these dynamics may be present in the Gospel of John. However, in this case, the gospel insightfully addresses the Judean leaders' *fear* of Rome and links that fear to their perception of Jesus.

And at least in this sense, John's gospel may be more historically accurate than the synoptic tradition. The opponents of the Johannine Jesus view belief in him as a threat, not primarily to their religious beliefs, but to their safety and survival under Roman occupation. For example, in the gospel narrative, the last sign of Jesus, the raising of Lazarus, results in a meeting of the Jewish leadership council.

So the chief priests and the Pharisees gathered the council, and said, "What should we do? This man is doing many signs. If we allow him to go on like this, all will believe in him, and the Romans will come and destroy our place and our people." (11:47–8)

Thus, the opponents of the Johannine Jesus in this story see him as a threat precisely because he may draw the unwelcome attention of Rome to their land. While we are intended to see the Jews and the Pharisees as the opponents of Jesus, a postcolonial reading can sympathize with these "chief priests and Pharisees" as they struggle to ward off imperial violence. Depicted as the leaders of the religious community, they are in fact powerless before the empire and can only hope to divert Roman attention from their nation by silencing Jesus and therefore the crowds he attracts.

In an ironic way, the gospel writer uses the occasion to put a fundamental Christological claim about Jesus into the mouth of the chief priest:

"You don't understand that it is more to your advantage to have one man die for the sake of the people than to have the whole nation destroyed." He did say this on his own, but being high priest that year he prophesied that Jesus was about to die for the sake of the nation, and not for the nation only, but so that the scattered children of God might be gathered into one. (11:50–2)

But again, even while asserting this Christological claim, the gospel writer gives insight into the fears of a colonized people. Of course, there is also irony in the fact that the gospel is written after the whole Jewish nation had been destroyed by Rome, but the gospel writer does not address that brutal reality.

John 17

FOCUS
TEXT

John 17 is a prayer that comes at the conclusion of the farewell discourse (John 14–16). There are a number of places in the gospel where the Johannine Jesus summarizes the message of the gospel (3:31–6; 5:19–24; 12:44–50), but only here does such a summary come in the form of a prayer. This artfully crafted passage has three sections: Jesus prays for himself in 17:1–5; he prays for his disciples in 17:6–19; and he prays for future believers in 17:20–4, before a concluding statement in 17:25–6.

In the opening section, the prayer points to the temporal dimension of the incarnation: At the time of his departure, the Johannine Jesus also takes the audience back to the prologue, recalling the glory he had as the pre-existent *logos* in the presence of God (17:5) and acknowledging that the "hour" has now arrived (17:1). While this hour clearly indicates his impending death, the Johannine Jesus prays for glorification from the Father so that he may glorify God in turn. Jesus recalls the authority given to him by God over "all flesh" (17:2), but also the qualified nature of this authority. The Johannine Jesus may give eternal life to those whom the Father has given him. Such language reminds the audience that Jesus does not act independently of God. It also provides an explanation for why not all have believed in Jesus, an issue that we have seen trouble other New Testament writers, such as Paul. Notably, while we have seen reference to eternal life throughout the gospel, the prayer goes further in defining this phrase. Here "eternal life" is precisely what has been central to the gospel: "that they may know you, the only true God and Jesus Christ whom you sent" (17:3). In this sense, having eternal life is not something that happens when one dies (i.e. "going to heaven"); according to the Johannine Jesus, it is a present reality in the life of the believer. That is to say, in the Gospel of John we find a **realized eschatology**. The idea of a future judgment and salvation in the "last days" that is evident in other Christian traditions is here transformed into an already realized state of affairs in the life of a believer. We see indications of this realized eschatology earlier in the gospel where the Johannine Jesus paradoxically proclaims, "the hour is coming and is now here" (4:23; 5:25; 16:32). Similarly, he refers to the present possibility of eternal life (5:24; 6:47, 54; 10:28; 11:25–6).

The second part of the prayer is a petition of the Johannine Jesus on behalf of his own disciples that will remain in the world once he is gone (17:6–19). These disciples are described as the ones whom God gave to Jesus "from out of the world" (17:6). They have received the basic message of the Gospel of John; they know that Jesus came from God and was sent by him (17:8). The Johannine Jesus prays for the same unity for them as he shares with the Father (17:11). Meanwhile, Jesus also reinforces their alienation from the world; the world hates them because they do not belong to it (17:14). In this way, the prayer of Jesus contributes to the inward turn of this gospel, constructing a community identity that draws strength through its perception of victimization and alienation vis-à-vis the world. Note that Jesus asks that God protect his followers from the "evil one." Primarily this designates a supernatural evil power, "Satan," but, as noted earlier, from the audience's perspective, such a reference could also include the particular earthly authority in whom this evil is manifest, e.g. the Roman emperor, or even a local governing authority.

Finally, the prayer reaches forward to the future to address believers who were not immediate disciples of Jesus but believe because of their word (17:20–4). This would include the audience of the gospel, but also future generations. Just the recognition of these future generations reveals a difference from the imminent apocalyptic expectations that we saw in earlier texts such as the letters of Paul. The hope for unity or "oneness" extends to these future believers as well. "The glory that you have given me I have given them so that they may be one, as we are one." This unified existence will also be a witness to the world of the identity of Jesus as one sent by God, and the identity of the believers as those loved by God (17:22–3).

The Johannine Epistles

READING
1, 2 and 3 John.

EXERCISE
What similarities do these writings have to the Gospel of John? What situation may have led to the writing of 1 John? (Hint: see especially 1 John 2:18–26.)

The texts of 1, 2, and 3 John, although quite different from one another, are commonly grouped together as the Johannine epistles. This is the case even though 1 John is not actually a letter, and none of the texts indicates the name of its author. Nevertheless, the language of each of the texts is so similar to the language and dualistic worldview of the Gospel of John that they seem linked to the gospel in some way. Perhaps they were written by the same person who revised the original gospel, or simply by someone familiar with the language and traditions of the gospel.

The longest of these three texts, 1 John, most closely reflects the ideas of the Gospel of John. In fact, the opening verse recalls the opening verse of the gospel, with its reference to what was in "the beginning" (1 John 1:1; see John 1:1). Likewise, the opening section of the epistle contains the dualistic language of the gospel. The world of 1 John is characterized by light versus dark, love versus hate, obedience versus disobedience, children of God versus children of the devil (1 John 1:5–7; 2:9–10; 3:10). The "Paraclete" is also mentioned, identified as Jesus Christ (1 John 2:1). The epistle shares the same animosity toward "the world" as we saw in the gospel (1 John 2:15–17; 3:13; 4:4–5), and it reiterates the commandment that the epistle's audience should believe in Jesus and love one another (I John 3:23; 4:11). Clearly, there is some relationship between this text and the Gospel of John.

Many scholars have focused on 1 John 2:19 as a clue to understanding the occasion for the writing of this text. Here the author refers to a group "who went out from us, but were not from us." This verse, in addition to the repeated references to those who "hate their brothers" (1 John 3:15; 4:20; see also 2:11), suggests that a break occurred in the author's community. There are several places in the text that are designed to bolster the group solidarity of the audience over against those who left. Those who do not do what is right, or do not love their brothers, are labeled children of the devil (1 John 3:10). Similarly, "every spirit that confesses that Jesus Christ is one who has come in the flesh is from God and every spirit who does not confess Jesus is not from God" (1 John 4: 2–3). The authority of the writer is reinforced with statements such as "the one who knows God, listens to us. The one who is not from God, does not listen to us" (1 John 4:6).

There is no certainty about the chronological relationship between 1 John and the Gospel of John. The dominant theory has been that 1 John was written *after* the Gospel of John, reflecting a later stage in the development of a particular Christian community. This theory suggests that the controversy in 1 John was no longer with the synagogue, but was internal to the community and involved differing ideas about Christ. But it may be that some of the community were returning to the synagogue, no longer confessing that Jesus is the messiah and Son of God. If this is the case, the controversy could well have generated the type of animosity toward "the Jews" that is reflected in the gospel. The fact is that the author's references to those who left are quite vague, suggesting that they were not the main focus of his composition. Perhaps the most we can say is that 1 John is concerned to shape and strengthen the identity of a group of believers, and he does so in ways that coincide with the worldview and language of the Gospel of John.

The brief letters of 2 and 3 John draw on the same language, but apply it to particular situations. For example, 2 John, written from "the elder" to an "excellent lady," uses the same language of truth and love versus deceivers and the Antichrist (2 John 1:4–7). But it also specifically discourages the recipient from offering hospitality to those who do not come with the "teaching of Christ" (2 John 1:10–11). Even more specific is 3 John. It refers to a conflict between the author and a certain Diotrephes who does not recognize the author's authority (3 John 1:9). These texts, together with 1 John, reflect an ongoing tradition that flowed out of a particular "Johannine" way of conceiving of Jesus, God, and the believers' role in relation to the world.

CHAPTER FOURTEEN REVIEW

1. Know the meaning and significance of the following terms:
- farewell discourse [in the Gospel of John]
- feminist criticism
- gender criticism [know the difference between this and feminist criticism]
- incarnation [especially for the Gospel of John]
- Paraclete
- realized eschatology
- signs source

2. How is the other-worldliness of Jesus expressed in both a spatial and temporal way in John? How does this emphasis on the other-worldliness of Jesus get reflected in John's retelling of Jesus's crucifixion?

3. In the Gospel of Matthew, one must obey to enter the kingdom of heaven. What does one need to do according to the Gospel of John? How is this shown in the gospel?

4. What is the dominant theory about why the Gospel of John depicts Jews rejecting Jesus, and Jesus as hostile to "the Jews"? What are the problems with this theory, and what might be an alternative understanding of the background to this theme in John?

5. How might postcolonial theory inform our view of tensions between Jews and Christians at the time the gospel was written?

6. How does Jesus's prayer in John 17 represent a shift from the expectation in some other New Testament texts (e.g. Paul) of the coming of the last days in the near future?

7. What similarities are there between the Johannine epistles and the Gospel of John?

RESOURCES FOR FURTHER STUDY

Brown, Raymond Edward. *The Gospel According to John*. Vol. 29, The Anchor Bible. Garden City, NY: Doubleday, 1966.

Brown, Raymond Edward. *The Gospel According to John*. Vol. 29A, The Anchor Bible. Garden City, NY: Doubleday, 1970.

Brown, Raymond Edward. *Anatomy of the Fourth Gospel: A Study in Literary Design*. Philadelphia: Fortress, 1983.

Culpepper, R. Alan. *The Gospel and Letters of John*. Interpreting Biblical Texts. Nashville: Abingdon Press, 1998.

Lieu, Judith. *I, II, III John: A Commentary*. New Testament Library. Louisville, KY: Westminster John Knox Press, 2008.

Reinhartz, Adele. *Befriending the Beloved Disciple: A Jewish Reading of the Gospel of John*. New York and London: Continuum, 2001.

Rensberger David. *1 John, 2 John, 3 John*. Abingdon New Testament Commentaries. Nashville: Abingdon Press, 1997.

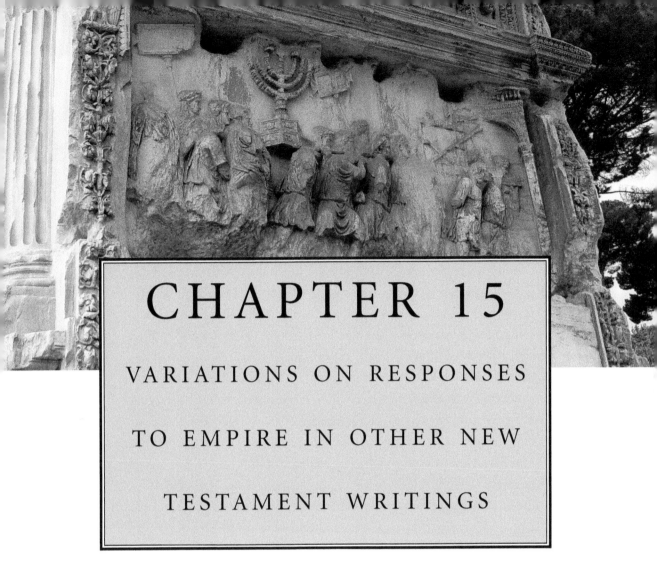

CHAPTER 15

VARIATIONS ON RESPONSES

TO EMPIRE IN OTHER NEW

TESTAMENT WRITINGS

Chapter Outline

CHAPTER OVERVIEW

As we come to the end of our study of the Bible, this chapter will focus on the diversity of early Christianity evident in some of the remaining New Testament texts, focusing in particular on the Revelation to John, Hebrews, and 1 Peter. Although there are some common elements to each of these texts, they reflect different responses to the experience of living under imperial rule. Like Daniel, our other major example of apocalyptic literature, the Revelation to John takes a resistant and hostile stance toward the empire. Indeed, even with its coded language, it is the most blatant of the New Testament writings in its attacks on Roman rule. Hebrews, on the other hand, seems less concerned with Rome than it is with the relations of the early Christian movement to the Jewish sacrificial cult. Nevertheless, the effects of living under imperial rule are apparent in Hebrews' appropriation of a Platonic worldview, as well as its emphasis on the alien status of believers. Our third text, 1 Peter, is an example of accommodation to life in the empire, though, like Hebrews, it adopts the language of exile and alienation.

The Revelation to John: Resistance through Imitation

READING
Revelation 1–5,
12–21.

EXERCISE
What is your emotional reaction to the book of Revelation? What do you
think the author is trying to accomplish with these images?

Many modern appropriations of the book of Revelation, whether in film, websites, novels, or sermons, are designed to instill fear in the audience. There is no shortage of frightening material on which to draw. Torturing locusts with scales and scorpions' tails (Rev 9:1–10), seven-headed dragons ready to devour a newborn child (Rev 12:1–17), and a multi-headed, leopard-like beast rising from the sea (Rev 13:1–3) are just a few of the images that come to us from Revelation. Yet juxtaposed with these images are visions of heavenly worship (Revelation 4–5) and promises of a future in which God will dwell with people and wipe away every tear (Rev 21:3–4).

In spite of the emphasis on fear and violence in most contemporary appropriations of the book of Revelation, the work was not intended to frighten its original audience. Rather, as is the case with **apocalyptic** literature in general, it was written to bring comfort and hope to believers who felt alienated from the synagogue and persecuted by Rome. We have seen responses to these two major pressures – living under Roman rule and relating to Jews who did not believe in Jesus – in the gospels and Pauline letters. We have also seen how these two pressures were related. The external forces of the Roman empire exacerbated the internal conflicts of the early Christian movement with the synagogue community. In the book of Revelation, the response to these pressures takes the form of resistance to the Roman empire, primarily through visions of Rome's utter destruction. Nevertheless, there is also imitation of Roman power in this work. As we have seen in other biblical writings, even as the authors resisted imperial power they did not escape the influence of living under it.

This imitation is apparent first in the seven messages to the churches in Asia Minor (Map 15.1). Although these are often referred to as letters, they are closer in form to imperial edicts. The imperial edict was used to issue instructions to local communities. It would begin with a formal introduction of the authority issuing the edict and then move to direct address to the addressees. This direct address begins with the Greek phrase meaning "This is what he says" (*tade legei*). The main body of the imperial edict would express decisions and sanctions, and then a final section was included to reinforce obedience. The seven messages in Revelation contain all of these elements. The issuing authority is identified in seven different ways in Revelation, all of which emphasize Jesus's power as the exalted Son of God, such as "the one having the sharp two-edged

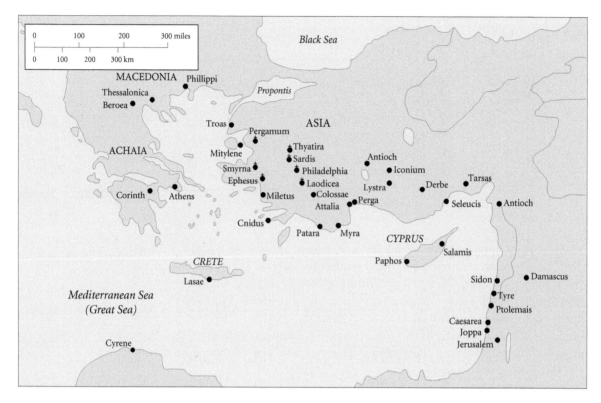

Map 15.1 Cities of Revelation. Redrawn from Steven L. Harris, *Understanding the Bible* (6th edition). McGraw Hill, 2003, page 597.

sword" (Rev 2:12), or "the Amen, the faithful and true witness, the ruler of the creation of God" (Rev 3:14). In each case, the authoritative voice of Jesus speaks directly to the local churches, identifying their merits and shortcomings and concluding with promises of punishment or rewards. The authority of this figure is exerted on multiple fronts – against those in the community who are accused of false teaching (Rev 2:14; 20–3), against those in the synagogue who are deemed to be non-Jews (Rev 3:8–9), and against those in the community who are going astray (Rev 2:4–5, 14–15; 3:14–19). In this way, the opening chapters of Revelation imitate imperial authority by presenting Jesus as one having the status and authority to issue formal "imperial" edicts with an expectation of obedience.

Throughout these messages, rewards are repeatedly promised to those who "conquer" (Rev 2:7, 11, 17, 26, 28; 3:5, 12, 21). A careful reading makes clear what is meant by this "conquering." Believers are to remain faithful to the point of death (Rev 2:10–11). If they do, like Jesus, they will be rewarded with authority over the nations, ruling them with a rod of iron (Rev 2:26–8; see also 12:11). They will be clothed in white robes (Rev 3:5) and given a seat with the risen Christ on his throne (Rev 3:21). Here then is another indication of imperial influence on a New Testament text, as the ultimate reward envisioned by those who feel oppressed by Rome, or the nations, is to become the one with ruling authority over others.

basics Revelation to John

Date and authorship

At one time, the "John" of Revelation was thought to be the author of both the Gospel and epistles of John, namely the apostle John. Now few would identify the apostle as the author of any of these texts, and scholars do not think the texts share an author. While there is no reason to doubt that the author of Revelation was named John, this was a very common name and we should simply consider him to be a leader among the churches of Asia Minor, writing from the island of Patmos (see Rev 1:9). The date of composition is uncertain. Many have tried to link the writing to the imperial reign of Nero, which would mean an early date in the 60s CE. Others have argued for linking the book to the reign of Domitian, which would mean the mid-90s CE. Both of these suggestions are based on trying to connect the suffering described in the book to state-sponsored, widespread persecution of Christians. Since most scholars are no longer convinced that such widespread persecution took place, there is little reason to date the book to a particular emperor. The most we can say is that the book was written sometime in the second half of the first century CE.

Here we might be more specific about the types of oppression the communities in Asia Minor might have been experiencing at this time. Most scholars now agree that there is no evidence for an official Roman policy of persecution of Christians. Indeed, for much of the first century CE there was little recognition of Christians as a group distinct from Jews. Still, following the crushing defeat of the Jewish revolt in 70 CE, there may have been hostility directed toward Jewish communities (including Jewish Christians) across the empire, including Asia Minor. Here one might consider the misplaced suspicions and ill will directed toward Arabs living in the US after 9/11. Also, as we mentioned in Chapter 11, there is one persecution of Christians under the emperor Nero. Tacitus, a Roman historian and also a despiser of Nero, gives an account of how Nero blamed the Christians in Rome for a catastrophic fire that destroyed large sections of Rome. Again, if rumors of this accusation spread across the empire, Christians might well have been subject to poor treatment in their local communities.

Tacitus's Account of Nero's Persecution of Christians in Rome

But neither human help, nor imperial benevolence, nor all the modes of placating Heaven, could stifle scandal or dispel the belief that the fire had taken place by order. Therefore to put an end to the rumor, Nero substituted as culprits, and punished with the utmost refinement of cruelty, a class of men, loathed for their vices, whom the crowd called Christians. Christus, the founder of the name, had undergone the death penalty in the reign of Tiberius, by sentence of the procurator Pontius Pilatus, and the pernicious superstition was checked for a moment, only to break out once more, not merely in Judea, the home of the disease, but in the capital itself, where all things horrible or shameful in the world collect and are celebrated. First, then, the confessed members of the sect were arrested; next, on their disclosures, vast numbers were convicted, not so much on the count of arson as for hatred of the human race. And derision accompanied their end; they were covered with wild beasts' skins and torn to death by dogs; or they were fastened on crosses, and, when daylight failed were burned to serve as lamps by night. Nero had offered his gardens for the spectacle, and gave an exhibition in his circus, mixing with the crowd in the habit of a charioteer, or mounted on his car. Hence, in spite of a guilt which had earned the most exemplary punishment, there arose a sentiment of pity, due to the impression that they were being sacrificed not for the welfare of the state but to the ferocity of a single man. (Tacitus, *Annals* 15.44, modified from the Loeb edition)

Following the seven messages, the text unfolds in a series of visions that are typical of apocalyptic literature. Beginning with the opening chapter, John relates nearly forty times what he "saw" and reiterates at the end of the text that he is the one who "heard and saw these things" (Rev 22:8). After the initial attention to the earthly affairs of the churches in Asia Minor in chapters 1–3, the text transports the audience to a scene of heavenly worship in the throne room of God (Revelation 4–5). Continuing the project of imperial imitation, the scene shares much with descriptions of Roman court ceremonials. The 24 elders casting their golden crowns before God parallel descriptions of Roman senators prostrate before the emperor's throne. The hymns and acclamations of God and the Lamb echo similar acclamations directed toward the emperor (Rev 4:10–11). But given the elaborate description of the heavenly throne room, which includes references to colorful jewels, flashes of lightning, peals of thunder, flaming torches, crystal, and golden crowns, it is clear that the vision is intended to surpass any description of an earthly court ceremonial. It also reinforces the idea that "the Lord

God, the Almighty" (Rev 4:8) is the real ruler of the universe and rightful recipient of "glory, honor and power" (Rev 4:10–11). Similar honors are given to the central figure in the heavenly throne room, the Lion/Lamb with seven horns and seven eyes (symbolic indications of strength and wisdom). He, too, is worthy "to receive power and wealth and wisdom and might and honor and glory and blessing" because of his self-sacrifice for people from every tribe and nation. Overall, the point of the scene is to confirm the ultimate ruling authority of God and the Lamb against the seeming authority of the emperor. It does so by providing a visual "parallel" to a court ceremony for the emperor, but one that surpasses in splendor and spectacle anything that could be found in Rome.

Having made clear who is actually ruling heaven and earth, Revelation goes on to display a cosmic conflict that occurs as the wrath of God and the Lamb is unleashed upon the earth and its inhabitants (Rev 6:15–17). There is no clear narrative sequence to the story of this conflict. Instead, the audience, along with the seer, John, "watches" gruesome scenes of war, death, and destruction that manifest God's final judgment over the unrepentant inhabitants of the earth. These judgments are deemed "true and just," as well as acts of divine vengeance on behalf of those righteous ones who were killed for "the word of God" and for their witness (Rev 6:9–10; see also 15:3; 16:5–7; 19:2).

One of the clearest allusions here to the struggle with Roman imperial power is found in the description of the two beasts (Rev 13:1–18). The first beast rises from the ocean much like the sea monsters symbolizing oppressive empires in prophetic texts (see Isa 51:9–11; Ezek 29:3–5; 32:2–6; Jer 51:34), and its appearance combines the features of the four beasts representing different empires in Dan 7:2–7. By combining these various biblical monsters into one beast, the author of Revelation implies that this beast/empire represents the worst of them all – the culmination of evil in the world. The question, "Who is like the beast and who is able to fight against it?" (Rev 13:4) might be exactly the question someone living under Roman domination might ask. The claim that the beast has authority over "every tribe, people, language and nation" (Rev 13:7) would feel practically true to those who were subjected to Rome's power. A further clue to associating the beast with the Roman empire is the claim that "all the inhabitants of the earth will worship it" (Rev 13:8). Particularly in the Eastern portion of the Roman empire, where Revelation was written, emperor worship became increasingly popular at both the state-sponsored provincial and the local city level. The men of the elite class in the cities of Asia Minor held political offices as well as priesthoods in various local civic cults dedicated to the emperor alongside other deities.

The powerful position of these men helps to explain the reference to the second beast in Rev 13:11–17. As Adela Collins and others have suggested, a beast that exercises authority on behalf of the first beast, and causes others to worship, matches the role of the elite class in the cities of Asia Minor. These affluent men controlled the political, religious, and economic affairs of their community in close association with Rome. Such power is reflected in the description of the second beast, which has authority to kill those who do not worship the first beast, or cut off their livelihood by denying them participation in the local economy (Rev 13:15–17). Of course, from a Jewish or

Figure 15.1 Fourth-century CE catacomb painting illustrating how early Christians viewed their own experience of the Roman empire through the lens of the biblical text. Though it depicts a scene from Dan 3:12–18 in which three men refuse to honor the image of the Babylonian king Nebuchadnezzar, the bust of the king looks like a Roman emperor and the officer demanding their veneration of the king is in Roman military attire.

Christian perspective, offering sacrifice to the emperor posed serious problems because it was a direct affront to their monotheistic beliefs (see Figure 15.1). But refusing to participate in these local imperial cults was the same as refusing to perform a civic duty. It was not just a religious practice, but also a political one. In this way the book of Revelation suggests that refusing to participate in sacrificing to the emperor produced tensions on a local level that could turn violent. Perhaps this is what happened with Antipas, the witness mentioned in Rev 2:13.

The rest of the book of Revelation provides graphic descriptions of the coming defeat and punishment of Rome and Satan. The call to worship "the one who made the heavens and the earth and the sea and the springs of water" (Rev 14:7) is juxtaposed with a picture of eternal torment of those who worship the beast (Rev 14:9–11). Throughout these violent scenes, the task of the faithful believer is to endure (Rev 13:10; 14:12). The violence against Rome and Satan is carried out by others, whether by the angels of God pouring bowls of his wrath or locking up Satan in a bottomless pit (Rev 16:1–21; 20:1–3), or the warrior rider striking down enemies with the sword of his mouth (Rev 19:11–18). And even though there are heavenly armies present, they are not shown engaged in the battle. The book takes us to the brink of the battle, but it is over before it starts (Rev 19:19–20). There is no question about who will win a contest between God and his opponents. Instead, the main point of these visions is to depict God's vengeance and punishment on his defeated enemies.

The final scenes complete the fantasy of a fallen Rome and the defeated evil power of Satan. A new holy city of Jerusalem comes down from heaven to a new earth. This new city will be home to God so that "God will dwell with humanity" (Rev 21:1–4). This is the hope offered to those living under the oppression of the empire.

FOCUS TEXT

Revelation 17–18

Although we will discuss two other New Testament texts below, the focus text for this chapter will be from Revelation, so we include it here. Revelation 17–18 expresses the most explicit anti-Roman sentiment in the entire New Testament. Up to this point, the author of Revelation has led the audience to visualize the wrath of God being exacted on Satan, "the beast," the earth, and most of its inhabitants. In these chapters, the focus is on the city of Rome itself, personified as "the **whore of Babylon**" (Figure 15.2). The image of the whore is introduced in chapter 17, where she is described as clothed in jewels and royal colors (Rev 17:1–6). She bears the name "Babylon the great, mother

of whores and of earth's abominations" on her forehead. The text also makes explicit that she is, in fact a city, "the great city that rules over the kings of the earth" (Rev 17:18). In the author's time, this could only have been Rome. Thus, the author draws on Israel's past trauma with a foreign empire, Babylon, which destroyed the first Temple, to symbolize the source of the community's present trauma. The figure of the prostitute is also familiar from Israel's scriptures (e.g. Hosea), but in Revelation it is used differently. Whereas Israel's prophets evoked the figure of the prostitute as a critique of wayward Israel, here the figure is used in reference to the enemy city. The fact that she is "drunk with the blood of the saints and the blood of the witnesses to Jesus" suggests the author is aware of instances of suffering at the hands of the Romans, perhaps under Nero. Revelation 17 concludes with an image of the destruction of the personified city. She will be stripped, devoured, and burned with fire (Rev 17:16). The fantasized scene indicates the levels of hostility directed toward Rome, but is yet another place in the Bible where the body of a woman is used in disturbing ways to convey the judgment of God.

Figure 15.2 The whore of Babylon, whose image has captured the imaginations of artists for hundreds of years. This 1809 pen and watercolor was done by the artist and poet William Blake.

MORE ON METHOD: CULTURAL CRITICISM OF THE BIBLE

Cultural criticism is interested in the interactions between the Bible and culture. In particular, it focuses on the use of the Bible in popular contemporary culture. Cultural critics might focus on appropriations of the Bible in Hollywood films, popular novels, television, comic books, advertisements, clothing, jewelry, and so on. Indeed, the possibilities for study are almost endless. On the flip side, cultural criticism also studies the way that popular culture influences the interpretation of the Bible.

The Revelation to John is a prime candidate for this approach to the Bible, given the ongoing popular fascination with end times. One might study the use of images from Revelation in artwork, such as the painting of the whore of Babylon shown in Figure 15.2. Or one might study the best-selling popular fiction series *Left Behind* by Tim LaHaye and Jerry B. Jenkins, exploring what images and ideas from Revelation are used in the novels and to what end. Conversely, one might examine how the interpretation of Revelation has been influenced by reading it through the lens of these novels.

For more on cultural criticism see J. Cheryl Exum and Stephen D. Moore, eds., *Biblical Studies/ Cultural Studies* (Sheffield: Sheffield Academic Press, 1998).

Revelation 18 reflects the deep frustrations at the wealth and luxury put on display by Rome and the longing to exact revenge from both the city and those who grew rich along with it. The chapter opens with an angelic announcement of the city's demise: "Fallen, fallen is Babylon the great!" The chapter is modeled on Ezekiel 27, which details the luxury and trading practices of the city of Tyre, and predicts the day of its ruin. Likewise, Revelation 18 details the luxury of Rome and its eventual destruction. Indeed, the entire chapter is a celebration of Rome's downfall and a call for God's people to come out from the city. Her punishment is viewed as what she deserves – "render to her as she herself has rendered" (18:6). The "sins" in view in this chapter are economic in nature. As we saw in the discussion of Revelation 13, the leaders of the Roman empire grew rich off the lands it conquered, as did those who cooperated with imperial expansion (see Rev 18:3). Notice the detailed list of the cargo sold to Rome by the "merchants of the earth," which concludes with a reference to trading in "human lives," that is, slaves (18:12–13). But while the rich grew richer, the poor grew poorer. As Adela Collins outlines in *Crisis and Catharsis*, we have reports of various types of disenfranchisement of the poor – cutting them out of local assemblies, denying citizenship to the working class, and hoarding grain to exact higher prices.

Although the chapter so far has spoken of the destruction of Rome as a past event, the concluding verses return to the future tense: "With sudden violence Babylon the great city will be thrown down" (18:21). This shift to the future exemplifies a tendency seen throughout the book of Revelation in which past, present, and future are mixed. Perhaps the point of this mix is to enable the audience to envision and fantasize about the utter demise of Rome, while also admitting that its destruction is still a future event.

Hebrews: Platonic Perspectives on Christ

READING
Hebrews 1:1–14;
4:14–10:39.

EXERCISE
What new image of Jesus do you see in this text? What does the text suggest about Jesus's relationship to the Jewish traditions? How does the heavenly sanctuary compare to the earthly one?

If the Revelation to John is the clearest example of resistance to Rome, Hebrews seems the most removed from such concerns. At first glance, there is little to suggest that the author has anything in mind but Jesus's relation to Jewish tradition, in particular the Jewish sacrificial cult. Nevertheless, the text is a fascinating combination of cultural influences and thus a clear example of the type of hybrid text generated in an imperial context. As we will see, the author is steeped in the multi-faceted Greco-Roman culture, combining a Platonic worldview with Jewish scriptural and cultic references in the service of his unique image of Christ. And, like other images of Christ that we have seen in the New Testament, this one too parallels images of Roman imperial authority. Moreover, Hebrews also develops themes of alienation and marginalization, suggesting that this author recognized the difficulty of living under imperial authority. Finally, as we will see, even the interest in the Jewish sacrificial cult may result from the pressures of colonization.

Hebrews first circulated with the collection of Pauline letters, although it nowhere purports to be by Paul. Nor is it really a letter, like the other Pauline letters. Aside from the concluding benediction and greetings (Heb 13:20–5), Hebrews is more of a homily than a letter. Even the earliest church writers did not think it was written by Paul. The second-century writer Origen asserted that "only God knows" who wrote it. Nor do scholars agree on when or where in the empire this text was written, although many see Rome as a likely possibility. The fact that greetings are sent from "those in Italy" (Heb 13:24) is offered in support of this view. What we do know for certain is that the author was well educated. The Greek of Hebrews is the most sophisticated of the New Testament writings, and its ideas are tightly woven together in an elegant style.

The central image of the text is a distinctive one: the author presents Christ as a high priest offering an atoning sacrifice for "the sins of the people" (2:17). Although there are certainly references in other New Testament writings to the sacrificial nature of the death of Jesus (see, for example, Paul's sacrificial language in 1 Cor 5:7 or Rom 3:25), only in Hebrews is Jesus presented as the priest who carries out the sacrifice. Specifically, Christ is depicted as high priest according to the order of Melchizedek (Heb 5:10; 6:20; 7:1–3). If you have never heard of Melchizedek, there is good reason. The name occurs *basics* Hebrews

Date and   Much about Hebrews remains unclear to modern scholars: author, date, place of
authorship composition are all difficult to determine with any certainty. As mentioned in Chapter
10, the author is unknown, in spite of the early association of this text with the
Pauline epistles. Proposed dates for the composition of Hebrews range from the 60s
to the 90s CE, with the debate centering on whether the text was written before or
after the destruction of the Temple in 70 CE. There is no explicit recognition of the
Temple's demise, but Hebrews' focus on the heavenly sanctuary and high priesthood
of Jesus could well be a response to its destruction. Similarly, the admission that "we
have no enduring city" (13:14) suggests an awareness of Jerusalem's destruction.
Given this, it seems most likely that the text was written post-70 CE. As for location,
most scholars now think the text was directed toward the church in Rome. There is
one reference to location in Heb 13:24 ("those from Italy greet you"), which may
indicate greetings from fellow Italians now living outside of Italy sending greetings
to the church in Rome. In addition, the earliest text that quotes Hebrews, *1 Clement*,
is a letter written by the Roman bishop Clement in the late first or early second
century.

in a brief account in Gen 14:18–20, where Melchizedek is described as both a king and
a priest who blesses Abraham. The only other reference to Melchizedek occurs in Ps
110:4, where the Davidic king is also called "a priest forever in the order of Melchizedek."
For the author of Hebrews, this double identity of king and priest was important. We
should not forget that a major role of the Roman emperor was that of high priest,
pontifex maximus, and thus mediator with the gods on behalf of the people. So too the
Jesus of Hebrews lives always to intercede for those who approach God (Heb 7:25). And
here we see the superiority of Jesus to earthly high priests, whether the Levitical high
priesthood (from which the author explicitly distinguishes the priesthood of Jesus), or
the high priesthood of the Roman emperor. In reading Gen 14:17–20, the author of
Hebrews notes the lack of a genealogy provided for Melchizedek and interprets this
lack as an indication of the eternal nature of his priesthood: "neither having beginning
of days nor having end of life, like the Son of God, he remains a priest forever"
(Heb 7:3). So, too, the priesthood of Jesus is permanent and eternal (Heb 7:23–4).

The reflection of the high priesthood of Jesus also reveals the fundamentally Platonic worldview of the author of Hebrews. The Greek philosopher Plato (427–347 BCE) believed that the objects that made up the earthly material world were imperfect reflections of the true ideal (and immaterial) forms of these objects. In Platonic thought, for example, a physical chair is merely a copy of the eternal idea of a more real and perfect chair. This **Platonic theory of forms**, as well as other aspects of Plato's thought, continued to influence Christian writers until well into the fifth century CE. The early stages of this influence are evident in Hebrews. In this text, the Levitical priests offer sacrifices in a sanctuary that is a "copy and shadow" of the heavenly one (Heb 8:5). But as high priest, Jesus has entered not an earthly sanctuary, "a copy of the true one," but rather what is truly real, "heaven itself" (Heb 9:24). Even the law is but "a shadow of coming good things, and not the form itself of these things" (Heb 10:1). Thus, the author uses this Platonic scheme to underscore the superiority of Jesus over various aspects of the Jewish cultic and legal traditions (see especially Heb 3:1–3; 7–9). In discussion of the gospels, we saw how such Christian assertions of superiority over Judaism were reflections of the sort of inter-group competition often created by colonization. The fact that Hebrews uses a Platonic structure to promote this view is another reflection of the effect of such imperial forces on inter-group relations, and also shows the persistent influence of Greek thought into the Roman period.

Finally, there may be a more direct link between the Platonic perspective of Hebrews and associations with imperial authority. In Heb 1:3, Jesus is described as an exact representation of God's real being. Here the author draws on a standard Greco-Roman political theory in which an ideal ruler is understood to embody reason and law, or, to use the Greek phrase, divine *logos*. To speak of the relationship between Jesus and God as one of "exact representation" highlights Jesus's own exact image of divine essence and authority, and offers a subtle critique of similar claims made of the Roman emperor. Moreover, the fact that Jesus is an exact representation stands in contrast to the shadows and copies mentioned throughout the text that do *not* convey the true essence of the form they copy.

While most of Hebrews is concerned with presenting a particular understanding of Jesus, there are also exhortations directed toward the audience. These sections show how the author understands the community's position in the world. For example, in a list of examples of faithful ancestors, the "great cloud of witnesses" (12:1), the author points to times when some lived as strangers and foreigners on the earth in search of a better homeland (11:13–14). But unlike the land promised to the ancient Hebrews, the better homeland of the Hebrews text is a heavenly reality (11:16). Still, at this point, the distance between the past wandering ancestors and the present believers collapses as the author switches verb tenses to declare that God "is not ashamed to be called God by them and in fact has prepared a city for them" (11:16). Later, the author reminds the audience that they have not come to a material reality that can be touched (12:18), but rather to the heavenly city of Jerusalem (12:22). Like Jesus, who was executed outside the gates of Jerusalem, believers are to go "outside the camp," for they have no lasting city, but are looking for the city that is to come (Heb 13:14). Thus, the author offers a subtle critique of present imperial rule. It is neither permanent, nor ideal.

Rather, drawing on the Platonic perspective of reality discussed above, the author suggests that the experience of earthly life in the empire only leaves them longing and searching for a better homeland.

1 Peter: Living as Aliens and Accommodating to the Empire

READING

1 Peter.

EXERCISE

How would you describe the situation of the intended audience for this writing? How does the author instruct the audience to live as believers in Christ?

Our third and final example of a variation in New Testament responses to empire is 1 Peter. Like Hebrews, 1 Peter introduces a theme of alienation – it opens with an address to "aliens in the diaspora" (1:1). **Diaspora** is a transliteration of the Greek word for "scattering," and in a Jewish context it refers to Jewish people living as foreigners in regions outside of Palestine. Like Revelation, 1 Peter is directed toward communities scattered across Asia Minor – Pontus, Galatia, Cappadocia, Asia, and Bithynia (1:1) are all Roman provinces in Asia Minor. Intended to circulate in a particular region, 1 Peter is an example of a "diaspora letter." It resembles other Jewish diaspora letters like Jer 29:4–23 and a number of Septuagint texts, such as Baruch (a letter associated with Jeremiah's scribe) and the epistle of Jeremiah. These texts often evoke themes of alienation and exhort those living in exile to conduct themselves in particular ways. So also, 1 Peter exhorts the readers to live "in fear" during their time of alienation (1:17) and to conduct themselves honorably as "aliens and strangers" (2:11). Some scholars have argued that this language should be taken literally, and that the letter addresses actual communities of exiles living in Asia Minor. But given what we have already seen in texts like the Gospel of John and Hebrews, it is more likely that the language of exile and alienation is used metaphorically to describe the relationship between believers and the world. They are no longer at home in the world, but live as aliens in a foreign land.

A second major theme of 1 Peter helps explain this feeling of alienation. Throughout the text, the author points to the experience of suffering on the part of the believers (1:6; 3:14; 4:12–19). There is no specific mention of physical suffering. Instead, the author suggests that the communities were experiencing the sort of local mistreatment

basics | 1 Peter

Outline:	I	Opening salutation and thanksgiving	1:1–12
an elder's letter	II	Letter body: the identity and proper conduct of the people	
to the churches		of God – accommodation and persistence	1:13–5:11
of Asia Minor	III	Concluding greetings and wishes	5:11–12

Date and authorship   The text purports to be from "Peter, an apostle of Jesus Christ," but few scholars believe that Peter was the author. Not only is it written in a sophisticated Greek style, but there is nothing in the text to suggest that Peter, a disciple of Jesus, wrote it. It is thus an example of a pseudonymous early Christian writing. Such texts would use the name of an esteemed figure in the tradition to enhance the authority of the text. Most scholars think the text was written in Rome, probably sometime after 70 CE.

that was discussed above. For example, the author writes of their being accused of doing evil (2:12), of fear, intimidation, and slander (3:14–17), and of insult (4:14–16). If this is their experience, it is no wonder that they feel alienated from the world!

But whereas the Revelation to John deals with the experience of alienation by adopting an openly hostile resistance toward Rome, the author of 1 Peter takes a different approach. He urges those suffering to live in ways that conform closely to the standards of Roman society. They are to live honorably (2:12) and subject to all authorities, whether the emperor or governors sent by him to punish evildoers and reward good (2:12–14). Indeed, they are to honor everyone and especially to "Honor the emperor" (2:17). Here is the fascinating possibility that the author may actually be advocating honoring the emperor in the sacrificial cult. Although many scholars have suggested that the author means to say "Do anything to honor the emperor *but* offering sacrifice," there are no such qualifications in the text. On the contrary, the author's overall stance – that his readers should not give cause for gentiles to despise them – would suggest conformity even to the imperial cult. Indeed, Warren Carter has made a compelling case that what the author advocates is precisely public accommodation to the civic demands of life under imperial rule while private convictions to Christ are maintained. Note, for example, the author urging believers to revere Christ in their hearts (1 Pet 3:15). They are to do so while being zealous to "do good." This doing good, Carter argues, likely refers to a general sense of civic good conduct, since no mistreatment will come to them if they conduct themselves in this way (1 Pet 3:13).

In addition to advocating "doing good," the author assumes that the community should embrace the same hierarchical relationships that shaped the social structure of the Greco-Roman world. Slaves should submit to the authority of their masters – "not only to those who are good and gentle but also to those who are perverse" (1 Pet 2:18). Wives should be submissive to their husbands (1 Pet 3:1). Husbands are to honor their wives, the "weaker female vessels" (1 Pet 3:7). The younger should submit to the elders (1 Pet 5:5). None of these exhortations would be unusual for the readers of 1 Peter, and this is not the first time we have seen these hierarchical relationships reinforced in an early Christian text. Similar household codes were used in the Deutero-Pauline letters (Col 3:18–4:1; Eph 5:21–6:9). Paul himself urged people to remain in whatever social position they were in when they became believers (1 Cor 7:17). In 1 Peter, the author draws on these standard codes of conduct to encourage cultural conformity among the community of believers.

Indeed, amidst the identification of the intended audience as aliens and strangers in the world, the general argument of the letter is to urge these believers to conduct themselves in ways that conform to the expectations of their society. It may well be that this was a deliberate strategy of accommodation, employed by the author to help the community avoid ongoing harassment by their neighbors and local authorities.

Conclusion: Three Different Relationships to the Roman Empire

Although we have not attempted here to discuss all the remaining texts of the New Testament, this chapter has shown diverse ways that certain authors outside of the gospels and Pauline traditions responded to the challenge of living as a follower of Jesus during the late first century in the Greco-Roman world. The Revelation to John, Hebrews, and 1 Peter all suggest that life in the empire was difficult at best, and a life of suffering at worst. However, each text presents a different approach to this reality. The apocalyptic text of Revelation takes a stance of hostile resistance toward Rome. It engages the audience in an extended fantasy in which they are invited to witness God's violent destruction of Rome. This vision of divine justice includes the ultimate promise of a restored Jerusalem where God will dwell alongside the people and wipe away their every tear. In contrast, Hebrews at first glance appears largely detached from the Roman political and economic sphere. It more directly engages the Jewish sacrificial cult, presenting an image of Jesus as a superior high priest and king. Nevertheless, even this image is a subtle way of pointing to Christ as superior also to the emperor. Similarly, the author's Platonic perspective allows him to highlight the perfection of Jesus, seated in the heavenly temple alongside God, in unspoken contrast to the imperfections of the present earthly imperial rule. Thus, Hebrews' more philosophical perspective results in a more subtle, intellectual critique of Rome compared to the bloody spectacles imagined in Revelation. Finally, 1 Peter urges accommodation to Roman authority and culture, even while it recognizes the alienated position of its audience. In stark contrast to Revelation, it looks toward a way of peaceful existence in the world, one that enables believers to fit into their cultural surroundings, while still maintaining their basic commitment to Christ.

CHAPTER FIFTEEN REVIEW

1. Know the meaning and significance of the following terms:
- diaspora
- Platonic theory of forms
- whore of Babylon

2. If Revelation was not designed primarily to inspire fear, what was it meant to do?

3. In what ways do the Revelation to John, Hebrews, and 1 Peter reflect distress in the audiences that they address? How does this compare with evidence in Roman sources for persecution of Christians?

4. What is the difference between the apparent positions of Revelation and 1 Peter on the issue of honoring and sacrificing to the Roman emperor? How does this reflect the different ways that Revelation and 1 Peter respond to alienation in their audiences?

5. How does the epistle of Hebrews, with its Platonic perspective, subtly critique the Roman empire through emphasizing how Jesus is an "exact representation of God's true being"?

6. How would you summarize in three sentences the different ways in which Revelation, Hebrews, and 1 Peter relate to their Roman imperial context?

RESOURCES FOR FURTHER STUDY

Attridge, Harold. W. *The Epistle to the Hebrews*. Hermeneia. Philadelphia: Fortress, 1989.

Barr, David L., ed. *Reading the Book of Revelation: A Resource for Students*. Atlanta: Society of Biblical Literature, 2003.

Carter, Warren. "Going all the Way? Honoring the Emperor and Sacrificing Wives and Slaves in First Peter 2.13–3.6," in *Feminist Companion to the Catholic Epistles and Hebrews*, eds A. J. Levine and Marianne Blickenstaff. London: T & T Clark, 2005.

Collins, Adela Yarbo. *Crisis and Catharsis: The Power of the Apocalypse*. Philadelphia: Westminster Press, 1984.

Horrell, David G. *1 Peter*. New Testament Guides. London and New York: T & T Clark, 2008.

Kovacs, Judith, and Rowland, Christopher. *Revelation*. Blackwell Bible Commentaries. Oxford and Malden, MA: Blackwell, 2004.

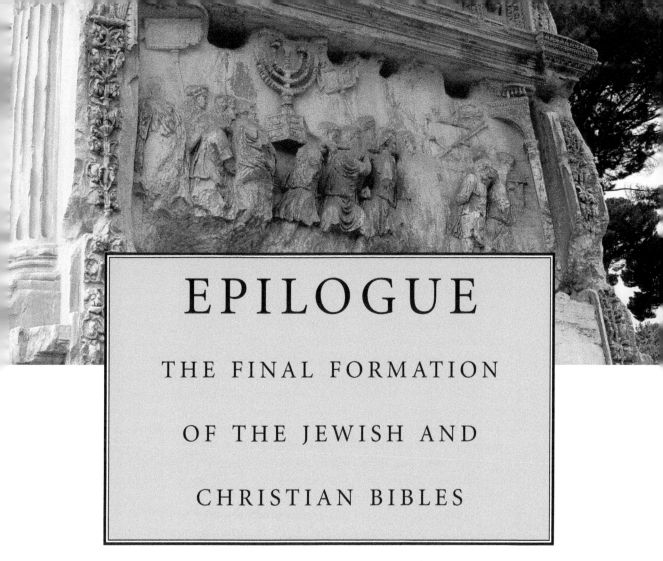

EPILOGUE

THE FINAL FORMATION

OF THE JEWISH AND

CHRISTIAN BIBLES

While we have come to the end of our study of the Bible, we have not yet discussed the final formation of the Christian Bible, or the shaping of the Hebrew scriptures into the "Tanach" used by Jewish communities. One of the most frequent questions about the Bible is how particular books got to be included, and others excluded. Was there a conscious decision to exclude certain books because of political reasons? Or was it a gradual process that was later ratified by church or rabbinic groups? Or something else? This epilogue addresses these questions.

Unfortunately, we do not have much direct evidence for the factors that led to the definition of what was in scripture in the Jewish and Christian communities. What we can say is that most scholars believe that the books in the Bible, including the books of the New Testament, were not originally written to be part of a separate "Bible." Indeed, some books, such as Paul's letter to Philemon about the slave Onesimus, seem to have started as private correspondence. As we saw in discussion of the origins of writing in early Israel, many early Israelite writings probably were meant to educate generations of students, serving as objects of study and memorization. Especially in a largely oral culture, such written works were seen as particularly old and holy, but they were not set apart from other texts. That is why prophets, royal historians, and others could keep producing new such writings up into the Hellenistic period. This shows that there is a significant distinction between the production and circulation of a work for reading and education and the process of "canonization." It is one thing to produce a work and for it to become popular. It is another to set up a collection of such works, a "canon," and thus separate it from all other books.

As we saw in Chapter 8, the first move toward such canonization came (at the earliest) in the latter part of the Hellenistic period, when the Hasmonean monarchs promoted a defined collection of *Hebrew* "Torah and Prophets" to counter the similarly sharply defined Greek curriculum of pre-Hellenistic authors (Homer and others). Yet even while the Hasmoneans promoted such an authoritative collection, there were other Jewish groups that did not recognize it. The Jewish community at Qumran who collected the Dead Sea Scrolls worked with a broader collection of scriptures, as did early Christian groups. For example, the New Testament letter of Jude cites the book of Enoch as if it were scripture (Jude 14–15). Not yet fully separated from Judaism, such early Christians worked with a collection of Jewish scriptures that included a variety of Jewish works not included in the narrower group of Hebrew "Torah and Prophets." This was especially true as Christianity became a largely Greek-speaking phenomenon. Indeed, quite early in the development of the church, Christians were working with the Greek versions of authoritative Jewish books (Genesis, Isaiah, etc.), as well as some works originally written in Greek (such as the Wisdom of Solomon). In sum, even if the Hasmoneans tried to define something like a Hebrew Bible, there still were plenty of Jewish groups – including early Christians – who worked with a broader and more flexible idea of scripture that included other books.

The books now in the New Testament were written and collected in this environment. Early on, the four canonical gospels began circulating together. Similarly the Pauline epistles soon circulated as a collection. Other texts were slower to gain universal acceptance and were more popular in one area or another. Revelation, for instance, was popular in the Western churches, but came under critique from some of the Christian writers in the East. Conversely, the letter of Hebrews was more popular in the Eastern church, and only reached acceptance in the West at a later point. Some early Christian works, such as the Shepherd of Hermas, seem to have gained initial acceptance in certain Christian circles, even though they were not ultimately included in the later New Testament. And still other works, such as an early form of the Gospel of Thomas, may have been in circulation as well. But there was no "New Testament."

So what, one may ask, led to the creation of the Jewish Tanach (Torah, Prophets, and Writings) on the one hand and the Christian Bible (Old and New Testaments) on the other? How did these communities find consensus on what books to include? Why did they seek such definition?

We cannot be sure, but it seems that unity on these questions of scripture was connected to the consolidation and unification of Judaism on the one hand and Christianity on the other. Judaism achieved a new level of unity in the wake of the first Jewish revolt (discussed in Chapters 11 and 15) and a second revolt that occurred in 132–5 CE. These revolts provoked a devastating Roman response, including the total destruction of Jerusalem, the elimination of dissident groups such as that found at Qumran, and the decline of diverse Jewish communities across the Mediterranean. Within this context, rabbinic scholars connected to the Pharisaic movement succeeded in unifying Judaism around a growing body of oral legal tradition that was later written down (particularly the Mishnah and Talmud). We first see regular references to an authoritative collection of "Torah, Prophets, and Writings," a "Tanach," in the writings of these scholars from the third and fourth centuries CE. To return to our theme of empire, this standardized three-part Tanach thus emerges as a unifying point for Judaism in the wake of imperial, Roman destruction.

Meanwhile, Christianity underwent its own form of consolidation during the same early centuries of the common era. We know from the diverse writings collected at Nag Hammadi in Egypt and other sources that there were many different sorts of Christian groups in the first and second centuries CE, some of which produced texts that were not included in the New Testament. Most early Christian groups seem to have worked with some form of the Jewish scriptures, usually Greek forms of Jewish books, but there was no standardized group of Christian writings. Indeed, the first generations of Christians actually seem to have valued oral traditions about Jesus passed down through authorities over written documents that could be falsified. Rarely, the earliest Christian authors would mention written authoritative works of the "Apostles" alongside Jewish books of "Prophets."

This situation changed as Christianity grew and consolidated itself as a centralized religious movement that was separate from Judaism (see Map 16.1). The Jewish scriptures were still valued, but came to be defined as part of a separate "Old Testament." Certain early Christian writings, ones valued in the church, used in the liturgy, and deemed to originate from one of the original apostles, came to be part of a "New Testament." In the third and fourth centuries theologians produced varying lists of what books were included in each part of the "Old" and "New Testament." Generally, theologians working in the Western Mediterranean included a broader range of books, while theologians working in the East had more restrictive lists.

By the end of the third century (200s) the church agreed on virtually all books to be included in the Old and New Testaments, but a new level of agreement came in the early fourth century when Constantine became the first Christian emperor of the broader Roman empire (Figure 16.1). At this point, Christianity started to make the final transition from being a movement under empire to becoming the religion of the empire. Divisions among Christians were threats to the unity of the imperial realm. Over the following century, a series of ecumenical councils was convened to resolve disputed theological matters. Most of these councils focused on issues of Christology, but several councils (such as those at Hippo in 393 and Carthage in 397 and 418) produced authoritative lists of which books were included in the Christian Bible. These lists included more Jewish texts in the Old Testament than were found in the Tanach of contemporary Judaism, and they included a range of early Christian works, such as Revelation and Hebrews, that were valued in different parts of the empire. Meanwhile,

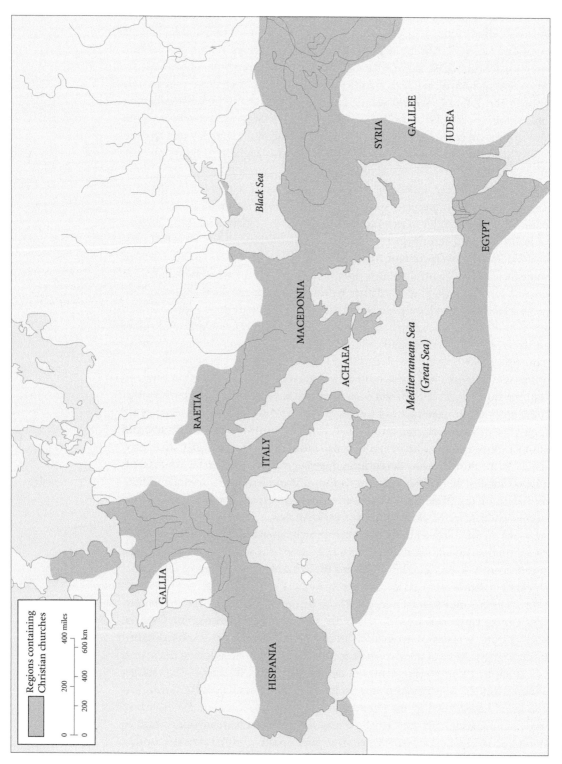

Map 16.1 Spread of Christianity across the Mediterranean world by 300 CE. Redrawn from Bart Ehrman, *The New Testament: A Historical Introduction to the Early Christian Writings* (3rd edition). Oxford: Oxford University Press, 2004, page 43.

Figure 16.1 Bust of Constantine, who acceded to the throne in 306 and secured control of the whole Roman empire in 324 CE. He ended persecution of Christians and began to use imperial power to resolve inter-Christian disputes.

some early Christian works associated with dissident Christian groups, and/or works whose connection to an apostle was not established, were excluded.

In this way the final definition of the Christian Bible was facilitated by the Christianization of the Roman empire, or one might say the imperialization of Christianity. Some forms of Christianity that developed outside the immediate orbit of the Roman empire, such as the Ethiopian, Armenian, and Syrian churches, went their own way in terms of canon and developed somewhat different lists of the contents of the Old and New Testaments. Nevertheless, by the third and fourth centuries the pattern was set. Judaism had a twenty-four-book, three-part Tanach of books largely written in Hebrew. Christianity had a two-part Bible, consisting of an Old Testament (generally the Greek Septuagint) and a New Testament (see Figure 16.2). And just a couple of centuries later, we would see the emergence in Arabia of another important text, incorporating some Jewish and Christian traditions and somewhat modeled on their idea of scripture: the Muslim Koran of the prophet Mohammed.

For the following centuries these scriptural corpora have played crucial roles not just in the religious communities where they have their home, but in the cultural and political contexts connected to those communities. From the eighteenth to the twentieth centuries, the teaching of the Christian Bible was a central aspect of European evangelization and colonization. Even now, debates about the Bible play a central role in disputes about the boundaries of the nation of Israel or the legality of same-sex marriage. In these ways and many others, the rich range of texts now collected in the Old and New Testaments continue to play a major role in people's lives, both religious and not. Deeper knowledge of those texts helps one become a more informed participant in a world still dominated by empires and infused with these scriptures.

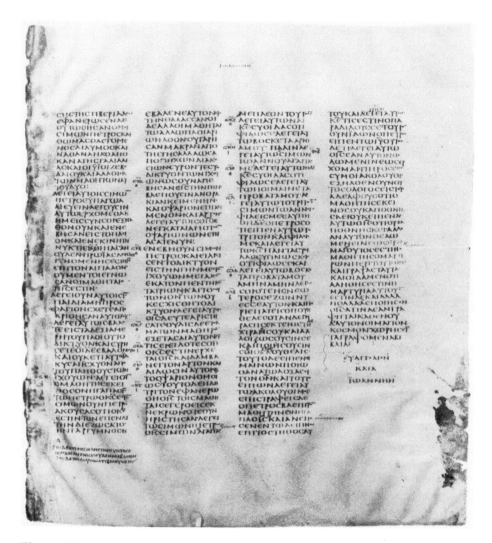

Figure 16.2 The Codex Sinaiticus. This Greek manuscript from the fourth century is one of the earliest complete copies of the entire Old and New Testaments.

GLOSSARY

Each entry includes (in parentheses) reference to the first location where a term is discussed, whether Prologue or chapter number, along with other major location(s). **Boldface** indicates terms that occur elsewhere in this Glossary.

act-consequence (3) – see **moral act-consequence**.

apocalypse (8) – a text commonly attested in the Hellenistic and later periods that describes a heavenly revelation to a human recipient, often a human recipient from Israel's distant past (e.g. Enoch, Levi, etc.; see **pseudepigraphy**). Such apocalypses appear in two main types, the heavenly apocalypse and the historical apocalypse, frequently show priestly connections, and feature much focus on esoteric knowledge.

apocalyptic (9) – predicting or describing the end of the current, unjust age and the arrival of a new age through God's direct intervention in history.

apocalypticism (9) – see **apocalyptic worldview**.

apocalyptic worldview (10) or **apocalypticism** (9) – a worldview, or social movement associated with the worldview, which emphasizes God's anticipated intervention in history, thus bringing the current, corrupt world order to an end. In this view, the unjust are punished, those who have suffered are rewarded, and a new, just world order is initiated.

apocrypha (Prologue) – Protestant term for **deutero-canonical books**, in this case designating books that are not viewed in the Protestant tradition as fully **canonical**.

apotheosis (13) – the raising of someone to divine status, typically after their death. This deification was common for deceased Roman emperors and their family members, who were posthumously given the title "*divus*" (for men) or "*diva*" (for women) before their names.

Asherah (2) – the mother goddess of the Canaanite pantheon, consort of the chief god, **El**.

Assyria (4) – a Mesopotamian state based in what is now northern Iraq.

Baal (2) – a storm god in the Canaanite pantheon.

Babylonian exile (1) – 586–538 BCE, a time when most of the elite living in Judah (especially Jerusalem) were forced to live outside the land in Babylon (with many never having the chance to return).

beginning of the Roman period (1) – 63 BCE: the end of the **Hasmonean monarchy** and the beginning of rule of Palestine by rulers appointed by Rome.

Ben Sira (8) – a collection of instructional texts authored in the early second century BCE (c. 200–180 BCE). It is one example of a **deutero-canonical** book included (under its Greek name **Sirach**) in the **Old Testament** of the Roman Catholic and Orthodox churches, but excluded from the Jewish **Tanach** and Protestant Old Testament.

book of the Twelve Prophets (4) – a book in the Jewish **Tanach** that includes the 12 **minor prophets** (Hosea through Malachi).

books of the former prophets (5) – the historical books of Joshua, Judges, 1–2 Samuel, and 1–2 Kings.

canon and canonical (Prologue) – "canon" is a collection of books that are recognized as divinely inspired scripture by a given religious community. Those books are recognized as "canonical."

chiasm (4) – a circular literary form that moves through a set of themes to the center (e.g. A, B, C, D) and then goes through similar themes in reverse order after the center (e.g. D', C', B', A'). Major emphasis is often put on the texts that occur at the center of a chiasm.

client kings (9) – Roman-appointed local leaders who ruled the provinces of Rome for the emperor (considered their "patron"), allowing some level of independence for the province and extended influence by Rome.

conjectural emendation (Prologue) – a correction of the biblical text proposed by scholars that is not based on any **manuscript witness**.

couplet (3) – along with the less common **triplet**, a basic unit in Hebrew poetry, where the first line is paralleled, contrasted, or otherwise **seconded** by the climactic second line. Many translations identify the second line of a couplet by indenting the beginning of the line a few spaces.

Covenant Code (3) – a set of early laws embedded in Exod 20:22–23:33 that (apart from some late additions) seem to predate later regulations asserting the requirement to worship Yahweh in just one place (e.g. Deut 12; cf. 2 Kings 22–3). The parallels between the topics of these laws and large portions of the Code of Hammurabi are an indicator that some form of this collection may have been composed already in the early monarchal period, e.g. tenth or ninth century BCE.

cultural criticism (1) – when applied to the Bible, study of the myriad ways in which biblical texts are reflected or used in popular culture. The focus on popular culture distinguishes the emphasis of cultural critical study of a biblical text from study of its **history of interpretation**.

cultural memory (2) – a common set of memories, taught to each generation and celebrated in common rituals, that help define a group by its shared past.

Cyrus cylinder (7) – a proclamation by the Persian king Cyrus that he was appointed by the Babylonian gods to liberate the Babylonians and rebuild their temples. It shows many parallels to the Cyrus proclamation quoted in Ezra 1:1–4 that Yahweh had appointed him to rebuild the Temple and allow the Judeans to return home.

destruction of Jerusalem (1) – 586 BCE: a climactic event in the history of Judah, including the destruction of Solomon's Temple and the end of the holy city many thought to be invulnerable.

destruction of the Second Temple (1) – 70 CE: occurred in the wake of a Jewish revolt against Rome and – along with the total destruction of Jerusalem in 135 CE after another revolt – repre-sented the end of the local Jewish temple state and the recentering of much Jewish life in the communities outside the land.

deutero-canonical books (Prologue) – books recognized as **canonical** by the Roman Catholic church, but not part of the Jewish **Tanach** or Protestant **Old Testament**.

Deutero-Isaiah (6) – see **Second Isaiah**.

Deuteronomistic (5) – adjective describing biblical texts that feature terminology and/or theology similar to that permeating the book of Deuteronomy.

Deuteronomistic history (5) – a history extending from Moses's speech to Israel on the edge of the land (Deuteronomy) through the books of Joshua, Judges, 1–2 Samuel, and 1–2 Kings to Judah's eventual exile from the land at the end of the books of Kings. Though incorporating potential earlier blocks of tradition (e.g. a possible early "succession narrative"), this broader history of Israel in the land is dominated by the later theology articulated most clearly in Deuteronomy, and is thought by most scholars to have been composed partly in the late seventh century and completed during the exile.

Deutero-Pauline (10) – designation for the disputed Pauline epistles 2 Thessalonians, Ephesians and Colossians. See **disputed letters** of Paul.

diaspora (15) – the "scattering" or dispersion of Jews throughout lands outside of Palestine, particularly during the **Babylonian exile** in the sixth century BCE and after the end of the **Jewish War** in 70 CE.

disputed letters (of Paul) (10) – Pauline letters whose authorship is disputed on the basis of difference in tone, language, or theological positions, or because the letter presupposes a stage in the development of the church that likely postdated Paul. These letters include 2 Thessalonians, Colossians, Ephesians, 1 and 2 Timothy, and Titus.

divided monarchy (1) – 930–722 BCE: a time when there were separate monarchies in the south (based in Jerusalem and ruled by descendents of David) and the north (ultimately based in Samaria and ruled by a variety of royal dynasties).

divine council (6) – the idea that the divine world is organized on analogy with a human monarchal court, with a divine king, his consort, his officials, and other parts of his administration. This idea is reflected in many non-biblical texts as well as in the Bible itself.

double tradition (9) – the material shared by Matthew and Luke (but not Mark or John), which contains the same wording and order in some places. Most scholars believe this material to be a now lost text that they call **Q**.

dynamic equivalence translation (Prologue) – a translation that aims to produce a meaning-for-meaning translation of a (biblical) text, as necessary diverging from a word-for-word translation to produce a more exact and understandable equivalent meaning.

E (6) – see **Elohistic Source**.

ekklesia (12) – a common Greek word, meaning "assembly" or "gathering," that was also a term for some Greco-Roman **voluntary associations**. It is often translated as "church," its later meaning.

El (2) – the name of the head creator god of the Canaanite pantheon, husband of **Asherah**.

election theology (2) – a set of beliefs surrounding God's choosing of and special protection of a people, Israel. Distinguished from **Zion theology** by its focus on God's relationship to a people rather than a place (Jerusalem).

Elohistic Source (6) – a *hypothesized* source of the **Pentateuch** (no separate copies have been found) that many scholars think is preserved in parts of Genesis 20–2 and other **non-Priestly** parts of the Pentateuch where the divine designation "Elohim" predominates (the **Priestly Source** also uses Elohim for God in Genesis, but is seen as distinct from this Elohistic Source). According to this hypothesis, this Elohistic Source was composed in the north of Israel sometime in the late ninth or eighth century, thus coming from a later time and different place from the **Yahwistic Source** (**J**). This textbook is one of a number of recent treatments that has discarded the idea that there is an identifiable **E** source in the Pentateuch, but there are still many references to this hypothesized source in past and some recent scholarship.

empire (2) – as analyzed in this textbook, a form of ancient social organization where a particular monarchal state dominated other states through amassed military power (often drawing on the resources of subject states), creation of interlocking economic networks, and propagandistic use of terror.

eschatology (9 and 10) – an aspect of theology that is concerned with the end of the world, the end of humanity, or the end of the current order of the world.

farewell discourse (14) – Jesus's departing words to the disciples in the Gospel of John (chapters 14–16) in which he prepares the disciples for his absence, describing how he, and thus his disciples, are at odds with the world, and how he will send the **Paraclete** to teach and comfort his disciples.

feminist criticism (1 and 14) – applied to the Bible, a range of methods aimed at analyzing biblical depictions of women (or lack of these depictions) and biblical use of feminine imagery.

formal correspondence translation (Prologue) – a word-for-word translation of a (biblical) text.

form criticism (1, 7, and 9) – the study of different types of texts, **genres**, in the Bible along with their typical social settings and purposes.

former prophets (5) – see **books of the former prophets**.

four-source theory (12) – the theory that the Gospel of Mark, **Q**, (**M**), and (**L**) were used in different combinations for writing the **synoptic gospels**. The four-source theory is the most commonly accepted solution to the **synoptic problem**.

fulfillment citations (12) – the repeated claim that aspects of Jesus's life story "happened in order to fulfill" or actualize the words of the **Torah** and the prophets. These citations constitute a distinctive emphasis in the Gospel of Matthew.

gender criticism (1 and 14) – applied to the Bible, the analysis of the ways gender categories function in biblical texts, not just in terms of male and female characters, but also with respect to gendered metaphors, images, and even sacrificial animals.

genre (7) – a type of text, such as a **lament psalm** or **prophetic call narrative**.

Greco-Roman period (9) – with respect to the New Testament, the period beginning with the Roman invasion of Palestine in 63 BCE, characterized by the ongoing influence of Greek culture (including art, architecture, social organization, and values) in the broader Mediterranean world during a time of Roman rule.

H (6) – a designation either for the **Holiness Code** in Leviticus 17–26 or for a broader layer of material in the **Tetrateuch** that is characterized by the central emphases of Leviticus 17–26 (e.g. the importance of Israel's holiness).

Hanukkah (8) – the Jewish holiday celebrating the rededication of the **Second Temple** by Judas Maccabeus in 164 BCE after it had been temporarily transformed by Antiochus Epiphanes IV into a temple to Zeus Olympius.

Hasmonean monarchy (1) – 142–63 BCE: the period of rule of members of the Hasmonean priestly family descended from Judas Maccabeus, who led a successful rebellion against the Hellenistic rule of Antiochus Epiphanes IV.

Hasmoneans (8) – a provincial priestly family who led a revolt against Antiochus Epiphanes IV and eventually founded the **Hasmonean monarchy**.

Hebrew Bible (Prologue) – scriptures shared by Jews and Christians.

Hellenistic period (1) – 332–167 BCE: a period when, following the conquest of the Persian empire by Alexander, Palestine was ruled by a succession of Greek kings based in Egypt (the Ptolemies), Anatolia (contemporary Turkey), or Mesopotamia (the Seleucids).

historical criticism (1) – a family of historical methods that analyzes how and where the biblical texts (and oral traditions in them) were composed.

historical Jesus (9) – the Jesus who is the person behind, but still separate from, the narratives about him in early Christian texts. Scholars have drawn conclusions about the historical Jesus by paying attention to the ways these texts contain overlapping and distinctive traditions about Jesus's life and teachings, and by applying the methods of **historical criticism** to these traditions.

history of interpretation (1) – study of how biblical texts have been interpreted, especially in faith communities (e.g. Judaism, Christianity, Islam). The particular emphasis on interpretation in faith communities distinguishes history of interpretation from **cultural critical** study of how such texts are reflected in popular culture.

history of religions (6) – a term used in biblical scholarship to refer to the study of ideas and themes relating to gods and ritual in ancient Near Eastern cultures outside Israel so that we might better understand biblical religious ideas and practices.

Holiness Code (6) – a collection of laws in Leviticus 17–26 *hypothesized* to have once existed separately (no separate copies have been found) and characterized by a frequent focus on the need for the people of Israel to preserve its holiness. Many recent scholars believe instead that the language and themes predominant in Leviticus 17–26 are characteristic of a broader layer of **H** material spanning the rest of material in the **Tetrateuch** assigned by others to **P**.

honor (vs. shame) (13) – a cultural value in the ancient Mediterranean that emphasizes personal or family status and reputation in the community.

household codes (10) – in Colossians (3:18–4:1), Ephesians (5:21–6:9), Titus (2:1–10), and 1 Peter (2:18–3:7), specific codes of conduct for how members of households in the community (including husband, wife, children, and slaves) should behave toward one another. These instructions generally mirror common expectations of behavior in Greco-Roman households, which means a strict social hierarchy of patriarch over wife, children, and slaves (in more or less descending order).

ideological criticism (1) – the analysis of ways that biblical texts can be, have been, and should be read in the midst of systemic structures of power. As such it overlaps with other methods (e.g. **history of interpretation**), but with a particular accent on analysis of ideology and power.

intercalation (11) – sometimes called a "sandwich" structure; a narrative technique regularly used in the Gospel of Mark, in which one story or episode is interrupted in the middle by another, complete episode, followed by the ending of the first one. The "inside" episode often offers an interpretation or complication of the story that enfolds it.

incarnation (14) – within the study of the New Testament, the idea of God becoming human and fully embodied in the person of Jesus, signaled especially by the Johannine phrase "word made flesh" (John 1:14).

intertextuality (6) – a word used to refer to the myriad ways different texts can be related to each other. It can refer to conscious or unconscious ways that texts draw on the wording of earlier texts, but also to the ways that the readings of any text can be influenced by what the reader (or reading community) knows of other texts, whether texts dated before or after the text being read.

Israel (1) – two meanings: refers more narrowly to the tribal groups settled in the northern highlands of Canaan or more broadly to Judah (in the south) along with those northern groups.

J (3 and 6) – the one-letter designation of the hypothesized **Yahwistic Source**. The prominent use of the divine "Yahweh" in the Yahwistic Source is only one indicator used to argue for the existence of the source, but it has led to the frequent designation of the source as "J" (the German letter for the "y" sound at the outset of Yahweh).

Jewish War (11) – the war between the Jews of Palestine and the Romans that began in 66 CE with an armed revolt by the Jews, and ended with the destruction of the **Second Temple** and the sack of Jerusalem in 70 CE.

Josiah's reform (5) – approximately 623 BCE: a socio-religious reform that Josiah is said to have undertaken in the wake of the decline of Assyrian influence over the area (2 Kings 23; compare 2 Chronicles 34), eliminating sanctuaries outside Jerusalem and laying claim to some of the territories of the former northern kingdom.

King James Version (Prologue) – an authorized translation of the Christian Bible completed under royal sponsorship by the Church of England in 1611.

Koran (Prologue) – the holiest text in Islam, seen in that faith as the collected recitations by Muhammad, the prophet, of his revelations from God. These recitations refer to biblical traditions, often as filtered through early Jewish and/or Christian interpretation of those traditions.

L (6) – see **Lay Source**.

(L) (12) – material that is found only in the Gospel of Luke.

lament psalm (7) – a type of psalm that is a cry for God's help and typically includes most of the following elements: complaint, plea for help, vow, statement of trust in God's help, and thanksgiving for God's help. Though some refer to such lament psalms simply as "laments," the cry for help typical of a lament psalm is distinguished from a lament

proper by the fact that it does not mourn something that is already finished (e.g. a death). Instead, it is a plea that things may get better. Because of this difference, some scholars prefer to call these lament psalms complaints or supplications.

Lay Source (6) – a term used in this textbook to designate a *hypothesized* source of the **Pentateuch** (no separate copies have been found) that included most of the material in the Pentateuch not assigned to the **Priestly Source** (**P**) in the **Tetrateuch**, along with Deuteronomy. In this book, this material is called the lay source or **L** because it seems to have been put together and transmitted by authors outside the priesthood. Most other scholars would designate this body of texts simply as **non-Priestly** (or **non-P**).

liberation theology (13) – a theological approach that emphasizes the importance of the perspectives of oppressed peoples as well as biblical themes of justice and emancipation from oppressive conditions.

literary criticism (1) – the use of methods from modern study of literary texts (e.g. attention to plot, characterization, signification) to illuminate the poetic-narrative dynamics of biblical texts.

LXX (Prologue) – an abbreviation for **Septuagint**.

(M) (12) – material that is found only in the Gospel of Matthew.

Macabbees (1 and 8) – another word for the **Hasmoneans**.

major prophets (4 and 5) – the three larger prophetic books: Isaiah, Jeremiah, and Ezekiel.

manuscript witness (Prologue) – an ancient copy of a biblical book or quotation of a biblical book (in the original language or translation).

Masoretic text (Prologue) – the authoritative version of the Hebrew text of the **Tanach** or Hebrew Bible produced by Jewish scribes in the medieval period and used as the base text in most translations.

messiah (7) – a Hebrew word meaning "anointed one," which during the **Second Temple** period came to designate a hoped-for anointed king who would deliver Jews from domination and/or a hoped-for anointed priest to replace the priests in Jerusalem who were perceived by some to be corrupt.

messianic secret (11) – a recurring pattern in the Gospel of Mark in which Jesus urges secrecy about his miracles of healing or about his identity.

minor prophets (4) – 12 smaller prophetic books (Hosea, Joel, Amos, Obadiah, Jonah, Micah, Nahum, Habakkuk, Zephaniah, Haggai, Zechariah, and Malachi) that follow the three books of the **major prophets** (Isaiah, Jeremiah, Ezekiel) in the Jewish **Tanach** and appear at the end of the Christian Bible.

monarchal city-state (2) – a state based in a walled city (and often supported by other fortified settlements) and ruled by a hereditary monarchic dynasty. This ancient form of social organization allowed an amassing of military resources and wealth not possible for more decentralized tribal groups.

monotheism (6) – a term referring to the belief that there is only one god and that all other gods are false. This is to be distinguished from the idea, attested up through the late pre-exilic period, that a given people should worship only one god among the various gods that exist, an idea sometimes designated as "henotheism."

moral act-consequence (3) – the idea that the cosmos is morally coherent; that is, morally good actions eventually lead to good results for the doer(s), while morally bad actions lead to disaster.

MT (Prologue) – an abbreviation for the **Masoretic text.**

narrative criticism (11) – applied to the Bible, a method of examining the gospels as literature, attending to such literary aspects as plot, characters, setting, point of view, and narrator.

non-Priestly and non-P (6) – term used to refer to texts in the **Pentateuch** (especially the **Tetrateuch**) not assigned to P. It is used by scholars who no longer believe in the existence of the early **J** and **E** sources.

Old Testament (Prologue) – Christian term for the scriptures originating in ancient Israel. It and the Jewish **Tanach** contain nearly identical books, but the order of the (Christian) Old Testament culminates in Malachi's prophecy of Elijah (leading into Matthew 3).

oral traditions (2) – traditions important at every stage in the formation of the Bible, especially if one includes the oral aspects of written traditions, since even the latter often were memorized and performed. More specifically, we see some reflections in the written traditions of the Bible of exclusively oral traditions, and these reflections are the typical focus of biblical **tradition criticism.**

P (3 and 6) – see **Priestly Source.**

parables (9) – brief, open-ended, comparative stories using metaphor that invite the listener to make conclusions about the nature of the comparison being offered. Jesus is depicted as speaking in parables in the **synoptic gospels**, often comparing the kingdom of God to everyday people, things, and events.

Paraclete (14) – the figure that Jesus describes in the **farewell discourse** of the Gospel of John, who Jesus promises he will send to comfort and guide his disciples after he departs. In 1 John 2:1, Jesus is described as a "paraclete" as well.

passion narrative (11) – from *passus*, a Latin word for "suffering"; the story of Jesus's trial, suffering, and death, which may have been an independent form that predated Mark's gospel.

passion predictions (11) – the instances in the gospels in which Jesus, referring to himself as the "son of Man," anticipates his own approaching suffering and death. Jesus does this three times in Mark, in keeping with Mark's preferred pattern of repeating important information in triplicate.

Pastoral Epistles (10) – 1 and 2 Timothy and Titus, called "pastorals" because they are addressed to particular leaders within Christian communities with instructions for those communities. The Pastoral Epistles were likely written in the second century CE. See **disputed letters** of Paul.

Pentateuch (Prologue and 3) – the first five books of the Bible, namely Genesis, Exodus, Leviticus, Numbers, and Deuteronomy, otherwise known as the (written) **Torah.**

Persian period (1) – 538–332 BCE: a time of Persian rule of Judah, when the Persians are recorded in the Bible as helping the Judeans who returned to rebuild the Temple and walls of Jerusalem and establish the **Torah** as the authoritative law of the returnee community.

Platonic theory of forms (15) – Plato's theory that non-material abstract forms possess a higher form of reality than the material world of sense perception.

postcolonial criticism (1 and 5) – study that examines ways in which texts such as the Bible were formed in imperial contexts and/or how biblical texts later functioned in colonial or imperial contexts (e.g. missionary efforts).

post-exilic period (1) – from 538 BCE: the period following the forced exile to Babylon, starting with the **Persian period**. Often the Persian period is the primary one meant when referring to the post-exilic period. Note: despite the term *post*-exilic, it is clear that many Judeans still lived outside the land after 538 BCE.

pre-state tribal period (1) – 1250–1000 BCE: a time when Israel lived in villages (joined loosely in larger tribal affiliations) in the hill country without any monarch over them.

Priestly Source (3 and 6) – a *hypothesized* source of the **Pentateuch** (no separate copies have been found) which most scholars agree contained texts such as the Genesis 1 creation story, genealogies such as Genesis 5, a strand of the flood narrative where no sacrifice happens (e.g. Gen 6:9–22 to 9:1–17), the covenant of circumcision with Abraham (Genesis 17), the second call of Moses (Exod 6:2–8), the whole section about Sinai (Exodus 19 to Num 10:10), and many other texts in the **Tetrateuch** with similar language and themes (though not all focusing on priests). Though this layer contains much earlier traditions, most scholars agree that the broader Priestly Source was not composed until the **Babylonian exile** or early **post-exilic period**.

primeval history (3) – the stories of creation, flood, and other events concerning early humanity in general found in Genesis 1–11.

pronouncements (9) – short, direct sayings in the form of sharp responses to tricky questions posed by one's rhetorical opponent. The gospels feature Jesus offering such retorts to his opponents.

prophetic call narrative (4) – a story, usually told in the first person, where a prophetic figure tells of how he was authorized by God to be a prophet, usually including some or all of the following elements: an appearance of God, introductory word by God to the one to be called, call of the

prophet, objection by the prophet that he is somehow unfit for the task, divine reassurance, and sign reinforcing the divine reassurance. Examples include Isaiah 6; Jer 1:4–10; and Ezekiel 1–3, though some scholars dispute whether some of these texts are proper "call narratives," and disagree about whether "call" (a term whose home is in later Christian theology) is appropriate for these ancient Hebrew narratives.

Psalter (7) – another word for the book of Psalms.

pseudepigraphy (8) – attribution of a later text to a more ancient author. This was particularly common in the Hellenistic period, when Judaism came into contact with a Greek culture that was more focused on establishing ancient authorship of authoritative texts.

pseudonymous (10) – adjective describing the common ancient literary practice of writing under someone else's name, typically a well-respected or famous author, even if that author were long dead.

Q (9) – a *hypothesized* source (Q stands for *Quelle*, the German word for source) for a set of sayings of Jesus found in Matthew and Luke, but not in Mark. Scholars have supposed that this **double tradition** stems from a Q sayings source, which the authors of Matthew and Luke adapted in different ways.

realized eschatology (14) – the notion in the Gospel of John that the judgment and salvation of the last days is an already present reality for the believer. This is particularly seen in Jesus's words to the Samaritan woman, "The hour is coming and is now here" (John 4:23), as well as in the "I am" statements that emphasize Jesus's incarnational presence.

rebuilding of the Jerusalem Temple (7) – 515 BCE (completion), described in the Bible as done over a period of years with Persian sponsorship: this **Second Temple** represented an important center of leadership and social organization in **post-exilic period** Judah in the years after the destruction of the monarchy.

reception history (1) – designates the study of the complete variety of ways that texts are used over time, in both textual and other (e.g. artistic) media and in various faith community and other contexts.

It thus encompasses the range of both **history of interpretation** and **cultural criticism**.

redaction criticism (1 and 12) – the attempt to identify the ways in which the author or redactors of the present biblical books created those books through arrangement, transformation, and extension of earlier source materials. It is a form of **transmission history**.

royal psalms (3) – a set of psalms in the **Psalter** that focus on the king and God's special relationship to him (see **royal theology**).

royal theology (3) – a set of beliefs and images surrounding God's appointing of the king as ruler and high priest, God's equipping of the king with power, justice, and blessing, and God's granting the king anything he wishes, particularly military victory and long life.

seconding (3) – a term coined by James Kugel in *The Idea of Biblical Poetry* (New Haven: Yale University Press, 1981) for the multiple and complex ways that the final line of a **couplet** or **triplet** can build on the meaning of the initial lines of the given poetic unit. Many find this to be a more flexible and accurate designation for this phenomenon in Hebrew poetry than older and more commonly used terms such as "parallelism."

Second Isaiah (6) – alternatively **Deutero-Isaiah**: term used to refer to chapters 40–55 of the book of Isaiah, a section that shows many signs of being composed during the time of **Babylonian exile** (with parts possibly even later). Almost no scholars today think that the author of these later chapters was named "Isaiah." The term "Second Isaiah" reflects the fact that this portion of the book of Isaiah was the first one to be distinguished from the words of the first "Isaiah," which are now to be found particularly in portions of Isaiah 1–11 and 28–32.

Second Temple (7) – the Temple rebuilt under Persian sponsorship by 515 BCE and eventually destroyed by the Romans in 70 CE, a center for Judean leadership and social organization throughout the intervening period.

segmentary society (2) – a term designating the kind of decentralized, horizontal social framework that tribal Israel had prior to the onset of the monarchy.

Septuagint (Prologue) – an ancient set of translations of **Old Testament** books into Greek.

Sermon on the Mount (12) – Jesus's mountaintop speech in Matthew 5–7, in which Jesus is presented as a figure like Moses, interpreting the **Torah** and giving instructions to his followers.

servant (6) – a term used in parts of **Second Isaiah** that seems to refer to a specific entity or individual, particularly in the **servant songs** of Isaiah. Scholars debate whether this "servant" is a reference to a particular individual or a metaphor in these texts for the people (or sub-group of the people).

servant songs (6) – a set of texts in Isa 42:1–8; 49:1–6; 50:4–9; and 52:13–53:12 that focus on a "**servant**" figure. Some scholars have thought these servant songs might represent a separate literary layer in **Second Isaiah**.

signs source (14) – a hypothesized text used in the composition of the Gospel of John. It contains seven miracle stories that are called "signs" by John, seemingly because they are meant to demonstrate Jesus's significance and identity. See John 2:1–11; 4:46–54; 5:1–9; 6:1–14, 16–21; 9:1–38; 11:1–44.

Sirach (8) – see **Ben Sira**.

social-scientific analysis ( ) – when applied to the Bible, analysis that draws on contemporary sociological and anthropological studies to provide a more nuanced picture of ancient Israel.

source criticism (1) – the attempt to reconstruct the (now lost) written sources used by the authors of the present biblical texts. It is a type of **transmission history**.

suffering servant (9) – the particular image of the **servant** in **Second Isaiah** found in Isa 52:13–53:12, an image that often has been interpreted by Christians to refer to the crucifixion and resurrection of Jesus Christ.

supersessionism (Prologue) – the idea that Christianity and the Christian church have superseded and thus replaced Judaism and the people of Israel.

synoptic gospels (9) – the gospels of Matthew, Mark, and Luke, which have a strong similarity in their story structures and content, as well as some instances of echoed exact wording. "Synoptic" means to "see together."

synoptic problem (9) – the question of how to understand the similarities and differences between the **synoptic gospels** of Matthew, Mark, and Luke. See **two-source theory**.

Syro-Ephraimite war (4) – a war occurring around 735 BCE in which Syria and the northern kingdom of Israel laid siege to Jerusalem and thus attempted to force Judah, under King Ahaz, to join a coalition of local states resisting Assyrian rule (though Judah was not yet under Assyrian rule). Ahaz appealed for and received help from Assyria in repelling the Syrian–Israelite alliance, but became subject to Assyria in return for the aid.

Tanach (Prologue) – the Jewish term for the Hebrew scriptures, referring to the three main parts of those scriptures: the **Torah**, Neviiim (Hebrew for "prophets"), and Ketuvim (Hebrew for "writings"). The arrangement of the Jewish Tanach culminates in Cyrus's promise to rebuild the Temple at the end of 2 Chronicles.

TaNaK (Prologue) – another way of writing **Tanach**.

Tetrateuch (3) – the first four books of the Bible, namely Genesis, Exodus, Leviticus, and Numbers. The portion of the **Pentateuch** that precedes Deuteronomy is formed out of combined **P** and **L** sources.

textual criticism (Prologue) – the collection and analysis of different manuscript readings, e.g. different readings in Hebrew manuscripts and early translations of Hebrew manuscripts of books in the Hebrew Bible.

Torah (Prologue) – the first five books of the Bible, namely Genesis, Exodus, Leviticus, Numbers, and Deuteronomy. Jews often distinguish between this "written Torah" and the "oral Torah" given to Moses, transmitted through the sages, and embodied in the Mishnah and other authoritative Jewish writings.

tradition criticism (1) – the attempt to recover, via the written texts of the Bible, the traditions that stand behind them, usually with a particular focus on the **oral traditions** reflected in the written texts.

tradition history (2) – a history of traditions that existed before and often alongside the written texts now in the Bible. Though such traditions can be written as well as oral, the term often refers primarily to the history of pre-biblical **oral traditions** reconstructed through **tradition criticism**.

transmission history (1) – an umbrella term for the study of the different processes leading up to the final composition of biblical books. It can include **tradition criticism**, **source criticism**, and **redaction criticism**.

trickster (2) – a character whose ability to survive through trickery and even lawbreaking is celebrated in religion, literature, or another part of culture.

triplet (3) – along with the more common **couplet**, a basic unit of Hebrew poetry. In it, the first two lines set the stage for the climactic third line. Many translations identify the second and third lines of triplets by indenting the beginning of the second line a few spaces.

tsedeqah (3) – a Hebrew word often translated as "righteousness," but perhaps better rendered as "social responsibility," fulfilling one's obligations to others in the society, particularly those most vulnerable.

two-source theory (9) – the theory that Matthew and Luke both drew directly from the Gospel of Mark and the sayings source **Q** to compose their accounts.

undisputed letters (10) – refers to the general scholarly agreement that Romans, 1 and 2 Corinthians, Galatians, Philippians, 1 Thessalonians, and Philemon were written by Paul himself. This conclusion is based on the letters' more or less common language, themes, and rhetorical style, as well as their assumed composition dates around the 50s CE.

united monarchy (1) – 1000–930 BCE: the time when David and Solomon ruled both north and south (and dominated some neighboring areas) from Jerusalem.

village (2) – an unwalled settlement inhabited by a few clans (50–300 people total) living in pillared houses in various extended family units. Though this ancient form of social life is introduced in the discussion of pre-state Israel in Chapter 2, it was the most common way for people to live throughout the history of Israel.

voluntary associations (10) – a variety of social clubs, professional guilds, unions, and religious groups that developed in the Hellenistic age. These associations (of which synagogues and churches were two) were the center of Mediterranean social life through the Greco-Roman period. The members of the associations met, often in the name of a god, over leisurely meals in which eating, drinking, singing, discussion, and storytelling all took place.

whore of Babylon (15) – female figure in the book of Revelation who personifies the corrupt city of Rome. Revelation 17–18 presents a vision of her violent destruction.

Yahweh (1) – the name of the god of Israel, often translated as "LORD" in English translations. This name came to be seen as especially holy in Jewish tradition.

Yahwistic Source (3 and 6) – a *hypothesized* early source of the **Pentateuch** (no copies have been found) that some scholars think starts with the garden of Eden and materials about Abel and Cain (Gen 2:4b–4:26), continues with a version of the flood story parallel to **P** (e.g. Gen 6:1–4; 7:1–5 to 8:20–2), and goes on to include the story of Noah and his sons, large portions of the Abraham story (the bulk of Genesis 12–13, 16–19) along with various **non-Priestly** portions of the rest of the **Tetrateuch** where the divine name **Yahweh** is used (translated as "LORD" in most English translations). According to this hypothesis, this source was composed in the early monarchal south, probably sometime during the tenth century. *Within this textbook* the probability of the existence of this broader **J**/Yahwistic Source is denied, though this book does affirm the probable existence of a J/Yahwistic strand exclusively in the **primeval history**, possibly composed in the early monarchal south.

Zion (3) – the name of a holy mountain on which the fortress and Temple of Jerusalem stood. It often comes to serve as a synonym for Jerusalem.

Zion psalms (3) – a set of psalms in the biblical **Psalter** that focus on **Zion**/Jerusalem and emphasize themes of **Zion theology**.

Zion theology (3) – a set of beliefs surrounding the idea that God lives in Jerusalem, holds Jerusalem to a high ethical standard, and will prevent Jerusalem from being destroyed by any enemy. Note: this is *not* "Zionist" theology.

INDEX

The letter b after a page reference indicates that the topic appears in a textbox. Page numbers in *italics* refer to illustrations.